GREEN DEVELOPMENT

THE WILEY SERIES IN SUSTAINABLE DESIGN

The Wiley Series in Sustainable Design has been created for professionals responsible for, and individuals interested in, the design and construction of the built environment. The series is dedicated to the advancement of knowledge in design and construction that serves to sustain the natural environment. Consistent with their content, books in the series are produced with care taken in the selection of recycled and nonpolluting materials.

Gray World, Green Heart: Technology, Nature and the Sustainable Landscape
Robert J. Thayer

Regenerative Design for Sustainable Development
John T. Lyle

*Audubon House: Building the Environmentally Responsible,
Energy-Efficient Office*
National Audubon Society
Croxton Collaborative, Architects

Design with Nature
Ian L. McHarg

Wind Energy Comes of Age
Paul Gipe

Tomorrow By Design
Philip H. Lewis, Jr.

Ecological Design and Planning
George F. Thompson and Frederick R. Steiner, editors

Green Development: Integrating Ecology and Real Estate
Rocky Mountain Institute

GREEN DEVELOPMENT

INTEGRATING ECOLOGY AND REAL ESTATE

ROCKY MOUNTAIN INSTITUTE

Alex Wilson • Jenifer L. Uncapher

Lisa McManigal • L. Hunter Lovins

Maureen Cureton • William D. Browning

333
.43

John Wiley & Sons, Inc

New York • Chichester • Weinheim • Brisbane • Singapore • Toronto

Library of Congress Cataloging in Publication Data:

Green development : integrating ecology and real estate / by Rocky
    Mountain Institute ... [et al.] : foreword by James J. Chaffin, Jr.: preface
    by Amory B. Lovins
        p.   cm. — (The Wiley series in sustainable design)
      Includes bibliographical references and index.
      ISBN 0-471-18878-6 (cloth : alk. paper)
    1. Real estate development — Environmental aspects — United States.
2. Land use — Environmental aspects — United States.   3. Building —
Environmental aspects — United States.   4. Green movement — United
States.   5. Sustainable development — United States.   I. Rocky Mountain
Institute.   II. Series.
HD255.G73   1998
333.73'15'0973 — dc21   97-28995

Printed in the United States of America
10 9 8 7 6 5 4 3 2 1

Contents

Foreword

My youth was spent in rural Virginia and my college years at the University of Virginia, acknowledged by most (including *National Geographic*) as the most beautiful academic environment in America. All of my adult life has been either in the Low Country of South Carolina or in the Colorado Rocky Mountains, both regions certainly steeped in natural beauty. I like to fish, hunt, bike, kayak, and backpack in these fragile ecosystems — and I develop real estate in both places. The land-use decisions we make have a dramatic impact on the very fabric of life in places I cherish. Not all of our decisions have necessarily been good ones, but I believe it is up to each one of us to be as well informed as possible about the potential consequences of our land-use decisions and about how to make them as creative and constructive as we can.

In early 1995, William McDonough, one of America's foremost "green" architects, gave an enlightening and stirring presentation to a group of Urban Land Institute leaders, ending with the exhortation: "Ignorance ends today, negligence starts tomorrow!" The reference, of course, was to our standard excuse of "not knowing any better." He was challenging us to be accountable, active, responsible stewards. A successful Denver-area residential developer approached McDonough with the promise that he would try to incorporate sustainable development and building practices into his communities, but that his toughest job, now that he was convinced, was educating and motivating his suppliers, subcontractors, and customers. And that, frankly, is the challenge of the environmental movement on all fronts — getting the proper information to those in positions of making a difference.

The CEO of a leading environmental nonprofit group recently stated, "The greatest challenge facing environmentalists is not global warming, or toxic waste, or habitat loss. The greatest challenge facing environmentalists is talking to people who are not environmentalists." Real estate developers, in particular, are caught in a never-ending paradox of moral complexity, balancing the competing imperatives of ecological sensitivity and economic sensibility.

Thomas Jefferson implored that we understand: "The earth belongs to each generation, and no generation can contract debts greater than may be paid during the course of its own existence." Today we call that sustainable development—meeting the needs of the present without compromising the ability of future generations to meet their own needs.

How do we do this? How do we adapt our planning, design, and construction methods toward sustainable ends, balancing the well-being of nature with continued growth and development? There are no simple answers. But one thing is sure: the answers must come from a proactive private sector, not overregulation from the government sector. The Urban Land Institute, a 13,000-member organization dedicated to responsible land use, has made environmental education a major priority in its meetings and publications. ULI agrees with Rocky Mountain Institute that there is a need for significant changes in the pattern of land use and construction that will result in communities that are better for people and at the same time less wasteful of natural resources and more accommodating of natural systems.

Improved technology and increased understanding are combining to dispel some initial misconceptions about green development practices. Early green architecture occasionally stressed "function over form," and green designs earned a reputation for being less attractive and less appealing to the market. In contrast, today's green architects are skilled designers who balance aesthetics with sustainability.

Another hard-to-shake myth is perceived higher costs. Constantly improving technology, and better research regarding operating efficiency and "payback" time, make sustainable development practices the right economic decision as well as the appropriate "conscience" decision.

In addition to this expanded knowledge regarding green development practices, there are significant marketplace trends that give developers greater opportunities to be responsible and profitable at the same time. Emerging psychographic, sociographic, and cultural trends indicate that the market is most receptive to products that are the result of responsible ecological stewardship. In the early 1990s, a Gallup Poll showed that more than 60 percent of Americans thought of themselves as environmentally sensitive. It is unlikely that almost two-thirds of Americans actually practice environmental sensitivity, but the fact is that they want to think of themselves as good citizens. In addition, individuals are becoming more principle-driven, and less status-driven. They seem to yearn for a greater sense of community that can nurture and support families and traditional values. Glitzier is not nicer, bigger is not better. They are seeking life experiences, not just life styles. There is a preoccupation with quality of life, with an emphasis on health over wealth, and a focus on well-being as opposed to being well-off. The market is in a time of wakefulness regarding our moral relationship with the land. There is a shift of consciousness as we begin to see the reality of our past behavior. The market, in short, is leading us to sustainable development practices.

E. O. Wilson, in his landmark book, *Biophilia,* proclaims a human tendency, indeed a genetically induced biological dependence, on nature and natural processes. Simply stated, people have a natural predisposition to feel better, perform better, and actually exhibit healthier physiological signs when looking at water, green vegetables, or flowers, versus "built" structures of glass and concrete. It is ironic that we often use our human creativity to destroy that which we truly need to live healthy, satisfied lives. If the natural landscape is indeed such a tonic, then we as developers must be sensitive to a greater sense of community—the web of life that links nature and humanity.

Rocky Mountain Institute is an effective, even-handed proponent of sustainable development practices. Its science-based research is the basis of its thoughtful recommendations regarding green development. RMI researchers and practitioners understand that even as we pursue the worthy goal of safeguarding the environment, we cannot compromise the principle that all citizens should be treated fairly. Many developers, including those who want to be responsible stewards, are understandably frustrated by the cumbersome web of regulatory directives. Thus, as professional stewards of our natural resources, as practical businesspeople, and as everyday citizens, we must strive to bring relative, rational, practical, and fair reasoning to the issues of protecting and restoring our natural resources, while producing living and working environments that provide a high-quality-of-life experience. We must apply these principles not only to our streams and forests, but also to our suburbs and inner cities.

In his essay, "The Community Concept," Aldo Leopold declared, "All ethics so far evolved rest upon a single premise: that the individual is a member of a community of interdependent parts...the land simply enlarges the boundaries of the community to include soils, waters, plants, and animals....In short, a land ethic changes the role of Homo Sapiens from conqueror of the land to plain member and citizen of it."

This enlightening book will surely help you more fully appreciate your role as "citizen" and thus, armed with new knowledge and insight, you will face the responsibility implied in McDonough's "...negligence starts tomorrow!"

James J. Chaffin, Jr.

President, Chaffin Light Associates
President, Urban Land Institute

For almost 30 years, Jim Chaffin has been engaged in developing numerous award-winning communities cited specifically for their environmental sensitivity. He is currently president of the Urban Land Institute and serves on the Board of Advisors of the School of Architecture (whose program emphasizes green development) at the University of Virginia.

Preface

Once upon a time, we erected statues to developers like William Penn and Beau Nash. They designed our cities and towns, and their creations shaped our lives. Perhaps more than any other members of society, they helped us conceive how we should live and interact with the world around us and make it better by our presence. A grateful public looked up to them as creators of something good and lasting: not buildings and streets, but communities.

What has led to developers becoming pariahs? Why are they now rewarded, not with statues, but with adversarial land-use processes and NIMBYism? It may be the cumulative impacts of development that sprawls across the landscape, destroys habitat, and causes gross social disruption.

Of course, this is not all the fault of developers. Car-oriented planning and zoning regulations dictate fragmented, dysfunctional landscapes. Lending criteria favor the tried and true, even when it clearly no longer works. Short-sighted purchasers prefer inefficient buildings that are cheap to buy but expensive to own. Yet merely "responding to the market"—the justification most developers give for doing what they do—is a peculiarly regressive competitive strategy, and one that would lead to ruin in almost any other industry. As this book will show, there is a better way, and those who practice it are gaining not only public acclaim but also competitive advantage.

Since 1982 we at Rocky Mountain Institute have been showing corporations how to gain competitive advantage and increase profits through resource efficiency. In the field of real estate development, we discovered vast opportunities for improving the comfort, aesthetics, resource efficiency, and value of properties while reducing pollution and saving money. In 1991 we launched Green

Development Services to assist architects, developers, and other real estate professionals in integrating energy-efficient and environmentally responsive design into specific projects.

The response has been enthusiastic. In a few short years, Green Development Services has had the privilege of working with—and learning from—such diverse clients as Monsanto, the White House, the Pentagon, the Grand Wailea Hotel and Resort, Ahmanson Land Company, the Smithsonian Institution's National Museum of the American Indian, the U.S. Naval Facilities Command, Wal-Mart, the Audubon Insectarium, Habitat for Humanity International, Continental Offices Ltd., the MERITT Alliance LLC, and the Sydney 2000 Olympic Village.

Originally, we thought this work would focus on energy efficiency, habitat protection, indoor air quality, environmentally preferable materials choices, and similar issues. But as we delved deeper, we began to see something even more interesting emerge—an entirely new way of thinking about the goals and the process of creating and modifying the built environment. This way of thinking transcends mere compliance strategies. It uses the process of addressing environmental concerns and opportunities as a catalyst to create fundamentally better buildings and communities. We have started to see developers, designers, corporations, and governments use real estate development as a financial engine for making profits and undertaking ecological restoration, community development, and even ethnic dispute resolution.

Real estate development was once a revered profession and a high calling. It can be so again. Indeed, the opportunity to create exemplary developments is greater than ever. What would it be like if developments produced more energy than they consumed? What if they increased habitat and biodiversity, produced food and clean water? What would they be like if they were deeply woven into the social and economic fabric of a community?

To quote the late Jim Rouse, one of this century's visionary developers, "Urban growth is our opportunity, not our enemy. It invites us to correct the past, to build places that are productive for business and for the people who live there, places that are infused with nature and stimulating to man's creative sense of beauty—places that are in scale with people and so formed as to encourage and give strength to the real community which will enrich life; build character and personality; promote concern, friendship, brotherhood."

Rouse said that in 1966. Perhaps he was ahead of his time, but that time has now come. We have reached a point where old ways of development have become intolerable—or, to put it more positively, the opportunities of green development are just too good to pass up.

Aldo Leopold, another of this century's great thinkers, said that to be an ecologist is to live in a "world of wounds," conscious of the environmental damage around us. The task of development in the twenty-first century will be to heal those wounds. And that process of healing may also restore a measure of respect and societal value to the profession of real estate development.

Amory B. Lovins

Director of Research and Vice President
Rocky Mountain Institute

Acknowledgments

The authors are grateful for the generous support, research assistance, and information from the many people who made this project possible.

Without the financial support of dedicated foundations over the three years of researching and writing this book, it could not have happened. With sincerest gratitude we acknowledge the Geraldine R. Dodge Foundation, the W. Alton Jones Foundation, the Emily Hall Tremaine Foundation, and Surdna Foundation, Inc.

The "green developers" we interviewed shared their vision and inspired us. In sticking their necks out to do something different, they have set a precedent for those who come after them. The following professionals patiently contributed valuable information, guidance, and inspiration, over several years' time in some cases: Jim Chaffin, John Clark, Michael Corbett, Rolanda and Kevork Derderian, Michael Horst, Harold Kalke, John Knott, Jonathan F. P. Rose, Stanley Selengut, and Bob Zimmer.

Through the process of writing this book, a number of professionals reviewed outlines and various drafts of the manuscript. For this we are indebted to the previously mentioned people, as well as to Bob Berkebile, BNIM Architects; Bill Brown, Veazey Parrott & Shoulders; Ian Campbell, Turner Construction; Kirsten Childs, Croxton Collaborative Architects; Roger Colwill, the Real Estate Institute of British Columbia; Judy Corbett, Local Government Commission; Guy Dauncey; Steve Loken, Center for Resourceful Building Technology; Nadav Malin, *Environmental Building News;* D. Scott Middleton, Urban Land Institute; Richard Ramella, the Planning Center; Richard Schoen, UCLA School of Architecture; Mark Smith, Pario Research; Robin Snyder, U.S. Environmental Protection

Agency; Harry Teague, Harry Teague Architects; and Kent Woodhouse, Turner Construction.

To the many members of green development teams who spent time discussing their projects with us for possible inclusion in this book as case studies—thank you for your dedication and perserverance. Many, many other people also deserve thanks for assisting us in the research and fact-finding process for this book.

Among our colleagues at Rocky Mountain Institute who contributed their time in research, we expressly thank Robert Alcock, Owen Bailey, Scott Chaplin, Rick Heede, Gunnar Hubbard, Dianna Lopez-Barnett, Kate Mink, and Dave Reed. We also thank our student interns Brian Cuff, Guy Harrington, Tanya Chan, and Swapna Sundaram, whose work was generously supported by the Konheim family in memory of their son, Eric. We also gratefully acknowledge the administrative support of Mardell Burkholder, JoAnn Glassier, Michelle Sinsel, and Lorraine Wiltse.

To Dan Sayre and Janet Feeney, our editors at John Wiley & Sons, who remained supportive of this project from its infancy through completion, we appreciate your patience and guidance.

Introduction

*G*reen Development: Integrating Ecology and Real Estate has been written for real estate developers, architects, planners, contractors, lenders, city officials, and all those who are concerned with the impacts of the built environment on the surrounding natural environment and larger community. It is a book that implicitly recognizes that financial reward is an important motivator for "doing the right thing." Green development is not an altruistic pursuit carried out by developers willing to lose money in the name of the environment. It is a way to achieve multiple benefits—for the developer, for the investors, for the occupants, and for the natural environment. Yes, developing properties in a manner that respects the environment *is* good for business.

Over the time that research for this book was being conducted, the concept of environmentally responsive development—"green development"—moved from the fringes of a few people's consciousness to become an accepted topic at professional conferences and workshops, the subject of dozens of journal articles, and the focus of several Internet discussion groups. The Urban Land Institute began including conference sessions on environmentally responsive development at its biannual conferences and formed a committee on environmentally responsive development, whose members prepared a white paper on the topic. A group of progressive, environmentally conscious architects within the American Institute of Architects formed the AIA Committee for the Environment. More and more green projects were being built within North America and elsewhere. Various universities have hosted conferences on green building for students as well as professionals. The U.S. Green Building Council, representing all facets of the building industry, was created to offer a comprehensive approach to creating green buildings. Several books on green architecture appeared, highlighting the features of certain special buildings that made them more sensitive to environmental concerns. Yet no one had yet examined how incorporating environmental concerns into the real estate development process would result in better places to live that were more profitable for their creators and investors. Rocky Mountain Institute saw a need to fill that void.

A firm belief in Kenneth Boulding's maxim, "Whatever exists, is possible," led us to fully explore the implications of the emerging art and science of green development, researching projects around the world. We wanted to examine what

Rocky Mountain Institute is located at 7,100 feet elevation in the heart of the Colorado Rocky Mountains in Old Snowmass. RMI is an independent, nonprofit research and educational foundation with a mission to foster the efficient and sustainable use of resources. *(Reprinted with permission from Rocky Mountain Institute.)*

worked in these projects, what problems came up, and how they were conceived, financed, designed, built, and marketed. Through site visits, interviews, and questionnaires, we elicited information from the development teams. We asked about environmental and social priorities and how the development team met the various challenges encountered throughout the process. We also examined the barriers experienced by developers and building professionals that currently impede widespread adoption of green practices.

This book was originally envisioned as a collection of case studies of green development. Each case study would report on the green features incorporated into the project and the specifics of how it was developed. As we dug deeper into our research, however, examining how environmental considerations affected site and building design, approvals, financing, construction, marketing, and occupancy, we began to see common threads that ran through the successful green developments. In general, we found that although projects with environmental goals might look like other developments, the development *process* was approached in a very different way. Extensive research confirmed our findings that the extent to which the design process was integrated inherently affected the first costs of green developments. We also found that the developers who are leading the way in this new approach to development are bottom-line oriented, but also guided by a desire to express their values through their work. These developers believe—and have demonstrated—that they can earn profits while doing good.

This book is organized as follows: Chapter 1 defines what Rocky Mountain Institute means when it uses the term "green development." Chapter 2 introduces and discusses the approach to the development process that lays the groundwork necessary for cost-effective green development to occur. Chapter 3 discusses overall land-use issues, examining how the location in which a project is sited affects its impact on the surrounding natural and built environment. Chapters 4 through 10 progress through the stages of developing a real estate project: market research, site planning and design, building design, approvals, financing, construction, and marketing. Then, Chapter 11 examines the importance of operating a building or development in an environmentally responsible way after occupancy. Finally, Chapter 12 offers a look into the future, sampling some exciting practices and trends in various locations that promise to help green development gain a broader foothold in the fabric of our cities and towns. These patterns of development will become the rule rather than the exception.

Through the process of our research, we examined some 130 case studies, and 80 projects were included in this book. Some projects are discussed in multiple chapters, while others appear only once. Many projects had a great deal to offer— much more information than could be contained in one book. We have attempted to distill the most important lessons gained from any one project and to include that project in chapters relevant to the various phases of the development process. To learn more about the more extensively covered projects, consult Appendix A, "Project Profiles and Contacts." The Case Studies Index provides easy reference to pages on which a given project is described. Boxed copy in the text provides additional information on specific aspects of projects or tells where to get more information on a given topic.

The case studies that appear in this book demonstrate various levels and elements of green development. No project built thus far is perfect, but each one described here offers valuable lessons. We hope that future green developers will not copy what others have done but, rather, will use their own creativity, dreams, and values to expand upon the models presented here and to venture even further.

Those who are already involved in green development have usually had to invest a great deal of time in educating themselves during their first few projects. While continuous education is needed to keep up with new technologies and methods and the learning must be fast, more and more resources are becoming available to assist in the process. We hope that this book will help to bring more developers into the fold of green development.

While remembering that modest goals and "baby steps" are vital links to start one on the path to more environmentally responsive development, also consider David Brower's exhortation to aim ever higher:

> What do we want the Earth to be like fifty years from now? Let's do a little dreaming and then see that this dream is not cut off at the pass. A future by design, not default. Aim high! Navigators have aimed at the stars for centuries. They haven't hit one yet, but because they aimed high they found their way.

GREEN
DEVELOPMENT

The Inn of the Anasazi hotel in Santa Fe, New Mexico showcases energy- and resource-saving technologies, strengthens the local community, and is profitable to its investors. (*Reprinted with permission of the Inn of the Anasazi.*)

CHAPTER 1

A New View of Real Estate

SANTA FE DEVELOPER ROBERT ZIMMER and his partners set out to build a hotel that would not only be successful financially and fit into its stylish Santa Fe surroundings, but would also embody their environmental and social ideals. Zimmer and partners Steve Conger and Michael Fuller cared deeply about the natural environment, and they were troubled by the impact of Santa Fe's growth on the city's Native American and Hispanic cultures. In building a hotel, they wanted to demonstrate that a business venture could showcase energy- and resource-saving technologies, strengthen the local community, offer first-class elegance, and financially reward its participants.

The Zimmer Group completed the Inn of the Anasazi in 1991. Located in the heart of Santa Fe's historic Plaza District, it is one of the premier hotels in the United States, rated four stars by Mobil and the American Automobile Association. The building's adobe exterior echoes the local Pueblo style. The interior design pays homage to the cliff-dwelling Anasazi Indians who flourished in the area centuries ago. Native American, Hispanic, and cowboy art grace the hand-plastered walls. Hand-loomed rugs, locally crafted furniture, and wrought-iron lamps help define the distinct Southwestern style. The restaurant is renowned for its locally grown organic food and gracious service.

Behind the scenes, the hotel has some unusual features. The developers capitalized on a prime Santa Fe location by reusing a 1960s steel-framed building that had housed the state penitentiary offices and served as a juvenile detention center. By doing this, they avoided the environmental impacts of building from the ground up. The central location reduces guests' dependence on automobiles during their stay. Local materials, of low toxicity, lend "authenticity," support the local economy, and provide good indoor air quality. Water-saving fixtures, natural daylight, and energy-efficient lighting help to make the Inn resource efficient. The restaurant supports the regional economy by purchasing produce grown by Hispanic farmers whose families have farmed in the area since Spanish Land Grant days but now struggle to maintain their land. To foster a strong community and cultural identity, the Inn promotes staff involvement in local nonprofit organizations and sponsors events to support diverse local cultures.

Despite being one of the higher-priced hotels in the area, the Inn leads all others with an 83 percent average occupancy rate. Hotels rarely begin paying back investors until their third year of operation, yet the Inn broke even by the end of its second year and began to pay investors in year three. By the end of year three, return on investment (after debt service) was running at an impressive 13 percent. While the owners attribute a great deal of the success to superior design and location, they also believe the development team's careful attention to environmental and community issues boosted hotel and restaurant performance by at least 15 percent.

What Is Green Development?

The Inn of the Anasazi is a very successful example of a new kind of real estate development that is emerging throughout North America and the rest of the world. Referred to as green development, it integrates social and environmental goals with financial considerations in projects of every scale and type.

Green real estate development has more than a single face. For one project, the most visible "green" feature might be energy performance; for another, restoration of prairie ecosystems; for yet another, the fostering of community cohesion and reduced dependence on the automobile. More significantly, though, green devel-

The restaurant at the Inn of the Anasazi features organically grown food and was listed in *Gourmet* magazine's "Top 50." (*Reprinted with permission from the Inn of the Anasazi.*)

opment is about the integration of all these features and many more. It is about *solution multipliers,* whereby one feature provides multiple benefits in reducing a project's impact on the environment. Green development is a very young and steadily evolving approach to real estate development. The perfect green development has yet to be built, but more and more projects today are demonstrating that the integrated elements of green development better serve the occupants, the developer, society at large, and the environment. Each of the projects described in this book is quite unique, illustrating the widely varying aspects of green development and demonstrating how far this rapidly growing field has come over a short span of time.

Green development is not a style, a trend, or a vernacular. Nor are all aspects of it even new. In many cases, it is more a merging of the old and the new. Many of the development patterns and designs used in green development have been employed for hundreds of years, though most have been largely forgotten in the half-century since the Second World War. On the other hand, some aspects of green development, such as highest-efficiency heating systems and emission-free paints, are brand new. According to developer John Knott of Charleston, South Carolina, green development is "a return to a climatically, geographically, and culturally appropriate way of architecture and building, in combination with new technologies."

For the developer and building owner, green development offers many potential benefits: reduced operating costs of buildings and landscapes, improved sales or leasing rates, higher property values, increased absorption or occupancy rates, reduced liability risk, better health and higher productivity of workers, avoidance of regulatory delays during permitting processes, and even reduced capital costs. Not all of these benefits will be realized in every project, but they appear frequently throughout the case studies presented in this book.

The Elements of Green Development

Common threads run through many green development projects. These can be grouped into three broad categories: environmental responsiveness, resource efficiency, and community and cultural sensitivity. These three elements manifest themselves in many different ways and often reinforce each other. For example, a development designed to reduce dependence on automobiles is likely to foster greater community cohesiveness and lower crime rates, since residents walk more and get to know their neighbors. A building designed in a regional vernacular style may be more efficient in its use of resources for construction because more local materials are used.

Environmental Responsiveness

Conventional development is frequently insensitive to the natural environment. Such projects may scar the landscape, take valuable agricultural land out of production, or destroy wildlife habitat. Many green development projects, on the other hand, are designed to restore and enhance natural habitats and resources.

A key to environmental responsiveness is respecting—and using—that which is already at a location or naturally belongs there. Environmental responsiveness is applied to land use by carefully siting buildings to blend in with the natural environment, by reusing already developed land, by restoring degraded land, and by preserving as much virgin land as possible. Environmental responsiveness is applied to infrastructure by capitalizing on natural features for storm water management, erosion control, and roadway design. And it is applied to buildings by using such natural resources as the sun, wind, landforms, and natural vegetation to provide heating, cooling, lighting, ventilation, and protection from the elements. Through the practice of environmental responsiveness, it is possible for a new development not only to minimize damage to the local ecosystem, but actually to improve the surroundings. In fact, some see green development as an "economic engine" for bringing about ecological restoration. This process of sitting lightly on the land, even when modifications to the landscape are made, is the essence of environmental responsiveness.

Resource Efficiency

Resources are the physical materials and energy flows we have access to and use: land, water, soils, minerals, timber, fossil fuels, electricity, solar energy, and so on. In real estate development, these resources are a form of capital that a developer works with in siting, constructing, and operating buildings. Resource *efficiency* is the process of doing more with less—using fewer resources (or less scarce resources) to accomplish the same goals.

Resource efficiency can apply to many aspects of real estate development, including land use, building design, material selection, waste reduction, water conservation, and energy efficiency. Clustered development patterns reduce infrastructure needs, saving resources and money simultaneously. Pedestrian-friendly and transit-oriented planning reduces automobile use and cuts pollution. Reusing existing buildings prevents unnecessary new land development and reduces building material use. Recycling demolished buildings and construction waste saves manufacturing energy and reduces landfill loading. Specifying energy-efficient appliances reduces fossil fuel and/or electricity use.

Resource efficiency offers financial savings. Buildings in the United States consume more than 30 percent of our total energy and 60 percent of our electricity. Good building practices can cut those numbers drastically. Besides directly saving money and resources, resource efficiency offers other benefits to society, including avoided pollution and improved health. Energy efficiency can enhance a building's comfort, beauty, quietness, performance, profitability, and occupants' productivity. Water-efficient plumbing fixtures and landscaping strategies can save money by reducing water and sewer bills, while reducing the need to dam rivers and expand wastewater treatment facilities.

COMMUNITY AND CULTURAL SENSITIVITY

According to surveys and media coverage, many Americans feel that their lives are lacking the quality they desire. This sense is linked in part to the physical environment. People say they are tired of the effects of suburban sprawl—the long commutes, auto dependency, and often monotonous, homogenous development patterns, all of which take their toll. People throughout America are mourning the loss of uniqueness, identity, and *community* in the places where they live. But what is this sought-after essence called "community"?

Community involves many things, including quality and quantity of human interaction, safety, and a sense of involvement and neighborliness. Robert Zimmer, developer of the Inn of the Anasazi, defines communities as "living patterns of relationships, comprised of individuals, families, friends, and institutions—all relating with their environment. Every living thing is connected, and all too often we fail to understand that interconnectedness. The result is that we attempt the impossible—trying to change one element or relationship in a community without having any effect on the rest of the community."

Community is voluntary. It cannot be forced. Developers cannot create community, but, with participation from stakeholders and end users, they can put together the pieces that encourage it to happen. Developers should recognize that *any* new development will influence the larger community. They can choose whether that influence will be positive or negative, subtle or intrusive.

Community exists on many scales, and community sensitivity is reflected through land use, building layout and design, and building operations. Green developments seek to be mindful of the larger community, complementing and connecting to it where possible. These developments use land appropriately in terms of both scale and function; they plan for pedestrians as well as cars; they provide convenient access to the existing infrastructure of services, schools, work, and shopping; and they offer a range of public and quasi-public spaces such as squares, porches, and courtyards for accidental or planned gatherings. Just as important, green developments address community in the way they are operated, including educational components in which concepts of sustainability are conveyed to occupants or users.

Cultural sensitivity means being responsive to the local history, the culture, and the existing built environment of a given location. This can mean using vernacular designs, purchasing local products and materials, respecting local customs and building practices, and honoring the cultural fabric of the region. Green developers usually support diversity—cultural diversity, economic diversity, or "market segment" diversity.

Both community and cultural sensitivity involve respecting and promoting a sense of place by recognizing the uniqueness that every setting offers. Atef Mankarios, president of Rosewood Hotels (for whom Robert Zimmer has developed resort properties), has praised Zimmer for his attention to cultural and community issues. "He doesn't parachute alien properties into a city. His hotels embrace the community. He preserves and highlights the cultural aspect of each hotel and trains the staff to be good neighbors."

INTEGRATING ECOLOGY AND REAL ESTATE

One of the key features of a successful green development is that it establishes and reinforces connections: between people and place, between people and nature, between buildings and nature. The Inn of the Anasazi is financially successful largely because it gives the people who stay there a sense of place and character, a connection with the locale that is very welcoming to travelers.

This process of establishing connections can be seen as the application of ecological thinking to real estate. Ecology describes the interconnections or mutual relations between living things—including humans—and their environment. In social theory, "ecology" describes the social and cultural patterns that result from relationships between people and resources. Ecological thinking means looking at things in their whole context, while seeking also to understand the interconnections between parts. It recognizes that nothing exists in isolation; everything is part of a larger system.

Green development is the application of ecological thinking to the business of creating places for people to live and work. Each of the three elements described earlier is, in its own way, a means of integrating ecology and real estate. Environmental responsiveness is a recognition that a development is part of the ecosystem in which it sits and should respect that position. Resource efficiency is a way to achieve a level of sustainability in our resource consumption. Community and cultural sensitivity addresses the fact that people, too, exist within a context—the network of human contacts on large and small scales and the historical and cultural milieu that defines what we are.

It is becoming clear in today's world that our actions have effects we would never have imagined. Over its life, a single compact fluorescent light bulb in a New York City office building can keep three-quarters of a ton of carbon dioxide out of the earth's atmosphere. Developers who understand and utilize these interconnections—who employ ecological thinking—are going to be the leaders of tomorrow's real estate industry. As they successfully integrate ecology and real estate, they are going to realize significant financial gain.

Doing Well by Doing Good: Benefits of Green Development

There is a widespread perception in the development industry that it is difficult to make money if a project is going to concern itself with environmental and social issues. Many developers fear that following a green agenda will delay project schedules and raise costs.

The reality, however, is that well-executed green development projects, such as the Inn of the Anasazi and dozens of others profiled in this book, perform extremely well financially. In fact, even though many of the leading-edge developers featured here have strong environmental backgrounds and ideals, the financial rewards of green development are now bringing mainstream developers into the fold at an increasing pace. It is possible—indeed, it is the norm—to do well financially by doing the right thing environmentally. For example, project costs can be reduced, buyers or renters will spend less to operate green buildings, and developers can differentiate themselves from the crowd—thereby getting a big marketing boost. These and other benefits of green development are introduced in the following paragraphs and are addressed in greater detail throughout this book.

Reduced Capital Costs

Undertaking a development in an environmentally responsible manner can reduce capital costs in a number of important ways: costs of infrastructure, such

Dewees Island®, off the coast of South Carolina, is a 1,200-acre resort and residential community with a build-out of 150 single-family residences. *(Reprinted with permission of the Island Preservation Partnership.)*

as storm sewers, can be lowered by relying on the land's natural features and mechanical systems can be downsized or even eliminated through smart energy design; and because approvals can be expedited if opposition to a project is reduced, faster approvals reduce carrying costs.

Land development and infrastructure costs for the environmentally sensitive development on Dewees Island®, off the coast of Charleston, South Carolina, were 60 percent below average because impervious roadway surfaces and conventional landscaping were not used. Residents get around this car-free island by walking or using electric golf carts on the porous sand roads. Common areas on the island are landscaped with low-maintenance native vegetation. "When you don't have all these manicured landscapes and paved roads, you end up with enormous reductions in infrastructure investment," notes John Knott, chief executive of Island Preservation Partnership, the island's developer. Reduced capital costs mean that Dewees' investors are enjoying a higher return on investment thanks to lower equity requirements.

The Body Shop, an international "cruelty-free" cosmetics chain, reduced site costs for its U.S. corporate headquarters in North Carolina by reusing an abandoned building that had adequate parking and vegetation already in place. It also saved money by reusing building materials and selling some for salvage.

In British Columbia, the architects of the University of Victoria's Engineering Laboratory Wing were able to cut capital costs significantly by eliminating the perimeter heating system in the 127,800-square-foot project. They did this by designing a high-performance building envelope. The project came in under budget.

In Davis, California, developer Michael Corbett saved $800 per lot in the 240-unit Village Homes subdivision by using natural swales for storm water infiltration in place of an expensive storm sewer system. The savings were put into landscaping for common areas and other amenities that have made the subdivision extremely popular since its construction in the late 1970s. In fact, properties at Village Homes command a substantially higher price, $10 to $25 more per square foot, than those of surrounding subdivisions, and homes sell faster when they come onto the market.

Prairie Crossing, a 667-acre residential development near Chicago, is saving even more. By designing the infrastructure to reduce environmental impacts, total savings of $1.4 million, or $4,400 per lot, were achieved. This was accomplished by designing streets that are 8 to 12 feet narrower than normal, by minimizing impervious concrete sidewalks, and by using vegetated swales and detention basins for storm water infiltration rather than conventional storm sewer systems. As with Village Homes, the infrastructure savings were spent to enhance the common open space and other project amenities.

REDUCED OPERATING COSTS

Most of the projects profiled in this book have far lower operating costs than conventional projects as a result of their greater emphasis on resource efficiency. Savings are usually easiest to quantify with energy, but can also be realized through reduced water demand, lower maintenance requirements, and a reduction in waste generation.

For businesses, savings in operating costs flow directly to the bottom line, increasing net operating income. This, in turn, can lead to higher return on investment and building valuation. Operating savings that are passed on to the tenant can result in favorable leasing arrangements and higher occupancy or absorption rates.

By incorporating energy-efficient measures, the Denver Dry Goods building is saving at least $75,000 per year in operating expenses, thus increasing the building's value by $750,000 when capitalized. In Vancouver, British Columbia, the developer of a 55,000-square-foot mixed-use development known as 2211 West Fourth saved $57,000 on energy in 1995 through careful energy design and use of ground-source heat pumps. The savings from the heat pumps are passed along to retail and office tenants, while residential occupants of the third- and fourth-floor apartments receive free hot water during a significant portion of the year. These operating cost savings enabled the landlord/developer to increase rents over the long term, thus sharing in the benefit.

Amory Lovins, cofounder and research director of Rocky Mountain Institute, has studied many buildings that have incorporated energy-efficiency measures. He has found that "avoidable present-valued energy costs can be comparable to a building's entire capital cost and can enhance its market value accordingly."

Reduced operating expenses for a building can also benefit the developer by reducing equity investments. Even if energy-efficiency features in a commercial building cost more, the owner may not have to invest more, because such measures increase the value of the project, and construction loan levels are based on building valuation. Often, the energy features do *not* increase capital costs (and the loan amount). In this case cash flow will improve, because cash flow is equal to net income less loan payments (see Chapter 8).

MARKETING BENEFITS: FREE PRESS AND PRODUCT DIFFERENTIATION

Developers of projects profiled in this book have derived enormous marketing benefits from their attention to environmental and community issues.

The developer of 2211 West Fourth, Harold Kalke, saved $850,000 in real estate agent leasing and sales fees by doing direct marketing rather than opening a sales center or hiring agents to lease retail and office space and sell apartments. This was possible because of the project's central location, allowing a lot of foot traffic, as well as extensive media exposure.

The Inn of the Anasazi has reaped free and unsolicited coverage from such major publications as Food and Wine, Traveler, and Travel and Leisure. This coverage increased business with travel agencies and individual travelers by about 20 percent over the Inn's projections.

Dewees Island® has generated an estimated $5 million in free press, greatly in excess of what was anticipated. Stanley Selengut, developer of three eco-resorts in the U.S. Virgin Islands, notes, "Press creates occupancy...so isn't it more sensible to spend money stretching the envelope of sustainability rather than on four-color ads competing with everybody else in the industry?"

Green developers have found again and again that the media like what they are doing and will promote it. Positive press coverage is the best kind of promotion available.

VALUATION PREMIUMS AND ABSORPTION RATES

In some markets, buyers will pay substantial premiums to be part of a development with identified green features. Harold Kalke attributed the outstanding absorption rates of 2211 West Fourth in part to its green features. Prior to completion, 100 percent of retail space and 85 percent of office space were leased, with contracts signed for 85 percent of residential space. Kalke's 12.3 percent return on investment was one-third-again higher than that of conventional retail/office

2211 West Fourth is located in the heart of the Kitsilano neighborhood in Vancouver, British Columbia. *(Reprinted with permission, ©Rob Melnychuk.)*

projects in his market. He attributes these premiums to "positioning the project as a green project, coupled with quality construction and integration of the project into the community."

In markets that cannot afford price premiums, green developments may enjoy faster lease-ups or sales rates because of differentiation from the competition. Production home builder McStain Enterprises is developing Greenlee Park, 170 units of affordable green homes in Lafayette, Colorado. Ideas were tested and refined on a demonstration home until the development team was able to get the total cost for green features (including replacement of the furnace with a heat recovery system) down to 1.5 percent of a home's total cost. Environmental consultant David Johnston pointed out that this cost is in the realm of a cabinet upgrade. Prior to Greenlee Park's grand opening, McStain Enterprises had already presold 75 percent of the first phase.

STREAMLINED APPROVALS

Gaining early respect and support from a community can greatly speed up approvals for a project. The developers of Central Market, a grocery store in Poulsbo, Washington, say that the decision to enhance an on-site wetland and offer it to the city as a park not only reduced maintenance costs, but also avoided delays by generating strong community support. Sam Clarke, executive partner of the Hattaland Partnership, noted: "The city of Poulsbo, and key community leaders, are well aware of our work—this establishes trust and respect, which translate eventually into financial advantages."

The environmentally sensitive restoration of the Denver Dry Goods building in downtown Denver garnered enormous community support, which helped the developers obtain financing and approvals for this mixed-use, adaptive reuse of a historic building.

By meeting directly with groups that had opposed any development of Dewees Island, developer John Knott was able to address their concerns and gain considerable support for the project, avoiding months, if not years, of delays.

Streamlining approvals and avoiding legal delays, in fact, is becoming one of the most important drivers of green development. The February 1995 issue of *Builder,* the official magazine of the National Association of Home Builders, recognized this trend in pointing out that building in an environmentally responsive way can hasten the development time line, saving money in the process by reducing carrying costs. The same argument is increasingly seen in the pages of *Urban Land,* the magazine of the Urban Land Institute, the leading association of real estate developers.

REDUCED LIABILITY RISK

By taking a responsible attitude toward the environment and occupants, green developments are sometimes able to reduce the risks of litigation, liability, and even such disasters as fires and floods.

The U.S. Environmental Protection Agency (EPA) has ranked "sick buildings" as one of the top five environmental threats to human health. EPA studies have found that indoor air is generally two to five times—and in some cases, up to one hundred times—more contaminated than outdoor air. According to a study by the American Medical Association and the U.S. Army in 1990, health problems caused by poor indoor air quality (IAQ) cost 150 million workdays and about $15 billion in lost productivity each year in the United States. An increasing number of building occupants are filing lawsuits claiming they are suffering from "sick building syndrome" (SBS). Unable to establish that any particular party is at fault, plaintiffs often sue everybody involved, including building owners, architects, contractors, and manufacturers of products used in buildings.

Ironically, a number of new county courthouses have been involved in high-publicity lawsuits over SBS. In 1995 a state jury awarded Polk County in Florida almost $26 million to enable it to correct design and construction flaws in its eight-year-old courthouse. The jury's verdict was directed against Reliance Insurance Company, which underwrote $29 million in coverage for Barton-Marlow, the general contractor for the project. (The actual renovations ended up costing $37 million.)

On the other hand, a 1996 jury found Dupage County, Illinois, responsible—as the *building owner*—for health-related complaints at its $53 million courthouse, calling the problems a result of improper operation and maintenance. The fact that some courts have held builders or designers liable for design flaws, while others blame the building owners for improper operation, highlights the importance of addressing indoor air issues in all stages of building design, construction, and operation.

Some building industry professionals believe the current number of IAQ-related cases is just "the tip of the iceberg." Lawrence S. Hirsch, an IAQ litigation expert with the Washington, D.C.–based law firm Cadwalader, Wickersham and Taft, noted in a *Building Environmental Report,* "Complaints concerning the quality of indoor air can affect the financial health of even the most prosperous owners. Building owners face an increasing risk they will be the target of a lawsuit by a building's occupants charging that myriad health effects have been caused by indoor air quality."

Lower insurance and/or workers' compensation policy premiums could potentially result from better air quality in buildings. In addition, some insurance companies are willing to offer lower premiums for buildings with high-mass walls because they reduce the risk of fire. As it happens, these walls can also save energy by storing heat and evening out temperature fluctuations. The Federal Emergency Management Agency (FEMA) gave all buildings in unincorporated areas of Charleston County, South Carolina, a 5 percent premium reduction on flood insurance, based on the voluntary efforts of the developers of Dewees Island to improve the county's flood management capabilities through actions undertaken on the island.

HEALTH AND PRODUCTIVITY

Several recent studies have revealed another compelling argument for green development. Improving office lighting, heating, and cooling—measures typically undertaken for energy savings—can make workers more comfortable and productive. According to a study by Rocky Mountain Institute, productivity gains of 6 to 16 percent, including decreased absenteeism and improved quality of work, have been reported as resulting from energy-efficient design (see the chart on page 18). Since companies spend an average of 70 times as much money (per square foot per year) on employee salaries as on energy, an increase of just *1 percent* in productivity can result in savings that exceed the company's *entire* energy bill. To a developer, these savings can mean higher lease rates and greater return on investment if the tenants understand the benefits. Most energy-efficient design practices are cost-effective just from their energy savings; the resulting productivity gains make them indispensable.

Often, the gains in productivity are an unexpected bonus. At the U.S. Post Office mail-processing center in Reno, Nevada, a $300,000 retrofit was carried out to improve energy efficiency. Combined energy and maintenance savings came to about $50,000 a year—a calculated six-year payback. But it turned out that

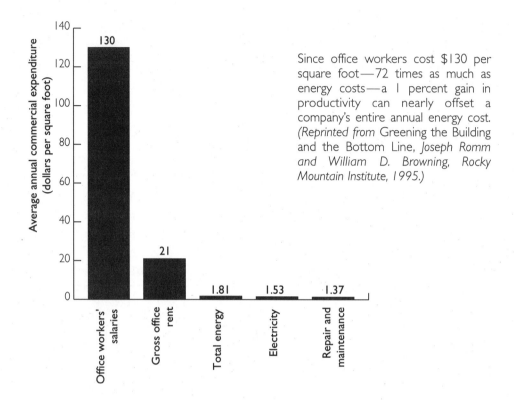

Since office workers cost $130 per square foot—72 times as much as energy costs—a 1 percent gain in productivity can nearly offset a company's entire annual energy cost. *(Reprinted from* Greening the Building and the Bottom Line, *Joseph Romm and William D. Browning, Rocky Mountain Institute, 1995.)*

improvements in employee productivity dwarfed the energy savings. With the new energy-efficient lighting, postal workers' output at the mail-sorting machines increased by 6 percent, while sorting errors dropped to 1 per 1,000—a rate lower than that of any post office in the western United States. These improvements were worth $400,000 to $500,000 a year. In other words, the productivity gains paid for the entire renovation in just seven to nine months.

Staying Ahead of Regulations

Few developers would deny that complying with regulations is expensive. Both national regulations, such as those dealing with asbestos and lead paint, and global regulations, such as the Montreal Protocol to phase out chlorofluorocarbons (CFCs), have necessitated costly and complex mitigation by the building industry. Since it is almost always more expensive to comply with regulations after the fact, those who stay ahead of future environmental regulations are likely to benefit down the road. Some of the green developments profiled in this book, for example, were among the first to specify totally ozone-safe chillers (chillers using refrigerants that do not harm the stratospheric ozone layer) and have thus protected building owners from the costs of future modifications when CFC and hydrochlorofluoro-carbons (HCFC) refrigerants become unavailable or prohibitively expensive.

Business consultant Michael Porter, of the Harvard Business School, cautioned in the *Harvard Business Review,* "We are now in a transitional phase of industrial history in which companies are still inexperienced in handling environ-mental issues creatively....The early movers—the companies that can see the opportunity first and embrace innovation-based solutions—will reap major competitive advantages, just as the German and Japanese car makers did [with fuel-efficient cars in the early 1970s]. While Detroit spent its dollars fighting fuel efficiency standards, German and Japan manufacturers dominated the market." In the development community, the innovators who embrace environmental respon-siveness, issues of occupant health, and productivity enhancement stand to gain, while those who stand still may be lost in the shuffle.

NEW BUSINESS OPPORTUNITIES

Some of the benefits to green developers are very difficult to measure. Many of the pioneering green developers are finding that their emphasis on protecting the environment and supporting local cultures is opening new doors. Based on what he did with the Inn of the Anasazi, for example, developer Robert Zimmer has been courted to duplicate that success with hotel projects in other areas.

Eco-resort developer Stanley Selengut has received numerous business oppor-tunities as a result of his environmentally sensitive development work. He has been offered resort properties all over the world that others salivate over, but which "aren't for sale." He has signed an agreement with the U.S. National Park Service to work on a series of prototypes for national park developments that will have minimum impact on the land.

SATISFACTION FROM DOING THE RIGHT THING

As illustrated throughout this book, substantial financial benefits are available to developers who are thinking of embarking on green projects. But most green developers do not do what they do entirely for monetary reasons. The other

Stanley Selengut developed Maho Bay, an ecoresort, on St. John. *(Reprinted with permission from William D. Browning, Rocky Mountain Institute.)*

reasons they give are many and varied: to provide "a better place to live," to prove that development can be done in a different way, to educate people about environmental issues, to make the world a better place for their grandchildren.

The Market for Green Development

A 1995 Roper Starch Worldwide poll (the annual "Green Gauge" done for Times Mirror) found that about three-quarters of Americans describe themselves as environmentally active or sympathetic, while 69 percent think environmental protection and economic development go hand in hand. Another recent Roper study commissioned by S. C. Johnson found that Americans increasingly understand the links between the natural environment, the social environment, and overall quality of life. While they might not understand exactly what "sustainable development" means, two-thirds of Americans agree with the idea that these three things "are inextricably linked and none should be sacrificed." Consumers continue to support environmentally responsible products and manufacturing practices, but does this support extend to the real estate market?

Developers and financiers often say there is no demand for green real estate, or they would be building it. But as management author Tom Peters points out, "Your customers are a rearview mirror." Customers respond to what is available on the market, and they do not always know what else might be possible. Conventional market research, by focusing on what already exists, often asks the wrong questions. Consumers are not asked whether they would prefer alternatives that are not readily available. Discerning market demand is a two-way street— customers need education about options available to them, while the building industry needs assurance that customers will indeed support greener projects.

Market surveys have shown that a surprising number of potential home buyers are willing to pay a premium for green or community-oriented amenities. The city of Tucson, Arizona, has been involved in promoting the concept of Civano, a planned 916-acre, mixed-use, environmentally responsible development. The city surveyed 300 heads of households and found that the concept of an energy-efficient community, like their vision for Civano, held a great deal of appeal for six out of ten respondents. More than 80 percent said they would be willing to pay a premium of $5,000 to $10,000 for a home with energy and community features if costs were recovered through lower utility bills. This level of interest came as a surprise to local builders, who, according to John Laswick of the city's Economic Development Office, "have historically viewed such developments as a tiny, and probably flaky, market niche. After years of battling with environmentalists, it still has not occurred to many of them that environmentalists live in houses too."

A 1994 survey by American Lives, a market research firm in San Francisco, found that 78 percent of 800 consumers who bought or shopped in master planned communities cited "lots of natural open space" as essential or very important. Other important factors that affected their purchasing decisions included walking and biking paths, ease in meeting people within the community, and public gardens with native plants.

In Dallas, average turnover of rental housing is high because people's needs are not being addressed. Columbus Realty Trust investigated to determine whether it could justify investing in the in-town rental housing market. It surveyed Dallas–Fort Worth residents, asking respondents whether they would prefer renting in a suburban setting or a mixed-use urban setting. Columbus was surprised to find that more than 50 percent chose the urban form even though no developer was building for that market at the time. By mid-1996 the company had completed almost 700 rental units just north of downtown Dallas and another 370 units in Uptown Village, according to its president, Robert Shaw. The developments are experiencing 97 percent occupancy and have added more than $38 million to the local tax base—in a city with no tradition of in-town rental housing. The average rent in the Columbus projects is $700, while average rent in the entire Dallas area is $530. Furthermore, turnover in the in-town units has been 25 percent lower than turnover in the local market in general.

Given the growing interest in the types of projects described in this book, there is almost certainly far more demand than can be met by what is available today, and there are few competitors. In February 1995, *Builder* magazine noted that "someday these principles will shape every new community," and profiled a number of developers and builders leading the "green crusade." Those with the foresight to enter the arena now will benefit in many ways: by serving as a model, by increasing profits, by generating publicity, by capturing market share, and by creating developments that they can feel good about.

So Why Aren't All Developments Green?

If green developments are so popular, so profitable, and so marketable, why aren't all developments green? There are many reasons, but the biggest is probably lack of awareness of the opportunities. There remains a widespread lack of understanding about what green real estate development is, the market for it, why it is beneficial, how to do it, and why it makes so much sense financially.

Green developments do take more time up front. There is a significant amount of learning required of leaders in any field, and this is especially true with green development. But today's pioneers, in breaking new ground, are finding that their up-front investment in education, planning, and design is saving considerable time and money down the line, while creating a superior, more marketable product.

A significant barrier to green development is financing. Financial institutions are conservative by nature and averse to risk. Anything new is considered risky. Chapter 8 covers some solutions to this problem and offers stories of developers who have surmounted it, but it is still a very real hurdle for the green developer.

Sometimes the barrier to green development is finding a willing partner. Visionary developers, for example, may want to put their knowledge and ideas to work but lack partners—designers and financiers—who can be persuaded to share their vision. Financiers are conservative by nature and are hesitant to invest in a developer without a successful track record, no matter what the nature of the project. Adding innovative or untested green features can further dampen their enthusiasm.

Other developers are waiting to see results of earlier projects before jumping into the fray, or they are simply unaware that it is possible to develop in a way that is economically *and* environmentally sound. Nonetheless, an increasing number of developers, builders, and architects are getting involved with green development and finding out that the benefits are substantial.

Many of those who would like to develop projects that are more environmentally responsive lack readily available information on materials, systems, techniques, and technologies. Fortunately, this information is becoming more accessible with the increasing number of good publications and Internet sites. As with most learning experiences, starting out is the hardest part.

Learning from the experiences of others is one of the best ways to overcome these barriers to green development. By seeing and hearing how these projects were envisioned, financed, built, and marketed, developers can gain confidence that this approach is possible. Such is the purpose of this book: to tell the stories of some of the first successful efforts at greening real estate development.

The Amsterdam headquarters for the International Netherlands Group bank is one of the most renowned green buildings in the world. *(Reprinted with permission from William D. Browning, Rocky Mountain Institute.)*

CHAPTER 2

Starting out Right: The Approach to Green Development

Sustainable design is not a reworking of conventional approaches and technologies, but a fundamental change in thinking and in ways of operating—you can't put spots on an elephant and call it a cheetah.

Carol Franklin of Andropogon Associates, Ltd.,
as quoted in *Guiding Principles of Sustainable Design*,
by the National Park Service, 1993

THE INTERNATIONAL NETHERLANDS GROUP (ING) bank in Amsterdam is an unusual place. The 540,000-square-foot headquarters of the country's second-largest bank, previously known as Nederlandsche Middenstands bank (NMB), is one of the most remarkable buildings in the world. It is largely daylit, highly energy efficient, and architecturally innovative with such features as curvilinear form, local materials, plants, artwork, and flowing water incorporated into the building in a highly integrated fashion. Many of the organic features and unusual building geometries were drawn from the teachings of Austrian philosopher Rudolph Steiner, whose ideas would hardly be expected to be found in a commercial office space. The building (really a series of interconnected towers) does not use conventional air-conditioning—a feat virtually unheard of for a building of this size—but relies primarily on passive cooling with backup absorption chillers. The building uses less than a tenth the energy of its predecessor and a fifth that of a conventional new office building in Amsterdam. The annual energy savings are approximately $2.9 million (1996 U.S. dollars), derived from features that added roughly $700,000 to the construction cost of the building—and were paid back in three months.

But what is perhaps most unusual about this building is the way in which it was created. In 1978 the bank was the fourth-largest bank in the country. According to Tie Liebe, who managed NMB's real estate subsidiary, the bank was viewed as "stodgy, and too conservative." Because it had outgrown its Amsterdam headquarters, the board of directors took this opportunity to create a new image for their bank. They laid out a strategy to deliver a functional, yet cost-effective, new headquarters that would be both appealing and environmentally responsive in design and function.

The board articulated a strong vision for the building: it would be "organic" and would integrate "art, natural materials, sunlight, green plants, energy conservation, low noise, and water." Next, the board assembled a multidisciplinary team to design the building. This team included architects, building engineers, landscape architects, energy experts, and artists. The team worked for three years designing the building in a process requiring that each step of the design be understood by every member of the team—so, for example, if the artists did not understand the natural ventilation system, its operation would be explained. There was frequent input from bank employees throughout this process.

As the planning proceeded, the board's vision was refined by the planning and design team with three criteria. First, the building must be thoroughly functional using the latest technology, including a specially designed security system and options for individual climate control. Second, the building had to be flexible, able to respond to inevitable changes in space needs over time. Third, the building had to be energy efficient, yet not cost "one guilder more" than conventional construction.

Employee input was used to determine where the new facility would be built. Construction began in 1983, and the building was completed in 1987—within budget. Not only has the bank building been a tremendous success financially, but employee absenteeism has dropped significantly. The bold new image of the bank —resulting from the building—is credited with elevating International Netherlands Group from fourth to second place among Dutch banks.

This flow-form sculpture is just one of the design elements that resulted from ING bank's strong vision for a building that includes the integration of art. *(Reprinted with permission, © POLYVISIE.)*

The ING Bank headquarters is one of the most significant green commercial buildings in the world. This achievement didn't just happen. It resulted from how the building was planned and designed. This was a process that included, first, a *vision* for what was to be created—this was not a vision of *what the building would look like,* but a vision of *the features and qualities the building would incorporate.* The vision came from the bank's board of directors.

Second, it was a process of *integrated* planning and design, in which the performance goals were identified *up-front.* This allowed designers to capture multiple benefits from design features and optimize overall building performance. This planning and design process can be divided into four overlapping components: whole-systems thinking, front-loaded design, end-use/least-cost considerations, and multidisciplinary teamwork, each of which is described later in this chapter.

Successful green developments are different from conventional developments. Whether or not they look different, they have different effects on their surroundings and use resources and materials in different ways. The key difference, however, that is found in practically all outstanding green developments—including most of those profiled in this book—is not always immediately apparent from the finished product. It is a difference in the *approach* that the development team uses. It is a process of creating a vision and then carrying out that vision through integrated planning and design. It surprises many to learn that this approach is consistent with financial performance goals for a project. Green developments need not cost any more than conventional developments. In fact, these four components of planning and design—whole-systems thinking, front-loaded design, end-use/least-cost considerations, and teamwork—help to reduce first-cost in development and ensure financial success for the developer and investors. While every green development is unique, these very aspects of planning and design are seen time and again in successful projects.

Visions and Visionaries

Like most new ideas, real estate development usually begins with inspiration or a vision. This is not necessarily a vision of what the finished project will look like, but rather what it will be—its features, its relationship to the environment and the community, its overall qualities. The vision is that first spark or idea that excites a developer, an architect, a corporation, or a community. According to Christopher Alexander and colleagues, in *A New Theory of Urban Design*, "Every project must first be experienced, and then expressed, as a vision which can be seen in the inner eye (literally). It must have this quality so strongly that it can also be communicated to others, and felt by others as a vision." The vision comes before any planning or design, and it is out of this vision that the project evolves. The vision should also extend throughout a development project and be adequately communicated to the rest of the development team, and even to the ultimate occupants —whether home owners, resort vacationers, or commercial tenants. In a sense, the vision becomes the filter through which planning and design decisions flow throughout the development process.

Sometimes it is a place that first inspires the vision. After 20 years as a recreational community developer, Jim Chaffin came across Spring Island, an island along the coast of South Carolina. From the first day Chaffin and his wife, Betsy, set foot on the island, they knew this was a special piece of property and that any

On Spring Island, the developers set about planning the development so that it would foster healthy interaction between people and the island's natural heritage. A mule wagon and riders are seen here at the island's ruins at dawn. *(Reprinted with permission from Betsy Chaffin.)*

development had to respect its natural beauty. Indeed, Chaffin initially offered to sell the property to the state for the same price he paid for it to establish a state park. Failing that, he set about trying to create a successful development that would minimize the impact on the island's ecosystem while providing residents and visitors with an opportunity to experience nature's gifts. That was, and is, his vision. Chaffin believes that the vision for a community will influence who will go there, and that it is critical to plan and design in a manner that represents these values in order to attract people who have the same values and desires to protect the land.

Together with Betsy and his partners in the Spring Island Company, Chaffin addressed three key issues that would help ensure that they met their vision. First they downsized the number of lots from 5,500 (previously approved) to 500. In running the numbers, they realized that adequate profits could be made while still protecting the fragile island ecosystem. Second, they established a trust to create a nature preserve on the property. Third, they set about planning the development so that it would foster a healthy interaction between people and the island's natural heritage. Chaffin credits Betsy as the major driving force behind the environmental agenda, and today she is the president of the Spring Island Trust, which manages the nature and archeological preserves on the island. Whenever Jim slipped back into his old conventional developer shoes, she would firmly nudge him back to the vision they held for the island and its residents 50 years into the future.

Today Betsy and Jim live on Spring Island and are active participants in the community and the environmental programs that they fostered. Chaffin believes it is the developer's responsibility to put in place programs or operations that will sustain the vision as a development evolves. His experiences with Spring Island changed Jim Chaffin's life and made him a leader in the fledgling green development field, actively promoting his ideas at the Urban Land Institute (the leading national organization of real estate developers, of which he was elected president in early 1997).

The key visionary and driver for a green development project is not always a developer or architect. In Tucson, Arizona, the city and local citizens have played an integral role in honing the vision for the Civano project. The idea for Civano —"Tucson's Solar Village"—a mixed-use development that is to include 2,600 homes and employment for 1,200 people on 916 acres of land, was initially the brainchild of builder John Wesley Miller. Miller had built solar homes for Tucson's high-end market in the early 1980s and was active with local and national building associations. But the vision evolved as other parties became involved. Miller's idea was to create an entire village that would capitalize on Arizona's sunny climate to provide energy-efficient housing for all income levels. Miller realized that because of the extensive planning and rezoning that would be required, the city's involvement was crucial. He worked hard to get city officials involved and to inspire the community. The full vision for Civano evolved through participation of the city and the public and, later, the development company (Case Enterprises) chosen to take over the development of Civano.

Detailed planning for Civano began in the late 1980s, with the Tucson Pima County Metropolitan Energy Commission serving as advisor to the city and the county. With help from the Arizona Energy Office, the Commission solicited input from 50 different public and private groups. Hundreds of local citizens were involved in broadening the vision to address pedestrian-oriented design, live/work opportunities in the new village, and protection of some of the desert lands. According to Miller in his essay in the 1992 book *Sustainable Cities*, the project is a "public-sector initiative responding to the increasing environmental and societal costs of urban growth. The public sector's role is to provide the leadership and incentives which encourage local builders and developers to build neighborhoods of this quality." John Laswick, the city of Tucson's project manager for Civano, noted that the inclusive planning process helped move the project along, without citizen revolt, and cut down on approvals time, because everyone worked toward a common goal.

An even more unusual origin of a vision is seen in the conception of a paper-recycling company in the Bronx. Allen Hershkowitz of the Natural Resources Defense Council (NRDC) had been investigating the idea of locating a recycled paper factory in New York City. In an urban location, raw material would be plentiful and transportation requirements minimized. Even so, the idea of an environmental group promoting industrial development is unusual. Hershkowitz proposed the idea to Yolanda Rivera, the head of a South Bronx community devel-

Local citizens were involved in broadening the vision at Civano in Tucson, Arizona, through charrettes such as this one with designer Sim Van der Ryn in 1990. *(Reprinted with permission from the City of Tucson.)*

opment organization called Banana Kelly Improvement Association, who was interested in creating jobs in the Bronx. Since the fall of 1992, Hershkowitz and Rivera have been refining their vision and moving the project forward, tackling zoning issues, financing hurdles, community reactions (both positive and negative), and contracts for paper supply. They dream of establishing the "worldwide environmental and community participation standard for how urban paper mills should be sited and designed, including issues related to environmental justice and minimizing technology impacts." Construction is scheduled to begin in 1997.

A few of the projects covered in this book did not have a vision or a real visionary at their inception, but generated one later. While this scenario is unusual today, it is likely to become more common as more mainstream developers enter the green development field. In this case, the developer needs only to recognize the requirement for a vision and to make sure that a visionary individual, or individuals, are brought into the project. Architect Bob Berkebile, FAIA, of BNIM Architects in Kansas City, Missouri, has played this role in several university projects, including the University of British Columbia's C. K. Choi Building for the Institute of Asian Research. Architects Greg Franta and Andres Duany have also played this role in other projects.

REFINING THE VISION

Once an initial vision has been put forward, it often must be refined. This is a larger, more participatory process, often involving extensive meetings with future residents, planning officials, and other stakeholders. Developer Jonathan Rose and his partner Chuck Perry have teamed up with architect Peter Calthorpe to turn a magical piece of prime real estate in Denver, Colorado, into a mixed-use community. First opened in the late 1800s, Elitch Gardens is now an abandoned amusement park, featuring old roller coasters, fanciful kiosks for games, a funky old theater, and a maze of gardens and tree-lined pathways. The 30-acre park is surrounded by dense urban neighborhoods. When the amusement park relocated to a new site, the owners of the property invited Rose and Perry's company, Affordable Housing Development Corporation, to submit plans for redevelopment. Rather than raze the old park, Rose and Perry plan to restore some of the old buildings, preserve the wonderful mature landscaping, and reuse the pathways and parks in a new mixed-use development.

Affordable Housing Development Corporation is redeveloping Elitch Gardens, an abandoned amusement park in Denver, into an intergenerational, mixed-income, mixed-use community. *(Reprinted with permission from Affordable Housing Development Corporation.)*

Rose is very good at considering the big picture, but he recognizes the value of bringing other people together to refine his visions. Soon after beginning contract negotiations to acquire the Elitch Gardens property, Rose assembled a group of 25 people from various backgrounds to view the site and spend a day brainstorming how to maintain the historic character of the park while enhancing and blending it in with the surrounding downtown neighborhood. This advisory team included local planning officials, historic preservation and land trust experts, environmentalists, spiritualists, consultants in social services (including elder care), and local residents.

Rose shared his vision and explained that before determining how to move the project forward, he wanted the group's help in refining the vision. What would an intergenerational, mixed-income, mixed-use community at Elitch Gardens look like, and how would it work? How could such a project fit seamlessly into the surrounding neighborhoods? How could the local community make its mark on the

The Vision of Jonathan Rose

Jonathan F. P. Rose, president of Affordable Housing Construction Corporation in Katonah, New York, (with a Colorado-based arm called Affordable Housing Development Corporation), is a visionary leader within the development field. "Ever since I was a child I've wanted to create villages," says Rose. His commitment to green development is exemplified in his company's mission statement:

> Our mission is to make cities, towns, and villages more viable while preserving the land around them. We think the best way to do this is to focus diverse sustainable development around interconnected nodes of transportation, leaving rural areas undeveloped. We believe that this model is not only more equitable, but more cost effective to society. We believe that communities are organic systems that evolve, and like organic systems, developed regions need boundaries to concentrate their energy effectively. Sustainability is not achieved by freezing the form of development but by intentionally planning and co-evolving an ever-changing harmony of infrastructure and culture.

Reprinted with permission from Jonathan F. P. Rose.

development? The group discussed everything from the commercial-residential mix to the layout of buildings, options for streets and parking, issues relating to restoration and building reuse, and the project's relationship to surrounding areas. While the group addressed how to preserve the history and character of Elitch Gardens, the focus was on the needs and wants of future occupants in a new community that would sit within an existing one.

While building owners and developers may have strong visions of a development, an advisory team — such as that assembled by Jonathan Rose for the Elitch Gardens project — can help expand and refine that vision. Not only will new ideas emerge from the process that can improve the vision, but the process brings more people into the loop and gets them invested in its successful implementation.

Establishing goals, principles, or specific guidelines can be a part of refining the vision. These may address both the product of real estate development and the process. Such fundamentals may be articulated prior to or during the planning process. Often they are used as guidelines for the development, as a framework for evaluating plans, and as a way to ensure that all the people involved in the project understand and adhere to the vision. On Dewees Island, for example, strict site planning guidelines dictate attention to tree preservation, view-shed analysis, passive solar orientation, and drainage impact. These principles guide builders and owners in planning the location of new buildings on the island. All plans are reviewed by the Architectural Resource Board of Dewees Island to ensure compliance with the development guidelines.

In planning Haymount, a 1,650-acre neotraditional town (with a projected population of 9,500) under development in Caroline County, Virginia, John Clark relied on years of experience and research, as well as consultation with experts to create a list of goals and principles for the project (see "Goals and Principles for Haymount" below). Clark selected his consultants and development team based on their reputation and commitment to the goals he had established for Haymount.

Goals and Principles for Haymount

Environmental Goals

- Design with humility and acknowledge the complexity of nature.
- Accept environmental responsibility for our work.
- Nurture the connection between nature and the human spirit.
- Design with sustainable objectives as a requisite.
- Design with flexibility to allow for environmental technology.

Social Goals

- Respect and involve current residents.
- Provide sites for spiritual life in design.
- Provide sites for civic life of community.
- Avoid privatization of public amenities.
- Provide affordable housing and avoid economic segregation.
- Preserve cultural heritage and provide access to archaeological information.

Reprinted with permission from John A. Clark, Haymount.

THE KEEPER OF THE VISION

The vision does not end when project planning and design is completed. Ensuring that the vision stays alive and flourishes throughout the project's development usually requires continued involvement by the visionary. Often, the visionary is also the driver who makes sure that key elements are not lost in design or construction phases of a project. Developer John Knott describes the visionary not as the "pearl in the oyster," but rather as the "irritant or grit that allows the pearl to grow." His role as a developer, he says, is to instill the vision in others on the project team. He calls himself a "vision keeper."

If the visionary—whether developer, architect, or other stakeholder—does not have adequate control over implementation, he or she may not be able to fulfill the vision. Such was the case at Laguna West, a 1,000-acre neotraditional development in Sacramento, California, where architect Peter Calthorpe was not empowered to ensure that all of his concepts were followed through. While many aspects of his vision survived, some were lost on builders who did not understand or share the vision and were not obliged to honor it. For example, the vision called for front porches. The builders tacked on porches, but they were too small to be functional.

In contrast, architect Anthony Bernheim played a lead role in ensuring that a green agenda was carried out in the new San Francisco Main Library, which opened in April 1996. Bernheim's position as project manager for Simon Martin-Vegue Winkelstein Moris (which worked with Pei Cobb Freed & Partners on the project) allowed him to play a leadership role in promoting and implementing the vision for a healthy building. While budgets were tight and the scale of the building required a large team and a complex process, Bernheim was relentless in adhering to the vision. He displayed political savvy in protecting design features key to healthy indoor air quality from the budgetary ax, and developed a cohesive and dedicated team by emphasizing education and communication.

Education plays an important role in Knott's "vision keeper" concept. Green development projects are different from conventional projects in ways that are unfamiliar to many architects, engineers, interior designers, and contractors. To create a successful green project, the entire development team needs to understand the vision. This may involve roundtable discussions with the team, suggested reading materials, even lectures by outside experts. John Knott has perhaps taken this effort furthest by organizing an annual green building conference and trade show that builders, designers, and others involved with his development are strongly encouraged to attend.

The Four Process Elements of Green Development

Once a project's vision has been developed and refined, planning is best done through an integrated process that includes the four elements of green development: whole-systems thinking, front-loaded design, end-use/least-cost considerations, and teamwork. These are terms Rocky Mountain Institute uses to convey key elements of green development; others may use different terms or practice these ideas without referring to them specifically. What matters is not what they are called, but that aspects of these elements extend throughout the development process.

WHOLE-SYSTEMS THINKING

> Business and other human endeavors are bound by invisible fabrics of interrelated actions, which often take years to fully play out their effects on each other. Since we are part of that lacework ourselves, it's doubly hard to see the whole pattern of change. Instead, we tend to focus on snapshots of isolated parts of the system, and wonder why our deepest problems never seem to get solved.
>
> *Peter M. Senge,* The Fifth Discipline, *1990*

Whole-systems thinking is a process through which the interconnections between systems are actively considered and solutions are sought that address multiple problems at the same time. Some refer to this process as the search for "solution multipliers."

Developer Michael Corbett is a master of whole-systems thinking. His 240-unit Village Homes subdivision in Davis, California, completed in 1981, was one of the first modern-era development projects to successfully create an environmentally sensitive, human-scale residential community. Designing narrower streets reduced storm water runoff and enabled simple infiltration swales and on-site detention basins to handle storm water. As a result, conventional storm sewers were not required, and the savings—nearly $200,000 (1980 dollars)—enabled Corbett to put in public parks, walkways, gardens, and other project amenities. The narrower streets also left more room for trees, which keep ambient air temperatures down and reduce the need for air-conditioning. Pedestrian paths and traffic-calming street designs have helped foster a strong sense of community with

The developers of Village Homes in Davis, California, incorporated narrow streets, resulting in numerous benefits. *(Reprinted with permission from William D. Browning, Rocky Mountain Institute.)*

extremely low crime rates and higher property values. "You know you are on the right track when your solution for one problem accidentally solves several others," observes Corbett. "You decide to minimize automobile use to conserve fossil fuels, for example, and realize that this will reduce noise, conserve land by minimizing streets and parking, multiply opportunities for social contact, beautify the neighborhood and make it safer for children."

Whole-systems thinking has also been put to use effectively by the MERITT Signature Development Alliance in Chicago. The MERITT Alliance is a consortium of major building product manufacturers, developers, energy experts, and others that was founded by Kevork and Rolanda Derderian (Kevork is president of Continental Offices, Ltd.) to renovate older, distressed commercial properties in environmentally sensitive and profitable ways. One of their first projects was

Continental Office Plaza in the Chicago area. The HVAC equipment in this early 1970s, 130,000-square-foot office building needed to be replaced. Simply replacing the mechanicals with new, high-efficiency systems would have had an unacceptable 111-year payback. Combining the HVAC upgrade with a major lighting system overhaul, however, made possible significant downsizing of the mechanicals and dropped the payback to slightly more than 7 years. Adding a sophisticated energy management system cut the payback to about 4 years. Finally, by "financing" the energy savings to commercial tenants—essentially selling the energy savings to outside investors—the building owner ended up with a 1.7-year payback. The retrofit was so successful because MERITT addressed the whole system, not just one aspect of the building.

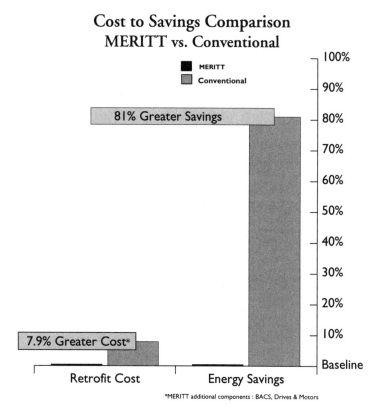

Reprinted with permission from Continental Offices, Ltd.

The benefits of whole-systems thinking can extend beyond buildings themselves. By using native landscaping in place of standard turf grass, the need for mowing, irrigating, and chemical treatments can be eliminated, while groundwater recharge and wildlife habitat are enhanced. Daylighting designs in office buildings can reduce the need for artificial lighting during the daytime, while improving worker comfort and productivity. Providing convenient access to public transportation and bicycling (including bicycle storage and convenient shower facilities) can reduce the space devoted to parking.

Unfortunately, as the various design and engineering professions have become highly specialized in recent decades, conventional development has moved further and further from a whole-systems approach. Architects think about building design, mechanical engineers about HVAC systems, lighting designers about electric lighting, and interior designers about how to utilize and beautify the resulting spaces. This separation of design functions and professions has largely prevented the use of whole-systems thinking.

Failure to practice whole-systems thinking is also seen in some supposedly "green" projects. Simple add-on packages of green features with little or no bearing on the *integration* of design features are examples of this failure. Some have called this the "Fifty Stupid Things" approach to green development. Consider the following illustration. A well-intentioned New Zealand developer offers buyers of his townhouse development "green specification" options, including double-glazed windows, heat-recovery ventilation, various energy conservation features, water-conserving plumbing fixtures, and solar hot water. Buyers who opt for the entire package pay about $10,000 (New Zealand dollars) on top of the $220,000 standard townhouse price tag. The problem is that the green features are not able to achieve their full potential. The development fails to capture the cost-saving opportunities that would have been identified through an integrated, whole-systems design approach. If cost-saving opportunities made possible by these options were captured, the units could cost even *less* than their standard counterparts, because mechanical systems could be downsized or eliminated.

Tom Hoyt, president of McStain Enterprises, the production home building firm that is developing the environmentally responsible 170-unit project Greenlee Park near Denver, believes that offering green features as an option does not work. "You have to decide what works, build it into the project, and make a commitment to it," he insists. Hoyt *integrated* green features into the house designs so that cost savings could be realized and passed on to the buyers.

Operation Cat Drop

While a lack of whole-systems thinking can mean lost opportunities, it can also result in unforeseen problems. Rocky Mountain Institute has a guiding parable that illustrates the folly of failing to consider the big picture.

In Borneo in the 1950s, the World Health Organization (WHO) attempted to solve the problem of malaria afflicting the Dyack people in Borneo. Its simple solution was to spray DDT to kill mosquitoes. The operation was considered a success, until the thatch roofs of people's houses started falling down. It was determined that the DDT also killed wasps that had previously preyed on thatch-eating caterpillars. Without the wasps, the caterpillars were rampant and ate the roofs of the village houses.

WHO then discovered a worse problem: the DDT built up in the food chain, poisoning insects that were eaten by lizards which, in turn, were eaten by cats. As the cats died, rats proliferated, and the area was faced with outbreaks of sylvatic plague and typhus. WHO eventually enlisted the Royal Air Force to parachute 14,000 live cats into Borneo. If WHO had considered the implications of spraying DDT from a whole-systems perspective, this entire fiasco might have been avoided and a more appropriate solution found.

Source: Rocky Mountain Institute.

The problems that result from not thinking about development holistically can be seen in the troubled Antelope Valley suburb of Palmdale, California, two hours outside Los Angeles. The area was dubbed "the next San Fernando Valley" in the late 1980s, and young working-class families flocked to Palmdale. Many people camped out and entered lotteries for the chance to buy a home in one of the many subdivisions going up. In 1996, however, nearly one in ten homes stood vacant; foreclosure rates had skyrocketed, and the social structure was in turmoil. The problem, according to the *Los Angeles Times,* was a failure to foresee the destructive impact of long commutes. Some home owners spend as much as 5 hours a day commuting to Los Angeles; 36 percent spend more than 2 hours per day in their cars. Many children are in day care as long as 12 hours a day. Child abuse is higher than here anywhere else in the state, marriages are unraveling, and teenage gang activity is mushrooming. The lesson is that developers and planners failed to consider the big picture—they sold a vision of contented home ownership without addressing the true impact of living in Antelope Valley while being dependent on employment in Los Angeles.

A side-by-side comparison in which whole-systems thinking was employed in one building but not in an identical building next door can be seen in a western

At Bentall Crestwood Corporate Centre in Richmond, British Columbia, Building No. 8 benefits from the whole-systems approach the architect used to improve building performance. *(Reprinted with permission from Teresa Coady, Bunting Coady Architects.)*

Canadian project. Among the eight office towers in the Bentall Crestwood Corporate Centre, in Richmond, British Columbia, stand twin buildings constructed and operated by Bentall Development Inc. Building No. 8, at 84,000 square feet, looks just like Building No. 7, built earlier. But they are very different. Building No. 8 benefits from the whole-systems approach the architect used to improve building performance through increased energy efficiency and more healthful indoor air quality. The biggest difference was the use of more expensive high-performance windows, which had excellent insulating value while maintaining good visible light transmittance. These windows allowed the design team to glaze nearly 60 percent of the envelope and still achieve twice the energy performance of neighboring buildings. The team also spent more money on extra insulation, while designing for 50 percent more fresh air than is standard to enhance indoor air quality.

When the owner questioned the higher cost of the windows and insulation, architect Teresa Coady of Bunting Coady Architects explained the whole-systems approach and justified the additional expense to the owner's satisfaction. Upgrading the building envelope allowed the designers to downsize the chiller from 200 tons—the size of Building No. 7's chiller—to 50 tons, saving tens of thousands of dollars and bringing the total building cost slightly *below* that of its twin.

FRONT-LOADED DESIGN

> Up-front building and design costs may represent only a fraction of the building's life-cycle costs. When just 1 percent of a project's up-front costs are spent, up to 70 percent of its life-cycle costs may already be committed; when 7 percent of project costs are spent, up to 85 percent of life-cycle costs have been committed.
>
> *Joseph Romm,* Lean and Clean Management, *1994*

By conducting the fundamental planning work up-front with all players at the table, the whole-systems thinking approach described earlier can be put to work by developers. In standard developments, resource efficiency and environmental impacts are often considered only as afterthoughts, if at all, despite the potential for substantial and continued savings throughout a development's life cycle. It is much easier and cheaper to maximize the benefits of green planning and design by addressing these issues in the initial stages of a project.

Developers often think front-loaded planning and design will cost more and delay project schedules. Greater up-front investments of time and money typically *are* required, but those costs are often recovered—with interest—by avoiding such downstream costs as expensive redesigns, drawn-out approvals, litigation, and stalled construction. As the saying goes: "If you can't afford to do it right the first time, how can you afford to do it twice?"

Florida's Department of Management Services, the "developer" of government buildings in the state, has reaped tremendous benefit from front-loaded planning. In 1995–1996 projects, it was able to save $2.5 million by increasing space efficiency from 77 percent in older buildings to 87 percent in new designs—equivalent to gaining $5.7 million in free office space, while saving $693,000 in energy costs. Meanwhile, construction costs dropped from an average of more than $80 per square foot to about $60 per square foot, saving $11.7 million for 800,000 square feet in the state's buildings. Standardizing certain design elements also helped them to reduce project development time for new office buildings by a year and a half.

The state has achieved these gains through a highly refined planning process. Once the project team for a given project is selected, but prior to fee negotiations, the Department of Management Services holds a "scope" meeting. The entire design team attends, including engineers, architects, and consultants, to hear the expectations and design requirements of the future occupant. Such issues as indoor air quality are addressed, and responsibilities of the project team are clearly delineated. This preparation avoids conflicts that might arise later if, for example, a team member budgets for fewer site visits than necessary and thus does not adequately address the client's or other stakeholders' concerns. All stakeholders, including maintenance and security personnel, have a say in planning a building. A room is dedicated to the project, and people can drop in to review and comment on the plans. Their comments are then collated and given back to the project team for incorporation into the building designs.

United Parcel Service wanted a new headquarters building that would minimize impact on their site. The project, a 623,000-square-foot, six-story office building with parking, was planned and sited so that the trees and other vegetation on the property around the building perimeter would not be removed or disturbed during construction. Environmental sensitivity was addressed in the siting and location of the building, but the logistics of the construction activities were not considered until preparation for construction began. To avoid damage to vegetation, construction plans called for cranes to sit atop the building while it was under construction. Yet, unaware of this building strategy, the architects had not designed a roof that could support the six very heavy cranes the scheme called for. Front-loaded design was inadequately employed. Roof redesign was required to accommodate the load so that the plans could adhere to the strict guidelines for site-sensitive development. Despite this error in planning, careful attention to logistics and ongoing communication among the owners, architects, and contractors enabled the project to be completed on time and under budget.

For the VeriFone project in Costa Mesa, California, the design team met the tight budget through a heavily front-loaded process. *(Photographer: Marshall Safron; architects: Croxton Collaborative Architects and Robert Borders and Associates. Reprinted with permission.)*

Recent evidence that a better building can boost worker productivity has made some companies more willing to invest in front-loaded planning and design. In 1991, VeriFone, an international corporation that manufactures electronic credit card verification equipment, decided to incorporate environmentally sensitive design in converting an old 76,000-square-foot industrial building in Costa Mesa, California, into a new manufacturing facility. The existing tilt-up concrete building had few windows, and its air-handling equipment was inadequate to filter out pollutants from the outside air.

The retrofit incorporated extensive daylighting, double filtration of the building's air supply, and selection of materials with the goals of minimizing toxins and maximizing resource conservation. The design team met the tight budget of approximately $39 per square foot through a heavily front-loaded process that paid close attention to integration, while using fairly simple materials but sophisticated design measures. VeriFone discovered an unanticipated benefit: the improved workplace environment led to a 45 percent decrease in absenteeism. The organization believes that its global competitiveness is being enhanced through reduced operating costs, improved employee morale and health, and an enhanced corporate image. VeriFone is now incorporating such green measures into its buildings around the world.

End-Use/Least-Cost Considerations

People talk about heating a building…a cathedral. But it isn't the cathedral that is asking to be heated, it is the people. To heat a cathedral, one should heat people's feet, not the air 120 feet above them.

William McDonough, adapted from a speech at the Cathedral of St. John the Divine, New York City, February 1993

End-use/least-cost planning is a decision-making approach that keeps the planning team focused on what the end users really want and need. It is a key component of green design and development because it identifies how to achieve the *greatest* benefits at the *least* cost in financial, social, and environmental terms. It is a way of thinking that considers costs over time as well as immediate costs. Although it is most commonly used to evaluate how energy, water, and other resources are used in buildings, this kind of planning can be applied more broadly to ensure that the full range of the end users' needs will be met by the project. What becomes clear is that there is never only one way to achieve a desired result.

This approach may seem obvious—common sense, really—but it is actually a fairly novel way of making decisions. Amory Lovins, cofounder and research director of Rocky Mountain Institute, coined the phrase to guide decision making in the energy industry. People don't want electricity or oil or coal, he reasoned; what they want are the services energy provides: illumination, cold beer, comfortable living rooms, hot showers, and so on. How can we provide these services, he asked, with the least overall cost? Lovins concluded that building multibillion-dollar nuclear power plants to operate baseboard heaters in drafty houses was not a least-cost solution to keeping people comfortable. Why not insulate the houses —for perhaps a hundredth of the financial and environmental cost—or build them right in the first place? His ideas prompted the electric utility industry to implement "demand-side management" and energy service programs that seek to meet customers' needs more cost-effectively through energy savings instead of providing more power at very high cost.

This approach has dramatic implications for real estate development. The examples that follow illustrate a few of the many ways development projects have benefited from end-use/least-cost planning. As Lovins and his colleagues have shown, these considerations extend far beyond energy efficiency to address such issues as water use, maintenance, and future adaptability.

Failure to focus on the end uses can result in projects that do not live up to their potential. This frequently happens in development projects because various stakeholders have differing, sometimes conflicting, goals for a project. Investors may need to get their money out of the project as soon as possible; first priority for the owner or operator may be to sell or lease the space right away; the architect may be focused on getting the project published in an architectural magazine; and the general contractor may be most concerned with project schedules. To add to the difficulty, the various players in development often speak different languages: developers speak dollars per square foot; investors, return on investment; electrical engineers, watts per square foot, construction workers, sign-off; and so on. Focusing on end use helps to maintain a common perspective in spite of these varied concerns and languages.

Keeping an end-use focus also helps to prevent shortsighted emphasis on the *creation* of a development to the detriment of its *operation*. Though most projects are initiated by market demand, it often becomes difficult to look beyond "opening day." This limitation results in buildings that may not meet occupants' needs, are difficult to maintain, detract from the surrounding community and environment, or are obsolete as soon as they are finished. Dewees Island developer John Knott concludes, "We focus on design and development, yet this is only 20 percent of a building's life; nobody talks about the 80 percent—the operation and life cycle of the building over time."

Incorporating end-use/least-cost considerations into the development process produces buildings that better meet the needs of occupants, maintenance crews, and the larger community. Such buildings may be more adaptable and thus may be either marketed more easily or reconfigured for the owner or tenant's changing needs. They often make better use of the natural landscape, minimizing impacts and costs associated with conventional turf grass and nonnative shrubs. They can eliminate the cost of expensive "fixes" to correct unforeseen problems. By better meeting clearly identified needs, they perform better in the marketplace over time. This approach implicitly addresses *people*—in commercial buildings, employee costs are by far the largest cost of doing business. Any measures that increase productivity and reduce absenteeism are end-use/least-cost solutions. Examples of how end-use/least-cost considerations can be incorporated into real estate development are described in the following paragraphs for the categories of energy, water, maintenance, adaptability, and human needs.

ENERGY

Energy planning is the most obvious application of end-use/least-cost thinking. By addressing operating energy use up front and considering how to meet energy needs at the lowest total cost, tremendous savings can be realized—not only savings in operating energy bills, but often savings in capital costs as well.

The Gap Corporation cleverly applied end-use/least-cost considerations to a 1995 renovation of its Banana Republic store on Santa Monica's Third Street Promenade. Faced with a large price tag for upgrading the electrical service to bring more power into the store, the company realized that it would not need more capacity if it reduced electricity demand through energy-efficiency measures. The effort succeeded. A rapid return on investment was attributed to system integration that reduced both peak electricity demand and total electricity use, while avoiding expensive infrastructure costs that the additional demand would have required.

The south elevation of the Engineering Laboratory Wing at the University of Victoria in British Columbia illustrates how daylighting is maximized through high-performance glazing, light shelves, and shading devices. *(Reprinted with permission from Wade Williams Young + Wright Architects in Joint Venture. ©Bob Matheson, photographer.)*

An excellent example of end-use/least-cost thinking is the use of "superwindows"—these are windows that use multiple glazing layers, two or more low-emissivity coatings, and often low-conductivity gas-fill to achieve very high insulating values (up to four times those of standard insulated-glass windows). Superwindows are significantly more expensive than standard windows, but they allow the developer to save money in a number of ways. Heating and cooling equipment can be downsized because of reduced heat loss and heat gain (which can reduce capital costs dramatically in commercial buildings if chillers are downsized). Because the windows are no longer going to be a major source of heat loss or drafts, baseboard radiators (or convectors) under the windows will not be needed, thereby reducing mechanical system costs and opening up a sizable amount of floor space that would have been lost to the heating units. Natural daylighting can be increased because more glazing area can be provided without the thermal penalties associated with conventional windows. This reduces the need for electric lighting during the daytime, strengthening occupants' connection to the outdoors and boosting productivity. Finally, superwindows will directly reduce energy use for heating and cooling. A typical developer will rule out the use of such windows because of their up-front cost. A green developer will insist on them, because they help achieve end-use/least-cost design goals.

Architect Terry Williams, a partner in Wade Williams Young + Wright, of Victoria, British Columbia, used superwindows in a 127,800-square-foot engineering laboratory wing at the University of Victoria (British Columbia) that was completed in 1995. He was able to maximize daylighting, eliminate perimeter heating, downsize heating equipment, and eliminate all mechanical cooling. To maintain comfortable summer temperatures, the building relies on automated nighttime ventilation.

WATER

While tremendous attention has been focused on energy since the early 1970s, water supply may ultimately prove to be a more difficult challenge for the development community. In many regions of the United States, aquifers are dropping more rapidly than they are being replenished. A few places in the West have even curtailed new development because of inadequate water supplies. Santa Fe County, New Mexico, restricts lot sizes based on amount of water available in county zones. In Old Snowmass, Colorado, water shortages are inhibiting buildout of previously approved developments.

While the usual approach to water shortages is to seek more supply, a few areas have begun to take an end-use perspective, requiring or encouraging water efficiency, promoting the use of graywater systems, and even providing tax credits for rainwater harvesting. In San Antonio, Texas, a city ordinance prohibits developers and owners of new homes from planting more than 50 percent of the yard in turf grass because the grass requires intensive lawn watering, which is a burden on the water table in this arid region.

The design team for the new C. K. Choi building at the University of British Columbia, completed in 1996, employed end-use/least-cost thinking to minimize water use and wastewater production. By using composting toilets throughout the 30,000-square-foot research building, they cut potable water use dramatically, saving 1,500 gallons of water per day, as compared with that of conventional buildings. While this measure reduced operating costs and conserved a valuable resource, the biggest benefits were realized through reduced burden on the university's sewage system and on the city of Vancouver's water supply, both of which were heavily overtaxed.

When Picayune, Mississippi, needed to upgrade sewage collection lines, it found that constructing a new wastewater treatment system would cost $10 million. Instead, the town built a constructed-wetland treatment system at a cost of $1.2 million. The developers used an end-use/least-cost framework to arrive at the best solution for the town, the taxpayers, and the environment. Not only did taxpayers save a bundle of money, but the wetlands gave the town a new visual amenity. Increasingly, developers recognize that wetlands can work to their advantage instead of being a liability.

Incorporating artificial or natural wetlands into a project is a great example of whole-systems thinking. Benefits can include reduced infrastructure costs, achieved by using the wetland for drainage or even biological wastewater treatment, visual appeal that can boost property values, compliance with wildlife regulations, and market differentiation that can help sales efforts.

Operation and Maintenance

Operation and maintenance are clearly end-use considerations, but they are often ignored. Chapter 6 addresses ways in which operation and maintenance considerations can be incorporated into design, and Chapter 11 discusses the long-term operation of green developments. However, these issues should also be considered in the early planning phases of a project.

The benefits of considering operations and maintenance up front (and the problems resulting from not doing so) are illustrated by two projects designed by architect Terry Williams. When Williams designed a new building for Malsapino College on Vancouver Island, British Columbia, he eliminated the need for mechanical cooling through an elegant design that relied on a passive nighttime ventilation strategy. When maintenance staff opened vents each summer evening, outside air would flow over concrete sheer walls, cooling them, and thus serve to keep the building temperatures comfortable during the day in this moderate climate—or so he thought. Unfortunately, the importance of opening and closing the vents was not adequately conveyed to maintenance staff at the college, and the desired effect was not achieved. Offices and classrooms overheated, and the college ended up installing an air conditioning system for south-facing rooms—instead of altering their operating procedures.

The lesson learned at Malsapino College was a powerful one for Williams: good design can be lost in operations. Convinced that passively cooled buildings are appropriate for his West Coast climate, Williams employed similar high-performance building envelope designs and ventilation strategies in designing the University of Victoria's Engineering Laboratory Wing. Instead of relying on daily operation by the maintenance staff, however, Williams ensured that nighttime ventilation cooling would be employed by incorporating automated controls. Says Williams, "The cost of control systems has come down in recent years. The systems are reliable and cost-effective." So far, the building has worked as planned, with operating savings of approximately $36,000 (Canadian) per year.

A large prairie restoration project at AT&T's Network Systems Campus in Lisle, Illinois, demonstrates the beauty of end-use/least-cost planning when applied to landscape design. Jim Patchett of the landscape architecture firm Johnson, Johnson & Roy outside Chicago, developed a landscaping plan whose *total* installation costs could be paid for out of the savings in landscape maintenance (mowing, irrigating, chemical applications, etc.). By replacing much of the conventional bluegrass turf with a native tall-grass prairie ecosystem, the designers reduced AT&T's maintenance costs by more than 75 percent while providing wildlife habitat, walking trails, and spectacular scenery for employees and town residents. The project has significantly boosted AT&T's environmental image. (Patchett later founded Conservation Design Forum in Naperville, Illinois, a firm that specializes in prairie restoration.)

ADAPTABILITY

End-use/least-cost planning can be used to design for the future adaptability and flexibility of a building project. It can also identify opportunities for remodeling existing structures rather than building from the ground up. Both strategies can reduce long-term costs, particularly for speculative buildings, whose owners may have to engage in expensive renovations to reconfigure spaces as clients come and go. European cities are full of buildings that have been successfully adapted throughout the centuries to accommodate changing uses and needs. American buildings, on the other hand, are often so specifically programmed that they are easier to raze and rebuild than to adapt.

At the C. K. Choi Building for the Institute of Asian Research at the University of British Columbia, adaptability is built into the roof, which is designed to accommodate photovoltaic panels. *(Reprinted with permission from Gunnar Hubbard, Rocky Mountain Institute.)*

Large retail stores are notorious for their short useful life spans. Wal-Mart and other discount chain retailers typically plan on a five- to ten-year useful life before moving on to a bigger store in a nearby location. While debate rages about the impact of chain retail stores on local economies, the future fate of these "big boxes" scattered throughout our suburban and exurban communities is another question that will soon need resolution. Architect William McDonough of William McDonough + Partners, based in Charlottesville, Virginia, pays careful attention to how a building can be adapted over its life as users' needs change. The firm contributed to the design of Wal-Mart's demonstration "eco-mart" in Lawrence, Kansas, adding features that will enable future conversion of the building into housing once its useful life as a retail store has ended. The ceiling height was raised by three feet, and the bay and coursing sizes were designed to permit adaptation to housing and to facilitate window installation if the space is someday converted to residential units.

Another example of intentional design to provide for future adaptability is found at the C. K. Choi building described earlier. The building houses the Institute for Asian Research at the University of British Columbia. In planning the building, the team worked with university officials and building users to help team members clearly understand building needs. The Institute has five program areas representing different regions of Asia. Research activities change every few years. Much of the faculty is composed of visiting professors from Asia, so turnover is high. The team both recognized the need to accommodate these changing uses and activities over time and respected the need for the different program areas to feel a sense of autonomy. The building's design allows for flexible classroom space as research requirements change. Walls are panelized, rather than permanently fixed in place, to allow rooms to grow or shrink as needed.

The architect developed a plan that gives each program area its own atrium and an open staircase to its second-floor offices. Within these areas, the plan accommodates flexibility of uses for offices, libraries, and meeting rooms. Recognizing that needs and technology change rapidly, state-of-the-art wiring was incorporated that can be easily accessed for modifications through a molded raceway. Adaptability is also built into the roof, which is designed to accommodate photovoltaic (PV) panels for electricity generation when the cost of this technology comes down.

While some measures that provide for future adaptability cost more up front, their inclusion can lower costs over time — both direct financial costs to the owner and costs to the environment resulting from reconstruction or major remodeling.

Designing for Human Needs

Perhaps the single most important end-use/least-cost consideration is how a development project meets the needs of the people it is designed for. In commercial office space, fairly simple modifications made during the planning and design stages (incorporation of natural daylighting, individually controllable climate systems, connections to the outside, etc.) can significantly increase worker productivity. A number of studies, including those by Rocky Mountain Institute, have shown that improvements in productivity can yield savings to the owners or tenants that dwarf savings from energy reductions, which have been the primary focus of end-use/least-cost planning to date. While energy costs for a commercial office building typically range from $2 to $3 per square foot per year, for example, employee costs are often much greater — $200 to $300 per square foot per year!

In residential developments, careful planning and design can create spaces that are more livable and that help to foster healthy community interactions. These benefits can, in turn, help to maintain or increase property value and improve financial performance over the long term. Success with this type of planning can be seen at St. Francis Square, a low-income housing project in San Francisco. Built in the early 1960s under strict cost constraints of federally funded low-income housing, the project has stood for decades as a model of community-sensitive design.

St. Francis Square is comprised of 299 low- to moderate-income apartments in three low-rise buildings on an 8.3-acre block in central San Francisco. Apartments are clustered in small groups so that residents will use common entryways and get to know their neighbors. Unlike most low-income apartment complexes, there are no long corridors or stairways serving dozens of units—places where crime is common. The units face away from the heavy traffic and fumes of Geary Boulevard. The buildings feature well-designed courtyards, each with unique character, surrounded by the creatively decorated balconies of residents' apartments. The square provides much-coveted opportunities for community interaction, and, contrary to the inner-city norm, St. Francis Square has fostered safety and trust among residents. It is a true melting pot of races—whites, African-Americans, and Asians. People come together in the public spaces, with no need for a security system or gated entrance. Neighborly interaction and the watchful eyes of the community ensure safe places for children to play and for people to meet.

Teamwork

For anything more than the most incremental change to occur, a reinvention of the manner in which all players in the development process talk to one another is imperative. The old model of the financier talking to the developer, who talks to the architect, who talks to the construction professional, who talks to the real estate broker, who talks to the tenant, in that linear a fashion, is counterproductive to the goals of sustainable development. Everyone needs to be communicating with one another simultaneously before a building or development project is actually considered.*

---

*Reprinted with permission by Neal Payton, CHK Architects and Planners, from the AIA/Nathan Cummings Foundation Roundtables, which were held to identify barriers to green architecture, 1992–1993.

In the conventional linear development procedure, key people are often left out of the decision-making process or included too late to make a full contribution. For example, buildings are often sited and oriented before the architect is ever brought in, precluding the opportunity to take advantage of passive suntempering opportunities that cost nothing. (Suntempering is the modest use of passive solar design and ought to be a part of all developments, even if more aggressive solar measures are not.) Through all parties' working together, on the other hand, both capital costs and operating costs can be reduced, and environmental and social goals met.

Front-loaded planning was addressed earlier in this chapter. To be most successful, that planning should be done by a broad-based team working together. Teamwork encourages an open exchange of ideas and generates integrated, whole-systems solutions. In the ING Bank building project described at the beginning of this chapter, the integrated team was one of the most important elements of success in converting the bank's vision into reality. Sunlight-reflecting sculptures in the atrium, for example, are an integral component of the building's daylighting strategy and could only have been designed through an integrated teamwork process.

Teamwork applies to all stages of development planning, not just architectural design. For green developments to be most successful, this team approach ensures that all key players on the development team support the overall environmental and social goals. Planning for the C. K. Choi building involved University project representatives, building users, contractors, and consultants. This team collectively established design, construction, and operation criteria. An electrical engineer at an early project team meeting noted, "I can see I'm going to have to learn about daylighting, not electric lighting." The benefits of this teamwork approach can be seen in the contributions of a mechanical engineer on the team who identified dramatic opportunities for using passive ventilation and reducing HVAC loads—opportunities that would have been missed had he not been involved in early discussions.

On the other hand, a single team member who is *not* invested in the team process or the environmental goals of a building can dampen the project's overall effectiveness. For example, a mechanical engineer who chooses not to account for the benefits of daylighting or reduced cooling loads and fails to downsize HVAC equipment accordingly can eliminate much of the benefit of energy-efficient, green design. Bringing key individuals into the teamwork process early on—especially individuals who are skeptical of the outcome—will help them become invested in the process and help to ensure a successful green development. But if, after investing in education efforts, a team member simply "doesn't get it," the best solution might be to replace that individual. At least that choice can be made before it is too late.

Green developers tell tales of very fruitful discussions that occur when the general contractor is brought in early and can point out opportunities for cost savings and waste minimization that might otherwise have been missed. For example, a contractor may suggest that slight changes in room dimensions would significantly reduce waste in wall sheathing products. As the people in the field, contractors come to a building project from a very different perspective and are invaluable team members.

The financial officer (if there is one) also needs to be part of the team. As keeper of the purse strings, this individual needs to understand the whole-systems approach being taken and the fact that extra up-front expenses can often reduce total project costs. Getting this person on board early can avoid delays and help to streamline the process.

Teamwork is important throughout every phase of the development process, but much of the team building occurs in the early planning stages. Assembling the appropriate team is critical to a successful whole-systems approach. Bringing all the right people to the table enables a more complete consideration of various needs so that the vision and goals can be realized. It is important to have consistent leadership and guidance, particularly for issues pertaining to the green plans and designs. Without that, follow-through may be lost if the team does not fully comprehend how to execute the plans for a green development. Teamwork in the planning phase may not necessitate face-to-face meetings of a group around a table—just clear communication and thoughtful review of all the issues. Much of the planning for some projects can be done via telephone and e-mail, but actual face-to-face meetings with the entire team at the table can prove invaluable.

When the Real Goods Trading Company began planning its new headquarters and showroom in Hopland, California, this largest catalog retailer of renewable energy and environmental living products in the United States wanted to practice what it preaches. After reviewing bids from several architectural firms, the company selected Sim Van der Ryn and Associates, a Sausalito firm well known for its ecologically responsible designs, to develop plans for the 5,000-square-foot showroom. Before any design work was initiated, the architects were invited to

Sim Van der Ryn and Associates developed plans for the 5,000-square-foot Real Goods Trading Company showroom in Hopland, California. This view shows the west side of the building and central oasis. *(Reprinted with permission from Jeff Oldham.)*

meet with Real Goods employees to share ideas about creating an energy-efficient and environmentally responsible showroom and to discuss preliminary plans for the project. The group examined ways to site the building to connect with the environment and to make the building an interactive educational experience as well as a showcase for Real Goods products.

While Van der Ryn's group came with ideas for the materials and design, it was project manager Jeff Oldham of Real Goods who suggested a straw bale showroom. Straw bale is a little known building material, recently regaining favor, that offers exemplary insulating value. Use of this undervalued material, in this case a by-product of California's rice growing industry, keeps it from being burned in fields. (Rice-straw burning is one of California's biggest air pollution problems.) The architects responded enthusiastically to this idea, and today the Real Goods Solar Living Center is one of the nation's largest straw bale structures.

Assistant project manager Tim Kennedy says that the best part of his experience in the Real Goods project has been the teamwork and the highly inclusive planning process. It was a community-based planning process, says Kennedy, in which "everyone was brought in to share the vision and help refine the plans." The company solicited the ideas of all the staff and even those of local residents. Staff members suggested that the scope of the project go beyond demonstrations of solar technologies to include integration with the local community. There was concern as to how the company could help some of the town's lower-income residents, and there was strong interest in supporting community efforts to recycle and compost wastes.

From all of these discussions blossomed the vision of Real Goods as it is evolving today. In addition to rice-straw bales, building materials for the passive and active solar buildings included old appliances (embedded in the concrete foundation), and salvaged and recycled wood from local mills. Visitors can interact with the passive solar building by opening and closing windows and louvers to influence daylighting and ventilation. Photovoltaic panels contribute to the power supply. The site features organic permaculture landscaping, a restored wetlands, aquaculture ponds, a closed-loop irrigation system, composting toilets, a grass amphitheater for presentations and gatherings, and tree planter boxes made from scrap automobiles. Community members are invited to participate in a "share food" program in which people can work two hours for a box of fruit and vegetables. Produce is also donated to the lower-income families in Hopland. Beyond demonstrating ecologically sensitive design, the company offers educational seminars on everything from renewable energy to organic gardening. And, of course, the showroom features the wide variety of products sold through Real Goods catalog. The inclusive planning process helped to create a green development that far exceeded the owner's dreams.

CHARRETTES

The term *charrette* is borrowed from the field of architecture and refers to an intensive workshop bringing together a group of stakeholders and experts to address planning or design. Charrettes may last a few hours or a few days and can occur as part of the initial planning process or as part of the building design process. Participants collaborate, sharing ideas and devising recommendations that can later be refined into specific designs. Charrettes for green developments typically address economic, social, and environmental considerations for a given project, then use this information to plan the type, mix, and location of buildings and other development elements (parks, gardens, parking lots, etc.). Outside experts and consultants such as biologists, ecologists, energy-efficiency experts,

T he *Environmental Design Charrette Workbook* provides summaries of intensive design workshops addressing energy efficiency, building technology, environmental approaches to landscaping, waste prevention, and resource reclamation, as well as planning and cultural issues. The workbook contains guidelines for organizers and facilitators of charrettes and a sample briefing booklet. The workbook is written by Don Watson and is published by the American Institute of Architects, 1996. $19.95.

See Appendices B and C.

green materials consultants, and representatives of a host of other disciplines may be brought into this forum. Together, the group identifies opportunities for integrating elements of green development and capturing synergies among various planning ideas.

Charrettes have played an important role in many green development projects. While the investment can be high—preparation for a charrette may take months and costs can run anywhere from $5,000 to $250,000—the benefits can be tremendous. Developer John Clark began designing Haymount by convening a small charrette to refine the goals of Haymount based on his environmental and social principles. This three-day meeting included the architecture and planning team Andres Duany and Elizabeth Plater-Zyberk, the engineers, and a few other consultants with expertise in various aspects of green development. A month later Clark held a larger charrette with a team of planners and architects, a landscape architect, energy and environmental experts for wildlife and vegetation analysis, fiscal analysis experts, an archeologist, a materials consultant, various state agency representatives, and a few community members.

Out of these charrettes came what promises to be one of the most comprehensive plans for a green development, encompassing many exciting strategies for the environmentally responsible and community-sensitive new town of Haymount. With ground broken in 1996 and a 20-year build-out, it remains to be seen whether this vision will fully come to fruition. From a planning perspective, however, success has already been realized, as approvals are solidly in place for even such unconventional items as a large-scale ecological wastewater treatment facility and a community greenhouse.

Another large-scale planning charrette focused on San Francisco's Presidio. For three days participants considered how to convert this historic landmark into an ecologically responsible mixed-use community while preserving much of the 1,480-acre property as a National Park. Many of the 115 participants in the charrette came from the local area, and all offered their services free of charge, as it was an opportunity to help create a model of environmentally sensitive land use and sustainable community economic development. One park volunteer, Aimee Vincent, described the experience. "Like the story of stone soup, we emerged from our offices at the Presidio, dragging our giant pot of water into the

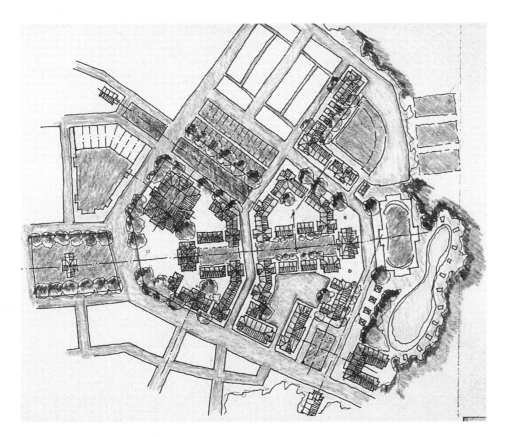

Preliminary plans for Haymount, a 1,650-acre neotraditional town under development in Caroline County, Virginia, began with a charrette process led by Andres Duany and Elizabeth Plater-Zyberk. *(Reprinted with permission from John A. Clark, Haymount. Drawing by Duany Plater-Zyberk.)*

town center (the charrette) where the team members arrived with veggies and spices—their expertise and experience—to flavor the broth. Everyone took turns stirring, and a community was united around a pot of hope for a sustainably evolving Presidio."

Planning and design charrettes for green development projects have provided a mechanism for significant "cross-fertilization" of ideas. Many of the leading green designers and green development specialists have participated in dozens of charrettes, taking ideas and successes from one project and applying them to others.

Engaging consultants and convening groups of people are viewed by some developers as cost-prohibitive and time-consuming. Yet time and again, green developers proclaim that time invested in front-end planning from a whole-systems perspective is time well spent. John Clark claims his front-end, team-oriented approach has saved him millions. He compares the $400,000 cost of Haymount's planning process to that of a nearby property where the developers spent only $135,000, but have been required to revise plans numerous times and to deal with zoning and entitlements costs that have pushed their planning cost up to $8 million. Says Clark, "Clearly, they spent more time and money by not using a front-loaded planning process."

Front-loaded planning does not necessarily mean spending more money; it means *thinking* more intelligently up front—considering all the issues and how they interrelate. It requires pulling together the right team of people who can help the developer think about all the pieces of the project puzzle and how to put them together. In many cases, the participants' time and advice is even free. Environmental groups, citizen's groups, town council members, local government officials, and planners typically welcome the opportunity to participate in project planning. In early planning stages, before hiring the team, some contractors and consultants may also be eager to participate in the planning process so that they can enhance their chances of being awarded the contract. The expense of providing donuts and coffee may be the only cost for bringing some participants to the table. Architects, contractors, and others involved with the project may participate in charrettes or other planning meetings as part of their services. If they are brought in strictly as consultants, they may require a fee for their participation. These expenditures can be worked into the project budget and are usually easily justified by the avoidance of costly mistakes or the realization of cost-saving opportunities.

During the Inn of the Anasazi's planning phase, a multicultural advisory board met to listen to one another's perspectives. *(Reprinted with permission from the Inn of the Anasazi.)*

THE COMMUNITY AS A TEAM MEMBER

Countless developments have stalled because the team failed to understand the needs of the community or did not consider the control and influence that local residents, government, and civil servants may have on the success of a bid to develop a property. Harnessing the ideas and influence of local government and citizens will foster development that is better suited to, and better accepted by, an existing community.

This approach rang true at Dewees Island, where developer John Knott demonstrated his concern and respect for the interests and ideas of the local community. Knott hosted a planning meeting where, instead of presenting plans and models and renderings of his vision for the property, Knott rolled out a blank site map of the island. He invited the neighbors to share their ideas for Dewees *before* the development team proceeded with honing their plans for the island.

Borrowing from progressive corporate managers, some developers are using conflict resolution strategies to bring parties together. In developing the Inn of the

Anasazi, Robert Zimmer met with Roberto Shané, an expert in conflict resolution, particularly in dealing with cultural conflict. During the Inn's planning phase, Zimmer and Shané established an advisory board of Hispanics, Anglos, Chicanos, and Native Americans. Recognizing that people come with different agendas, board members met to listen to one another's perspectives in order to foster greater understanding of the needs and interests of people of other cultures. The purpose of this committee was to help resolve the conflicts that often result from a lack of understanding of other cultures and to bring the cultural groups together to help plan a hotel development that would financially and socially strengthen Santa Fe's community.

Community members are the people who will ultimately have to live with the development, even if they do not live or work within its immediate borders. Soliciting their ideas and opinions will better serve the end-use goals and increase the likelihood of a successful development. All too often today, developers and residents are at odds. Growing concern for the preservation of dwindling open space is often in conflict with developers' quests to fulfill their visions. Developers are viewed with suspicion because of past failures to consider the impacts on existing communities. Demonstrating his concern for a thorough and inclusive planning process for Haymount, John Clark held numerous meetings, inviting community groups, local church members, and local and regional government representatives to attend. Clark shared his ideas for a multicultural development and invited suggestions from the area's predominately African-American residents. As a result, the local communities have supported his efforts, and the three Baptist churches in the region have openly backed the project. At a public hearing, 550 people voiced their support for Haymount.

Putting It All Together: Greening the Plan

None of the process elements of green development described in this chapter works alone to create successful real estate products. Instead, they are mutually reinforcing. A strong *vision* is the initial step. Effective *whole-systems thinking* is required to ensure that integrated solutions are found. By *front-loading* the planning and design process, the benefits of whole-systems thinking can be realized. Throughout this process, *end-use/least-cost* considerations ensure that optimal, cost-effective solutions are generated. And, finally, effective *teamwork* throughout the planning and design process draws the best from all players and helps them to become invested in the outcome.

Integrating these elements is the key to developing an effective plan for a given development project. The plan delineates how a project will unfold and identifies all the parties who will need to be involved in executing it. Careful front-end planning informs all other phases of development. It considers all the issues involved in design, construction, operation, and other phases of real estate development, as well as the timing, sequencing, and other needs and constraints of these activities. The development plan addresses *how, when,* and *by whom* various goals and strategies will be executed. Planning considerations and decisions made (or *not* made) early in the project influence other decisions and activities throughout later stages of development.

The 55,000-square-foot 2211 West Fourth project in Vancouver is a remarkable example of mixed-use infill development, featuring locally owned retail shops and professional offices on the second floor, with apartments above. *(Reprinted with permission, © Norman Hotson.)*

CHAPTER 3

Land Use: Considering the Big Picture

THE PLIMY FAMILY HAD OPERATED A Chevrolet dealership in the heart of the Kitsilano neighborhood of Vancouver since the 1950s, while homes, shops, and light commercial activities had blossomed all around it. In 1990 developer Harold Kalke was invited by the heiress of Plimy Motors to redevelop the site. The auto dealership just did not fit into the neighborhood anymore, and large retail stores were itching for an opportunity to locate on this prime piece of infill real estate. Kalke knew that any plans to redevelop the old car dealership in Vancouver would influence the local community. He also knew that with the development of 2211 West Fourth Avenue, he had an opportunity to influence in a very positive way the character of Kitsilano, one of Vancouver's most popular neighborhoods.

Kalke was determined that development of 2211 West Fourth, as the project is known, should enhance the neighborhood and preserve its friendly atmosphere. As a first step he spent many hours personally getting to know the area, its people, and its activities. Through this process, Kalke formulated a vision of what the development should be and began a planning process in which integration with the larger community was a driving priority.

Today, 2211 West Fourth is a splendid example of mixed-use infill development that fits into the neighborhood as if it had always been there. The 55,000-square-foot building blends small, locally owned retail shops, professional offices on the second floor, and residential (condominium) apartments above. When the project was completed in 1994, 85 percent of the space had already been leased or sold, and the remainder was under contract within three months of completion. Today the project is working just as Kalke had envisioned. Residents share cappuccino in the bakery and browse the bookstore during free time, chatting with their neighbors; the development truly engenders community cohesiveness.

The phase "green development" often conjures up images of individual buildings that are constructed from earth-friendly materials, that meld into the landscape, or that rely on passive solar heating and natural daylighting. But green development is much more than individual buildings and the products and technologies that go into them. A building can be very energy efficient and environmentally sensitive, for example, but if the occupants of that building face long commutes to get there, or if the development pattern contributes to the dissolution of neighborhoods, its negative impact can outweigh any environmental benefits.

This chapter focuses on the broader land-use context into which a development fits. Implicit in the concept of green development is the idea that land, as well as other resources, will be used as efficiently as possible and in a manner that supports healthy interactions between people and the environment both in the immediate location and in the region. Existing and planned green developments have employed a wide assortment of progressive land-use strategies in the pursuit of resource efficiency, environmental sensitivity, and community sensitivity. These strategies can be broken down into two broad approaches. The first is to avoid development on "greenfields"—open space or other undeveloped lands—by making the best use of what is already there. The second is to minimize environmental impacts caused by development when building on greenfields cannot be avoided. Both strategies will be addressed throughout this book.

Assessing Sprawl

Since World War II, real estate development in America has been characterized by inefficient use of land and resources. This practice can be traced to several factors.

Why Communities Pay for Growth...
but Prosper from Development

A Rocky Mountain Institute paper, *Paying for Growth, Prospering from Development*, details why growth virtually always costs communities more than it returns to them in tax revenues. The paper describes how communities can choose alternative forms of development with lower overall costs.

Widespread construction of highways and the surging use of automobiles makes it possible for people to live farther from their places of work. For developers, open space (whether farmland or wild) is often less expensive than other sites and is relatively easy to develop into large, highly profitable developments. Current zoning and other land-use regulations usually push developers toward rural, open lands because existing communities often resist more growth. Standard "Euclidean" zoning specifies that residential districts must be separated from commercial districts—resulting in increasingly separated development patterns.

While often highly profitable to the developer, sprawl development has many hidden costs to occupants and to society. Residents become more dependent on their cars, downtown areas fall into decay, neighborhood cohesiveness may break down, and prime agricultural lands are lost.

Various studies have recently begun to quantify the direct and indirect costs of sprawl development. A 1992 study by the Center for Urban Studies at Rutgers University suggests that if 500,000 new residents come to New Jersey over the next 20 years, each new home owner will pay $12,000 to $15,000 more, as a result of sprawl development, than they would if development patterns were more compact. In 1995, the Bank of America released a report, "Beyond Sprawl: New Patterns of Growth to Fit the New California," that challenged the wisdom of conventional development patterns. Among its conclusions, the report warned that "sprawl has created enormous costs that California can no longer afford. Ironically, unchecked sprawl has shifted from an engine of California's growth to a force that now threatens to *inhibit* growth and degrade the quality of our life." The report called for California to grow in a smarter way by inventing mechanisms for directing growth in compact and efficient patterns that respond to people's needs at all income levels, as well as maintaining economic competitiveness and quality of life for California's residents.

The American Farmland Trust reported in July 1996 that expanding suburbs will consume a million acres of California's Central Valley—the richest farmland in the United States—by the year 2040. Developers are turning farmland into housing to meet demand from home buyers priced out of the San Francisco and Los Angeles markets. Farmers, conservationists, and politicians, while acknowledging that growth in the Valley is inevitable, are fighting for smarter development patterns and coordinated zoning. They recognize that sprawl means scarcer water and higher taxes because it stretches municipal services.

As described in Chapter 2, sprawl development in Antelope Valley, a suburb two hours outside Los Angeles, has eroded family life and led to increases in crime. The impact is greatest on those who are too old, too young, or too poor to own a car, because sprawl inhibits adequate public transit options. In *Visions for a New American Dream,* Anton Nelessen identifies other psychological and economic effects of sprawl development. "Sprawl is privately expensive to maintain. The financing of home and car ownership is getting more difficult for most wage earners. Both members of a couple must work in order to cover the high suburban costs, including the house mortgage, credit payments, insurance, taxes, and two or more cars. Commuters move along at stop-and-go speeds, spending one hour or more per day—totaling five weeks per year—in their cars traveling between their subdivision house and the office park or the mall."

Working with What's Already There

As development is examined in the larger context of land-use patterns, the first question should be whether that development needs to be from the ground up. Channeling future development onto already developed areas rather than building on undeveloped rural land has numerous benefits. From an economic standpoint, it can save developers, taxpayers, home owners, and businesses billions in avoided infrastructure and service costs as well as travel costs. Avoiding greenfield development can slow the rate of urbanization of rural lands, preserve agricultural and forest lands, protect wildlife habitat, and maintain recreational opportunities. It can also enrich communities by adding diverse, energetic, and people-friendly environments and can offer opportunities to restore buildings, creeks, and vegetation.

A number of strategies for redeveloping existing buildings or sites are described in the following paragraphs, along with examples of how green developers have used them effectively. These strategies, which make the best of existing development, include adaptive reuse and/or renovation of buildings and communities, urban infill, and brownfield redevelopment.

ADAPTIVE REUSE/RENOVATION OF BUILDINGS AND COMMUNITIES

The nation's existing building stock offers tremendous opportunity to developers. There are estimated to be some 4.5 million existing office and public buildings in the United States. Hundreds of thousands of office buildings are functionally obsolete and need either extensive renovation or replacement. As many as 150,000 federal buildings are scheduled to be demolished over the next decade, according to Peter Yost of the National Association of Home Builders Research Center.

Developers often ignore the opportunity to reuse existing building stock, despite a myriad of economic, environmental, community, and cultural benefits. Underutilized, run-down buildings and neighborhoods can be transformed into

The Inn of the Anasazi reused a building that once housed state penitentiary offices and a juvenile detention center. *(Reprinted with permission from the Inn of the Anasazi.)*

vibrant living and working spaces. These areas are often best suited to public-transit-accessible housing and offices and can provide people with convenient and affordable alternatives to automobile dependency. At the same time, by lessening the pressures on suburban sprawl, redevelopment can protect farmland, forests, and natural areas.

The Inn of the Anasazi in Santa Fe is an excellent example of adaptive reuse. Looking at the tasteful, vernacular design , one would never guess that the original building once housed state penitentiary offices and a juvenile detention center and was "the ugliest building in downtown Santa Fe," according to architect Michael Fuller. Recognizing the building's potential, Fuller and his partners transformed it into a four-star hotel and restaurant that has succeeded admirably.

Renovating old buildings preserves a sense of history and generally results in less environmental impact than constructing new buildings. Because most of the structural elements and, frequently, the sheathing, siding, and finish materials are

Veazey Parrott & Shoulders, Architects and Planners, renovated the American Trust and Savings Bank on Main Street in Evansville, Indiana, allowing its employees to enjoy the convenience of the downtown location. *(Reprinted with permission, © Fred Reaves, Light and Ink.)*

maintained in building renovation, less energy is required for renovation than for new construction. This includes the "embodied energy" in building materials, which is the energy required to extract, manufacture, and ship materials.

Renovating an existing building can be an excellent way to demonstrate ecologically responsible and community-sensitive development to clients as well as to the larger community. When planning to expand their firm, the principals of Veazey Parrott & Shoulders, an architecture, planning, and engineering company in Evansville, Indiana, first considered suburban locations with appealing land prices. Ultimately, however, they settled on a historic building in the heart of Evansville.

According to partner Mike Shoulders, the old limestone building they found had inherent value—historical and embodied—and "the sale price was a bargain." When the company compared the costs of renovating the downtown building with the costs of building a new office, the renovation came out way ahead. In addition, the quality and character of the finished product was greater with the historic building because the old marble wainscoting, ceramic mosaic floors, and beautiful wood detailing were restored in the renovation. If the firm had chosen to build a new building, it would have had to cut corners in the detailing quality and would never have been able to capture the beauty that a historic building offers.

There were other benefits as well. The building is located on a main downtown street, placing the firm within a couple of blocks of major clients, consultants, banks, government agencies, a public library, and an athletic club where staff frequently work out. The architects are now able to walk to most of their appointments, as well as to nearby retail shops and

The main stairwell at the restored Veazey Parrott & Shoulders offices features marble wainscoting and daylighting from the original skylight. (Reprinted with permission, © Fred Reaves, Light and Ink.)

At Mashpee Commons on Cape Cod, Massachusetts, developers converted an auto-oriented shopping center into the main street of a mixed-use, pedestrian-oriented project. *(Reprinted with permission from William D. Browning, Rocky Mountain Institute.)*

restaurants. Today, Veazey Parrott & Shoulders employees enjoy the convenience of their downtown location and are proud of creating a workplace that is both ecologically responsible and an impressive showpiece of their architectural expertise.

On a larger scale, Mashpee Commons on Cape Cod in Massachusetts was one of the first projects to redevelop a failed shopping center. The developers sought to transform a five-acre auto-oriented shopping center into the Main Street of a mixed-use, pedestrian-oriented project, whose design echoed the traditional town center. They believed that modern shopping centers lack character, while the small-town communities in which they had grown up had qualities that could be incorporated into today's retail centers. Neotraditional planners Andres Duany and Elizabeth Plater-Zyberk were hired to design a new community around the old shopping center. The first phase built was the new Main Street, which includes retail stores and restaurants, with offices above, a movie theater complex, a bank, parks, and a U.S. Post Office.

Mashpee Commons is evolving into the town center for the city of Mashpee. The city has moved its library and its police and fire headquarters to the Commons, and various community amenities are proposed nearby. Although the housing originally envisioned for the project has so far failed to materialize, because of financing problems, the owners have been pursuing approvals for their master plan, which will include housing, more retail, and a performing arts center.

Although Mashpee Commons remains an auto-oriented destination with stores dependent on a regional customer base, and although the center still lacks a residential component, it shows how new life can be breathed into a derelict project whose useful life seemed to be over.

Even some of the discount retailers, notorious for "big box" stores on the fringes of towns, are recognizing the benefits of adaptively reusing and renovating old buildings within urban areas. Target, a discount retail chain, departed from its usual practice by renovating a vacant department store in Pasadena, California. Target was not driven by resource efficiency, but rather by recognizing that this downtown location was several miles away from Target's nearest competitors and readily accessible to extensive pedestrian traffic. The company has since pursued this strategy with several other stores, realizing considerably higher sales revenues in the process.

The city of Pasadena's leaders recognized that Target's strategy could revitalize downtown Pasadena's retail area, which had been largely killed off by regional malls. The city supported Target's efforts by sharing tax revenues, a fairly common practice in California whereby a portion of sales tax revenues are rebated back to select retailers. The efforts have paid off handsomely for both Target and the city. Pasadena's annual sales tax revenues from this source are about $250,000 after Target's share is deducted.

On the commercial front, Continental Offices, Ltd. (COL) of Chicago is among the first developers to recognize the financial windfall that can result from renovating some of the hundreds of thousands of glass and steel office buildings erected in recent decades. "Buildings developed 10 to 20 years ago are becoming functionally obsolete," observed Kevork Derderian, COL's president. Many of these buildings need reglazing and mechanical-system upgrades. Reflecting on the tremendous opportunity to increase the value of real estate—while greening buildings and providing more comfortable spaces for tenants—Derderian asks, "Do we need to start planning from the ground up, or can we just move from the inside out?" He founded the MERITT Alliance, introduced in Chapter 2, to pursue these opportunities more fully.

THE PROMISE OF REUSED MILITARY BASES

The closure of military bases nationwide offers tremendous opportunity for creative redevelopment. A half-million acres of military property are currently being transferred into civilian hands through the U.S. government's Base Realignment and Closure (BRAC) program. Although the transfer process for a given facility usually takes about 10 years to complete (owing to cleanup, reuse planning, infrastructure upgrading, and property transfer), the Clinton Administration instituted a fast-track program for hazardous waste remediation to speed up the transfer. In another effort to make these deals more enticing, the 1994 Pryor Amendment to the Department of Defense's congressional budget authorization allowed property transfer to local authorities at *below* appraised values—even at zero return to the government—if such transfers will create jobs.

Hamilton Field, a former army airfield located near the city of Novato in Marin County, California, includes a small town of Spanish-influenced architecture built in the 1930s. The base had a reputation as one of the best places to be stationed in America's armed forces, thanks to its beautiful bayfront location and proximity to San Francisco. After the base was abandoned in the 1970s, the local community debated its ownership and future for 20 years, declining numerous redevelopment proposals that failed to capture their imagination. In 1991 the city of Novato began collaborating with the New Hamilton Partnership on an extensive community planning process. The project management team carefully wove together ideas from the key players—including the city, the Hamilton Reuse Planning Authority, and the Hamilton Advisory Committee—to reach a level of consensus unusual in the military base reuse project.

Today, Hamilton Field has been divided into three zones with three different owners. One zone will include 1,000 homes, 750 of which will be renovated from military housing. Another zone of 800 acres that formerly included the airport runway will most likely be restored as wildlife habitat and wetlands. The third zone of 400 acres, under the leadership of the New Hamilton Partnership, will evolve into Hamilton, a mixed-use, mixed-income community. Responding to the community's concerns regarding environmental and historic preservation, the developers of Hamilton have included more than 160 acres of open space and wildlife habitat. The beauty of reusing this military base, among other advantages, lies in the ability to make use of existing infrastructure and amenities, including a street grid already established by the military. The developers plan to restore many of the old buildings as well as the main gate and bridge.

Hamilton Field, a former army airfield located in Marin County, California, is just one of many military properties currently being transferred to civilian hands through the U.S. government's BRAC program. *(Reprinted with permission, © EXL Imaging, Inc.)*

The New Hamilton Partnership wants to transform the old army airfield into the mixed-use, mixed-income community of Hamilton. *(Reprinted with permission from the New Hamilton Partnership.)*

Hamilton will feature six distinct neighborhoods, containing a total of 950 new homes, while historic town-center buildings will be preserved and reused. An existing row of airplane hangars will be transformed into a commercial center, offering hundreds of new jobs in enterprises ranging from start-up businesses to large corporate facilities. New residents will be able to use existing tennis courts, hiking trails, and biking paths. As of autumn 1996, construction of additional infrastructure had begun, with home construction, neighborhood parks, and the town center expected to follow soon.

INFILL DEVELOPMENT

Done well, infill is a flexible and opportunistic approach well-suited to what architect Dan Solomon calls the "dirty work" of repairing existing urban and suburban fabrics that are often riddled with difficult existing conditions. In contrast to well-publicized proposals to develop new areas in the image of older towns, infill focuses on reworking existing built-up areas to better meet the changing needs of American households and workplaces.

Peter Marshall Owens, On the Ground, *fall 1994*

"Infill development" means increasing the density of already-developed areas through the addition of new buildings. Harold Kalke's 2211 West Fourth project is one example of infill, in which an old car lot in an existing neighborhood was redeveloped into a mixed-use project offering housing, stores, and offices. Infill development can be applied to single-family neighborhoods, local commercial districts, live/work situations, downtowns, and warehouse districts. Appropriately sited and carefully carried out, infill can strengthen existing neighborhoods while capitalizing on existing infrastructure. On a per-lot basis, this approach can be more cost-effective than sprawl development, because the impact on sewers, roads, water, and other infrastructure is likely to be lower.

While developers and planners cannot create community, they can plan and design to foster it, as Harold Kalke did so effectively at 2211 West Fourth. Infill development offers greater opportunity to connect with the existing community and to complement the culture, style, and vernacular of a project's surroundings.

Current regulatory constraints, however, often make infill development more difficult than lower-density suburban development. Some communities find infill threatening, because they have no experience with it. They fear loss of open space or negative impacts from increased density. Others remember bad experiences with "urban renewal" (urban removal) infill in the past. Peter Marshall Owens, in *On the Ground* magazine, charges that "forty years of indiscriminate demolition and infill of motel-like apartments, strip commercial buildings and housing projects have eroded neighborhood structure through their failure to relate to the street, domination by parking and lack of human scale." Fortunately, more people now recognize that infill development should be a way to enrich the urban environment in cities with decaying, depopulated downtowns. The next step is revision of outdated zoning ordinances to reflect this new-found awareness.

The new San Francisco Main Library, which opened in April 1996, was built on an infill site in San Francisco's Civic Center district. A parking lot previously occupied the site, along with a small building that had served various government uses over the years. This site is right across the street from the BART (Bay Area Rapid Transit) system and is easily accessible by foot or by bus. Bike racks for patrons and staff, and showers for staff, encourage bike transportation. This central location means that the new library strengthens—and benefits from—the existing civic character.

The San Francisco Main Library, built on an infill site in San Francisco's Civic Center District. *(Photography by Timothy Hurley. Reprinted with permission.)*

Another type of infill, which diversifies neighborhoods while providing more affordable housing, is the "Granny flat" or carriage home—a small apartment in the rear yard of single-family homes. These accessory units can incrementally raise the density of a neighborhood without negatively affecting the neighborhood's character, especially if they blend in with the area's prevailing architecture.

Live/work projects, in which people can work where they live, offer another effective application of infill—and a wonderful example of a solution multiplier. Time that residents would normally spend commuting is freed up, allowing them to spend time with their families, to work with local volunteer organizations, or to enrich their lives in other ways. The environment and the larger community benefit from reduced automobile energy use and its associated air pollution.

Over the last decade, architect Thomas Dolan has designed a dozen live/work infill projects in San Francisco's East Bay area. These projects, with four to eighteen units each, are either very near mass transit or in pedestrian-accessible urban neighborhoods. Dolan has found that "because they are designed as communities, usually around courtyards that seem to successfully encourage interaction, they lead to the formation of friendships and a social structure characterized by a significant percentage of the residents' total social interaction happening right there in the community."

The city of Pasadena is committed to infill as a strategy for meeting one of the guiding principles in its general plan—to be a city where people can circulate without cars. One such project is Holly Street Village Apartments, a successful transit-oriented development that includes mixed-use, mixed-income housing, historic preservation, and attractive site planning and architecture. Holly Street Village Apartments is located between Old Pasadena's revitalized historic commercial core and the Civic Center, near a future light rail station. The infill project includes 358 units of new housing along with 16 loft apartments created through adaptive reuse of the historic former police headquarters. Also included are 11,000 square feet of ground-floor retail, comprised of a deli, a convenience store, and an art gallery.

The success of Holly Street Village Apartments has sparked a 70-unit senior project on the other side of a community park and a 24-unit market-rate condominium project nearby. Developed by the Janss Corporation, these projects received support from the city of Pasadena, which sold the land and assisted in project financing. The retail space is master leased by the city.

Communities and neighbors often resist the higher density that comes with infill, believing that it will reduce their quality of life. The benefits of infill projects sometimes get lost in contentious community debates over density and related issues. But denser development need not be worse development. Higher density is

Pasadena's General Plan Supports Infill

In 1992 Pasadena adopted a general plan based on seven organizing principles. These principles were not only unanimously adopted by the city council, Transportation Commission, and Planning Commission, but were also approved by voters in the November 1992 election. The principles of the plan include the following:

- Growth will be targeted to serve community needs and enhance the quality of life.
- Change will be harmonized to preserve Pasadena's historic character and environment.
- Economic vitality will be promoted to provide jobs, services, revenues, and opportunities.
- Pasadena will be promoted as a healthy family community.
- Pasadena will be a city where people can circulate without cars.
- Pasadena will be promoted as a cultural, scientific, corporate, entertainment, and educational center for the region.
- Community participation will be a permanent part of achieving a greater city.

Source: City of Pasadena, California.

very appropriate so long as quality of life is protected. Carrying out effective infill development depends on careful planning and design that helps to make dense residential neighborhoods safe, community-oriented, highly livable, and environmentally responsible (see "Design Strategies to Make Density Livable" in Appendix D). Jane Jacobs, an astute commentator on the built environment's impact on humans, reminds us that it is the *quality* of space that is essential to vibrant communities:

> In orthodox city planning, neighborhood open spaces are venerated in an amazingly uncritical fashion. Ask a zoner about the improvements in progressive codes and he will cite incentives toward leaving more open space. Walk with a planner through a dispirited neighborhood and though it be already scabby with deserted parks and tired landscaping festooned with old Kleenex, he will envision a future of more open space. More open space for what? For muggings? For bleak vacuums between buildings? Or for ordinary people to use and enjoy? But people do not use city open space just because it is there and because city planners and designers wish they would.
>
> *Jane Jacobs,* The Death and Life of Great American Cities, *1961*

Toolbox for Infill and Redevelopment

Redevelopment for Livable Communities. The Washington State Energy Office makes available this informative and useful booklet that provides retrofitting techniques and tools for creating livable communities. It also includes case studies of successful redevelopment projects that reduce sprawl development. To obtain a copy, contact the Energy Outreach Office, 503 West 4th Avenue, Olympia, WA 98501, or call (360) 943-4595.

The Local Government Commission's (LGC) Tools for Planning Infill Development

Building Livable Communities: A Policy Maker's Guide to Infill Development. This guidebook suggests a number of ways to create infill development in a community, including proactive planning, assuring public participation, using public facilities and development fees to attract investment, assisting with project financing, and zoning for mixed-use and higher-density development.

Participation Tools for Better Land Use Planning. This guidebook discusses ways to improve the level and quality of citizen participation in land-use planning. It describes tools such as computer simulation, role-playing games, Visual Preference Survey™, and facilitated meetings. Several case studies are featured throughout the book.

The LGC also offers other infill tools including a slide library, video library, and conference proceedings. For more information, contact the LGC at (916) 448-1198, or write to the LGC at Center for Livable Communities, a Project of the Local Government Commission, 1414 K Street, Suite 250, Sacramento, CA 95814.

BROWNFIELDS

Cities offer many opportunities to build on land that was previously occupied by industrial facilities or uses. Known as "brownfields," these sites are defined by the U.S. Environmental Protection Agency (EPA) as abandoned, idle, or under-used industrial and commercial facilities where expansion or redevelopment is complicated by real or perceived environmental contamination. Brownfields are often in prime locations with easy access to public transit, infrastructure resources, and the work force. Such sites are often inexpensive, relative to prime undeveloped land. Their development can also spearhead the revitalization of deteriorating neighborhoods. There are as many as 450,000 official brownfield sites around the country, most of them in urban areas.

It is hard to imagine now that the new Real Goods Solar Living Center in Hopland, California, was, until recently, the site of a California Department of Transportation dump. Real Goods Trading Company carefully transformed the land into a hybrid farm/park with climate-appropriate landscaping, wetland areas, ponds, organic demonstration gardens, orchards, and olive groves.

Farther up the coast, Portland's successful RiverPlace project was once home to a freeway, a plywood mill, and other industrial uses. The city of Portland reclaimed the site more than 20 years ago and guided its transformation. Today one finds a bustling 10-acre mixed-use development that offers a popular walkway to Waterfront Park and is a vital link in Portland's comprehensive downtown pedestrian plan. RiverPlace features a long row of small retail shops and restaurants that face the Willamette River, apartments above the shops, and, in the project's interior, office space, a hotel, a marina with floating restaurant, an athletic club, and a grass amphitheater on a riverfront park.

RiverPlace was created through a public-private partnership in which the Portland Development Commission selected Cornerstone Columbia Development because of the firm's previous experience with mixed-use projects and its management capabilities. The city offered the developers 10 years of property tax relief if they would build at high density and include affordable housing. While the project's density is high (47 units per acre), it is very livable. Retail and office spaces are fully leased, and the hotel has the highest occupancy rate in the area (95 percent year-round).

The brownfield site that became RiverPlace required some complex cleanup solutions, demonstrating the benefits of public-private partnerships. The city's Department of Environmental Quality paid for an extensive site assessment and remediation report, while the developers paid for the actual cleanup of toxic materials.

Long-range transportation planning played an integral role in the development of RiverPlace. Currently there is insufficient mass transit serving the project and insufficient parking for the high level of automobile use. So the newest addition has been designed for adaptability. A new 135,000-square-foot Pacific

Portland's RiverPlace project was once home to a freeway, as depicted in the photograph at the top. Today it has been transformed into a vibrant mixed-use area. *(Reprinted with permission, © C. Bruce Foster.)*

Gas Transmission office building includes a parking deck that will later be converted into office space once additional mass transit becomes available and automobile pressures ease. (The building was financed, incidentally, through an energy-saving program of the Oregon Economic Development Office; net savings in energy covered the financing and fees of 5 to 6 percent.)

Many prospective developers fear that if they become part of the chain of ownership of a brownfield site, they will be liable for cleanup of previous contamination. Under federal Superfund regulations, owners and users who unknowingly purchase contaminated sites can still be liable for full cleanup costs. The threat of liability has slowed both the cleanup and the economic redevelopment of many sites. That roadblock may be disappearing, however. A number of states have already established initiatives that minimize liability risks and encourage brownfield redevelopment.

The U.S. Environmental Protection Agency has also established the Brownfields Initiative to encourage investment in the cleaning up of brownfields to reduce risk to surrounding communities while promoting their redevelopment and beneficial reuse. EPA hopes to use market mechanisms to facilitate more property cleanups while discouraging first-time development and potential contamination of greenfields. In 1996, EPA committed to funding 50 pilot projects with up to $200,000 each for site assessment, characterization, and development of remediation plans prior to cleanup.

Responsible Greenfield Development

From an environmental standpoint, it is usually better to develop on already-disturbed land. At this point, however, market pressures often necessitate greenfield development. Moreover, government policies still subsidize greenfield development through existing taxes, zoning regulations, infrastructure grants, and other actions that encourage developers to seek greenfield sites for their projects. When development of greenfield sites is undertaken, there are various strategies to minimize environmental impacts. These include clustering buildings on just a portion of the site, downsizing the project, protecting significant ecosystems and wildlife corridors, and reducing automobile dependence through compact land-use patterns.

OPEN SPACE AND CLUSTERED DEVELOPMENT

Conventional development covers fields with a Euclidean pox of house lots and streets, and it barricades the roadsides with strips of jumbled commercialism. The creative way [to develop] places houses at the treeline or in the woods, keeps roads to a minimum and puts those roads on the least environmentally sensitive terrain. The target is to leave half of the space open, often by reducing lot size and clustering houses together.

William A. MacLeish, New England Monthly, *September 1990*

The strategy of protecting portions of a site as open space while increasing density on the developed areas is often the best way to preserve or restore land. Open space provides an opportunity for people to learn from and better appreciate nature, while protecting biodiversity of species and native habitats. But it is important to note that open space is more than a park bench plopped on an expanse of Kentucky bluegrass. This should not just be random space left blank on a plan and labeled "open space," but useful, well-thought-out, meaningful space that serves multiple purposes. In green developments, open space should be planned and located to balance such needs and opportunities as recreation, preservation of wildlife habitat, carbon dioxide sequestering (using vegetation to take carbon dioxide out of the atmosphere), food production, storm drainage, and noise reduction.

More than 65 percent of Dewees Island ®—784 acres—has been set aside as a wildlife refuge and will remain undeveloped forever. The master plan developed for the island by Burt Hill Kosar Rittlemann Associates of Washington, D.C., protects more than 550 acres of land by conservation easement to minimize disruption of fragile ecosystems and wildlife habitat. Even the land that is developed is well protected by development covenants that limit the area of impact on each lot to 7,500 square feet. By early 1997, 60 lots had been sold and 20 homes completed, with another 11 in design or construction. Although lots in the first phase sold somewhat more slowly than initially expected, income greatly exceeded the pro forma, demonstrating that some home buyers are willing to pay a premium for the benefits of protecting habitat.

In identifying open space set-asides, it is important to consider not only those areas themselves, but also how they interconnect. Careful layout of a site offers an opportunity to provide contiguous wildlife corridors and habitat areas—reversing, for at least that parcel, the widespread trend of ecosystem fragmentation that is occurring nationwide. When possible, open spaces on one parcel should be

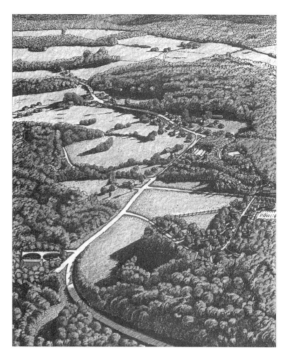

In his book, *Rural by Design*, Randall Arendt illustrated conventional development land-use patterns with this aerial view, as compared with more compact, creative development seen in the image on the right. *(Reprinted by permission from* Rural by Design, © *1994 by the American Planning Association.)*

linked with open space set-asides on surrounding properties. Keeping wide buffer areas along streams and valley bottoms is another important way to provide this sort of unbroken corridor.

Clustering is particularly valuable and applicable when farmland is under development pressure. Randall Arendt, author of *Rural by Design* and *Conservation Design for Subdivisions* and a national advocate of clustering, endorses this approach. "Whole sections of rural towns can be developed in a manner that will preserve significant tracts of open space for agriculture, forestry, and wildlife habitat," he says. "There are even ways to enable rural landowners to realize their equity without having to slice their entire property into house lots."

A 1990 study conducted by Jeff Lacy of the Center for Rural Massachusetts found that open space pays off. A comparison of real estate values in clustered subdivisions versus conventional site plans showed that people are willing to spend significantly more for the amenities and benefits of common open space with smaller individual lots.

The study looked at 800 property transactions over a 21-year period in two Amherst, Massachusetts, subdivisions: Orchard Valley (a conventional development with half-acre lots) and Echo Hill (a clustered development with quarter-acre lots and open space). Both had average densities of two units per acre, the same basic floor space (1,600 square feet), and similar average prices. The main difference between the two subdivisions was the site plan. Orchard Valley had very little open space except for a small area surrounding a pond. In contrast, half of the Echo Hill development was retained as open space, which included a playing field, a woodland trail network, ponds, a swimming area, a tennis/basketball court, and a baseball diamond. In the mid-1970s, homes in both developments sold for about $26,600. After 20 years, both had appreciated significantly, but the average price of an Orchard Valley home went up to only $134,200, while the Echo Hill homes increased to $151,300.

Clustering homes can substantially reduce infrastructure costs for developers —apparently without reducing property values. Arendt points to a Howard County, Maryland, study showing that the local housing market would value one-acre residential lots with plenty of open space the same as conventional large lots of three to five acres. By clustering the homes, the developer would save $3,500 per home in infrastructure cost. Thus, for a 25-acre development with five houses, clustering the homes on just five acres saves the developer $14,000. Savings can be achieved, for example, by reducing paved area, minimizing the length of utility lines and sewer systems, and reducing the amount of earth removal. Meanwhile, the remaining 20 acres of land can be permanently protected as open space.

The National Association of Home Builders found that clustering development, along with narrowing streets and using natural drainage, can protect land and cost as little as one-third as much as conventional development. This study, titled *Cost Effective Site Planning: Single Family Development,* compared two land-

---

Resources on Protecting Open Space Through Clustered Housing

Rural by Design, by Randall Arendt et al. Planners Press, American Planning Association, Washington, D.C., 1994. 460 pages, hardback.

Conservation Design for Subdivisions: A Practical Guide to Creating Open Space Networks, by Randall Arendt. Island Press, Covelo, California, 1996. 160 pages, paperback.

use plans for the same hypothetical site: the first plan had uniform sites of three to four houses per acre; the second plan had the same overall density but clustered a mixture of housing types to preserve open space. Costs were compared for site preparation (clearing and grading), roads, driveways, street trees, sewers, water, and drainage. The study also assumed that the cluster design would use 20-foot-wide streets instead of the usual 30-foot width and would shift from full curb-and-gutter drainage to swale drainage. Land development costs per unit came to $13,102 (updated to 1987 dollars in a 1989 report, *The Costs of Alternative Development Patterns,* by James Frank for the Urban Land Institute) with the conventional scenario, and only $4,600 for the innovative approach.

Prairie Crossing, in Grayslake, Illinois, 45 miles northwest of Chicago, is seeking to integrate residential development with the preservation of natural areas and agriculture. The developers are using a creative land-use strategy to preserve as much open space as possible on this 667-acres of rolling farmland. Upon build-out, Prairie Crossing will comprise 317 single-family homes—far fewer than the 1,500 considered in earlier plans by other developers—while protecting nearly two-thirds of the land as open space. The property had been involved in protracted litigation in the 1970s over a development plan "that would have destroyed the rural character of the neighborhood," according to Victoria Post-Ranney, of Prairie Holdings Corporation, the current developer.

The hybrid development plan for Prairie Crossing includes several land-use configurations: large-lot residential areas, clustered homes, and mixed-use neighborhoods. Several native habitats are being restored as part of the site's development, including tall-grass prairies, wetlands, and a lake. One hundred fifty acres of existing farmland remain in production, including a 10-acre community-supported organic garden. About 75 acres have been set aside for industrial and commercial uses. A commuter rail station at the southern edge of the site provides transit service to downtown and the airport. Prairie Crossing broke ground in 1994, and by January 1997, 50 homes were occupied with another 30 under construction. While sales started out slowly, positive press coverage and the addition of such amenities as the lake and a community center in a restored century-old dairy barn have increased the sales pace.

The value of open space is hard to quantify. Developers often consider only the revenue lost by keeping a portion of a project undeveloped. But good-faith efforts to protect habitat and open space, while concentrating development in prescribed areas, can offer both direct and indirect financial benefits to developers. Tens or even

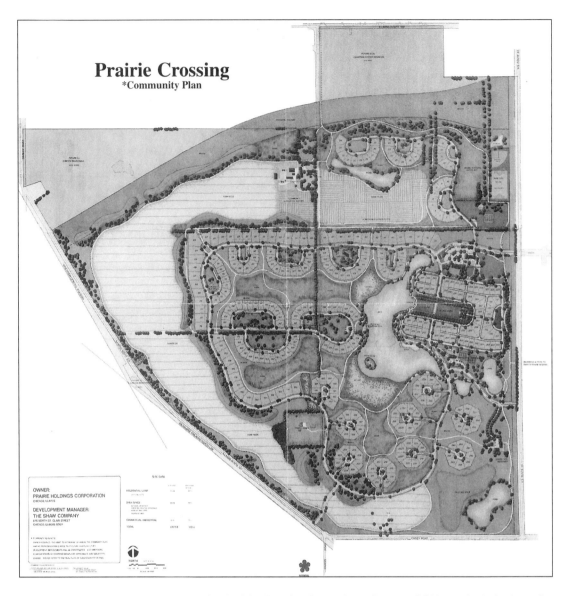

The development plan for Prairie Crossing, located northwest of Chicago, includes large-lot residential areas, clustered homes, and mixed-use neighborhoods. *(Reprinted with permission from Prairie Holdings Corporation.)*

hundreds of thousands of dollars in legal battles with community and environmental activists can be saved by gaining early support for land protection efforts. And, as the developers of South Carolina's Dewees Island have found, protected open space can dramatically increase the desirability—and value—of property.

NEOTRADITIONAL DEVELOPMENT PATTERNS

> Unlike the typical suburban PUD [planned unit development], where high densities are viewed with less enthusiasm, the neotraditional town leverages higher density development to achieve a sense of community....higher densities of the neo-traditional development can be used to offset land and infrastructure costs.
>
> Haymount Project Market Analysis, *Economics Research Associates,*
> *February 1996*

The conventional wisdom in regard to residential development in America since the 1940s has been that every home needs to be its own private little estate—even if only a single lot. Properties are typically surrounded by fences or neat rows of cultivated shrubs imported from foreign climates. Prevailing zoning laws usually prescribe this pattern of development. Increasingly, however, progressive developers and community planners are challenging this approach. They recognize that large-lot zoning encourages automobile dependence while precluding the establishment of cohesive neighborhoods—tight-knit communities where neighbors can get to know one another.

The idea of creating compact towns or village centers in which people can walk to basic services, access public transit, and feel part of their community is variously referred to as neotraditional development, transit-oriented development, traditional neighborhood development, pedestrian pocket planning, or New Urbanism, depending on the context and application. While these concepts remain controversial in some architectural circles, the basic idea is gaining momentum among developers, town planning officials, and home buyers. Neotraditional development is an approach that aims to create more livable communities by designing them to resemble and function as traditional small towns or urban neighborhoods, land-use patterns that have worked well for centuries.

Neotraditional developments are designed to be less dependent on the automobile, with compact, pedestrian-friendly neighborhoods and mixed-use areas of retail shops, professional offices, and even light industry. They are designed on a pedestrian scale so that many activities of daily living are within easy walking distance, allowing accessibility for those who do not drive, including the elderly and the young. These concepts are expressed through civic architecture that includes public and semipublic spaces, narrow streets to slow traffic and minimize the impacts of pavement, plus porches and shallow front yard setbacks to encourage neighborly interaction.

The fact that most neotraditional developments completed to date are on green-field sites has led to criticism that this is just a prettier form of suburban sprawl. But neotraditional projects can run the gamut of size, location, and development strategy—including infill, adaptive reuse, and even brownfield development. Victorian Gate in Columbus, Ohio, is a two-block neotraditional development with approximately 160 units of market rental housing plus 6,000 square feet of retail space on High Street. All of the space has been successfully leased and rented, with no subsidies or government assistance. At the other end of the spectrum is Haymount, a new town being developed outside Washington, D.C., that will, upon build-out, include 4,000 homes and up to three-quarters of a million square feet of commercial space. The scale of Haymount is large enough that development will be laid out in smaller neighborhood pockets based on neotraditional design principles.

Neotraditional practitioners have also contributed to the successful revitalization of a number of historic downtowns. The town of Stuart, Florida, invited leading New Urbanist architects and town planners Andres Duany and Elizabeth Plater-Zyberk to apply their concept of small-town life to Stuart. The renewal project won a Governor's Award as a model for other Florida cities and spurred cities around the country to consider redevelopment as a way of preserving and emphasizing traditional aspects of their downtowns, rather than making way for yet another mall.

In 1988, when Duany and Plater-Zyberk were hired, less than half of Stuart's downtown commercial space was occupied. The downtown was decaying, with shoppers choosing nearby malls instead and retail stores abandoning the area. But the design team found that the town had characteristics similar to those of the new towns they were designing: distinctive regional architecture, mixed-use buildings, and pedestrian-oriented neighborhoods.

Under the architects' guidance, Stuart enacted new codes that regulated building colors, materials, landscape features, and designs to enhance the town's historic image. The new approach attracted dozens of new businesses and boutiques, as well as new downtown residents. In just five years, from 1987 to 1992, the number of businesses in downtown Stuart jumped from 25 to 87, while the number of employees tripled. Buildings are now fully occupied, and townspeople enjoy such new amenities as a series of waterfront parks, a pathway along the river, a pier, and two other parks. Three public structures have been restored. One of these is a 1937 art deco courthouse, which had been taken out of service when a new courthouse was completed in 1986. The new $10 million building

Victorian Gate in Columbus, Ohio, is an example of a small neotraditional infill development project. *(Reprinted with permission from Continental Real Estate Companies.)*

ended up causing health problems for people working there, and even the expenditure of another $13 million could not make this sick building habitable. The county had planned to build yet another courthouse—outside the city limits—and tear down the historic one. Duany convinced the county to restore the old one, which now lends extra character and function to the downtown area.

In 1996, the Congress for the New Urbanism (CNU), a loosely structured body of planners and architects committed to neotraditional development, adopted the following as part of a new charter: "The Congress for the New Urbanism views disinvestment in central cities, the spread of placeless sprawl, increasing separation by race and income, environmental deterioration, loss of agricultural lands and wilderness, and the erosion of society's built heritage as one interrelated community-building challenge."

The Charter of the New Urbanism calls for the creation of neighborhoods that are diverse in use and population, communities designed for pedestrian and transit as well as the car, cities and towns shaped by physically defined and universally accessible public spaces and community institutions, and urban places framed by architecture and landscape design that celebrates local history, climate, ecology, and building practice. The charter includes 27 specific principles dealing with policy, development practices, urban planning, and design.

Some observers mistakenly believe that neotraditional development is synonymous with green development. That is not the case. While neotraditional, or New Urbanism, planning and design includes some elements of a green agenda — such as pedestrian orientation, increased density, mixed-use development, and pockets of open space — most built New Urbanist projects have fallen short when it comes to energy efficiency, building orientation, building materials selection, water efficiency, and landscaping. The CNU's charter suggests that "architecture and landscape design should grow from local climate, topography, history and building practice" and "natural methods of heating and cooling can be more resource-efficient than mechanical systems." However, unless these concepts are actively pursued in the planning and design of neotraditional communities, the projects will fail to meet their full potential as models for the kind of development needed to lead us to a more sustainable future.

For more information on New Urbanism:

Congress for the New Urbanism
The Hurst Building
5 Third Street, Suite 500A
San Francisco, CA 94103
(415) 495-2255; (415) 495-1731

New Urban News (a bimonthly newsletter on neotraditional developments
across the United States)
P.O. Box 157
Emmaus, PA 18049
(610) 965-4623; (610) 966-3434 (fax)

CORPORATE CAMPUSES

Increasingly, large corporations are moving their headquarters from urban centers into expansive, rural "corporate campuses." This trend has serious environmental implications, including dependence on automobile commuting and destruction of farmland and open space. Even the most energy-efficient, site-sensitive office building, if located outside an urban core and requiring employees to drive to work, reflects the failure to use a whole-systems approach. The energy consumption of employees' vehicles will likely negate any savings generated by the building. Such factors should be considered in the planning process before a site is even selected.

United Parcel Service (UPS) and Duracell Corporation have both recently developed large corporate campuses—UPS in Atlanta, Georgia, and Duracell in Meriden, Connecticut. These companies have been conscientious about preserving woodlands and other natural areas, limiting total impact area on the sites, shielding the facilities from the surrounding communities, and designing buildings that are models of energy efficiency and environmental responsiveness. Yet, by locating on large plots of land outside urban centers, they have increased the automobile dependence of their employees while consuming large tracts of land that might otherwise have remained undeveloped. While these facilities are often profiled as examples of environmentally responsive building design, they raise the broader question of location. Could these facilities have been planned as urban infill projects? Could they have been built on restored brownfields? What is the net cost to society, to the environment, and to employees of a facility that increases automobile use and consumes large expanses of previously undeveloped land?

In contrast, aerospace industry giant Boeing Corporation recently built a new corporate campus, Longacres Park, that addresses some of these land-use concerns. Conscious of the impact on Seattle's already overcrowded roadways, Boeing chose to locate on 214 acres outside the city. But instead of building way out in the sticks, the company located the new facility adjacent to a metro transit route in Renton, a Seattle suburb. Once a forest and a dairy farm, the site had most recently been home to a racetrack that destroyed such original landscape features as creeks and wetlands.

The new development is organized around a central park. Wherever possible, the site plan clustered buildings to create common entries and outdoor terraces that face the park. A network of paths and covered walkways encourages walking between buildings. Boeing downsized the parking area, provided buses for students and visitors, and implemented ride sharing and other incentives to minimize automobile use. Full build-out will include 2.9 million square feet in 13 buildings housing 12,000 employees. As of January 1997 almost 20 percent of the project was complete.

Can Development Be Good for the Environment?

The idea of using development as an engine to protect open space, strengthen communities, reduce automobile use, and even restore damaged ecosystems is an exciting one. Environmentalists are used to thinking of developers as the enemies of land preservation and other environmental goals, but responsible developers are beginning to be recognized as allies of the environment. Participants of the American Institute of Architects/Nathan Cummings Foundation Roundtables on Sustainable Development noted that it will require a paradigm shift to move society "from the thinking that the best it can do is minimize impact, toward a view in which development is seen as both contributing to the growth of healthy human communities, while simultaneously restoring (not merely sustaining) the natural environment."

Developers cannot single-handedly serve as the engine of environmental and social gains. Success is most likely when a collaboration is established with municipal officials, environmental organizations, and citizen groups. Working together increases the prospect of everyone's benefiting, including the environment.

In some areas, residents assume that sprawl is the natural outcome of economic growth, and they passively accept it as a given. In other places, community frustrations with sprawl have led to no-growth policies that stop virtually all development. The development community often responds with litigation, followed by countersuits, and everybody loses in the end. But development does not have to be synonymous with physical expansion or growth. Instead of increasing a community's physical size, developers can improve the quality and complexity of a community by thinking about how the project will link to uses in the immediate surroundings, and what is missing from the neighborhood. The best green developments—on every scale, from a single building to a large mixed-use project—strengthen and enhance existing communities.

With the use of conventional development patterns ruled by zoning mechanisms, every acre ends up being somebody's private fenced-off space. Because it is often politically difficult to enact open space preservation regulations, many communities adopt large-lot zoning with the intention of preserving some open space. Low-density development, however, is not the best answer for preserving land, because single-family homes sitting square in the middle of larger lots, be they one, two, or ten acres, still interrupt land-use patterns necessary for wildlife habitat, farming, or other land-based activities. Low-density, large-lot development instead usually exacerbates sprawl, while the advantages of protected open space—economically and as an amenity—are lost. Planned, responsible development of large parcels of land, on the other hand, at least offers the *possibility* of protecting significant areas of open space.

There are some sites that should not be built on. But for most land, development on greenfield sites can be implemented in a manner that protects and restores significant portions of the land. Even on developed portions of a site, careful planning and design can foster community, reduce automobile dependence, and minimize environmental impacts from storm water runoff, erosion, and pollution.

At Maho Bay on St. John, guests sleep in rustic, screened-in tent-cabins perched on wooden platforms. *(Reprinted with permission from Maho Bay Camps, Inc.)*

CHAPTER 4

Market Research

WHILE ECO-TOURISM IS POPULAR TODAY, it was a radical departure from the status quo in the mid-1970s when Stanley Selengut got his feet wet as a resort developer and helped to launch the industry. In 1976, Selengut risked $250,000 of his own money to create a private campground-like resort on an in-holding within Virgin Islands National Park on St. John, largest of the U.S. Virgin Islands. His Maho Bay resort features 114 wood-and-canvas "tent-cabins" perched on wooden platforms and accessible by wooden walkways above the fragile tropical forest floor. Guests sleep in rustic screened-in tent-cabins, shower in a common bathhouse, and either cook their own food on gas burners or dine in an open-air restaurant—always close to the island's rich natural environment. Although this is not a resort for everyone, tourists wanting to be close to nature while keeping their environmental impact to a minimum have made the Maho Bay resort highly popular.

Selengut's bold move to create and expand his three Virgin Islands resorts demonstrates his visionary brilliance. But his success is also a result of careful research. He is a master of getting to know his clientele and responding to their needs with his product offerings—in short, market research.

Visitors to Maho Bay are among the 43 million people, according to surveys, who are willing to pay a premium to patronize green hotels or resorts. Selengut

Tent-cottages at Maho Bay are accessible by wooden walkways above the fragile tropical forest floor. *(Reprinted with permission from Maho Bay Camps, Inc.)*

invests considerable time and money in learning exactly what it is that this growing submarket of the tourist sector wants. He makes extensive use of customer surveys to determine what his visitors are looking for, and what they are finding at Maho Bay. Each year he personally examines 2,000 to 3,000 surveys completed by guests, using that information to refine the visitor experience, improve customer service, and guide him in planning new developments.

Selengut's decision to seek a different clientele from the usual sunbathing-and-beach-house set seemed risky when he founded Maho Bay. But Maho's very high occupancy rates have given him remarkable profits of 25 percent on his gross revenue. He has done well because he figured out—through personalized market research—what his visitors wanted and how to provide it. Today's rapidly growing eco-tourism industry is proof that his ideas have broad applicability.

Whether developing a resort facility in the Virgin Islands, a residential subdivision in Tucson, or an office building in Chicago, market research is crucial to refining the product and providing confidence that it will succeed in the marketplace. Market research helps developers understand whom to target as buyers or renters, what features they are looking for, where they want to live, and how much they are willing to spend. Market research informs the planning and design phases of real estate development and provides direction for positioning the product in the marketplace. Finally, market research provides critical information about the economic climate that will help the developer and any investment partners determine whether to risk moving ahead with a project.

Market researchers employ various tools to determine whether certain products and features will succeed. In real estate development, the process typically entails examining the demographics and characteristics of the market area and reviewing long-term national, regional, and local customer preference trends for a given product. Traditional market research, however, compares existing products serving similar customers, often overlooking the possibility of new products or new customers. Market research for green development projects must venture beyond conventional market research into these new areas.

Some of the most important tools of market research are described in this chapter. Such basic tools as comparables and surveys are useful, whether examining a conventional real estate development or a green development. Yet because these tools may fail to identify real markets, green developers often turn to more innovative market research strategies to help them determine market demand, market preferences, and which specific product features to include in their projects.

Limitations of Conventional Market Research

Conventional market research asks questions only about historic market performance of comparable products ("comps"). This practice can be one of green development's greatest barriers, because comps may not give an accurate reading of the appeal of the new, greener product. The information presented by conventional market research can stymie innovation and encourage risk-averse developers and financiers to shy away from entering the world of green development. This "rearview mirror" approach to market research that bases feasibility studies on an extrapolation of the past often portrays innovative green developments as inherently less feasible, because there is no way to evaluate them using traditional methodology.

In *Competing for the Future,* author Gary Hamel tells the story of a U.S. auto company that used intensive market research to guide new product development. The result, however, was the creation of a new compact car that competed against three-year-old Japanese models. Meanwhile, Japan had designed and introduced exciting new cars that continued to capture the market. The U.S. car company's market research identified customer satisfaction for *existing* products but failed to draw out ideas for innovations. Studying historical market segments and determining what customers like about available products may help fine-tune a product's specific features to meet the needs and wants of a particular market segment, but it seldom leads to product innovation. Hamel suggests that "insight into new product possibilities may be garnered in many ways, all of which go beyond traditional modes of market research."

In an interview with *On the Ground* magazine, Philip Langdon, author of *A Better Place to Live,* criticized market researchers and developers for their inability to seek ecologically responsible products. "One of the things that bothers me is the assertion that there's nothing wrong with the kinds of houses or communities that people are getting because this is what consumers choose. That's a fallacy. Many people simply take what's available." In reference to risk-averse developers who balk at change, Langdon compares them to office equipment manufacturers 20 years ago who said there was no need for personal computers as the public was satisfied with typewriters. "At any given time people are buying what's available. To leap from that to say that therefore there's no need for anything different or better is, I think, illogical."

Market research validates Langdon's opinion. According to Laurie Volk and Todd Zimmerman, managing directors of Zimmerman/Volk Associates, a firm that conducts strategic analysis for the real estate industry, the best and most rigorous qualitative analysis consistently indicates that in the new home market — even in very conservative regions — people are buying conventional new housing because it is the only thing offered, not because it is what they want. One of the benefits of taking a risk with an innovative product, according to Zimmerman and Volk, is that developers will *avoid* the risk of being caught in a flat market with a product that is no different from all the others that are available. "When development programs are based on what has succeeded in the past, they are susceptible to market shifts. It is the 'rearview mirror' approach to research that is in large measure responsible for the dramatic boom/bust cycles to which American real estate has been prone."

Comps—When They Work and When They Don't

Despite their limitations, comps remain one of the most important tools for real estate development, both in figuring out what buyers are looking for and in securing financing. Comps typically provide information about market demand for products or product features and what the market has accepted in regard to price, size, design, quality, and amenities. But what if there are no comps to examine? Market researchers tend to focus only on what they can compare: square footage and other traditional attributes. This practice tends to overlook the features that make any project unique—information that could help the developer distinguish the product when marketing it. Worse, unless the project offers all that conventional developments do *and more,* a comp limited to square footage may penalize what is really a more appealing product. For many developers, this has been a reason not to touch innovative projects—making green development and other new ideas in real estate and building slow to catch on. As more developers are discovering, however, the lack of comps need not be a reason to give up on green development, but it will require digging a little deeper to determine the market potential of a project.

In seeking comps for new development plans, market researchers collect detailed information about the value of buildings or space in terms of price, size, demand, and the value of particular features. These features are evaluated as negative, positive, or neutral (a neutral attribute being one that all products of that type would necessarily have, such as a roof on a house). For example, a home owner may purchase a house because of such positive attributes as the floor plan, unique design features, or proximity to work, schools, and shops. Negative attributes, such as an inefficient heating system, may be tolerated if the positive attributes are judged to be of greater value or the customer does not perceive that he or she has another option. However, given a choice between two houses with the same positive attributes, if one also has a more efficient heating system, this attribute may differentiate the product enough to give it an advantage in the marketplace. The product has all the comparable features of a conventional product *and* some green features as well.

Developers and market researchers who focus only on determining the primary needs of customers may fail to value the additional positive attributes of green developments. In real estate, the customer's primary need is for space. Conventional market research that only compares square footage to square

The market research for the new town of Haymount in Virginia included discussion of the benefits of the project's neotraditional features. *(Reprinted with permission from John A. Clark, Haymount. Drawing by Duany Plater-Zyberk.)*

footage may not ask enough questions to uncover additional needs and wants of potential customers.

Despite the many features and value-added attributes of green developments that attract buyers, it is often the conventional and easily comparable features of a project that entice investment from risk-averse financial institutions. Without this financing the project will not be built. Comps remain the most important market research for lenders, who want to see historic examples of success.

When developer John Clark shared his vision for Haymount with a private investor, he brashly revealed his plan to create a development unlike any on the market through his attention to ecologically responsible building and land use. Yet when Clark hired the well-known firm Economics Research Associates (ERA) to prepare a conventional project market analysis report, a vehicle for raising more capital to finance $10 million in infrastructure costs, hardly a mention was made of the project's green elements. Why? Because the ideas were new and different, and most banks will not lend if there are no comps.

ERA's report compared housing values, sizes, and historical market performance for existing Northern Virginia housing submarkets going back as far as

1980. Some discussion of the benefits of the new town's neotraditional features was included along with statistics about population, job market trends, and existing and projected commercial and retail activity in the region. But the fact that Haymount was carefully planned to capitalize on the benefits of mixed-use development was not addressed. In fact, the commercial and retail activities were treated as separate projects from the residential development for the purpose of this feasibility study. Clark's vision for an integrated design that creates a community of homes, commercial and retail businesses, civic buildings, and recreation amenities got lost in a maze of data that only compared houses to houses, and commercial and retail plans to existing conventional commercial developments, but he recognized what the financiers wanted, and he provided it.

Market Research Tools Applied to Green Development

Green developers are moving beyond the bounds of conventional market research. The breadth of these approaches used to gauge market potential is indicative of the newness of this field and the creativity of the pioneering players.

DIRECT OBSERVATION

Direct observation can enable developers to understand the community and the context in which a new development is to be sited. Spending time at the location —lots of time—is one of the best ways to do that.

Developer Harold Kalke has spent 25 years studying the Vancouver real estate market and observing the people of various neighborhoods in order to plan new projects that will fit in well. Before redeveloping the land at 2211 West Fourth Avenue, Kalke spent long hours observing the activities of surrounding businesses and people on Fourth Avenue. He observed the demographics of the Kitsilano neighborhood and the patterns of use at the businesses. Kalke visited the site at all hours of the day, sometimes dragging his wife along after an evening out, so that he could observe the change in activities throughout the day and listen to the sounds of the street. This information filled Kalke with ideas about the attributes that would make 2211 West Fourth a successful development.

It was those long hours of observation that led Kalke to incorporate such design features as a double-wall, rainscreen construction detail to block out street noise. Direct observation also influenced his decisions about the mix of businesses and activities appropriate for the project. During the development process, a national retail store and the provincial Liquour Board came to Kalke, offering to prelease space. The banks urged him to take advantage of these opportunities, but he was determined to create a more appropriate mix of retail and commercial tenants that would protect the strong sense of community he had observed in Kitsilano. As far as Kalke was concerned, liquor and chain stores did not fit this criterion.

Kalke hand-picked retailers that he believed would blend in and add to the long-term vitality of the neighborhood. At street level, a natural food grocery store/restaurant is situated beside a credit union, a bookstore, and a long-established Vancouver outdoor sporting goods store (which relocated to this site). These businesses draw clientele from the densely populated neighborhood surrounding 2211 West Fourth and from the 78 condominium apartments that make up the third and fourth stories of the complex. On the second floor, the offices of famed environmentalist and television personality David Suzuki are located next to various health practitioners and Kalke's own offices, Salt Lick Productions, Ltd.

Target Market Analysis: Finding the Green Buyer

Market research for a green development entails careful analysis of who the customers are and what products they want. The target market for a green development may be quite different from the target market for a conventional development. Or it may be a smaller subgroup of a recognized larger market.

Zimmerman/Volk Associates uses a tool it calls *target market analysis* to find specific markets, or submarkets within conventional market categories. This firm goes beyond demographically based customer profiles to "put human faces on the numbers." For example, in studying residential demand for new towns, the company examines in detail the life-style characteristics and housing preferences of potential customer types. For residential development, it has classified 39 unique household types according to life stage (empty-nesters, retirees, families, younger singles, etc.) and geographic locations (cities, suburbs, small and edge cities, town and country, rural/agrarian, etc.). Each of these groups has its own specific economic and demographic characteristics, consumption patterns, lifestyles, and housing preferences.

Retailers that would add to the vitality of the neighborhood were chosen for the 2211 West Fourth mixed-use project in Vancouver. *(Reprinted with permission, © Norman Hotson.)*

Zimmerman and Volk's research for an urban redevelopment project in Norfolk, Virginia, designed by Duany Plater-Zyberk, yielded results quite different from those of conventional market research. Because the investigators examined several household types that had not originally been considered likely customers, their research forecast higher overall demand and higher absorption rates. Their findings convinced the developer that housing that accommodates a greater mix of household types would attract customers from a larger range of target markets, including home buyers who would otherwise be seeking housing in suburban locations.

Jim Chaffin used a similar approach when he began work at Spring Island in the late 1980s. Even though Chaffin is a strong advocate for the environment, when it comes to business he is just as concerned about risk as any other developer. When he began exploring the opportunities for a greatly downsized, environmentally conscious development on Spring Island, he did not know whether there would be a market for it. The idea of a private recreational community emphasizing environmental preservation had not been tried before. Golf resorts were the development of choice for South Carolina's Low Country islands. Chaffin had to prove to himself—and to his partners—that there was a market for the product he envisioned.

As he began planning the basic elements of this new project, Chaffin conducted extensive market analysis. "Real estate development is market identification and product development," says Chaffin. So why, he wondered, were there no products of this specific type in the marketplace? Was there no market? Or did the previous absence of a similar product keep people from realizing that there really was a market niche to be filled? Chaffin set about identifying and quantifying potential submarkets that he could target for his initial vision for Spring Island.

Chaffin started with conventional market research by studying demographics. He learned that the 78 million baby boomers in the United States would begin turning 50 in 1996—one every six seconds. He also learned that a population shift was bringing more people to the Southeast to retire. Further research revealed that people over 50 take the most vacations and begin searching for retirement homes. Earning power is also peaking at age 50. Chaffin next turned to opinion polls to learn more about this population's market needs, interests, and mind-sets— sociographic and psychographic research. A 1989 Roper poll indicated that 67 percent of Americans thought of themselves as environmentalists. In 1991 another Roper poll found that for the first time people were more preoccupied with leisure and quality of life than with work. Chaffin describes this as a shift from being "status driven" to being "principle driven." People were caring for themselves, their community, and the environment, instead of simply striving to make more money. Other studies showed that more money was now being spent on cultural activities than sporting activities, and that people were expressing a greater feeling of individual responsibility and concern for the environment.

All this information helped Chaffin and his partners assure themselves of a market for their Spring Island development. Having paid $17 million for the property, he and his partners were still concerned about risk and decided to include a golf course in the development plans. Nearby Hilton Head and other successful island golf resorts provided ample evidence of the demand for golf club recreational properties. They felt that the risk was too great to rely on nature trails alone as the recreational amenity. The golf course was a "safety valve," says Chaffin, to assure the developers and their financial backers of the market demand for this product.

If the project were to be developed today, Chaffin believes it would be a success without the golf course, because nature has proven to be the number one amenity for Spring Island's home owners. Today the island is home to a thriving community whose occupants agree that it is the stands of old-growth oak trees and subtropical forests, the bald eagles, deer, fox squirrels, and other wildlife that have drawn them to the island to enjoy the connection with nature. Fewer than half the occupants play golf, and the average age of home owners is 54 — Chaffin's numbers were right.

By identifying new customers or market niches that would not otherwise have been recognized, Chaffin was able to succeed with his innovative style of recreational community development. Similarly, by studying environmental trends and emerging consumer interest in eco-tourism, Stanley Selengut developed a new product that connected tourists with the natural environment. Selengut is drawing new customers to St. John, expanding the island's popular tourism industry by appealing to the eco-tourism niche market, and establishing comps for future products.

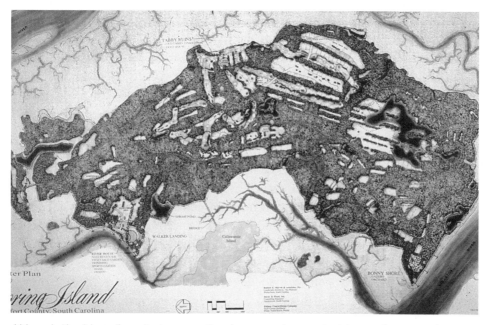

Although the idea of a private recreational community emphasizing environmental preservation had not been tried before, developers of Spring Island decided to create a nature preserve in their 500-home development. *(Reprinted with permission from Betsy Chaffin.)*

SURVEYS

The real estate industry has long relied on surveys as a key component of market research. They can be useful to green developers when the right questions are asked and the information is used creatively and in the proper context. Countless surveys of the housing market have tried to provide enough information to help developers avoid the risk of building products the market does not want. Surveys can provide information about product types and characteristics and about needs and wants of potential buyers of a product or service. They can be done on any level: national, state, regional, local, or even individual neighborhoods.

Surveys can be of tremendous benefit to green developers. But, like analysis of comparables, they can also provide misleading information. Many assumptions about market preferences have been derived from surveys. Some have contributed to the lack of variety in real estate development and to the trend toward cookie-cutter real estate development throughout the United States. For example, the industry assumed that condominiums attract divorced singles or middle-aged couples after the kids move out, and that apartments attract only young people. Recent studies have shown that these simple rules of thumb about the marketplace overlook the complex patterns and profiles of real estate consumers today. There are trends and patterns in housing preferences that can be gleaned from surveys, but surveys are most useful when employed in conjunction with other types of market research.

Surveys often fail to ask the right questions to guide ecologically responsible development and to demonstrate a demand for its products. Green development seeks to provide a better quality of life and to encourage safe, healthy human interaction while protecting the environment and preserving natural resources. Even if people do not overtly express a desire for green living, they seek the qualities that green developments deliver. For example, golf is increasing in popularity, and a growing number of residential golf course communities are cropping up throughout the United States. Developers find that lots adjacent to golf courses sell faster and at premium prices. But is it the sport or the space that is drawing home buyers? In an informal survey done by the *Philadelphia Inquirer,* four out of five residents in two new golf course developments in Montgomery County, Pennsylvania, indicated that they have little or no interest in playing golf. They chose the homes primarily because they prefer the parklike setting and attractive views from their windows.

Brooke Warrick, president of American Lives, Inc., a San Francisco-based market research firm, had a hunch that people wanted something other than golf course communities. American Lives has been asking home buyers what elements of communities are important to them, to determine people's interest in environmentally responsible and community-sensitive development. In 1994 the company surveyed 2,300 people in regard to various characteristics of real estate and community development. The survey showed an overwhelming interest in such community-sensitive features as walking and biking paths, natural open space, and quiet, low-traffic areas. However, the survey may have biased its outcome by asking whether people liked particular features with which they were familiar, rather than asking their preference between two ways to achieve the same result. For example, most respondents replied "yes" when asked whether they like cul-de-sacs. But do they really like cul-de-sacs, or are they seeking the end-use qualities and life-style they think accompany cul-de-sac development patterns: quiet neighborhoods, safe places for children to play, lower automobile traffic, distance from polluting industries, and so on? All these qualities can be achieved as well—if not better—through compact, mixed-use neighborhoods. But the survey did not inquire about such alternatives, and the respondents may not have been aware of, or understood, this type of development. Surveys that ask questions that do not allow respondents to really understand and express their preferences from an end-use perspective may fail to accurately reflect customer needs and wants.

Recognizing that real estate surveys may not be asking the right questions to gain insight into green development demand, some developers have drawn on surveys outside the realm of real estate. Chaffin and others have used data from consumer interest surveys on environmental awareness and concern, for example, to extrapolate demand for environmentally responsible developments. Selengut created his own surveys so that he could draw out information about consumer interests and preferences in green development. His surveys document customer feedback on positive as well as negative features of Maho Bay. These surveys and his reviews of visitor demographics encouraged Selengut to develop Harmony, a second eco-resort on St. John, for the traveler willing to pay a higher price for a more upscale eco-tourism experience.

After reviewing customer surveys, however, Selengut canceled plans to add 20 more cabins at the Harmony site. He learned that many visitors enjoyed the comforts provided by Harmony's solar-heated showers, low-flow toilets, and fully functioning kitchens, but they missed the closeness to nature provided by Maho Bay's low-tech tents. Claims Selengut, "Harmony turned out to be on the way to the next stage." He used customer feedback to shape plans for Estate Concordia, a

On St. John, developer Stanley Selengut used customer feedback from his two earlier developments to shape plans for Estate Concordia, featuring lightweight tentlike structures and high-tech strategies. *(Reprinted with permission from Maho Bay Camps, Inc.)*

hybrid of Maho Bay and Harmony. In partnership with the U.S. National Park Service, Selengut is now developing this project, whose lightweight tentlike structures and high-tech strategies merge the comfort and environmental education opportunities of Harmony with the closeness and connection to nature experienced in Maho Bay's airy tents. Will the new project be successful? Only time and Stanley Selengut's surveys will tell.

In planning Civano, the mixed-use development currently under construction in Tucson, Arizona, the city was unsure whether its plan to create a community with energy-efficient residential and commercial development was really what its residents wanted. The city commissioned a market research study to find out. Three hundred full-time Tucson-area residents were surveyed to determine their attitudes about resource-efficient homes and environmentally responsible development. Experienced, professionally trained telephone interviewers asked about interest in such features as solar water heaters, water-efficient appliances and landscaping, graywater systems, pedestrian pathways, protective greenbelts, and natural areas. Questions addressed the specific location of Civano, a number of design and land-use issues, and whether buyers would pay a premium for homes with "energy and community features" if higher costs would be recovered through lower utility bills. The results of this survey showed that 80 percent of respondents would pay a premium of $5,000 to $10,000 for such homes. This convinced the city that it was appropriate to proceed with plans for Civano—the "Tucson Solar Village."

Southern California Gas Company has been supplying natural gas to commercial and industrial users since 1957, but in the early 1990s the company discovered that something was wrong. The company's commercial customers were moving their businesses out of state, as a result of both the slumping economy and the cost of complying with southern California's toughened environmental regulations. The Gas Company turned to customer surveys to learn how to turn this situation around. Customers said they needed help in learning how to deal with the state's environmental regulations and how to keep their costs down in a tight economy. This feedback led to the creation of the Energy Resource Center (ERC). The building showcases innovations in resource-efficient designs, materials, and equipment to help businesses make informed choices about energy consumption and conservation. The ERC opened its doors in June 1995 and quickly gained acclaim, not only for its message but also for the building itself. Its cost-effective, energy-efficient design, water-conserving landscaping, attention to indoor air quality, and use of recycled and salvaged building materials go well beyond the original goals of showcasing energy-efficient design, serving as an excellent educational resource for the company's customers.

Southern California Gas Company's Energy Resource Center demonstrates energy-efficient design and serves as an educational resource for the company's customers. This photograph illustrates the building envelope display in the Climate Control Room. *(Reprinted with permission, © Milroy/McAleer.)*

The Perfect Office Space?

Continental Offices Limited is a Chicago development company that has looked for opportunities to differentiate its products by proactively satisfying customer needs. Continental has teamed up with Carrier Corporation, General Electric, Herman Miller, and Rocky Mountain Institute to form the MERITT Signature Development Alliance. Continental's president, Kevork Derderian, explains the Alliance's impetus: "Real estate is being thrust into rapid change to respond to advancing technologies and a more demanding, better-educated clientele."

MERITT surveyed its own team, as well as hundreds of Fortune 500 company executives and real estate leasing agents, inquiring about their satisfaction with existing office stock and asking, "How do you envision the perfect office?" By both asking about what works and allowing building occupants to dream about the ideal development, the MERITT Alliance discovered a huge opportunity to improve customer satisfaction and differentiate its products by creating commercial and institutional spaces that offer cost savings through energy efficiency, improved thermal comfort, and better indoor air quality.

MERITT is developing and retrofitting its own speculative properties and offering build-to-suit services to other corporations and institutional investors. By adding value to the products it delivers, MERITT is positioning itself to capture a market that is only now beginning to realize the many benefits MERITT's products will offer.

VISUAL PREFERENCE SURVEYS

Finding out what the market wants may sound simple, but it can be a challenge for green developers if their products are unfamiliar to the market. How can customers articulate preferences for a product of which they have no knowledge? Peter Palmisano of Pacific Union Marketing, explains: "Consumers don't have the vocabulary to describe what they want. Instead they rely on images from existing developments. We need to educate customers about the full set of values and differences between existing and new products."

Anton Nelessen, who is an associate professor in planning and policy at Rutgers University, developed the Visual Preference Survey™ (VPS) to enable developers, planners, and community members to visualize potential new developments before

Anton Nelessen's Visual Preference Survey™ enables developers, planners, and community members to visualize potential developments before planning and design decisions are made. During a VPS session, a slide showing the image on the left might receive negative remarks, while the image on the right might receive positive responses. *(Reprinted with permission from Michael N. Corbett and Rocky Mountain Institute.)*

planning and design decisions are made. His consulting company, Nelessen Associates, Inc., of Princeton, New Jersey, presents slides of photographic images and computer-enhanced drawings of various planning and design elements of buildings and communities, accompanied by questionnaires and other analysis techniques. While viewing slides of various urban settings, participants evaluate the images and select their preferences. This survey is most typically used in town planning to help communities consider various options for new development and the potential impact on their town. However, VPS can also be an effective market research tool to explore customer interest, especially for new land-use approaches. Some neotraditional developers have begun using this tool extensively because they recognize the importance of having the surrounding community clearly understand a project, and because it enables survey participants to express their preferences without having to come up with the words to describe it.

Since 1979, Nelessen's firm has evaluated more than 50,000 surveys from a broad spectrum of people ranging in age from 17 to 88. Such surveys have been conducted all over the United States for master planning, site planning, downtown redevelopment projections, transportation planning, and public education. In Nelessen's book, *Visions for a New American Dream,* he discusses the purpose of a

VPS in enabling people to visualize two- and three-dimensional spaces and their impact on the user. Says Nelessen, the images he uses are not arbitrary but rather the product of a public process representing "consensus from people who have experienced the place." The results of these surveys clearly indicate that though people throughout various regions of the United States may not know the real estate industry jargon for their development preferences, they share a common vision of community in which people are brought together in pedestrian-friendly, nonsprawling patterns of development.

The benefits of visual surveys to a green development can extend beyond simple market research. Not only can survey participants from the community provide valuable information on the market for the project, but if they find it attractive, their support will be helpful during the approvals process.

LET'S TALK

In conducting market research for their project to redevelop 400 acres of the Hamilton Field military base in Marin County, California (described in the preceding chapter), Pacific Union Marketing Company looked at the neighborhoods within a short radius of the base. Pacific Union's research determined that the smallest and oldest homes in the heart of the traditional towns sold for 25 percent more than the new houses out on the suburban fringes. Peter Palmisano of Pacific Union Marketing believes that this is because the older houses come with an enhanced quality of life: the walkability of the neighborhoods and the closeness and connection to a multitude of attractions in the towns. "Given a choice," says Palmisano, "most people are looking for this, so Pacific Union is going to create this small community on the old air force base." His research supported the goal of the Hamilton Field redevelopment—to create a mix of homes, businesses, civic and recreation amenities, and bring back the positive characteristics of older California towns.

Many developers hold press conferences and make presentations to the community, but how many actually use feedback from the community to help determine the specific features of the product or the mix of product types? For their Hamilton project, the Martin Group, the developer, and Pacific Union Marketing "went out to the community and listened with both ears....The community has very high expectations, but we have found them to be realistic and achievable," noted David Martin, chairman of the Martin Group. A citizens'

Modeling Attributes to Create Green Developments

Modeling is used by researchers in many fields seeking to evaluate impacts of actions or the popularity of new products before taking risks. Modeling typically entails collecting information (through observation, interviews, focus groups, etc.) about the salient attributes of a variety of existing products. Modelers map attributes of products that are similar to or associated with the new product, then analyze the combined information to project the resultant outcome (such as market demand for a new product).

Mark Rodman Smith, president of San Diego-based Pario Research, uses this approach to assess the potential impacts of environmentally responsible attributes on real estate developments. He uses his own model, the Ecologically Accountable Building Process Model (EAB ProModel), to assess such attributes as enhanced energy performance. He also quantifies tax credits and other financial incentives for energy-efficient buildings. He models the costs and benefits of site character-istics that may foster green development strategies and may save money for the developer, as well as such information as levels of local expertise that could ease the green development process.

Smith used this market research tool to conduct a feasibility study for improving the environmental features at Grandview, a new mixed-use industrial redevelopment project in East Vancouver, British Columbia. Among other attributes addressed, he collected information about green projects in the city that had benefited from funding and design assistance for improving the energy performance of buildings. This assistance—available through the province's utility, B.C. Hydro—can help persuade local investors and banks to fund green development. Information of this kind is not typically collected and quantified in conventional market research, yet it can significantly improve the capital and operating costs of a development.

Source: Personal correspondance with Mark Rodman Smith of Pario Research, fall/winter 1996.

advisory committee representing a broad cross section of the people of Novato was established to represent the interests of the region's residents. This advisory group provided input for two and a half years, reviewing the environmental studies and all the plans for development. Prior to any discussions about specific

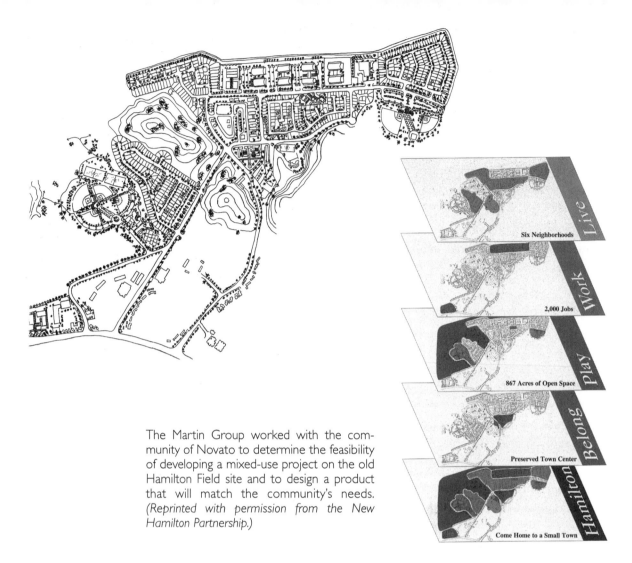

The Martin Group worked with the community of Novato to determine the feasibility of developing a mixed-use project on the old Hamilton Field site and to design a product that will match the community's needs. *(Reprinted with permission from the New Hamilton Partnership.)*

Within the images (labels):

Six Neighborhoods — Live

2,000 Jobs — Work

867 Acres of Open Space — Play

Preserved Town Center — Belong

Come Home to a Small Town — Hamilton

project plans, the 12 advisory group members were required to attend five three-hour sessions giving them background on the project in order to establish a common base of understanding about the economic realities, the environmental constraints and opportunities, and the community dynamics and needs.

Martin explains that most developers specialize in a specific kind of product — commercial, residential, or resort, for example. They come to a community and try to sell that product. Big-box retail development is a glaring example of this practice. But because his firm engages in all types of real estate development, it is able to ask the community to describe the kind of development it wants and how this can fit with existing development. The Martin Group then works with the community to determine the feasibility of these ideas and to design a product that will match the community's needs. This reduces the risk of not satisfying the customer's needs and enables Martin to create a product that will fit with the existing culture and community in which it is located.

With a clear directive from the community that the proposed development not place an economic burden on the community of Novato, the developers have been seeking commercial tenants to commit to buy land and establish operations in Hamilton, to provide residents of the new community with employment opportunities. Citizens also voiced concern about the amount of traffic the new development would generate. By creating a mixed-use community with jobs, shops, houses, parks, and recreation amenities, all connected by walking trails, bike paths, and transit access, the developers' plans reflect the surrounding community's preferences.

With a portfolio of more than five million square feet of development valued at over $1.6 billion (1996), Martin is perhaps justified in believing that his approach makes more sense than the "top-down" development practices still often seen today.

Focus Groups

One of the most widely used market research tools for many products, focus groups are gaining popularity in real estate market research. They can help the developer understand market preferences and figure out which products and features will entice people to buy or lease property. A group of individuals who share similar demographics and socioeconomic profiles are invited to a roundtable discussion of a given product. A facilitator leads the discussion, in which participants are asked a wide range of questions relating to the product and its competitors. However, as with surveys, the right questions must be asked if a focus group is to provide useful answers.

Not all experts accept the value of focus groups in conducting market research. In his interview with *On the Ground* magazine, Philip Langdon suggested that "using focus groups to find out what excites people and what motivates them to buy...concentrates on whipping up desires and fantasies rather than on identifying people's real needs." Yet, if conducted properly, developers can use focus groups to support—and further—their visions of green development. Peter Palmisano of Pacific Union Marketing says he always uses focus groups in doing market research for new developments. He does not use outside firms to conduct these sessions, however, because he wants to be directly involved with the participants so that he can clearly understand their needs.

Prairie Holdings Corporation first began market research for Prairie Crossing in 1986. On this 667-acre site northwest of Chicago, the company believed they could create a successful development that preserved surrounding farming activities to enhance the residential environment and that, in turn, the development could support the region's agricultural base. With no other developments of this type for comparison, the market research firm hired by Prairie Holdings Corporation set about doing conventional research by collecting information on the average price per square foot of homes in nearby existing subdivisions. Using only a simple comparison of existing housing values and other basic comparables, this market research produced results indicating that the project would fail because the prices would be too high as compared with other homes in the area. This standard review of comps overlooked the special attributes of Prairie Crossing, however, such as conservation easements to protect open space, and trails, gardens, and other amenities that will help residents enjoy the land.

Prairie Holdings recognized the limitations of this research, yet the company needed information about consumer interest in order to calculate the risk and determine potential price ranges, target markets, and customer priorities. The company shifted its attention to focus groups. A professional facilitator was brought in to assemble focus groups in three different categories: potential home buyers under 40 years old, potential home buyers over 40 years old, and real estate agents. Through answers to pointed questions and back-and-forth dialogue about the development envisioned, the focus groups helped Prairie Holdings Corporation assemble profiles of potential buyers. The focus groups confirmed the company's hunch that its target market was not simply the empty-nesters that earlier market research had identified. Information from the focus groups provided valuable input on how to design houses that would appeal to a mix of age groups.

In the focus group discussions, slides of farmlands and pastoral scenes were shown, and participants were asked whether they would like to live next to a farm. Surprisingly, the reaction was negative. Was it the smell of manure and livestock that was a deterrent to the potential home buyers? By asking the right questions and encouraging a discussion, the facilitator was able to discern that the participants were not opposed to living next to farms. Rather, they were suspicious that these agricultural lands would soon be replaced by development, and they did not want to live in homes engulfed by sprawl. When the participants learned that Prairie Holdings Corporation planned to establish conservation easements to protect the adjacent farmland from ever being developed, they were not only enthusiastic about such a development, but believed these properties to be worth a premium. The concerns, values, and preferences expressed by the focus groups helped Prairie Holdings Corporation identify the most important attributes or unique selling points of this development, which guided the firm in preparing marketing materials.

CREATIVE FEASIBILITY

Just as product innovation in other markets relies on more creative market research to determine customers' needs and wants, green development may require more innovative strategies in order to demonstrate viability. Michael Horst, president and founder of InSpire Enterprises, a San Francisco-based real estate consulting firm, uses a market research methodology he calls "creative feasibility" to carry market analysis of demand for new real estate products beyond conventional analysis. Creative feasibility uses such standard market research strategies as focus groups, surveys, and interviews with potential buyers. This information is then combined with analysis of analogs—similar products or features—in other developments, usually outside the local market. Analogs are used to compare and assess the best practices of various real estate products and development methodologies of existing successful projects with new project ideas. While the comps used in conventional market research examine similar projects, the analogs used in creative feasibility enable the researcher to pick and choose among projects, or even specific features, much more widely.

According to Horst, analogs are an important means of creatively evaluating the feasibility for such new products as green developments. Analogs may be models, prototypes, or ideas developed by others that are analogous in some way to the planned elements or features of a new real estate product. He cites as an example industrial firms who benchmark competitors' products, "ranging from Ford and Xerox dissecting other producers' machines, to accountants modeling other firms' service policies." Architects, too, regularly use analogs, either consciously or unconsciously, in assessing and comparing building designs and construction details to figure out whether a feature that was successful in one application can be used successfully for their particular application. In real estate, analogs are useful for developing and validating ideas for specific features or attributes for a new product or feature that may not yet have been tried in the region. Instead of simply copying the development patterns of neighboring residential developments, for example, a developer may mirror some of the better features of a project in another state. Says Horst, "In creative feasibility, the key is not necessarily to duplicate other ideas, but to learn the lessons and transfer or translate them to the subject property."

The pioneering market research done by Harrison A. (Buzz) Price at Stanford Research Institute represents one of the earliest creative feasibility studies. In the 1950s, Price was charged with conducting market research for a new project idea — Disneyland. There was no other project like it in existence, so Price looked to such analogs as amusement parks, main streets, and public parks. Then he linked together the best aspects of each and decided that it was worth the risk to proceed with Walt's dream. And the rest is history.

Creative feasibility studies enhance rather than ignore traditional market analysis. Horst worked with the market research firm Economic Research Associates to prepare a feasibility study for a low-impact land-use strategy at the

Michael Horst used a market research methodology called "creative feasibility" to review sales programs for such land stewardship projects as the Shenoa Retreat and Learning Center in Mendocino County, California, where this straw-bale house is located. *(Reprinted with permission from Michael L. Horst.)*

Santa Lucia Community Preserve, a high-end residential development near Monterey, California. In an area where there is much resistance to growth, the developers, Rancho San Carlos Partnership, plan to incorporate extensive land preservation strategies in the 350-home development. Using creative feasibility, the team combined conventional market research methodologies (including focus groups) with careful examination of analogs. The analog study reviewed sales programs for high-end residential development projects in other states, including Colorado and Montana, as well as such land stewardship projects as Shenoa Retreat and Learning Center in Mendocino County, California. Primary demographics research provided some demand analysis, focus groups explored the target market's preferences, and the analogs embellished the market research report's supply section by showing the viability and success of projects in other states. Results of the research assured the Rancho San Carlos Partnership that there is a market willing to pay a substantial premium for homes that play a part in an environmental protection program.

WHAT'S AHEAD?

The market research needs of green development projects will change over time. Today there are very few comps to draw upon in convincing developers and their financial backers that such projects can succeed. But that will change as more projects are built and prove successful. If Jim Chaffin could have pointed to a development like Spring Island that already existed and was earning money for its investors, he would have had an easier time bringing investors on board and he might not have had to hedge his bets by incorporating the golf course. But now that Spring Island and other similar projects *do* exist and *are* successful, they will serve as models—or comps—for future projects.

Today's green developers have gone out on a limb to do what they believe in. Using conventional and creative market research, they base their decisions on strong visions, brash optimism, intuition, and deep commitment to their environmental ideals. While it is likely that green developers of the twenty-first century will share the environmental ideals of the leaders profiled in this book, the work of their predecessors will have made it far easier for more conservative developers to get involved with green development, and it will allow the pioneers to go even further in making their developments more environmentally and socially responsible.

On Dewees Island® the impact area is limited to 7,500 square feet per lot, and conventional lawns and other nonnative landscaping is prohibited. *(Reprinted with permission from the Island Preservation Partnership.)*

CHAPTER 5

Site Planning and Design

LOCAL REAL ESTATE AGENTS THOUGHT that the environmental restrictions placed on the proposed Dewees Island® development would be the kiss of death. Preventing people from building right by the shore…prohibiting gasoline-powered cars… limiting the "impact area" (the area affected by putting in a driveway and constructing a house) to 7,500 square feet per lot…restricting overall building size to 5,000 square feet…prohibiting conventional lawns and other nonnative landscaping…telling home owners they cannot pave their driveways or water their plantings with anything but collected rainwater—these restrictions just were not going to help developer John Knott sell his 150 home lots. Or so the area realtors thought.

As it has turned out, the island development off the coast of South Carolina is doing just fine. By early 1997, 60 lots had been sold, completing the first phase of development and a portion of the second. Roads were going in for Phase Three. Even more significant, lot prices had gone up substantially since 1992 and net profits were exceeding pro forma targets by about 90 percent.

By all accounts, Dewees Island is a remarkable place. The 1,200-acre island 12 miles northeast of Charleston is one of the last barrier islands that will be developed. But at build-out, the island will be far different from its well-known neighbor, Isle of Palms, or Hilton Head Island, farther down the coast. Dewees Island is as much a

Dewees Island offers miles of nature trails and shoreline, salt marsh estuaries rich in wildlife, freshwater lagoons, and birding opportunities. *(Reprinted with permission from the Island Preservation Partnership.)*

nature preserve as a resort development. Instead of a golf course as the main attraction, Dewees Island boasts miles of nature trails and shoreline to explore, extensive salt marsh estuaries that are rich in wildlife, freshwater lagoons with alligators, superb birding opportunities (including several elevated observation platforms), and forests that are home to bobcats and foxes. Sixty-five percent of the island, including a 200-acre tidal lake, was set aside as a wildlife refuge—to be left forever wild. An extensive land stewardship program is supported by a 1.5 percent premium on each lot sold.

The master plan for Dewees Island was developed by the architectural firm Burt Hill Kosar Rittelmann Associates, which is well-respected for its environmental designs. Planning and site design were guided by input from numerous experts, including a wildlife consultant, beach and dune management engineers, representatives from the Department of Natural Resources and Wildlife, a soils engineer, a civil engineer, environmental consultants, and architects, all of whom participated in a planning charrette with the development team. It was a collective planning process, but, says Knott, "Dewees Island told us what should be done with her. We just have to respect what Dewees says about herself."

Site design is intended to minimize disturbance of the natural environment, protect the island's resources, and capitalize on the advantages of the coastal climate to help conserve energy. Before construction begins on any new home site, representatives from Dewees Island's Architectural Resource Board review plans to guide homeowners through sustainable development practices. Homes are required to "nest" within their habitat and to take advantage of winter sun, summer shade, prevailing breezes, and natural lighting in order to minimize energy use. The absence of impervious (paved) surfaces on the island means that rain and runoff will feed into the island's underground aquifer. Sewage is treated with a biologically based, closed-loop wastewater system that keeps discharges out of local waterways.

"Letting the land and nature do the site planning is always less expensive," says Knott, who claims that the buildings and other infrastructure on the island will last longer as a result of climatically appropriate siting and materials choices. The development has received numerous awards and was the first ever to be honored by the President's Council on Sustainable Development for environmental sensitivity.

While Dewees Island boasts many environmental features, the site design elements are perhaps the most striking. Ecological site design respects and works with the land's natural processes and features, adapting the development components—buildings, utilities, infrastructure, and other features —to the patterns of the place. In the case of urban developments, ecological site design blends with and enhances the existing fabric of the community and strengthens the character of the built environment by accommodating activities and healthy human interactions. In the case of rural sites like Dewees Island, ecological site design involves developing a close relationship with the environment —protecting, restoring, and celebrating the biological diversity and beauty that only nature can produce.

An important facet of green developments is that these projects are not isolated entities; they exist within a broader ecological and cultural context. No site can be understood and properly evaluated without considering its relationship to the broader region. As part of the early planning process for a development, the site's interconnections with regional ecosystems and communities should be examined, as was discussed in Chapter 3.

This chapter introduces the elements of ecologically responsible site design and the benefits of such practices to developers, to the human occupants of these sites, and to the environment. By necessity, this is a cursory review, but it should convey the tremendous potential of developing with—instead of against—nature.

Planning and Teamwork

Site design determines how a project will interact with and affect the immediate environment. Keeping that impact to a minimum necessitates starting out with an understanding of what is already there—which means conducting a careful site assessment. It then requires developing a thorough plan that can include the following components: protecting existing ecosystems and historic or cultural features, repairing damaged areas and restoring valuable ecosystems, responsibly dealing with water on the site to maximize infiltration and reduce pollution and runoff, developing management strategies that will result in minimal environmental damage (relative to water use, fertilizers, pesticides, lawn mowing, etc.), and establishing a sense of culture and community.

The value of teamwork and the need for landscaping specialists to be involved with the development team at the earliest stages of planning cannot be overstated. Andropogon Associates, Ltd., a Philadelphia firm specializing in environmentally responsible site design, recommends a participatory design process that includes a broad spectrum of ecosystem experts, landscape architects, landscape contractors, and grounds managers along with the full design team. It is a process of education and communication—as are many other aspects of green development.

The developers of Dewees Island used a multidisciplinary team of participants and consultants as well as input from local residents. Before any design was even put down on paper, Knott invited locals to participate in discussions on the use and layout of the site. Teamwork—bringing landscape architects together with developers, engineers, future occupants, local community members, and others—can promote front-loaded planning and whole-systems thinking. These, coupled with an end-use perspective that seeks to minimize costs and ecological damage to the site, lead to a development that is more attractive, both visually and financially.

Understanding the Site

No matter what is to be done with land development, the first step should be a careful assessment of what is already there. Site assessment entails collecting information about existing features and conditions so that potential impacts from development can be understood and examined throughout the development process. Specific data describing the topography, soils, hydrology, microclimate, vegetation, wetlands, biodiversity, wildlife habitat and corridors, and the site's

Ecological Site Design Guidelines

- *Create a participatory design process.* Participatory design is an ongoing process of education and communication. It involves a broad spectrum of users and managers who will ultimately promote stewardship of the landscape.
- *Preserve and reestablish landscape patterns.* Rebuilding whole systems requires connecting landscape fragments and establishing networks beyond a site.
- *Reinforce the natural infrastructure.* Ecological design respects and works with the large-scale processes, adapting the site development components—building, utilities, circulation—to the patterns of the place.
- *Conserve resources.* The natural hydrologic patterns, terrain, and native plant communities represent the fullest and most efficient use of resources.
- *Make a habit of restoration.* Each site intervention presents an opportunity to encourage recovery and to promote the ecological health of the larger environment.
- *Evaluate solutions in terms of their larger context.* Site interventions should look outward to the larger context and confront potential impacts to the community.
- *Create model solutions based on natural processes.* Sustainable solutions modeled on natural processes reflect the efficiency and elegance of biological systems.
- *Foster biodiversity.* Preserving and enhancing indigenous landscapes fosters biodiversity by helping nature reestablish the functions that support a rich complexity of species.
- *Retrofit derelict lands.* Today the choice is often between restoring and reusing neglected lands or destroying the few remaining rural or natural areas. Much of the work of the future will be "pioneering in reverse."
- *Integrate historic preservation and ecological management.* Renewing historic landscapes integrates many overlapping and interrelated values with contemporary use and ecological management.
- *Develop a monitored landscape management program.* Creating sustainable landscapes requires a revolution in landscape maintenance. A monitored management program ensures that policy and practice are informed by science and fulfill long-term goals.
- *Promote an ecological aesthetic.* A place that is understood, preserved, repaired, and celebrated as an integrated whole can become a powerful and memorable work of art.

Reprinted with permission from Andropogon Associates, Ltd.

connection with surrounding lands are among the types of information to be collected during a site assessment. The assessment not only considers natural features, but also the built environment and examines a project's impact on the character and quality of life of existing communities. This can be thought of as taking due diligence to a more comprehensive level, identifying not only potential problems, but also potential opportunities.

Careful site assessment can enable developers to capitalize on the land's potential—views, solar access, natural drainage opportunities, natural shading through vegetation, cooling from prevailing winds—while minimizing or avoiding damage or disturbance to the site and surrounding areas. Assessment data is used to guide decisions about the location, layout, footprint, and orientation of buildings, as well as to inform the location and design of landscaping, infrastructure, parking lots, parks, and other outdoor amenities.

One of the most important tools for site assessment is the Geographical Information System (GIS), a computerized mapping system that includes a wealth of physiographic information on different "layers." Individual layers contain information about such features as topography, hydrology, and vegetation. Green development teams are using GIS to prepare detailed inventories of the land to guide development. GIS data can be directly transferred to many computer-aided design (CAD) programs, allowing team members to evaluate appropriate building and infrastructure placement and design. Modeling of site design options and planning decisions enables the project team to compare and assess potential environmental impacts and determine the best ways to integrate native landscapes, existing features, and community elements into the plan.

When Jim Chaffin first began developing Spring Island, he knew that to protect the land he first had to understand it. He brought together a team that included a biologist, a naturalist, a forester, a landscape designer, and an environmental scientist to conduct an extensive inventory and assessment that included baseline data on natural resources, soils, and topographic features. The information was entered into a highly detailed GIS data base. The team even created individual species maps to better understand animal habitats.

The team of scientists delineated critical wildlife habitat, wetlands, and important vegetation areas. Chaffin set this land aside in a 1,000-acre nature preserve. The GIS assessment guided site planning and design decisions to minimize the impact of trails, dirt roads, buildings, and a golf course and to allow maximum diversity of plants and animals. While the island already had approvals to build 5,500

For the Spring Island development, a team of scientists delineated important areas of the natural preserve. Two members of the team are shown here reviewing detailed vegetation maps. *(Reprinted with permission from Skip Meachen.)*

units, Chaffin felt that this many homes would ruin the island and reduced the number of lots to 500. The result of these decisions is a successful development where plants, animals, and people all thrive in the natural beauty of Spring Island.

With more than 25 years of experience in real estate projects, Chaffin has learned that developers can realize the greatest outcome from their investment in the land through comprehensive site assessment and design integrated with the natural environment. "As developers, we need to have humility regarding the importance of a property's natural amenities. We often believe that we can 'improve' the value of property, or enhance the customer experience through man-made facilities. I believe that the first goal should be the thorough assessment of, and the protection and enhancement of, a property's natural features."

For Chaffin, the highest and best use of the land extends far beyond greatest net financial return. "Providing the opportunity for personal connection with the natural environment offers more personal nourishment and spiritual fulfillment than any of our 'developer' amenities," he says. "What greater product can we offer our customers?" The Spring Island Trust has received awards from such organizations as the South Carolina Wildlife Federation, the South Carolina Department of Natural Resources, and Renew America. And even with all this emphasis on the ecosystems at Spring Island, Chaffin's development is highly successful financially.

Site assessment was even more extensive at Haymount, John Clark's 1,650-acre new town under development in northern Virginia. Within the GIS mapping framework, the site assessment team inventoried all trees 18 inches in diameter or larger, identified 302 animal species, delineated vegetation types and wildlife corridors, and mapped all wetlands. Archeologist Jay Harrison was hired by Haymount's development team to piece together the land's archeological past

Biodiversity Gap Analysis Program

In part developed by the University of Idaho, the Biodiversity Gap Analysis Program is a scientific method of mapping the degree to which various vegetation types and individual bird and animal species are or are *not* present in a particular region. The purpose of this tool is to identify critical land and habitat for protection of biodiversity and endangered species. It is being used in one of the first state and nationwide efforts to map public land ownership and private land conservation. This information will provide an objective basis for local, state, and national decisions in managing biological resources. For developers concerned with environmentally sensitive planning, Gap Analysis provides valuable information for better understanding a site and region.

For data and contacts, see the Gap Biodiversity Homepage on the Worldwide Web.

from prehistoric times through the Civil War. Through this extensive site assessment process, developer John Clark and architects and planners Andres Duany and Elizabeth Plater-Zyberk identified areas that could be developed with minimal disruption to the site's natural ecosystems.

More than two-thirds of the Haymount site is to be preserved in its natural state (restored in some areas) or maintained as productive organic farmland. Development at Haymount—4,000 residential units and up to 750,000 square feet of commercial space—will be concentrated in discrete villages around the site. Development is planned on only 12 percent of the riverfront, with no private docks or homesites. There will be only one dock on the river to minimize impacts to the sensitive riparian environment. Efforts will be made to minimize storm water runoff and encourage pedestrian modes of transportation. More than 17,000 artifacts found on the property will be housed in a museum at Haymount to give residents and visitors an understanding of the rich history and prehistory of the area.

In addition to capitalizing on the natural features and amenities of a site, a thorough assessment can help avoid costly mistakes. Horror stories abound of developments that failed or encountered huge cost overruns because of inadequate site assessment. At Portuguese Bend near Los Angeles, 156 homes slid down the hillside, lubricated by underlying septic tank effluent. The team that assessed the site failed to recognize that the shale would be unable to absorb sewage effluent.

Protecting What's Already There

A large part of environmentally responsible site design for new development is the protection of important natural and other features that already exist on a site. Many greenfield sites are rich with woodlands, prairies, or wetlands. Other greenfield sites include farmland that, while not natural, is nonetheless important and usually worthy of protecting in some form. Rural and urban sites may include historically or culturally important features. Once the features of a site are fully understood, the next step is to do the planning and design work needed to maximize ecosystem protection while still meeting the economic needs of the project. Even areas of the site that are to be kept in their natural state can be damaged during construction if care is not taken. Conversely, many sites may contain degraded areas that need restoration.

Careful site assessment and planning were required for United Parcel Service's corporate office park in Atlanta, Georgia. Through this process, a large portion of the native woodland on the property was protected. *(Reprinted with permission, © Brian Gassel, Thompson, Ventulett, Stainback & Associates.)*

The first architecture firm to offer a design for the United Parcel Service (UPS) corporate office park in Atlanta, Georgia, suggested that the best way to maximize the value of the property would be to clear the heavily wooded 26-acre site and landscape from scratch. UPS disagreed and brought in another firm, Thompson, Ventulett, Stainback & Associates. This firm recognized that by integrating features of the native landscape into their design, much of the site's ecosystem could be protected while enhancing the buildings' aesthetic value. This required careful site assessment and planning, which influenced building layout and design. Through this process, a large portion of the native woodland on the property, including a natural ravine, was protected. Utility lines and the entrance drive were carefully placed outside preserved areas, and a drainage line was designed in a zigzag fashion around the building foundation to avoid damage to a stand of large oaks. Such design and construction techniques enabled trees to come within 15 feet of the buildings. The forest and ravine offer attractive views from the many windows throughout the three main buildings. Several layers of silt fencing were used to prevent sediment and runoff from clogging the wetlands. Storm water is filtered before it can enter the creek. A bridge between two buildings is nestled among the trees, and woodland paths and benches invite staff to step out of the buildings into their natural surroundings.

Native landscapes were a successful part of the site design at both the UPS office complex and on Dewees Island. Yet in most developments today, manicured lawns, mulched shrubs, parking lots, and paved sidewalks have replaced native landscapes. Instead of reliance on natural systems to absorb storm water and control erosion, sophisticated engineering is required to deal with these issues (see "Managing Water on the Site," a later section in this chapter).

The site for the proposed C. K. Choi Building for the Institute of Asian Research at the University of British Columbia presented the design team with a number of challenges. The property featured a magnificent stand of Douglas fir trees. The team wanted to preserve them, but doing so would severely restrict the building's footprint. The solution was to situate the 30,000-square-foot building on a narrow strip of land, barely 60 feet wide, that had been a parking lot. Architect Eva Matsuzaki and her design team accommodated the site's constraints by integrating the building design with the native landscape. They created a long, narrow footprint, placing tall picture windows in the front meeting and confer-ence rooms. Not only were the trees saved, but they became an important component of the design aesthetic. Upon entering the building, people are treated

A remaining 1800s tabby, a structure built of crushed shells and mortar, serves as a reminder of Spring Island's history. *(Reprinted with permission from Betsy Chaffin.)*

to a picture-perfect view of British Columbia's famed temperate rain forest. The narrow footprint and windows also helped to reduce the building's energy load by about $15,000 per year, because the design provides ample daylighting and opportunities for natural ventilation.

The conflicting needs of protecting natural vegetation and, at the same time, providing good southern exposure for passive solar heating and daylighting can pose a significant challenge. It requires careful siting of buildings, based on orientation, topography, and vegetation. Some municipalities, such as the city of Carbondale, Colorado, now have zoning laws that mandate solar access in the layout of residential developments.

In addition to preserving the natural features that exist on the land, historic and culturally significant elements can also be protected. At Spring Island, an old 1800s tabby, a structure built of crushed shells and mortar, was left to serve as a reminder of the island's rich and varied history of past settlements and enterprises. Horse-drawn carts carry residents and guests around the island to visit such special remnants of the past.

At Prairie Crossing in Grayslake, Illinois, the development team preserved a sense of cultural history by salvaging an old barn and moving it to an appropriate place on the site to be used as a community center. An old one-room school house was also relocated and will be used as a nursery school.

Restoring Damaged Sites

> If every development could just reconnect the fragments in the landscape—the swale and the hedgerow—it would begin to tie back into the landscape, initiating the healing process in an unpretentious way.
>
> *Carol Franklin, Andropogon Associates, Ltd., 1996*

An increasingly important component of many green developments is the restoration of damaged sites. In some cases, sites have been damaged by previous building or industrial activities; these brownfield sites may require extensive remediation to remove toxins from the soil. In other situations, land that appears "natural" is actually very different from the native ecosystem that existed prior to human settlement; at these sites, "ecological restoration" can be carried out to bring back ecologically diverse landscapes. Careful site assessment can identify the restoration needs and opportunities.

The use of brownfield sites is attractive from an environmental standpoint, because in conjunction with good land-use polices, it permits greenfields to remain undeveloped. Brownfield sites have already been disturbed, so further development—coupled with environmental cleanup—can result in a net improvement. But brownfield development poses many challenges.

In 1988 the province of British Columbia sold 202 acres of prime waterfront property, known as the Expo Lands, in downtown Vancouver to Concord Pacific Developments, Ltd. As a gesture of support for the proposed redevelopment project, the city agreed to foot the bill to clean up site contamination resulting from decades of industrial operations by companies that were long gone. The city anticipated expenditures of about $5 million but by 1994 had spent $27 million removing heavy metals and other toxins or otherwise decontaminating the soil, and the bill is expected to reach $75 million before cleanup is complete. Despite the costs, the city hopes to reap the benefits of this mixed-use development through the increased tax base that will result and by the project's serving as a model for other redevelopment around the old Expo Lands.

As described in Chapter 3, both federal and state programs are addressing the concern that purchasers of brownfield sites might subsequently be held liable, and increasing interest in brownfield development is likely. After all, many of the contaminated brownfield sites in American cities could be the most valuable for development—riverfront sites, for example, with easy access to public transportation and center-city activity.

At Boeing's Renton, Washington, site much of the original landscape features had been obliterated by years of human activity. Creeks had been diverted into underground culverts, and wetlands had been polluted or destroyed. Today the 214-acre corporate office park has a plan for 2.9 million square feet of office space, a 30-acre park, a 3-acre lake, and miles of walking and jogging paths amid woodlands, meadows, creeks, and an apple orchard. While the continuing landscape restoration at Longacres Park is not always easy—reestablishing healthy wetlands has proven to be especially challenging—Boeing is setting an important example by identifying ecological restoration as a priority in a large commercial development project.

Not all land restoration efforts are focused on industrial brownfield sites. Some lands have been damaged by drainage for farming or decades of overgrazing by livestock. In 1990, the Rancho San Carlos Partnership purchased 20,000 acres of rolling coastal hills and valleys near California's Carmel Valley. The Partnership plans to sell 300 homesites at $1 to $4 million apiece as the vehicle to permanently protect nine-tenths of the land in a nature preserve, known as the Santa Lucia Community Preserve, and to restore vegetation throughout the site.

Most of the Rancho San Carlos Partnerhsip's 20,000 acres of rolling coastal hills and valleys will be permanently protected in the Santa Lucia Community Preserve. *(Reprinted with permission from Lisa McManigal, Rocky Mountain Institute.)*

Using detailed GIS information, planners identified areas for preservation and limited development to only the most degraded parts of the property. Much of the valley floor is degraded from decades of intensive cattle grazing, clearing, logging, and cropping. All buildings and development will be sited along existing ranch roads, and an innovative design for a "golf trail" system will also follow the old dirt roads. By siting on already-disturbed areas of the property, the developers are minimizing environmental impacts while providing a golf course amenity. The development also established a native plant nursery and a "heritage seed program" to raise plants and seeds for restoration projects on the property. The developers want to restore most of the land to the natural environment that existed here 200 years ago. (Chapter 7 describes this project's contentious approvals process.)

In Zeeland, Michigan, furniture manufacturer Herman Miller is paying similar attention to landscape restoration. The company brought in architects William McDonough + Partners and landscape architects Pollack Design Associates to design a multi-purpose facility, called Simple Quality Affordable (SQA), for their subsidiary that remanufactures office furniture. The location was

Herman Miller's SQA building in Zeeland, Michigan, was sited at the property's high point along a natural ridge line, but the undulating topography helps the building blend in with its surroundings. *(Reprinted with permission from Don Van Essen, photographer.)*

chosen for its proximity to an existing Herman Miller warehouse facility and to public transit, but the land was an old industrial site that had been extensively damaged. After careful study of the land and soils, the design team called for the restoration of much of the original topography and preservation of any undisturbed areas on the property. The building is located at the property's high point, situated along a natural ridge line, but the undulating topography helps the building blend in with its surroundings. Water naturally drains away from the building down to the river, eliminating the need for artificial drainage systems. Sculpted tiers and sedimentation basins prevent erosion of the hillside, and more than a mile of continuous wetlands help to purify runoff water.

The integration of the building's shape with the topography, and the landscaping measures, make the facility nearly invisible to nearby residents. Roadways and parking lots on the property were designed so that headlights from cars would not be directed at homes in the adjacent subdivision. McDonough proposed a staff tree-planting program that will eventually create a forest around the building, enhancing the visual appeal of the property while restoring some of the native vegetation. Trees also shade the buildings and buffer prevailing winds, helping to lower energy use. How appropriate for a company renowned for its wooden chairs and other fine furniture to plant trees to replace some of the many it uses in its daily manufacturing activities.

RESTORING THE PRAIRIE

Tall-grass prairie is a unique American ecosystem. Yet such prairies, which once spanned the land from the Mississippi River to the Great Plains, are now almost entirely gone. Jim Patchett is a champion of ecologically responsible land management, especially prairie restoration. His firm, Conservation Design Forum, in Naperville, Illinois, comprised of landscape architects, water resources experts, land planners, and environmental scientists, is at the leading edge of prairie restoration.

Prior to founding Conservation Design Forum, Patchett worked with Johnson, Johnson & Roy (JJR), a landscape architecture firm, on a number of projects to reintroduce native tall-grass prairies into corporate campuses. His work with JJR for AT&T, Sears, and Tellabs headquarters has demonstrated the economic benefits of tall-grass prairie landscaping. In addition to restoring the indigenous vegetation and helping to reestablish a healthy and diverse ecosystem, using native plants reduces maintenance and landscaping costs.

Near Chicago, AT&T's headquarters features a tall-grass prairie landscape, which restores the indigenous vegetation and helps to reestablish a healthy and diverse ecosystem. *(Reprinted with permission from William D. Browning, Rocky Mountain Institute.)*

At two AT&T office parks in the suburban Chicago area, Patchett proposed prairie restoration as a way to deal with the high cost of maintaining 50 acres of turfgrass. The facility also had problems associated with geese and limitations on irrigation during droughts. The first phase of the work in 1993 converted 18 acres of turf to prairie at AT&T's Lisle, Illinois, campus. To ease company concerns about the high cost of prairie restoration, Patchett agreed to a $2,000-per-acre budget ceiling for the work—the annual amount the company had been paying for turfgrass management (irrigation, fertilizing, pesticides, mowing, etc). The project came in at budget, resulting in a break-even the very first year. Today, annual management costs are less than $500 per acre—one-quarter of what they had been.

AT&T was so pleased with the results and the positive media attention received as a result of this work that it carried out an even larger project at its nearby Naperville campus, converting more than 30 acres of turfgrass to tall-grass prairie in 1994. Geese are no longer a problem in areas converted to prairie, because the tall native plants prevent the birds from being able to look around as they can on mowed turfgrass—so they move on to "greener pastures." Today the company is saving about $75,000 per year on landscaping costs at these two facilities.

The premise behind these savings is simple. If vegetation is native to an area, it is likely to thrive in the climate naturally with little need for irrigation or other artificial enhancements. The diversity of plants and animals provides far greater ecological balance, so any one species is far less likely to proliferate and become a problem. By avoiding costly infrastructure needs, reducing water and energy use, and saving labor, ecologically sensitive site design is inherently cost-effective.

Patchett is applying these same strategies in retrofitting 12 acres of the University of Wisconsin Research Office Park's Charmany Farm parcel in Madison, Wisconsin. He designed open space and a commons area, eliminating most of the maintenance needs by reintroducing native prairie. With the success of this project, Patchett developed a master plan to redesign an additional 200 acres at the university. His natural landscaping design enabled the university to avoid storm water infrastructure costs by relying on natural drainage patterns. Building on these landscaping improvements, Patchett and the university have teamed up with the MERITT Alliance to develop a sustainable office demonstration project on a 28-acre portion of the university.

Managing Water on the Site

Water is likely to become an increasingly significant environmental concern as aquifers are depleted, groundwater contamination worsens, and fresh water in general becomes more precious. Dealing more responsibly with water on a development property can not only help to alleviate these environmental concerns, but can also provide significant financial benefits. Carefully designed storm water infiltration systems, natural wastewater treatment systems, and water-efficient landscaping strategies all can save the developer money. In fact, these water-management strategies can be one of the most significant economic drivers of green development, helping to pay for a much broader green agenda.

STORM WATER MANAGEMENT

Conventional practice in storm water management is to carry the water off the site as quickly as possible through underground storm sewers, or to collect it in extensive retention ponds. These are expensive solutions and can be detrimental to the environment. More environmentally attractive strategies that rely on infil-

Root Systems of Prairie Plants

(Reprinted with permission from the Conservation Design Forum, Inc. Illustration by Heidi Natura, Conservation Design Forum, Inc.)

Conservation Design Forum, Inc.
Heidi Natura 1995

Integrating Natural Plant Communities into Conventional Landscape Areas: Benefits All Around

Environmental

- Promotes long-term landscape stability and sustainability
- Increases biological diversity
- Enhances groundwater recharge through increased absorption
- Regenerates organic soil layer with decomposition of above ground growth
- Reduces soil erosion with soil-holding root systems
- Reduces downstream flooding by virtually eliminating surface water runoff
- Preserves and/or restores existing plant and seed banks; maintains genetic memory
- Improves air quality through permanent carbon fixing in the soil
- Improves water quality through filtering of dirty water and slowing of surface water velocities
- Reduces maintenance impacts through reduction or elimination of herbicide, pesticide, and fertilizer applications, mowing emissions, and irrigation

Social

- Creates a strong sense of place and regional pride
- Promotes a sound development ethic
- Provides public education and interaction opportunities
- Develops aesthetic richness
- Provides emotional and physiological relief from the built environment
- Promotes stewardship of the earth's plant and animal communities

Economic

- Significantly reduces maintenance costs
- Significantly reduces infrastructure costs
- Offers comparable installation costs
- Creates new markets for related services
- Promotes environmental responsibility with improved public relations

Source: Conservation Design Forum.

tration (to recharge aquifers) and detention of water behind naturalized swales can save hundreds of thousands of dollars in infrastructure costs and can also speed up the approvals process.

When the owners of Westfarms Mall, just west of Hartford, Connecticut, began designing a 310,000-square-foot mall expansion that called for four acres of additional overflow parking, they ran into opposition from the West Hartford and Farmington zoning boards. The biggest obstacles were the ratios of permeable surfaces to impervious surfaces and the amount and quality of runoff that would be generated by the development. Designing the detention pond to adequately handle the extra runoff was not a popular idea in the community—nor was the estimated price tag of $1 million appealing to the mall owner.

The solution that emerged was elegant and environmentally attractive: the four-acre parking area would be "paved" with turf, allowing storm water to soak in and recharge the groundwater. Roof-top storm water would be collected in an underground tank beneath the grass parking area, and the collected water used to irrigate the turf. The system used consists of a honeycomb-like grid of recycled plastic that is laid in a bed of crushed stone, then filled with sand and soil and planted with turfgrass. The grid contains the soil and prevents compaction when driven over. The material cannot be driven over every day without damaging the grass, but it works very well in an overflow parking lot, which is used primarily during the Christmas shopping season—when grass is dormant. For snow removal, plow trucks were fitted with special rollers that keep the blades slightly above the ground surface. The system was completed in the fall of 1995 and has been working well.

The $500,000 cost of the installation was somewhat more expensive than asphalt paving, but the system meant that expansion of the detention pond was not required, resulting in an immediate savings of at least $500,000. Even without that initial savings, lower maintenance costs would have enabled the installation to break even with asphalt after five years, according to Westfarms Mall. Perhaps even more significant, once the developers began promoting the system used in the parking lot, they were quickly able to get the support of neighboring property owners, local planning commissions, and the West Hartford Wetlands Commission.

At the 240-unit residential Village Homes subdivision in Davis, California, innovative strategies to reduce the amount of storm water runoff and to provide for natural infiltration of that storm water saved the developers $800 per lot as compared with the use of conventional storm sewers. The savings derived from this more environmentally responsible groundwater recharge approach was put toward the creation of common spaces and landscaping.

At Village Homes in Davis, California, innovative strategies such as the use of infiltration swales reduced the amount of storm water runoff and provided natural infiltration of that storm water, saving the developers substantial costs. *(Reprinted with permission from Michael N. Corbett.)*

In 1970 developer George Mitchell wanted to build a new town, Woodlands, on 200,000 acres of flat land in Houston. Mitchell approached landscape architect Ian McHarg for site planning because of McHarg's reputation as an environmentally conscious designer. McHarg and his team carefully inventoried the property, examining the hydrology, soils, and vegetation of the pine-oak forest. They found that the soil did not drain well and that the flat site was prone to extensive flooding during storms. At other developments in the area, engineers had applied a conventional solution of lowering the water table to solve this flooding problem. This solution not only required ugly drainage ditches, but also killed trees.

McHarg's team proposed a natural drainage system that offered many benefits, including protection of trees and elimination of off-site storm water discharge. As described in McHarg's autobiography, *A Quest for Life,* the team's natural solution included defining primary and secondary drainage easements to handle storm water runoff; minimizing erosion by specifying that no ground cover, understory, or trees were to be removed in the drainage easement areas; creating natural swales by layering native plants and vegetation; and designing temporary water storage ponds, check dams, and swales so that water would slowly flow over permeable surfaces, allowing it to infiltrate into the ground and recharge aquifers. They delineated open space that was to remain undeveloped and specified that all new construction was to be designed at densities that would permit on-site absorption of all rainwater. The team's findings regarding the geological properties of the soil determined these densities and land use.

McHarg and his team showed the developer how this system would save him $14 million in the first phase alone, as compared with building a conventional storm drainage system. In addition, by choosing this system the developer was able to take advantage of a $50 million loan guarantee under the Urban Growth and New Communities Development Act of 1970. Woodlands currently has about 30,000 residents, and its natural drainage system has been performing without a hitch for more than two decades.

On Dewees Island the cost of drainage systems was avoided by using only compacted sand roads and carefully designing swales and detention ponds to handle runoff. Impervious paving of driveways and walkways is not permitted in the island development, and even runoff from roofs is minimized because only collected rainwater can be used for irrigation and filling pods and spas. These carefully planned regulations serve to recharge the island's precious freshwater aquifer while minimizing soil erosion that can result in sedimentation and pollution of the waterways, which in turn harms wildlife habitat.

WASTEWATER MANAGEMENT

Better wastewater management on a site can be achieved by the use of constructed wetlands and contained aquatic systems to purify wastewater (sewage and/or graywater). In the constructed wetland complex, ecosystems containing microorganisms, aquatic plants, crustaceans, and other organisms eliminate various harmful bacteria and remove nutrients from wastewater—in an attractive naturalized wetland that actually improves the visual appeal of a development. By mimicking one of nature's most effective ways of purifying water, constructed wetlands can reduce treatment costs 60 to 95 percent, as compared with conventional mechanical systems. Constructed wetlands eliminate the need for chemical treatment and reduce the flows of treated—but still environmentally damaging—effluent from wastewater treatment plants into surface waters. Even though the system functions "naturally," it is necessary to set up a proper maintenance plan to ensure that the created ecosystem keeps working effectively.

A growing number of green developers are employing this and other strategies in both residential and commercial real estate projects. Modular home developer Richard E. Scott installed a constructed wetlands system for wastewater treatment at two of his housing developments near Rockaway Beach, Missouri. Scott claims his system cost $150,000 and replaced the need for a $10 million mechanical sewage treatment plant.

Constructed wetlands were used on a much larger scale for treating municipal wastewater by the northern California town of Arcata along the Humbolt Bay. Originally composed of thousands of acres of wetlands teeming with vegetation and wildlife, the area had been drained over the past hundred years for pastures and farmlands. When the 1972 Clean Water Act banned the town's practice of dumping wastewater discharges into the bay, the town council had to make a decision—either invest in an expensive and energy-intensive regional sewage treatment system or go with an alternative natural system proposed by several local university professors. The professors eventually convinced the council and the state Water Quality Board to consider the town's sewage as a resource instead of a disposal problem. They showed how wastewater could be used to nourish a constructed wetland, restoring valuable habitat and improving the quality of the water discharged into the bay. The cost of the completed system was a fraction of the projected costs for a conventional system. In the end, 154 acres of freshwater and tidal wetlands were restored, and the marsh has become a haven for wildlife and a popular birding area. This project provides another example of a solution multiplier: the project educates people about better ways to treat wastewater, improves water quality, creates wildlife habitat, and supports Arcata's aquaculture project in which salmon are raised in treated wastewater.

In the design team's efforts to make the C. K. Choi building more environmentally sustainable, a number of innovative strategies were employed to reduce water use and treat wastewater. Composting toilets were installed throughout the 30,000-square-foot building, and a simple biological treatment system was built to treat the very limited wastewater flows generated in the building. These strategies allowed the building to be independent from an already overloaded municipal sewage treatment plant.

Because of the small lot and the importance of protecting huge Douglas fir trees, there was little land available for a biological wastewater treatment system. The treatment system was cleverly designed as a narrow strip of landscaping along the front of the building. Bulrushes and iris set in gravel overlaid with loose stones process graywater from the building and the liquid "tea" from the composting toilets. After flowing through this biological filter, the purified water is used to irrigate vegetation around the site. Testing has shown this water to be cleaner than water supplied to the university by the conventional sewage treatment plant.

More compact biological wastewater treatment systems, such as John Todd's Living Machines (also known as Solar Aquatics™ systems) are also gaining popularity as environmentally responsible and cost-effective sewage treatment systems. These systems channel wastewater through a series of ponds or tanks containing diverse aquatic ecosystems. The aquatic tanks are typically located inside a greenhouse to maintain temperatures high enough for optimal biological activity year-round. The systems effectively remove nitrogen, pathogens, and other contaminants from water. Because these treatment systems are odor-free (unlike conventional sewage-treatment plants), they can be located close to municipal centers, saving the expense of piping effluent to more remote locations. The facilities are also appealing enough to be significant tourist attractions; thousands of people annually tour the several dozen biological wastewater treatment plants now operating in North America.

John Todd's Living Machines, such as this one in Frederick, Maryland, are recognized as environmentally responsible and cost-effective sewage treatment systems. *(Reprinted with permission from William D. Browning, Rocky Mountain Institute.)*

In December 1995, the Haymount project received a permit from the Virginia Department of Environmental Quality for construction of what will be the largest biological wastewater treatment system built to date. If the development proceeds as planned, a Solar Aquatics wastewater treatment system will be built by Ecological Engineering Associates of Marion, Massachusetts, to treat 1.2 million gallons of wastewater per day. The final cleansing of the effluent will be done through a constructed wetland, resulting in tertiary-treatment-quality water. It will help to create wildlife habitat and will function as an educational tool in promoting environmental awareness. It will also serve as a civic park. The facility is being designed to rely on photovoltaic (solar electric) power for its operation. All capital costs for the system will be borne by the Haymount project, but upon completion it will be turned over to the county.

In addition to constructed wetlands and biological wastewater treatment systems like Solar Aquatics, there are various improvements to conventional practice that are gaining popularity among green developers. Intermittent or recirculating sand filters provide an attractive option for smaller projects not connected to municipal sewage treatment plants. Installed between the septic tank and a downsized leaching field or filtration trench, the sand filter provides a concentrated bacterial ecosystem in which both aerobic and anaerobic bacteria thrive. The bacteria oxidize (break down) organic matter and remove nutrients from the effluent. Sand filter systems are currently being used in the Pacific Northwest, the upper Midwest, and Texas, and are being actively tested in other areas where soil conditions prevent the installation of conventional on-site wastewater systems.

Professional engineer David Venhuizen of Travis, Texas, has been designing sand filtration systems since 1987 and suggests that they are most cost-effective when designed in conjunction with water-efficient drip irrigation. Venhuizen installed intermittent sand filtration systems on Washington Island in Wisconsin for a number of homes and a grocery store. This system enabled builders and developers to achieve code compliance for water treatment at a much lower cost than with a conventional sewage treatment system. In a study being done for the Texas Water Development Board, Venhuizen has found that sand filtration is cheaper than extending sewage lines to the Colonias, areas of Mexican migrant worker housing, in Hidalgo County. Most of these low-income housing areas do not have any sewage treatment, and concern over groundwater contamination is growing. Venhuizen's findings indicate that at $4,000 per house, sand filtration systems cost about half as much as extending the sewage lines.

Landscaping for Low-Impact Management Practices

Carefully planned and designed landscapes can dramatically reduce the economic and ecological costs of landscape management. Planting climatically appropriate vegetation can eliminate the need for irrigation and chemical herbicides and insecticides. The savings in landscape maintenance costs at the two AT&T corporate facilities previously described more than paid for the cost of the prairie restoration work within one year. Moreover, their ongoing landscaping costs today are just a quarter of what they were prior to the work.

Savings can be achieved with far less involved landscaping strategies than prairie restoration. Simply selecting the right trees, shrubs, and turfgrass can greatly reduce maintenance costs. Vegetation patterns at corporate campuses are surprisingly uniform across the country. "Basically the same 15 species of trees are being planted, even though the ecosystems are highly varied," said landscape architect Jim Patchett. To keep a tree or shrub that is adapted to a moist temperate climate alive in Phoenix takes lots of water and chemicals. Turfgrass provides an even more striking example. Despite its name, Kentucky bluegrass is not from Kentucky, but has Euro-Asian origins. Yet this is what we expect to see around houses and office buildings, whether in Nevada, Florida, or Montana. Keeping the grass alive and healthy consumes precious water and far exceeds the per-acre chemical loading of average American farmland. When landscape irrigation is needed, there are automated drip-irrigation systems that are far more water-efficient than standard spray-irrigation systems. Incorporation of such systems into standard landscapes can provide significant savings to the owner—though not as much as plantings that require no irrigation.

ENVIRONMENTALLY RESPONSIBLE GOLF COURSE MANAGEMENT

Nowhere is the potential for improved turf management more obvious than on the 1.5 million acres of the nation's 15,000 golf courses. Extensive irrigation of golf courses, coupled with high rates of chemical application, results in high pollution runoff. With hundreds of new golf courses springing up around the country each year, public outcry over their impact on the natural environment has prompted a number of developers to seek ways to develop this recreational amenity in a more environmentally responsible manner. Some golf courses have been built atop industrial waste sites, municipal landfills, or abandoned quarries. Others are using permaculture techniques, integrated pest management, and various organic management strategies to minimize the need for irrigation, chemical fertilizers, herbicides, and pesticides. An increasing number of golf courses are using treated effluent for irrigation, thereby reducing the discharge of this effluent into surface waters and saving millions of gallons of water per year. A few golf courses now have on-site biological treatment systems to purify wastewater. The Pebble Beach Company in arid central California used to use 8,000 acre-feet of water per year —2.6 billion gallons—for irrigation, fountains, and other uses. Along with employing many other low-impact strategies, management has now switched to irrigating the course with treated effluent.

According to Pat Jones of the Golf Course Superintendents Association, developers are beginning to embrace the concept of environmentally responsible golf courses. Spring Island's golf course earned certification by Audubon International, which administers the Audubon Cooperative Sanctuary Program for Golf

Dunes, marshes, and grass buffer zones provide wildlife habitat and collect filter runoff on the Spring Island golf course. *(Reprinted with permission from Betsy Chaffin.)*

Courses. (This program is not affiliated with the National Audubon Society or local Audubon chapters.) Spring Island has enjoyed lots of positive press for its ecologically sensitive golf course. In planning this course, the team paid careful attention to preserving archaeological and historic sites and protecting coastal areas and wildlife habitats. The facility incorporates a lagoon system to collect and filter irrigation water runoff for reuse on the golf course. Dunes, marshes, and grass buffer zones collect and filter runoff, providing wildlife habitat while offering natural hazards for golfers. The course design and layout accommodated native grasses, aquatic plants, and many trees. Trees removed from the course site were transplanted throughout the island.

More than 2,000 golf courses have been certified by Audubon International since 1991. To comply with the program, which is sponsored by the U.S. Golf Association, courses must demonstrate that they have made a real effort to improve environmental quality in six areas: habitat management, water conservation, water quality, integrated pest management, environmental planning, and public/member involvement. Although it constitutes an important step forward, the Audubon International program has been criticized by some because no site visits are made to ensure compliance and certification is based solely on information supplied by the golf course.

Better Golf Courses

Resources to improve the environmental performance of golf course developments:

- The U.S. Golf Association and the National Fish and Wildlife Foundation have launched a program called Wildlife Links—providing research, education, and management to encourage developers to protect or create habitats for endangered species on golf courses.

- Audubon International operates the Audubon Cooperative Sanctuary Program as well as the "Signature" program to certify new golf courses that follow its design and construction guidelines.

- The Golf Course Superintendents Association of America is disseminating a set of environmental principles for golf courses in the United States. The principles were developed by an alliance of golf associations in cooperation with leading environmental organizations.

Fostering a Sense of Community and Culture

A place that is understood, preserved, repaired, and celebrated as an integrated whole can become a powerful and memorable work of art.

Ecological Design Guidelines, *by Andropogon Associates, Ltd.*

According to developer Michael Corbett, "planning for a good social environment can be even more difficult than planning for a good physical environment, simply because human behavior is even more complex and unpredictable." In creating the landmark ecologically responsible development Village Homes, Corbett focused on creating a project that would encourage people to get out of their cars and meet their next door neighbors. The site design includes pedestrian walkways, trails, and common spaces for community gatherings. Neighbors come together to plant and harvest food in the community gardens and orchards. Despite having twice the housing density of nearby Sacramento, open space (agricultural and recreational land) comprises 25 percent of Village Homes' acreage, and much of it is designed to encourage residents to interact with one another.

Corbett narrowed the streets to create quieter, pedestrian-scale spaces. Less pavement meant that more land was available for green belts, and narrower streets slow traffic. The many pathways encourage walking and biking. These features have made Village Homes the most popular neighborhood in the area; residents keep their houses longer than average, often adding onto them as needed. Housing values average 13 percent higher than in neighboring subdivisions.

Rancho Santa Margarita in Orange County, California, is often acclaimed as one of the county's greatest master-planning successes, providing affordable housing and jobs while preserving open space and fostering community. In 1979, Rancho Mission Viejo, a local development company, hired planner Richard Reese to create a master plan for the remaining 43,000 acres of its ranch, which included the land on which Rancho Santa Margarita now sits—a stream-fed valley with 100-year-old oak and elm trees. Ground was broken in June 1985, and the first homes were completed in 1986. Once the final phase including the Town Center is complete, the 5,000-acre development will contain 30,000 to 35,000 people in a blend of 50 percent permanent open space (required by Orange County) and 50 percent devoted to what planner Richard Reese calls "urban lifescape village—a blend of man and nature." The neighborhood is pedestrian oriented with wide walkways and bikeways, while amenities such as a "swimming hole," an amphitheater, and lots of carefully sited benches provide community gathering places.

Developer John Podmajersky in Chicago is demonstrating that one can use common spaces, outdoor meeting places, and careful design to foster healthy human interaction in redevelopment projects too. Podmajersky grew up in Pilsen East—one of Chicago's oldest working-class districts, with modest one- and two-story frame buildings dating back to the 1870s. After college, he returned to the area to discover that a highway had torn a hole through the community, causing urban decay and a mass exodus of families. The streets soon filled with taverns, pool halls, gangs, and violence. Buildings were falling into decay.

Podmajersky has spent more than 40 years restoring this neighborhood into a vibrant inner-city community. He says his inspiration comes from his tenants, some of whom have lived in the neighborhood for more than 20 years, and from the old buildings he calls "sweethearts." "My goal is to create powerful buildings that have great spaces, great environments—you can't do this sitting in an architect's office. You need to be there on the site—use the space to find opportunities."

John Podmajersky has spent more than 40 years restoring the Pilsen East neighborhood in Chicago into a vibrant inner-city community. *(Reprinted with permission from David Johnston.)*

In addition to renovating old buildings into rental suites, artists' studios, and a small community theater, Podmajersky has created courtyards and malls out of old alleyways. "I create spaces so people can't help but meet each other," he says. Podmajersky redesigned the old stores, factories, and row houses to put their entrances in the back. Garden-level apartments open onto courtyards, and suites on the upper stories look down onto community gardens and inviting public spaces. Once dingy alleys with dumpsters

Revitalized garden-level apartments open onto courtyards, and upper-story suites overlook community gardens and inviting public spaces in John Podmajersky's project. *(Reprinted with permission from David Johnston.)*

and oil slicks, these courtyards are now home to community gatherings and outdoor art galleries showing the work of local artists. Residents tend the gardens, and in 1995 one courtyard was named Chicago's "Garden of the Year." Indeed, by designing to bring people together in this moderate- and lower-income redevelopment project, Podmajersky has not created Chicago's grandest neighborhood, but for the tenants who live in this community—it is a real home.

"Involve Me, I Understand."

John Knott set out to create the kind of development at Dewees Island that would inspire all who came to the island community to cherish it. An inclusive planning process and ongoing educational and communications programs ensure that this "ecological aesthetic" will be preserved at Dewees Island.

Says Knott, "You can't orchestrate every aspect of people's lives in your development. Education and understanding of the property's natural features is important in order for residents to gain an appreciation of the value of this land and its ecosystem." For example, before designing and constructing homes on the island, residents must participate in the site analysis of their homesite. This helps them learn about environmental issues, and it enables them to understand and accept design strategies that protect the property's sensitive features. Knott quotes the old Eastern proverb, "Tell me, I forget; show me, I remember; involve me, I understand."

The siting of The Way Station creates a parklike setting, enhancing the "main-street" feel of the Frederick, Maryland, historic district. *(Reprinted with permission from Harriet Wise, photographer.)*

CHAPTER **6**

Building Design

THE WAY STATION IS A PRIVATE, NONPROFIT health care facility in Frederick, Maryland, devoted to the rehabilitation of people with mental illnesses. When the company began planning a new healthcare facility, it wanted a building that would contribute to the patients' psychological and physical health. It also wanted a building that would be both cost-effective and ecologically sound.

The first architect produced a design that was too institutional, did not seem to speak to the concerns of the residents and staff, and did not reflect the organization's concern for the environment. Wanting more from its building, The Way Station scrapped the plan and brought in Boulder, Colorado, architect Greg Franta of the ENSAR Group, an internationally recognized expert on environmentally responsible design.

Completed in 1991, the 30,000-square-foot building Franta designed satisfies The Way Station's end-use goals beautifully. Located in the heart of Frederick, it is sited to create a parklike setting that enhances the main street feel of the sur- rounding historic district. The building's whole-systems-based design is highly energy efficient, with energy consumption just a third that of a conventional building. Extensive use of superwindows with multiple low-emissivity coatings on suspended plastic films enables the facility to have large window areas without the energy penalty that usually results from extensive glazing. This provides warm, relaxing spaces that are bathed in natural light. An innovative mechanical system recovers heat from the exhaust air to provide plenty of fresh outside air without losing much energy. Water-efficient plumbing fixtures lower water use and lessen the impact on the municipal sewage system. Nontoxic materials and finishes ensure a healthy indoor environment for both patients and workers.

The building's lighting design is particularly noteworthy, making use of high-tech products and systems, but providing the low-tech feel of a warm, friendly environment. The design provides for high-quality lighting from multiple sources, optimum light levels for comfort, minimum glare, appropriate levels of contrast between light and dark surfaces, and pleasing aesthetics. Natural daylighting comes from a blend of light shelves, light scoops, skylights, and high-performance glazings. A sun-tracking lighting system on the roof is linked to an efficient electric lighting system that adjusts light levels according to outside conditions. Daylight streams through skylights on the second level. Daylight is brought deep into the building by bouncing it off light shelves located in the windows on the south side, which also act as shading devices to reduce unwanted heat gain from summer sun. In the

On the Way Station's roof a sun-tracking lighting system, like this one, is linked to an efficient lighting system that adjusts light levels according to outside conditions. *(Reprinted with permission, © Milroy/McAleer.)*

The Way Station: Reducing Operating Costs While Healing People

The architecture of The Way Station creates a unique physical environment that is ecologically sound, comfortable to occupants, and cost-effective. This chart compares the energy-efficient Way Station to a standard building of the same size and in the same climate.

	Standard Building	Energy-Efficient Way Station
Space and Water Heating	$8,800/yr.	$2,939/yr.
Lighting and Cooling, Electric	$47,100/yr.	$16,672/yr.
Water Heating	$2,100/yr.	$734/yr.
TOTAL	$58,000/yr.	$20,345/yr.
Energy Use	66,100 Btu/SF/yr.	22,700 Btu/SF/yr.

Source: Burke Miller Thayer, "Way Station," *Solar Today Magazine* (July/August 1994). Reprinted with permission from the American Solar Energy Society, 2400 Central Avenue, G-1, Boulder, CO 80304; (303) 443-3130.

center of the building a light court serves as the central organizing feature while allowing light to bathe the traffic circulation areas and adjacent rooms.

The highly integrated design of The Way Station did not just happen. At the beginning of the process, Franta brought together lighting designers, health care designers, landscape architects, historic preservation experts, and engineers to participate in the design. He also involved The Way Station staff and residents from the beginning, knowing that their insights were vital to the design process. The team developed "health-promotion techniques," such as full accessibility for disabled persons and open space designed to aid those with perceptual difficulties.

The real proof that Franta's team process succeeded is the sense of community that emerged at the new Way Station. It has improved the residents' outlook on life. The Way Station staff find that patients progress through rehabilitation programs much more quickly here than in conventional facilities. As one patient noted, "There are no dark corners in the building." Franta stresses the importance of this aspect "for people who are already troubled with dark shadows in their minds."

The most effective building designs emerge through careful attention to the four elements outlined in Chapter 2: whole-systems thinking, front-loaded design, end-use/least-cost considerations, and teamwork. All four of these elements were used in designing The Way Station, and the results are evident in the finished product.

This chapter takes a cursory look at specific aspects of environmentally responsible building design. A more complete description of building design would easily require an entire book. The following are the basic elements of designing a green development:

- Design to fit the site.
- Design to foster community.
- Design for resource efficiency.
- Design for a healthful indoor environment.
- Design for adaptability.
- Design for durability and easy maintenance.

The process of designing a green building is different from that of conventional design. Design teams must be aware of difficulties that may arise. This chapter describes some of the barriers and solutions experienced in taking a green development approach to designing buildings.

Green Building Elements

The elements that tend to make a building project turn out green apply to both new construction and renovation. Renovation generally imposes fewer burdens on the environment than new construction, so the possibility of fixing up an older building instead of building from scratch should always be examined before new land is disturbed. The energy and materials that it took to create the building may be retained, rather than having to invest in "new" embodied energy. Existing buildings are more likely to be found in populated areas that offer easy access to public transportation and allow future occupants to walk to stores and other services.

Portland Metro, the department that handles transportation and waste management in Portland, Oregon, put the city's recycling and waste-avoidance program into practice by moving its offices into the old Sears building, a 60-year-old retail complex that had stood vacant for eight years. The project reused such components as doors, railings, and plumbing fixtures. Any new products were required to be made of at least 50 percent recycled material. The floor tiles, for example, were made of ground glass from old fluorescent lamps, and the toilet partitions from recycled plastic milk jugs. Including the shell of the building, some 7,900 tons of construction materials were reused that would otherwise have been disposed of. According to project manager Berit Stevenson, the renovation saved $2 million over the cost of a new building.

DESIGN TO FIT THE SITE

Issues relating to site design were covered in Chapter 5, but it is important that the schematic design of a building be developed with an understanding of how that building will interact with the ecosystem(s) on its specific site. Surrounding vegetation, for example, will inform decisions on passive solar and daylighting design. An exposed site suggests the use of a design that blocks entrances from prevailing winds, while a sheltered site offers opportunities for natural wind-breaks.

The Boyne River Ecology Center in Shelbourne, Ontario, is the environmental education center for the Toronto school system. Located near the bottom of the ecologically diverse Boyne River Valley, the Center is surrounded by hardwood trees, streams, meadows, ponds, and a waterfall. To avoid cutting trees, the project team located the building very carefully, using a site where beavers had felled trees. This opened up a clearing that provided solar exposure in winter, yet left enough trees standing for summer shading. The building was built into a south-facing hillside to moderate temperature fluctuation and was designed to benefit from the available energy sources on the site, including not only solar energy (roof-mounted photovoltaic panels as well as passive solar), but also a micro-hydropower plant, and a wind generator.

DESIGN TO FOSTER COMMUNITY

The places where we spend our time affect the people we are and can become. These places have an impact on our sense of self, our sense of safety, the kind of work we get done, the ways we interact with other people, even our ability to function as citizens in a democracy. This means that whatever we experience in a place is both a serious environmental issue and a deeply personal one. Our relationship with the places we know is a close bond, intricate in nature, and not abstract.

Tony Hiss, The Experience of Place, *1990*

People are beginning to recognize that buildings can play an important role in helping to strengthen a sense of community. While the primary way in which development can promote community is through land-use planning issues (see Chapter 3), building design and specific building elements can also promote or discourage interaction with neighbors and the broader community. In this way, building design can help to slow down or reverse the dissolution of community that has been happening since the automobile became such a significant force in shaping the built environment. Building design can also foster an understanding of, and integration with, diverse cultures that may exist in a community.

Developer Harold Kalke renovated six 1908 townhouses in the heart of Vancouver's Chinese community. Kalke strove to keep the cultural integrity of the structures, and he recycled as much of the building materials as he could. The townhouses were revitalized according to the ancient Chinese way of doing things—a "refining of the past rather than a bold building of new." Because there was little ground around the townhouses and because the residents value their gardens, Kalke's development team created rooftop gardens that are accessible by a pull-down ladder above the second landing.

The ING bank in Holland took people-oriented building design further than perhaps any other company. Through careful attention to human-scale elements throughout the headquarters building in Amsterdam, architect Anton Alberts achieved unique, inspiring spaces where people can feel comfortable. In a 1991 *Architect and Builder* article he described his thoughts about the design. "An office is really like your third skin. Everyone knows what your real skin is; your clothes are your second skin, and the third layer is the building in which you work. If that third skin doesn't fit, people start to feel uncomfortable in it. Our aim is to allow people to go to work in a relaxed manner." Instead of stacking the building's 2,400 employees in a typical monolithic skyscraper, the 538,000-square-foot building is broken up into a snaking series of 10 slanting, brick-faced, interconnecting precast-concrete towers. The ground plan is an irregular S-curve, with gardens and courtyards interspersed over the top of a structured parking lot and service areas. "Flow-form" sculptures, which create a pulsing, gurgling stream from a constant flow of water, are used extensively throughout the interior of the buildings, even as handrails for multistory ramps. This is one of the few buildings in the world in which bankers in three-piece suits can be found splashing in the handrails. Restaurants and meeting rooms line the internal street that connects the 10 towers, giving occupants opportunities to interact.

The ground plan of the ING bank in Amsterdam is an irregular S-curve; gardens and court-yards cover the structured parking lot and service areas. *(Reprinted with permission, © POLYVISIE.)*

DESIGN FOR RESOURCE EFFICIENCY

Using energy, water, and materials efficiently is one of the most important strategies for creating an environmentally responsible building. It also makes the building more affordable to own and operate.

Many environmental problems result directly or indirectly from inefficient use of resources, particularly energy. Careful design of the building envelope, lighting systems, and heating, ventilation, and air-conditioning (HVAC) systems is important, as all of these elements affect the energy use of the building. If heating and cooling loads are kept low through careful envelope design, glazing selection, and lighting design, heating and cooling equipment can be significantly downsized or, in some cases, even eliminated. This can make the building cheaper to build or, at a minimum, offset any price increases that the additional energy-saving equipment may impose.

Developer Harold Kalke believes that energy prices are headed for significant increases, and he plans for that possibility through careful designs. Says Kalke, "Anything we can do to make our commercial tenants and residential buyers more equipped to deal with that increase in the future, we should do it." And, of course, reductions in energy use significantly benefit the environment by reducing pollution generation.

BUILDING ENVELOPE

Getting the building envelope right the first time is particularly important, because future modifications will be difficult, expensive, and environmentally costly. Envelope decisions will likely determine the energy consumption of the building for decades to come—perhaps even for a century or more.

Many building professionals assume that if a building complies with code, then it must be energy efficient. But as Randy Croxton of Croxton Collaborative Architects in New York City (and designer of the Audubon headquarters renovation) points out, building to code means that if the building were designed any worse it would be against the law.

At the University of Victoria in British Columbia, architect Terry Williams designed the new 127,800-square-foot engineering laboratory wing, which relies primarily on passive solar heating and natural cooling. With a high-performance building envelope and the use of high-tech controls, the building's interior environment can be controlled naturally. The systems were designed to be as simple and efficient as possible. Carefully selected windows and effective use of light shelves minimize electric lighting while keeping heat loss to a minimum. This strategy enabled the designers to eliminate perimeter heating throughout the building. The extra cost of the high-performance glazing was more than paid for by the elimination of perimeter heating. Heat loss calculations showed that more heat will be generated through light fixtures and equipment than will be lost through the envelope. Fresh air is introduced through a high-velocity ventilation system that provides double the normal fresh air quantity; operable windows also aid in cooling. Together, the energy systems are saving 723,000 kilowatt-hours each year, worth $36,150 (Canadian).

LIGHTING

Twenty-five percent of the electricity consumed in the United States is for lighting. The air-conditioning required to take away the heat produced by inefficient electric lighting can amount to 3 to 5 percent of the total energy use (according to

E SOURCE's *Lighting Atlas*). In homes, incandescent lighting prevails, despite the fact that roughly 90 percent of the energy used in the bulb is directly converted into heat and only 10 percent into light. In commercial and institutional buildings, fluorescent lighting is more common, but most of that uses older technologies that waste energy and produce unpleasant light quality, hum, and flicker.

With careful design, natural daylighting can provide most needed ambient lighting, along with a significant percentage of light needed for fine work. Light shelves and reflective ceilings and walls can help to direct daylight deep into a building. By coupling daylighting with dimmable fluorescent lighting controlled by photocells, the lighting controls (and savings) can be automated.

Natural daylighting was used extensively in a new 600,000-square-foot office building in Sunnyvale, California, built by the Lockheed Missiles and Space Company in the early 1980s. Lockheed's Building 157 houses 2,700 engineers and support staff. The building was designed by the San Francisco-based architecture firm Leo A. Daly and is one of the most successful examples of day-lighting use in a large commercial office building. Fifteen-foot tall window walls with sloped ceilings bring daylight deep into the building. "High windows were the secret to deep daylighting success," says the project architect, Lee Windheim. "The sloped ceiling directs additional daylight to the center of each floor and decreases the perception of crowded space in a very densely populated building."

At Lockheed's Building 157 in Sunnyvale, California, daylighting is enhanced by a central "literium." *(Reprinted with permission from William D. Browning, Rocky Mountain Institute.)*

Daylighting is also enhanced by a central atrium, or "litetrium," as the architects call it (*atrium* sounded too much like an amenity for Lockheed's tastes). The litetrium runs top to bottom and has a glazed roof. Workers consider this the building's most attractive feature. Other light-enhancing features include light shelves on the south facade that operate both as sunshades for blocking direct sunlight and as reflectors for bouncing light from the high summer sun onto the interior ceiling. Researchers from Lawrence Berkeley National Laboratory explain, "In the winter, the interior light shelves diffuse reflected light and reduce glare during lower winter sun angles."

The overall design separates ambient and task lighting, with daylight supplying most of the ambient lighting and individual fixtures supplementing the light at each workstation. The continuously dimmable fluorescent ceiling fixtures with photocell sensors were installed to maintain a constant level of light and save even more energy by dimming lights when natural daylight is available. Daylighting has reduced lighting energy use at Building 157 by about 75 percent, as compared with a conventional office building. Since daylight generates less heat than office lights, the peak air-conditioning load has also been reduced. Overall, the building uses about half of the energy of a typically constructed building of this size. The energy-saving features added roughly $2 million to the $50 million cost of the building, but provided direct energy savings worth nearly $500,000 a year—paying back the energy investment in less than five years. Productivity improvements resulting from the high-quality lighting have yielded far greater savings for Lockheed. Absenteeism dropped 15 percent, which paid back 100 percent of the extra costs of the building within the first year.

HVAC

The selection of heating, ventilation, and air conditioning (HVAC) systems provides another opportunity to reap the benefits of energy-efficient design. In large buildings, the savings in mechanical systems can more than pay for the energy improvements and actually reduce the total cost of a green building.

The Queens Building at the New School of Engineering and Manufacture at De Montfort University in Leicester, England, is one of the most remarkable institutional buildings in existence. Designed by Short, Ford, and Associates of London, this 100,000-square-foot building for mechanical and electrical engineering students is the largest naturally ventilated building in the United Kingdom. It serves as a living laboratory for mechanical engineering design,

The Queens Building at the New School of Engineering and Manufacture at De Montfort University in Leicester, England, is passively ventilated through carefully designed building geometries and thermal chimneys that induce ventilation through the building. *(Reprinted with permission from William D. Browning, Rocky Mountain Institute.)*

providing (ironically) a training facility for mechanical engineers while using almost no mechanical HVAC strategies.

Passive ventilation at the Queens Building is achieved through carefully designed building geometries and *thermal chimneys* that induce ventilation through the building. This "stack effect" draws warm air up through eight large towers capped with ornamental metal louvers. The airflow, in turn, pulls outside air into vents and through the building. Occupants can open or close windows to adjust the comfort level in their spaces. Sixty percent of the glazing area is operable. To ensure that the temperature stays within acceptable levels, an automated management system was incorporated to adjust dampers, louvers, and heating controls. Calculated overhangs and the heavy masonry walls minimize cooling loads. Construction cost of the building was $184 (U.S. 1995) per square foot, which is considered low for an engineering school building.

While the Queens Building did not require a chiller, chillers are used in most large buildings, particularly in climates with larger cooling loads, and they provide an excellent opportunity for energy-efficiency improvements in most commercial buildings. As well as being the largest users of electricity in many commercial buildings and representing approximately 23 percent of installed electrical capacity in the United States, chillers are also leading emitters of ozone-depleting CFCs and HCFCs into the atmosphere. Replacement of CFC-based chillers with newer, environmentally safer products offers an opportunity to significantly improve energy performance. Chiller energy consumption can be reduced 50 percent by using direct digital controls, variable-frequency drives, improved heat exchanger design, and proper maintenance practices.

WATER EFFICIENCY

Conserving water should be a key design goal in any green development. Reducing water consumption not only conserves a valuable resource, but it saves money directly and reduces the financial and environmental costs of treating wastewater. Rocky Mountain Institute estimates that an average of 20,000 gallons of water per home per year could be saved in the United States if water-efficient fixtures were widely used.

At the Boston Park Plaza Hotel the simple measure of replacing old plumbing fixtures with new water-efficient models has dramatically reduced water consumption—and saved the hotel a bundle of money in the process. The hotel installed tankless toilets with "flushometers" that control the water use. It also initiated a water conservation system for its in-house laundry operations (one of the largest in Boston). These initiatives reduced water consumption by 65 percent, saving $45,000 annually. The water conservation retrofits had a payback of just 1.9 years.

The United States uses 5 billion gallons of water per day flushing toilets. Annually, 1.4 billion pounds of nitrogen, 456 million pounds of potassium, and 194 million pounds of phosphorus are flushed down our toilets with the water. Sewage treatment plants try, with only moderate success, to remove those nutrients, then use 1.2 billion pounds of chlorine to "purify" the water.

Source: Earth Island Journal (Spring 1996).

Having no sewer connection was one of the goals for the C. K. Choi building at the University of British Columbia. Designers eliminated the use of water for toilet flushing by choosing composting toilets. These had to be carefully incorporated into the building design, because the toilets required a straight shot to the basement with 14-inch-diameter chutes that extended as high as three stories. Composted solids are applied on the land. Liquids (urine and graywater) pass through a constructed wetland, where nutrients are removed and the water is purified. (Biological wastewater treatment systems are discussed in Chapter 5.) An added benefit is that the cleaning staff only has to throw a few handfuls of sawdust down the chutes each day; they do not have to deal with harsh cleaning agents.

EFFICIENT USE OF MATERIALS AND SPACE

Regardless of their particular features, smaller buildings nearly always use less material in construction, occupy less land, and require less energy to heat and cool. They are thus better from an environmental standpoint (as long as size constraints do not force later expansion, which also has environmental impact.) By reducing overall building size, bottom-line savings can be realized, or—within a given budget—more money can be put into finishing details and higher-quality components, furnishings, and amenities.

In residential construction wood use can be reduced through "optimum-value engineering" (OVE) or "advanced framing." Nearly all strategies that reduce material use or waste result in bottom-line cost savings for a construction project. The OVE strategies promoted by the National Association of Home Builders National Research Center can save approximately $2 per square foot in construction costs with light-frame buildings, according to Peter Yost of the Center.

Chicago home builder Perry Bigelow uses OVE to reduce construction costs and improve energy performance. He uses such strategies as 24-inches-on-center framing, single top plates, single 2×12 headers above windows, trusses, and two-stud corners. "We get rid of every piece of wood we don't need for structure," says Bigelow. "The savings pay for upgrading from conventional 2×4 to 2×6 framing." More insulation can be installed with 2×6 framing, creating a better building envelope.

At Prairie Crossing, near Chicago, builder Shaw Homes was able to get approval for a package of advanced framing construction practices that were not generally accepted by the local building department. Engineer Joseph Lstiburek of Building Science Corporation in Chestnut Hill, Massachusetts, developed a cohesive package of energy conservation, moisture control, and material optimization details that the builder took to the building department. Lstiburek presented the case and obtained acceptance of the entire integrated package by the local county building department. Subsequently, the Prairie Crossing development has become part of the U.S. Department of Energy "Building America" demonstration program; resulting homes should achieve a 50 percent reduction in heating and cooling energy consumption, as compared with conventional subdivisions in the Chicago area.

SELECTION OF THE APPROPRIATE MATERIALS
New buildings carry a heavy environmental burden by virtue of the materials used in their construction. Some materials cause resource depletion during harvest or extraction, others give off pollutants during manufacture, emit pollutants into the occupied space, or contribute to solid waste problems at the end of their useful life. Most building materials consume large amounts of energy during their pro-

Architects for the U.S. headquarters for The Body Shop in Wake Forest, North Carolina, analyzed materials for indoor air quality impacts and other environmental considerations. *(Reprinted with permission from Doug Van de Zande, photographer.)*

duction. Understanding these various issues involves a process referred to as "life-cycle assessment," or LCA. One goal of environmentally responsible development is to reduce the life-cycle impacts associated with materials used in construction.

So-called "green building materials" are those that, for one reason or another, are attractive from an environmental angle. Some are made out of recycled waste products. Others are "natural" materials, produced without synthetic or petroleum-based constituents. Still others are environmentally attractive because they are salvaged, locally sourced, sustainably harvested wood, easily recyclable, or responsible for fewer pollutants emitted into the air.

It is the designer's job to carefully weigh these environmental considerations while still addressing such conventional selection criteria as performance, durability, and cost. A green material should have certain attractive environmental features while performing as well as, or better than, the more conventional product. If the green product has to be replaced twice as quickly as the conventional product, any environmental benefit is probably lost. Some green building materials cost more than conventional counterparts; others are the same price or even less expensive.

The U.S. headquarters for The Body Shop, a manufacturer of environmentally and animal-friendly body products, in Wake Forest, North Carolina, was designed by Clearscapes Architecture with environmental design and materials consulting by Design Harmony of Raleigh, North Carolina. The 153,700-square-foot office and manufacturing facility, completed in 1993, began its life as a fire extinguisher manufacturing plant. Reusing an existing building fit perfectly with The Body Shop's environmental goals. Foundations, exterior concrete wall panels, roofing, and windows were all reused. Materials going into the building were carefully analyzed for indoor air quality impacts and other environmental considerations. The paint used in the manufacturing wing was a new, zero-volatile organic compound (VOC) product. Several materials used in the remodel were produced from recycled waste, including tile in the lobby produced from crushed light bulbs and carpet made from 100 percent post-consumer polyethylene terephthalate (PET) soda bottles. The designers relied on Material Safety Data Sheets, on-site testing, and direct communication with manufacturers to provide a basis for evaluation of materials.

Fifty percent of the total materials used in the C. K. Choi building have recycled content or were salvaged. Originally, the structure had been planned as a concrete building, but when the design team learned that a neighboring building was to be torn down, they arranged to salvage the 100-foot-long heavy timbers of its frame. Because the frame was joined using mechanical fasteners, disassembly

Hundred-foot-long heavy timbers were salvaged for use in the C. K. Choi Building at the University of British Columbia. The frame for the new building was joined using mechanical fasteners so that it can be disassembled in the future. *(Reprinted with permission from Gunnar Hubbard, Rocky Mountain Institute.)*

was easy; the designers carried forward that feature in the new building so that it too can be disassembled in the future. A timber grader examined the timbers individually and specified where each could be used in the structure. The total cost of the salvaged wood was $40,000 (Canadian), including $10,000 for grading. As the project progressed, word got out that salvaged materials were being used, and people started offering materials to the design team. Brick cladding for the building came from a brick-paved street in downtown Vancouver. When a nearby golf course building was demolished, its handrails were salvaged for the balconies of the atrium and its doors were reused for the new offices.

Tools for Materials Selection

Understanding all of the factors pertinent in selecting appropriate materials can appear to be an overwhelming task for a design team. A number of books and newsletters provide useful up-to-date information on green building products. The American Institute of Architects devotes a large section of its *Environmental Resource Guide* to the subject. *Environmental Building News,* a monthly newsletter published in Brattleboro, Vermont, is another leading source of information.

Specific product data bases are available from several different sources, including:

- *Harris Directory,* 522 Acequia Madre, Santa Fe, NM 87501 (data base available on disk only)
- *REDI Guide,* Iris Communications, www.oikos.com (Web site—data base available on-line)
- *Guide to Resource Efficient Building Elements,* Center for Resourceful Building Technology, P.O. Box 100, Missoula, MT 59806; (406) 549-7678

See Appendix C for more sources.

DESIGN FOR A HEALTHFUL INDOOR ENVIRONMENT

Americans spend upwards of 80 percent of their time indoors, so ensuring that an indoor environment is safe and healthful should be a high priority for every designer. Indoor air quality (IAQ) is now listed as the fourth-largest health threat to Americans by the U.S. Environmental Protection Agency (EPA). According to the EPA, indoor air can be a hundred times more polluted than outdoor air. The Occupational Safety and Health Administration (OSHA) claims that 25 to 50 percent of all commercial buildings have IAQ problems. A study published in the *Journal of the American Medical Association* stated that the sickest buildings are typically those built or renovated in the 1970s and 1980s because their "sealed box" designs had poor ventilation and air circulation.

IAQ is affected by such factors as the choice of materials and finishes in a building, activities like smoking and open combustion of gas- or wood-fired appliances, high moisture levels that permit mold growth, and the amount (and quality) of fresh air introduced through ventilation. Carpets, paints, and adhesives have been among the worst offenders. Scientists have identified 1,500 bacterial and chemical air pollutants given off by paints, carpets, manufactured products, and office equipment. Selecting from more environmentally benign building materials and designing to provide effective ventilation will help alleviate IAQ problems.

"Sick building syndrome" (SBS) has increasingly made the news in recent years. This illness is characterized by widely varying symptoms, including dizziness, headaches, irritated eyes, nausea, throat irritation, and coughing. When a person with these symptoms leaves the building, these reactions go away. SBS was first highly publicized in the 1980s when, ironically, a large number of employees at the newly remodeled EPA building in Washington, D.C., became sick. Off-gassing from new carpeting was ultimately implicated as the culprit. Nineteen employees filed suit for $1 million and won their case.

In renovating the National Audubon Society headquarters in New York City, a great deal of time and effort was put into selecting building materials and finishes that would ensure a healthful indoor environment. One of the early goals for this major remodeling of the hundred-year-old building was "to eliminate as much as possible the risk of sick building syndrome." All furniture, fabrics, and wall and floor coverings were carefully researched by Croxton Collaborative Architects, with input from Jan Beyea of the National Audubon Society. Testing was used to avoid materials that off-gassed such chemicals as formaldehyde, benzene, xylene, and toluene. Low-VOC paints and adhesives, and carpeting and carpet pads made of natural materials, were used throughout. The ventilation system delivers high rates of fresh air, exceeding ASHRAE (American Society of Heating, Refrigeration and Air Conditioning Engineers) standards by 30 percent.

Design for Adaptability

> Any design element that has only one function is probably a mistake or a missed opportunity. We ought to strive for multiple and diverse functions of each element so we pay once and get many benefits.
>
> *Amory B. Lovins, Rocky Mountain Institute*

Building uses and needs change over time, particularly for commercial spaces. A new building should be constructed to facilitate relatively easy, low-impact conversion to new uses. Architects use the term *programming* to describe the process of identifying the type, size, use, and requirements of spaces for a project. This process can be used in green developments to help designers identify and understand the users' current needs, as well as changing needs over time. Unfortunately, this latter step rarely happens.

Author Stewart Brand examined how buildings evolve over time. In his book *How Buildings Learn,* he presented the ideas of British architect Francis Duffy, who suggests that buildings have several layers, evolving at different rates. Building exteriors tend to change every 20 years or so, while new wiring, plumbing, and climate control systems might be added every 7 to 15 years. Floor plans can change as often as every 3 years. The key to making buildings last and adapt is to clearly separate these layers, according to Brand, so that the slow-changing ones do not impede alterations to the fast-changing ones.

The country's leading green architects and planners consider adaptability of buildings to be a high priority in their designs. During schematic design, they plan for what that building might become once its current use ends. When the environmentally conscious outdoor clothing retailer Patagonia began planning a new distribution center and office facility in Reno, Nevada, it specifically asked that the building be designed with adaptability in mind. So Miller Hull Architects of Seattle, designers of the 185,000-square-foot building, incorporated the structural capacity to add a second floor that could someday be converted into office space. The front third of the building was specifically designed to be adaptable because it had most the access to daylighting and natural ventilation. Providing for this adaptability did not cost any more up-front, because it was incorporated early enough in the design process. But it will save a great deal of money if building modifications are made in the future.

DESIGN FOR DURABILITY AND EASY MAINTENANCE

Ongoing maintenance can cause environmental impacts over time. If one siding option for a house, for example, requires a coat of paint every five years, while another option will last fifty years with no maintenance, the environmental impact of those 10 coats of paint should be weighed in deciding which siding to specify. Even if the latter option has somewhat greater environmental burdens associated with its manufacture, it might be a better choice on a life-cycle basis.

The use of cleaning fluids, pest control practices, and other maintenance can have significant impacts on IAQ as well as on the outdoor environment—even if natural materials were used extensively in the building. To ensure low environmental impact, issues of ongoing maintenance and durability should be considered throughout the building design and materials selection process. Designers should also provide building owners with recommendations on low-impact maintenance procedures (see Chapter 11).

Architect Lynn Froeschle, AIA, was the consulting environmental architect for the Ridgehaven Building, an older building renovated for the city of San Diego's Environmental Services Department in 1996. The 73,000-square-foot building is the most efficient commercial building in San Diego, even though it was renovated on an extremely tight municipal budget. Froeschle incorporated numerous green materials into the building and developed detailed guidelines for the city on building maintenance and pest control. The department has several employees who have chemical sensitivities, so IAQ was an important criterion throughout the design process.

Overcoming Barriers and Seeking Opportunities in Design

Building design is at the heart of most real estate development. Creating environmentally responsible buildings—whether single-family homes or million-square-foot corporate towers—entails careful attention to green building issues at every step of the design process. The design phase is where the critical decisions are made that will make or break a project. There are many opportunities that designers can take advantage of in creating buildings that achieve high levels of comfort while using a minimum of energy, ensuring healthful indoor air, and minimizing overall impact on the environment.

THE GREEN DEVELOPMENT PROCESS VS. CONVENTIONAL METHODS

Architects and engineers are comfortable with conventional design. They have developed practices and rules of thumb that they have come to rely on. These rules of thumb, many of them obsolete, continue to produce greatly oversized HVAC systems that are not optimally addressing the needs of buildings and their occupants. In his paper "Energy-Efficient Buildings—Institutional Barriers and Opportunities," Amory Lovins noted, "Price competition…creates a widespread tendency to buy, accept, and expect the lowest common denominator—'catalog engineering,' which is only the application of crude and outmoded rules of thumb to selecting common listings from major vendors' catalogs. This procedure is at the root of today's appallingly low mechanical-system efficiencies." Lovins identifies many obsolete design and engineering rules of thumb. They are misleading, he claims, for many reasons. For instance, they often assume outdated electricity prices that are far below today's; they seldom take into account interactions with and within the HVAC system, such as the fact that lighting and fan power add to

Energy Savings Opportunities and the Design Sequence

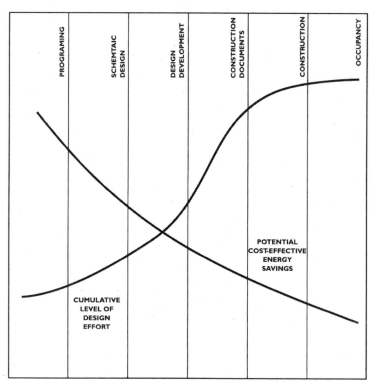

Time of Design Process

(Reprinted with permission from the ENSAR Group and E SOURCE.)

the cooling load; and they do not count indirect benefits of energy efficiency, including the fact that more efficient mechanicals can increase net rentable space, decrease floor-to-floor height, and reduce noise, maintenance, and structural requirements. Furthermore, energy plug loads are driven by elements of the real estate industry, including leasing agents, who want to ensure that even the most energy-intensive client's needs will be more than met.

In contrast, environmentally responsible design asks designers and engineers not only to consider a whole range of new and unfamiliar information, but also to incorporate most of these concerns from the start of the design process. As the design proceeds from programming to schematic design to construction documents, it becomes increasingly difficult and more costly to incorporate energy efficiency and other green measures. Opportunities to save capital costs through downsizing or elimination of mechanicals sharply decrease (see the figure on page 177).

In the process of designing the Queens Building, described earlier, the designers explicitly made the decision to use a passive ventilation strategy from the outset of their design process. It would have been nearly impossible to incorporate this strategy later on. The passive ventilation strategy was integral to the development of the rest of the design. Because the appropriation that funded the building was a lump sum, the savings from the passive system could be applied to other areas of the project, such as bigger classrooms. Part of the program for the mechanical engineering school required a diesel engine test cell room. Normally, such a room costs well over a million dollars to insulate acoustically. By fundamentally rethinking *up-front* what had to be done to achieve the desired end use of good acoustic separation, the designers came up with a solution that cost one-third as much. They designed a solid masonry "chimney" for the test room, surrounded by a stand-alone serpentine masonry wall, both of which contribute to the building's airflow dynamics.

As described in Chapter 2, in a typical design process the design is passed from one party to another, like a baton in a relay race. The developer defines the parameters, the architect designs the project, and the engineers each add their respective systems. A successful green real estate development, in contrast, results from the whole-systems, end-use thinking that comes from having all team members work together from the outset to capture the interconnections.

In her design for the Crestwood Corporate Office Centre's Buildings No. 2 and No. 8, architect Teresa Coady included mechanical engineers in discussions to define the basic systems the building would use even while the buildings were in an "embryonic" phase. Electrical engineers set the parameters for indoor light levels and were asked to design light shelves to enhance the daylighting strategies. These engineers were part of the team from the beginning. Working together, the team achieved its goal of 70 percent energy reduction in the final design.

Some design teams fall into the trap of using a value engineering approach for system or product selection, instead of a whole-systems approach. This piecemeal approach prices design elements one by one to find the cheapest available product. It fails to capture the benefits that can be achieved by recognizing that even though certain parts of the design may be more expensive, the whole project can cost less and be of greater value. Rocky Mountain Institute calls this "tunneling through the cost barrier."

This idea of tunneling through the cost barrier was employed at the ACT[2] house, a demonstration project in Davis, California, that was funded by Pacific Gas and Electric Company. Using an integrated design approach, the project team created a 1,672-square-foot single-family tract house that combines a number of efficiency measures. These measures allowed the designers to eliminate most of the major mechanical equipment—including furnace, air conditioner, and related components (ductwork, pipes, controls, and wiring). This whole-systems approach resulted in an aesthetically pleasing, livable home that reduces total space conditioning, water heating, lighting, and refrigeration energy use by more than 75 percent over a conventional home of the same size. If the products and technologies were widely produced and available off-

An integrated design approach was used to create the ACT[2] house in Davis, California. The project team combined a number of efficiency measures (including increased insulation), which allowed them to eliminate most of the major mechanical equipment. *(Reprinted with permission from Rocky Mountain Institute.)*

the-shelf, as they are coming to be, construction cost savings of $1,800 would have been realized for the house. Savings will also be achieved through reduced maintenance requirements. Though many of the individual components were more expensive than their conventional alternatives, their inclusion permitted other systems to be eliminated entirely, leading to a lower total cost.

The designers of the new American Association for the Advancement of Science (AAAS) building in Washington, D.C., paid careful attention to energy performance and also realized the benefits of tunneling through the cost barrier. The building's design incorporates two deeply cut glazing bays that extend the full height of the 10-story building and draw light into the atriums. Light shelves bring daylight into workspaces. The integration of high-performance windows and energy-efficient lighting have cut energy consumption to half that of a typical building: 90,000 Btus per square foot per year versus 183,000 Btus per square foot per year for a conventional office building of the same size. Energy use for lighting in the building is less than 1 watt per square foot—well below the U.S. average of 2 watts per square foot. Project architect Henry Cobb, of Pei Cobb Freed & Partners, stated, "The AAAS building is no high-priced gimmick. While the costs of some of these features are more expensive initially, they save money in the long run, making the building a strong investment for a nonprofit association and readily marketable if AAAS should decide to leave."

Using a whole-systems approach can also bring about solution multipliers—solutions that serve many purposes. The new 381,000-square-foot, seven-story San Francisco Main Library, completed in 1996, includes extensive measures to ensure healthful indoor air. "The quality of the indoor air was a major concern," according to project manager and architect Anthony Bernheim, who collected comments at numerous meetings with individuals, organizations, agencies, commissions, and the library staff. It became apparent early in the schematic design phase that an overall approach was needed to satisfy these concerns and ensure a healthful building. After negotiation with the city, an IAQ specialist was hired onto the design team. The library's five-story atrium was designed not only to provide the superior ventilation that the librarians wanted, but to provide other benefits as well. It brings light deep into the building and adds an aesthetically pleasing design element. The air returns along the linear atrium and the central atrium double as emergency smoke control exhausts. These multiple purposes ensured that the atrium would not be cut from the budget as merely an aesthetic element. Further measures were taken to ensure good indoor air, including the installation of air intakes on the roof to avoid air pollutants present at street level. The design provided a high ventilation

Designers for the San Francisco Main Library took extensive measures to ensure good indoor air. *(Photography by Timothy Hursley. Reprinted with permision.)*

rate of 25 cubic feet per minute per person. The team selected limestone floors for the building's three main entrances instead of carpet, because they feared that chemicals, dirt, and dust being tracked in might cause IAQ problems.

THE MATERIALS BARRIER

Sometimes the best intentions of a designer in choosing materials do not work out as planned. In deciding what on the materials he would use for an office project in Kansas City, Missouri, architect Bob Berkebile of BNIM Architects chose granite for the walls and floors because it is durable and attractive. By specifying a material from nearby Minnesota, he sought to minimize energy and pollution associated with transportation. However, he later learned that after the granite is mined in Minnesota, it is trucked to the Gulf of Mexico, transported by ship to Italy to be cut and polished, then shipped back to the Gulf and trucked to Kansas City! His initial goal of saving energy by using a relatively local material fell a bit short.

Herman Miller's SQA

From the beginning, the design process for Herman Miller's SQA (Simple Quality Affordable) building brought all members of the design team to the table. Design of the facility intended to house the company's subsidiary, Phoenix Design (a remanufacturer of office furniture), was at times "a lively and intense process." Design discussions included the project architect and support staff, project manager, general contractor and subcontractors, interior designers, Herman Miller facility and environmental engineers, maintenance and landscape staff, a landscape architect, corporate and financial representatives, health and fitness experts, and food service personnel. This team included local practitioners whom Herman Miller had either worked with before, or felt it could trust. The architects, McDonough + Partners, were focused on "practical realism" instead of theoretical design or what might work. Using the expertise of the local people, the workability and "buildability" of solutions were discussed up-front. The people with hands-on experience compared the innovative but do-able solutions created by the team with their conventional practice. They found that the new way made better sense.

This varied team had the expertise to deal with a wide range of facility issues, from material use to the shape of the building. Design sessions usually consisted of three days of meetings, with time between design sessions used to refine and develop the ideas generated. The team kicked off the process by saying they wanted to create "a building that was a living machine." From the outset, Herman Miller was receptive to the green design measures, giving the design team few barriers to overcome.

Design discussions for Herman Miller's SQA building included a diverse team, representing a wide range of disciplines, to explore innovative solutions. *(Ed Nagelkirk, photographer. Reprinted with permission.)*

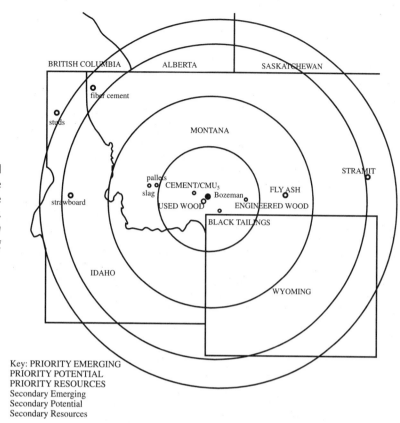

Priority resources were identified within a 350-mile radius for the National ReSource Center at the Montana State University campus. *(Reprinted with permission from the Center for Resourceful Building Technology.)*

One way to overcome this kind of barrier is through a process called resource mapping. In planning for a new Montana State University National ReSource Center, the design team decided that the materials must come from within a 350-mile radius of the site, to help promote local industry and stimulate the local economy. The team hired Pliny Fisk of the Center for Maximum Potential Building Systems in Austin, Texas, and Steve Loken of the Center for Resourceful Building Technology in Missoula, Montana, to draw a resource map of available materials found within the specified radius. For example, regional salvaged wood was specified for all structural timber in the building. This was sourced in the nearby town Gallatin Gateway by Big Timberworks, a company specializing in remilled wood.

Taking this concept further, Pliny Fisk is working with the EPA and a consortium of universities to develop an economic development data base of environmentally responsible U.S. businesses, cataloging what they buy, sell, and produce. This data base will be linked to a Geographical Information System (GIS) to identify places where products and by-products are being manufactured, assisting those who would want to specify local materials.

Education Is the Key

> Sustainable building demands a commitment to well-informed thoughtful choices about design, material specs, and construction practices. To do it right you have to invest in educating yourself (and your team) about the issues.
>
> Environmental Building News, *1995*

Designers committed to reducing the environmental impact of their buildings have to invest in education. Leading practitioners in the field stay current with green design through a variety of publications. They keep up with developments, products, and building practices through conferences, workshops, and Internet discussion groups. Architect Bob Berkebile, known as a leader in environmental design, worked with members of the design team for the C. K. Choi building at the

This ariflow analysis for Montana State's National ReSource Center illustrates that when summer temperatures are reached and nighttime flush is not sufficient to cool the building, a hydronic system in the slab will be used to cool the slab, creating radiant cooling. *(Reprinted with permission from BNIM Architects.)*

Building Design Tools

The following are a few of the more useful design tools that have been employed by green designers:

- *Physical building models.* Many architects rely on physical models to help a client understand what a finished building will look like and to understand such aspects of the building as daylighting and passive solar design. While many architects are switching to three-dimensional computer modeling for these functions, some still insist that physical models do a better job. Sophisticated sun models with high-intensity lights that travel in an arc over the building are sometimes used to simulate an exact time of day and year.

- *Three-dimensional CAD models.* Sophisticated computer modeling is increasingly used by architects to provide careful analysis and visual images of the finished space. Daylighting models, for example, demonstrate how deeply sunlight penetrates into a building and how shadow patterns change throughout the day at different times of year.

- *Mock-ups.* Actual full-size mock-ups of wall sections or building elements can be constructed to help designers and clients understand how a building will look and perform. The design team for the United Parcel Service headquarters built models of various aspects of the building, including a 30-foot wide, two-story mock-up of an interior office space.

- *Energy modeling programs.* Sophisticated energy modeling programs are widely used in building design, including DOE-2, Energy 10, Power DOE, REM-Design, and HOT-2000. It is advisable to model energy performance precisely rather than rely on rules of thumb or simple calculations to determine mechanical system sizing and building energy loads. The simulation results often differ from the designer's intuition. At the Crestwood Corporate Center's Building No. 8, a sophisticated version of DOE-2 was used. "Our instincts were not always right," said one of the designers, "and the computer simulation helped us to avoid designing a 'problem building.'"

- *Computational fluid dynamics.* When designers need to know how air will move in a building (when sophisticated passive ventilation designs are being used, for example), computational fluid dynamics provides a means for doing so. Complicated equations are translated into easy-to-understand visuals that show fluid flow patterns, eddies, airflow velocities, pockets where cold or warm air would collect, and so forth. This fluid mapping exercise was used in both Montana State's National ReSource Center and the Queens Building in England, both of which rely on passive ventilation.

University of British Columbia. Matsuzaki Architects was selected for the project because it had a sincere belief in green architecture and wanted to learn. Even though very few of the team members had ever participated in a green building project, each understood the overarching green vision. The project began with a two-day charrette for the whole team, led by Berkebile. The multidisciplinary team set ambitious goals of 50 percent less water, no sewer connection, 50 percent recycled materials, and high energy performance. Allowing people to share their ideas and concerns before any concrete plans were made helped everyone to start from the same place.

The architects reported that their firm took three times as long to design the building as compared with a conventional building because they had to educate themselves all along the way. Now they have this knowledge, and have gained a reputation as green designers. A number of magazines have featured articles on the project, and a book has been published about the building. Matsuzaki Architects has been sought out for more environmentally responsive work. Their education not only helped them overcome the barriers they encountered, but also helped them acquire a new expertise that they could market.

GETTING PAID FOR BETTER DESIGN

Despite the possibility that education can help a firm's reputation to grow, the extra investment of time can be a barrier, because such costs are not reimbursed in conventional design fees. Energy-efficient design is a worthy goal for all designers, for example, but achieving exceptional efficiency requires architects and engineers to invest more time, both initially and throughout the project. Conventional compensation not only provides no payment for that extra effort, but the conventional fee structure for architects may actually provide a *disincentive* to design better buildings. Many efficient buildings need smaller and simpler mechanical systems for cooling, heating, and air handling. This makes the whole building cost less, reducing the designers' and engineers' fees, which are typically based on a percentage of total building cost. Even if the fee is fixed in advance, the designers get the same fee for more work. Either way, their profits decline.

The concept of performance-based fees is an important step toward remedying this situation. With this approach, the architect and/or engineering firm is paid a bonus if the building exceeds energy performance targets set in an initial agreement with the client, and pays a penalty if it falls short. The targets are determined through well-established computer energy models. Once the structure is built, occupied, and commissioned (has received its final systems check), the building's actual performance will be compared with the preset goal, factoring out such interfering variables as weather and occupancy. The results determine whether there is a bonus or a penalty due, and if so, how much.

In 1996, Charles Eley Associates of San Francisco began a test of performance-based fees with a $78 million new administration building for the city of Oakland. A baseline standard has been set at 20 percent better energy performance than required by the California Title 24 Energy Code (the highest standards in the nation). If the building surpasses this minimum goal, the design/build team will receive the financial equivalent of five years of energy savings. However, if the building does not meet the baseline, then the team will be financially liable for fifteen years' worth of the shortfall. Both reward and liability are capped at $250,000.

For a Ciba Geigy building completed in New York in 1996, the designers agreed to gamble a percentage of their design commission on the satisfactory results of an employee survey. The 150 employees were overwhelmingly positive, with 84 percent reporting high satisfaction. The extra compensation—$300,000 —was awarded.

This performance-based compensation idea could be applied to other measures of performance, including health, worker productivity, and overall satisfaction. The problem is that these attributes are more difficult to measure.

DESIGN AND DEVELOPMENT GUIDELINES

Design and development guidelines can help developers ensure that their designs stay on track and that design decisions made by others are in keeping with the overall project intent. This strategy can work particularly well in the case of large developments when there are a number of architects and builders involved. These guidelines do not restrict creativity, but they ensure that the green goals are not lost in the design and construction phase.

One way to guarantee that guidelines are followed over time is to institutionalize them through codes, covenants, and restrictions (CC&Rs). These legal restrictions should be good for people living in the development, should provide a mechanism for occupants to change them, and should not be too restrictive, while still ensuring that the elements of green development are honored.

The Architectural and Environmental Guidelines for Dewees Island seek to ensure green design and site sensitivity measures for each project. *(Reprinted with permission from the Island Preservation Partnership.)*

The Dewees Island comprehensive review process requires builders to incorporate green design measures and site sensitivity measures into each project before it is built. Architectural and Environmental Guidelines, included in the Island's CC&Rs, stress reduced dependency on resources from outside the island and improved efficiency in utilizing all resources. Each home buyer is asked to sign off on the guidelines when he or she signs a contract to purchase a property. The covenants also empower the Architectural Resources Board (ARB), which reviews design submissions and determines whether the Dewees Island environmental principles are adhered to—from site design to building material selection and landscaping. The board includes home owners, an architect, a landscape architect, an environmentalist, and a Dewees staff person. The ARB has the final call on all design decisions and is the only appeals board.

At Spring Island, an architectural review board also scrutinizes all home plans, including siting, landscaping, and alteration of natural foliage, to see that each proposed residence meets the strict environmental control standards established for the development. The intent is to guide the design of the houses so that a community of dwellings is created that is rooted in local building traditions. The guidelines also ensure that the houses will have a low impact on the island from both a visual and an environmental standpoint. They call for efficient appliances, high-performance windows, passive ventilation from the indigenous "Low Country"–style architecture, recycling centers, and sustainably sourced wood. The development's community office keeps an updated data base of sources for various other products considered appropriate to use.

A Palette of Design Options

Many of the decisions that lead to successful green developments are made in the design phase. To make the right decisions, a mutlidisciplinary team capable of whole-systems thinking is needed from the beginning. Ideally, the team will be educated regarding the many elements of green building and will understand the various options for integrating them into the design. Usually, there is not one right answer for how a building should be designed, or what features should be incorporated into it. There is a large palette of options. Making appropriate choices— factoring in environmental performance, conventional performance, and cost— depends on the skills, knowledge, and experience of the design team.

Developers Michael and Judy Corbett encountered many difficulties in seeking approvals for their Village Homes project in the mid-1970s. *(Reprinted with permission from William D. Browning, Rocky Mountain Institute.)*

CHAPTER 7

Approvals

MICHAEL AND JUDY CORBETT STRUGGLED to get the approvals they needed for Village Homes, the innovative 70-acre, 240-home subdivision they built in Davis, California. This was the mid-1970s and many aspects of the project were new and unfamiliar, including use of natural-drainage swales in place of storm sewers, the incorporation of agricultural areas, and narrower streets. The Corbetts might have given up and retreated to the status quo, except that they believed in the value of their ideas.

The Corbetts faced opposition not only from the city of Davis's planning department, but also from the public works department and the Federal Housing Authority (FHA). Police had reservations about patrolling the narrower streets, while fire officials worried that they would not be able to maneuver fire trucks. The FHA questioned the wisdom of combining agricultural uses in a residential area, fearing it would risk the project's value by departing from a traditional residential appearance.

The Corbetts went to great lengths to make their case. They wrote point-by-point rebuttals to reports that recommended against approval of various features of the proposed development. They surmounted some objections by taking their case directly to the city council. At the time Village Homes was going through approvals, three of Davis's city council members were environmental activists who, Corbett said, were "willing to read the reports and our written rebuttals, and then make up

Despite all of the approvals battles, Village Homes today is a popular community in Davis, California. Homes sell for $10 to $25 per square foot more than standard homes in the area. *(Reprinted with permission from William D. Browning, Rocky Mountain Institute.)*

their own minds." Going through city council instead of the standard design review process for landscaping and buildings gave the Corbetts greater flexibility with design choices.

The natural drainage system proved to be the toughest part of the project to get approved. In Michael Corbett's 1981 book, *A Better Place to Live,* he recalled the resistance from city staff and the FHA. "They all said it wouldn't work; that it would require continual maintenance and wouldn't significantly reduce the amount of runoff. The planning director said it would harbor vermin—an engineering term for wildlife, I suppose." The Corbetts could not convince officials that the infiltration swales would really handle storm water runoff and had to put up a bond to pay for retrofitting storm sewers in case the natural system failed. Soon after, Davis was hit with a one-hundred-year storm—the ultimate test of drainage capabilities. Not only did the Corbetts' system work just fine, but it also proved itself by having to handle runoff from neighboring subdivisions whose conventional storm sewers failed. After two years the bond was deemed unnecessary.

Many of the difficulties the Corbetts encountered in seeking approvals for Village Homes in the mid-1970s remain just as challenging for green developers today. But at least today, nearly a quarter-century after the Corbetts struggled to gain support for their radically new ideas, green developers can point to numerous examples where innovative development configurations, environmental restrictions, clustering, and natural storm water management systems are working beautifully.

There is much that we can learn from the pioneers in green development regarding how they gained the necessary approvals for their projects. Here are their stories.

The Challenge

Today, many communities continue to rely on a legislative framework that was created for a very different pre–World War II America. As a result, the planning and growth management mechanisms in force in most states in the 1990s are woefully out of step with the times. They frustrate nearly everyone—developers and business people, conservationists and preservationists, community and regional planners, design professionals, housing advocates, environmentalists, and citizens.

American Planning Association, 1992

Two important stakeholders in any development process are governing bodies and citizens. Getting approvals for a green development is not always easy. Local government and community or environmental groups may oppose green developments because they do not understand them, because they oppose new development in general, or because they are mistrustful of any developer's claims. They may be leery of claims about environmental benefits because they have been exposed to "greenwash" before.

Unfortunately, the legitimate concerns of local governments can backfire. All too often they have in force obsolete codes, zoning laws, and other regulations that are excessively restrictive and will inhibit even the best development. The approvals process is often identified as one of the most frustrating barriers to developing more environmentally responsive and community-sensitive projects. Innovative projects may get bogged down simply because they are unique. This can lead to costly delays or changes to plans and designs. Developers may even be dissuaded from innovation altogether when facing the prospect of lengthy approval battles.

Green developments *have* been approved, however, often with the vision fully intact. Furthermore, they frequently have a distinct advantage in communities that are sensitive to issues of the environment and community. Many green developments, in fact, have had lower carrying costs in the approvals process because their projects were approved much faster than normal.

ZONING AND BUILDING CODES

Zoning was first introduced in 1869 in New York City to prevent unhealthy and odorous industrial land uses from locating near residential areas (glue factories near apartments, for example). Building codes were also established to regulate construction at the local level, mainly to protect safety, health, and property. In *The Geography of Nowhere,* which traces the evolution of land use in America, author James Howard Kunstler points out that "these controls made sense from the standpoint of seeking stability in a time of explosive and destructive growth, but they would establish some nasty precedents and lead to unpleasant repercussions once the automobile came along."

The legacy of these well-intended controls is *sprawl*—a pattern of land development characterized by the decentralization and separation of land uses. This pattern can be traced to the 1927 landmark Supreme Court case *Village of Euclid vs. Ambler Realty Company,* in which the establishment of separate zones of single-use buildings was deemed legal. This case upheld a municipality's right to designate single-use zones to prevent mixing polluting, unhealthful industries and residential areas—to keep "the pigs out of the parlor." Since the late 1920s land-use zoning has generally carried forward this idea of separation of uses. Anton Nelessen, in *Visions for a New American Dream,* noted with irony that the separation of uses on which the *Euclid* case was based today causes tremendous pollution and natural resource destruction. "What was validated for health, safety and welfare in 1927," he wrote, "has destroyed communities and created negative visions which today are the catalyst for the reformulation of small communities."

Zoning prevents compact and mixed-use development in many towns, even those with older, vibrant downtowns that have worked well for decades (but would not satisfy zoning regulations today). Worse, many public works codes are based on serving the automobile rather than pedestrians. According to Kunstler, in *The Geography of Nowhere,* streets in suburban areas were "designed so that a car could comfortably maneuver at 50 mph no matter what the legal speed limit is. The width and curb ratios were set in stone by traffic engineers who wanted to create streets so ultra safe (for motorists) that any moron could drive them without wrecking his car."

While local governments around the United States are beginning to realize that land use and building codes often prevent them from evolving into the kinds of communities their citizens want, change is slow to happen. Some of the opposition is simply a resistance to change—to doing things differently—even though, as one green developer noted, "We must change in order to stay the same …staying the same will lead to great, unwanted change." Such resistance is sometimes based on experience—many of the developments that have changed people's landscapes have not brought about positive change. Sometimes it is based on a lack of understanding. Ed Starki, a Portland landscape architect, tells about trying to get a land restoration proposal approved in northern California. He met with resistance from local "environmentalists" who did not want the land touched; however, they failed to realize that what they sought to protect was not a native ecosystem but a landscape that had been altered by humans over the years.

Blanket zoning and prescriptive codes mean that the approvals process is often ill-equipped to deal with projects that incorporate unconventional land-use patterns, building forms, or technologies. Stanley Selengut, eco-resort developer, has found that the approvals process is "the toughest part of all." He went on to explain, "I think the one rule about sustainability is that you are breaking all the building codes…you are really a maverick, trying to do things that on first impression look like you are trying to get away with all sorts of stuff…like letting water run into the ground, using local materials, or recycling trash."

Easing the Approvals Process

Fortunately, committed green development teams are educating local governments about the benefits that can accrue from more environmentally responsive elements in development plans. In some cases, persistent and visionary green developers have been able to set new standards for local jurisdictions. And, increasingly, local governments are working to create more progressive and flexible codes or to create incentives for developers to build more environmentally responsible projects.

How long the approvals process takes is an important consideration. A longer-than-usual approval process, as sometimes occurs when the development incorporates innovative or unusual features, increases carrying costs and, thus, expense. This extra cost may be recouped through reduced costs in other areas, such as marketing, which balances out the overall equation. Other green developments have enjoyed faster approvals as a result of the environmental features. In fact, in some cases, speeding up the approvals process has been one of the most important benefits of green development.

This latter effect—more rapid approvals—was a key advantage of green features at the new 2,050-acre Abacoa development straddling Palm Beach County and Martin County, Florida. When complete, Abacoa will have 6,000 residential units as well as three million square feet of light industrial, commercial, and retail space, including a corporate park and a town center. New winter training facilities for the Montreal Expos and the Saint Louis Cardinals will be located here, as well as the Florida Atlantic Campus, part of the Florida State University system. Green elements addressed in Abacoa's plan include energy- and water-efficient homes, walkable, neotraditional-style neighborhoods with community centers and locally based commercial uses, environmentally sensitive landscaping practices featuring native plants, and habitat protection.

A 60-acre parcel in the southeast corner of Abacoa with the highest biological and ecological significance has been preserved as a gopher tortoise refuge. Exotic species have been removed to restore natural vegetation. According to Bill McCalpin, director of Program-Related Investments for the MacArthur Foundation (a partner in the project), setting aside this parcel took a real commitment to environmental values. "Nobody in their right mind would give up this corner—it's the kind of land developers drool over." But this act helped the developers sail through the approvals process in just one and a half years, which is considered rapid for a parcel of this size in Florida, a state with stringent development and environmental regulations.

Strategies: How to Obtain Approvals

The strategies green developers have used to obtain approvals are varied and often overlapping. A number of the most important strategies are covered in the following paragraphs.

INVOLVE STAKEHOLDERS

The local community is an important stakeholder in any development project. Its members are those who will be affected daily by aspects of new development, ranging from obstructed views and traffic congestion, to increased demand on infrastructure and schools. While development plans often pit developers against the surrounding community, this does not have to happen. Green developers have found that involving the community in the process *from the beginning* will help to promote mutual understanding while ensuring that the development addresses community needs. Listening to citizens early on can avoid prolonged difficulties created later by people determined to have their say—one way or the other. Stanley Selengut cautions developers that it is imperative to involve the community in any development plan: "Before you have the arrogance to say 'this is what we want to do'…go to the local community and say 'this is what we'd like to do.'" He says that unless a developer is willing to work with a community from the beginning, he or she is "dead in the water."

The Urban Ecologist, a bimonthly publication focused on ecological urban development practices, counsels developers and cities to involve stakeholders in discussions and site walks early in the development process. People should be involved before a project's design and economics are worked out, while there is still time for neighborhood mitigation measures and design and density changes. Developers, planners, and other city representatives should go out and talk to neighborhoods on an ongoing basis and truly listen to what they hear.

As plans for redeveloping Elitch Gardens, the abandoned amusement park in Denver, moved through the approvals process, developer Chuck Perry of Affordable Housing Development Corporation reserved a table at a neighborhood cafe every Tuesday night to discuss the mixed-use infill project with any locals who wished to drop by. He was willing to go through the development proposal and studies, translating esoteric information into everyday language about how the development would personally impact nearby residents—how many more cars would drive past their houses in a day, for example.

John Clark went to great lengths to garner local support for his concept of Haymount, a 1,650-acre new town development in rural Caroline County, Virginia. Although he still faced extended difficulty in gaining approvals, public hearings on Haymount typically had more supporters than detractors. The Haymount team started by doing its homework on the property. By thoroughly assessing the site and carefully developing a master plan that fit the site, they headed off much potential opposition. Through this up-front work, they were able to avoid expensive redesigns or new environmental impact studies throughout the approvals process. Clark then held numerous meetings with community groups, local church members, and local and regional government representatives to hear their suggestions. He made a special effort to reach out to the large African-American community in the area, and those efforts paid off with support, including the backing of three local Baptist churches. At one public hearing, 550 people showed up to support Haymount.

The major objections to Clark's plan were that the property was located on the pristine Rappahannock River and that the development would attract too many people to this rural area. Getting the required amendments to the county's land-use plan took about 30 months. While the project received strong support from some elements of the community for the far-reaching aspects of its environmental sensitivity, it still faced opposition from local environmental groups, as well as three lawsuits from adjacent landowners. Efforts to block Haymount included claims that Clark's plan to donate land to 14 churches violated separation of church and state. One farmer even argued that when he sprayed pesticides, they drifted onto the Haymount property, making it unfit for future human habitation.

Haymount was also contentious because it did not fall under Caroline County's comprehensive plan, whose intent was to channel sprawling growth along the Interstate 95 corridor and away from the river terrain. Caroline County residents, shocked by earlier development atrocities, gave Haymount a thorough going-over. Some, along with the Chesapeake Bay Foundation, conceded that it was the "right plan, wrong place." Estie Thomas, the Foundation's natural resources planner, told the *Washington Post*, "Although the environmentally sensitive design within Haymount is the type of thing we would like to see, it will be going into a rather pristine neck of the Rappahannock, in a rural area that was never slated for development. It's going to cause leapfrog development and encroach upon surrounding farmland."

Clark disagreed, seeing Haymount as a superior alternative to the planning models that have produced wasteful sprawl throughout Virginia's suburbs and once-rural areas. He finally persuaded Caroline County's Board of Supervisors to approve the project in a close 3-to-2 vote. Clark continually points out that the land will be developed in some fashion. Formerly, it was zoned for 10-acre "martini farms"—too small to farm and too big to mow. He argues that his plan will make far better use of the land.

Developer John Clark held numerous meetings with community groups, local church members, and local and regional government representatives to obtain their comments and suggestions on the proposed Haymount project. *(Reprinted with permission from John A. Clark, Haymount. Drawing by Duany Plater-Zyberk.)*

When explaining their vision for Haymount, Clark and one of his attorneys, Dan Slone of Maguire Woods Battle Boothe, asked county planners a key question about the zoning that existed before Haymount: Where will people shop? What kind of environmental impact will their travel have? They pointed out that when built-out, Haymount will offer the services and goods its residents need, providing local jobs and eliminating commuting and long drives for errands wherever possible.

There is no doubt that Caroline County, with its close proximity to Washington, D.C., will grow. County officials now plan to integrate some of the best ideas offered by Haymount into their new zoning regulations and subdivision policies to encourage more innovative development countywide, including design standards, buffers, and density issues addressed by Haymount. In rezoning the property to a master planned, mixed-use community, the Planning and Community Development Department asked the Haymount team to look at the comprehensive plan for the entire river valley and offer proposals on how to prevent sprawl growth from following in Haymount's wake. The Haymount team proposed some language for the river corridor that designates certain areas as environmentally sensitive to ensure that future development impacts will be minimized through land-use patterns. The language in the comprehensive plan should limit Haymount's sphere of influence by restricting new development to within Haymount's boundaries. This growth boundary will remain in effect until 75 percent of Haymount is complete (at about 2003), in order to limit speculative development along the river corridor. Michael Finchum, director of planning and community development for Caroline County, opined that "Haymount works if it protects the corridor." Finchum believes that once the revised zoning ordinance is in place, emphasizing clustered development patterns, proposed new developments will carry less threat of undesirable spin-off development.

In a demonstration of good faith, Haymount's team put their environmental performance criteria into the development proffers, which will become covenants upon construction. This act binds the commitment even if the development team should change.

Regarding roads and wastewater, Clark experienced resistance by regulators "at every turn." He was engaged in a long and not entirely successful battle with the Virginia Department of Transportation (VDOT) to eliminate curbs and reduce paving width, to implement traffic-calming measures, and to increase on-street parking. The Haymount team worked at all levels, even up to the state Secretary of Transportation, to try to improve the legislated road design. At present, the road network design does not go as far as Clark wanted, but is better than standard. Clark's strategy was to convince VDOT to agree that this project would serve as a demonstration project to test his theory. The team received approval for the first phase of the project and agreed to be responsible for metering traffic. Should Clark's team be wrong on traffic impacts, this could jeopardize the future of the other phases of the project, and they might have to revert back to old standards. But if it works well, the development team could get further concessions and bring this aspect of the project back to its original intent.

Haymount also struggled to get approvals for its innovative Solar Aquatics™ sewage treatment plant. In December 1995, Haymount finally received a permit from the Virginia Department of Environmental Quality entitling the development to treat 1.2 million gallons per day of wastewater using this biological treatment system pioneered by John Todd. The system will route effluent through a series of translucent tanks containing plants, snails, fish, and other organisms. The tanks, along with a constructed wetland that accomplishes the final cleansing, or "polishing," will be housed in a greenhouse. The treatment plant will function as an educational tool for wildlife and environmental awareness, while also serving as a civic park. Although the state approved the system as designed, Haymount also had to get county approval. The county, distrustful of this innovative system, required the team to put in a conventional oxidation ditch and blending tanks as backup. Clark believes the backup system, at a capital cost of $400,000, will never be used, but he incorporated it into the design. The county then required him to go back to the state for final approvals, further extending the approvals period. All costs for the treatment plant are being borne by Haymount. Upon completion, it will be turned over to the county after training staff how to operate it.

Throughout the approvals process for Haymount, Clark made himself available to anybody wanting to talk about the project. His willingness to work with even vocal opponents was one reason that the project ultimately succeeded in obtaining approvals. Clark believes that when people drop by his office and see the model of Haymount, they walk away more convinced that it will be a great place. In early 1997, the project was securing financing, with the first phase of construction expected to begin by summer 1997.

Haymount struggled to get approvals for its innovative Solar Aquatics™ sewage treatment plant that will treat 1.2 million gallons of wastewater per day. *(Reprinted with permission from from John A. Clark, Haymount. Drawing by Neal Payton.)*

WIN OVER LOCAL ENVIRONMENTALISTS THROUGH IMPECCABLE DETAILS

Big Sur, home of crashing surf, pine forests, and craggy cliffs overlooking the sea, is one of the most antigrowth places on the planet, thanks to a population hell-bent on preserving the stunning natural beauty. This is a community, according to the *New York Times,* where "environmental activism approaches militancy." So it was truly notable when the Post Ranch Inn became the first commercial development in almost 20 years to get approvals, and that it happened with "scarcely a ripple of dissent."

The 98 cliff-top acres on which Post Ranch Inn sits were formerly the home and ranch of the Post family, one of the two oldest families in Big Sur. Joseph William Post III, a retired transportation engineer, provided the land for the inn as well as his clout as a descendant of Big Sur's founding fathers. He partnered with Michael Freed, a prominent California real estate lawyer, and Myles Williams, a local retirement hotel owner. For eight years, the three developers participated in debates and hearings and carried out biological surveys, traffic analyses, environmental impact reports, and a myriad of other studies in order to build the small jewel of an inn. Local environmentalists wanted to ensure that the plan strictly conformed to the Big Sur Coastal Land Use Plan, which limits the number and size of rooms, bans golf and tennis courts, and carefully protects coastline and mountain views. The strong environmental sentiments expressed in Big Sur's plan persuaded the developers not to ask for variances or request a waiver on an environmental impact report, but to work within the existing framework to create an environmentally acceptable project.

They went to great lengths to win over the local government and community, beginning by hiring local architect Mickey Muennig, who specializes in houses that are carefully concealed in the landscape. Muennig lived on the site for five months before creating an organic design that was unanimously approved by the county board. His plan sited some rooms on stilts to avoid disturbing roots or removing trees. Others were sunk in the earth and covered with sod roofs that would grow lettuce and wildflowers. Only one tree, identified as a fire hazard by the county, was removed. Local residents were invited to view and comment on Muennig's drawings.

To reduce impacts, the developers limited the number of guest rooms to 30 and banned gasoline-powered vehicles from their site. Instead, guests are transported in electric carts. The developers provided hiking trails for visitors and

Developers of the Post Ranch Inn in Big Sur hired architect Mickey Muennig because of his highly regarded skill in carefully concealing buildings on the landscape. There was virtually no opposition to the project because of the development team's sensitivity to the site. *(Reprinted with permission from William D. Browning, Rocky Mountain Institute.)*

agreed to donate land to the volunteer fire department and provide low-cost housing for hotel staff. The result of their care was the virtual absence of opposition. In fact, *Los Angeles Magazine* reported that "at the final meeting of the county planning commission, which practically begged to hear a contrary voice, the developers breathed a collective sigh of relief when the inn's nearest neighbor stood up...and proceeded to declare her absolute support."

The general manager of the competition, Ventana Inn's Bob Bussinger, who battled 15 years to expand his operation from 40 to 59 rooms, complimented Post Ranch Inn's "very shrewd" team who hadn't "put a foot wrong." Even former Monterey County supervisor and ardent conservationist Karin Strasser Kauffman praised the Post Ranch Inn. "It's refreshing to see a quality, small-scale project come through...it sends a message to other interested people that they can build in Big Sur provided they respect the rules and regulations." Owner Post notes that although there are those in Big Sur who believe there should be no development along the coast, he is "just as happy to see a project that tries to fit into the area and will pay tribute to our heritage." Partner Freed believes that the unopposed approvals process demonstrates the value of working with the community. "The big mistake developers make is that they are not open with the process," he said. "People are going to find out what you are doing, so you have to be open and not try to sneak it by."

SOMETIMES THEY JUST CAN'T BE CONVINCED

Just up the coast from Big Sur, the Carmel Valley is also an area in which it is difficult to get approvals for any development because of the stance of conservation-oriented citizens and local government. Here, in 1990, the Rancho San Carlos Partnership purchased Rancho San Carlos, which had been a working ranch for 200 years. Most recently owned by the Oppenheimer family, the 20,000-acre parcel had once had approvals for 11,000 homes. Because the Oppenheimer heirs did not want to see the land divided into many parcels, they decided to sell it to a limited partnership whose principal partner and manager, Pacific Union Development Company, was able to buy the whole parcel. The developers announced early in

Rancho San Carlos is one of the last existing large California ranches and the largest single piece of private property on California's central coast. This hacienda from the original ranch will be used as a community center for the 300 future home owners in the development. *(Reprinted with permission from Lisa McManigal, Rocky Mountain Institute.)*

the process that they were going to preserve 18,000 of the 20,000 acres within a conservation trust. They spent three years in the approvals process, trying to convince local residents and municipal officials of the sincerity of their commitment to preserving the beautiful land. They ultimately succeeded in permitting most of their plan only after a contentious public process.

As it is one of the last large California ranches and the largest single piece of private property on California's central coast, development of this massive and beautiful chunk of real estate has been controversial for many years. Two hundred residents jammed county chambers to hear the developers describe their plans at a March 1993 Board of Supervisors hearing. Three years later, the board unanimously approved the project, after fine-tuning a list of more than 200 conditions that the developers must meet. Soon thereafter, however, a group of local environmentalists mounted a signature-gathering campaign to put Rancho San Carlos before the citizens in the November 1996 election.

The new owners expressed their intention early in the approvals process to limit construction to 300 free-market homes, 50 employee housing units, and a 150-unit hotel, as well as some commercial development to serve the residents. They also announced their plan to set aside 90 percent of the land as permanent open space by forming the Santa Lucia Conservancy, which would oversee the land's protection. The Trust for Public Land, a national nonprofit land conservation organization, agreed to help establish and manage the preserve and become owner of the land title should the Conservancy disband. This protection, however, is contingent upon capital coming from the development to support the conservation goals. A local newspaper quoted Jeffrey B. Froke, president of the Santa Lucia Conservancy, as calling the project's ultimate success a "roll of the dice," dependent upon "developing the financial capability to manage the land"—and that, he said, "is tied to the forward success of the project."

In April 1996, the *Christian Science Monitor* noted that bitter differences of opinion over the Rancho San Carlos plan are "more deeply a war among environmentalists... [than the] classic struggle between a developer and the defenders of nature." Some prominent conservationists supported the plan as a nationally significant model demonstrating that ecology and development can coexist. Opponents, including the local Sierra Club chapter, call it one more public relations scam in which environmental concerns are used to conceal less altruistic aims.

The most contentious approvals issues for Rancho San Carlos revolved around water supply and transportation. In addition to required traffic mitigation efforts (including funding $4.4 million in roadway improvements), the developers offered additional mitigation strategies: carrying out limited commercial development within the project to reduce local trips, and implementing an employee trip-reduction program. However, local opponents remained concerned that the development would still add heavy traffic impacts to Carmel Valley Road and Highway One, already overcrowded during peak commute times. And despite confirmation by three county agencies and three independent hydrologists that the Santa Lucia Preserve has a long-term, sufficient water supply that would not adversely affect Carmel Valley's water supply, opponents remained unconvinced. On election day the public voted by a narrow margin to overturn the board's approvals.

The irony of this outcome is that the referendum does not block the development; rather, it blocks some of the features that would have strengthened its role as a model of environmentally responsible development. The referendum overturned the board's rezoning of some of the ranch to permit a 150-room hotel, a village store, and a ranch operations center. According to Tom Gray, president of the Rancho San Carlos Partnership, Measure M overturned low-density residential zoning that was actually more restrictive than the former "resource conservation" zoning. Since the hotel and village store had not been permitted under the original zoning, these pieces cannot now become a part of the development. This does not concern Tom Gray and his partners. Gray saw the hotel as one way to increase public access to these beautiful lands, but believes the lack of a hotel will not bother future home owners. He finds it ironic, though, that residents will now have to drive off-site for their everyday needs that could have been met by a small store in the development.

Gray's lesson from this frustrating experience differs from the conclusion of the Post Ranch Inn developers. He believes that by offering the entire, thoroughly thought-out vision at once, the development team won the approvals of the county government, yet increased public opposition. He sees the current land-use approvals system as fundamentally adversarial in nature. "Doing such a thorough job increases the pressure by the system. . . . Unless they get an extraction from you, they don't feel like they are satisfied. It appears we did too much mitigation." Although the people of Monterey County said they wanted to know everything up-front rather than having the developers piecemeal the property through the development process, Gray found fault with their zealousness: "We couldn't use an analog to show what we were doing, because nothing like it has been done before. A small group of people [such as county supervisors and staff] can take the time to get educated, but when it went to a countywide vote, most of the people didn't even know what or where Rancho San Carlos was."

DARE TO BE DIFFERENT

Certain types of development are difficult to permit owing to preconceived notions held by authorities and citizens as to what the impacts or appearance of such projects will be. Mixed-use projects, for example, are often resisted because municipalities lack mixed-use zoning provisions or because residents have the misperception that nearby commercial uses will necessarily have a negative impact on them. The same concerns can apply to low-income housing. The New York-based Affordable Housing Construction Corporation (AHCC) and its western arm, Affordable Housing Development Corporation (AHDC), have succeeded with affordable housing projects—alone and as part of mixed-use developments —through their careful designs and persistent approach to the approvals process. The company is willing to buck the trends and work closely with local government, effectively setting precedents in the process.

When Jonathan Rose of AHCC and his partners proposed Second Street Studios—a live/work project in Santa Fe—the site was zoned for commercial use and the city had no mixed-use policy. This did not stop the development team,

The site of Second Street Studios in Santa Fe, a live/work project, was originally zoned for commercial use. Zoning codes were modified to permit residential uses in commercial and light industrial areas. *(Reprinted with permission from the Affordable Housing Development Corporation.)*

however. They worked closely with the city to modify existing zoning codes to permit residential uses in commercial and light-industrial areas. Now, residential occupancy is permitted as a principal use if the units are occupied by owners, employees, or tenants of other permitted principally commercial or light-industrial uses. The development offers flexible use of space, including light-industrial, studio, office, retail, and residential uses. Most of the units can include separate work, storefront, and living areas.

Santa Fe also had no parking policy for mixed-use development. Initially, the city calculated the development's parking requirement by tabulating and combining the maximum amount of parking required for each use that might occur in each unit. This led to an average of one parking space per 150 square feet (four parking spaces for even the smallest space). Wanting to avoid a sea of parking, the developers negotiated parking standards, which resulted in a final plan of one space per 420 square feet.

BE PROACTIVE AND RESPONSIVE TO GOVERNMENT EARLY

When The Body Shop renovated a building in Wake Forest, North Carolina, the company was proactive in demonstrating its desire to be a good neighbor, assuring the community that the environmental impacts of its operations would be minimized. The Wake Forest facility serves as the company's U.S. headquarters and also bottles bulk cosmetics and soaps for distribution. The Body Shop initiated a review procedure, although this was not required, with the Town of Wake Forest Public Utilities to demonstrate that the facility would not impose any additional burden on the local wastewater treatment plant, even in the event of a product spill. The town was provided with information on compounds the company uses so that the utilities staff could determine any impact from a spill. The Body Shop also maintains a testing lab and regularly monitors its products for the presence of bacteria and problem chemicals. The town determined that there would be no negative impacts on the wastewater system, which smoothed The Body Shop's way through the approvals process.

While individual buildings do not incorporate environmental sensitivity, the overall plan at Rancho Santa Margarita, in Orange County, California, does a good job in addressing open space, pedestrian issues, and wildlife habitat protection within this 5,000-acre master planned community. Bringing the county in as early as possible and quickly gaining an understanding of its primary concerns guaranteed the developers smooth sailing through the approvals process. Prior to any planning, the development team asked county planners what their "immutables" were (issues they would not compromise on). The county's biggest concerns were retention of regionally significant open space, provision of a subregional community center to serve the surrounding foothill communities, and cooperation and support for a private toll road planned to run through the area (which has since opened). Rancho Santa Margarita's team walked the bluff with county staff to determine the proper edge for the built community. At the very first meeting, in 1979, they carved out wildlife corridors with the county's input. All plans were processed simultaneously, and approvals were completed by September 1982.

GO BEYOND THE MINIMUM REQUIRED

Beaufort County, South Carolina, home of Spring Island, includes fairly stringent environmental protection in its local ordinances. Spring Island met or exceeded the requirements on all points. The Spring Island approvals process was smooth and simple, with little opposition. The developers never submitted a Planned Unit Development (PUD). Instead, they platted single-family lots one phase at a time. Charles Gatch, a longtime employee of the county's planning office, had hunted on Spring Island as a child. Yet, despite seeing his childhood hunting grounds turn into luxury homes, Gatch believes Spring Island's developers have exceeded expectations, "given the reality that the island eventually would be developed."

The lack of opposition may be attributed to the fact that the island was already approved for four units per acre (5,500 homes) and the developers' plan had a far lower density. Gatch, however, also praised Spring Island's strict codes, covenants, and restrictions (CC&Rs), conservation easements, efforts to protect trees (notably, a unique live oak forest), archeological preservation, and artfully designed golf course. He noted that Beaufort County draws people who are looking for "peace, quiet, trees, and scenic vistas," so a developer would be "stupid to destroy what draws people."

PROVE YOU CAN MEET AND EXCEED CODES THROUGH PERFORMANCE

Unlike Spring Island, Dewees Island®, further up the South Carolina coast, encountered numerous obstacles in the approvals process. Although many other barrier islands had been developed, Dewees had remained relatively pristine for a

Getting Approvals for Clustered Development

Although many communities are receptive to clustering, they often have trouble figuring out how to encourage it. What are the appropriate lot size reductions? Should they rely on the carrot (density incentives) or the stick (prescribed clustering)? While Randall Arendt calls for local planning jurisdictions to adopt design requirements for open space development (in his book *Rural by Design*), he also suggests a technique that savvy developers can use to open minds to the benefits of clustering. He suggests that developers submit a plan using open-space development design standards as an option along with a conventional plan, then let the planning department or commission and the community make up their own minds after seeing the difference between the two plans.

This happened in Grafton, Massachusetts, where opponents of clustered development became allies once they understood the results. As described in *Rural By Design,* a clustered housing layout increased the total number of homes on one site from 57 to 68 while simultaneously preserving 43 percent of the site as open space and reducing road lengths from 5,800 to 4,700 feet. The community won with protected open space; the developer won with an increased number of units, reduced infrastructure costs, and community support. Future residents got a more cohesive community built on closer interaction of neighbors.

Source: Information from *Rural by Design,* by Randall Arendt, 1994.

surprisingly long time. In the 1970s and 1980s, three attempts to develop the island failed, and, according to *Charleston Magazine,* rumors began to circulate that the island was "undevelopable, and only a fool would sink another dollar into trying because the local environmental groups had gained such strength, they'd kill the project in its tracks." In such a climate, how on earth did Dewees Island's owners manage to get approvals to develop 150 homesites on the island?

Island Preservation Partnership, formed in 1990 to develop Dewees Island, brought John Knott on board to accomplish its goal of developing the island in a way that was dedicated to environmental preservation. They believed that a man who had spent his life doing historic preservation would bring with him the process of "inventorying available assets and building from within" rather than starting over from ground zero. Said Knott, "I jumped at the chance. Here was this magnificent boat-access island, and the owners wanted to do the development right: unpaved roads, no golf course, no cars, and prearranged investors to position the project as an equity-based development. It was the once-in-a-lifetime chance to show that environmentalism and development can go hand in hand. I couldn't wait to start."

Knott took great precautions to ensure that the project's environmental sensitivity would be genuine and endure over time. The partnership set up very strict covenants that, among other things, limit the total number of homes to 150 and permanently protect two-thirds of the island from any development.

Yet several local groups were not so happy. The nonprofit South Carolina Coastal Conservation League (SCCCL) and several other concerned groups filed an appeal to block the permitting of the Dewees Island sewage system. Even though it was well designed, they feared that the sewer system would overload, contaminating ground and surface water. Knott was concerned by the suit. He told the local consultants he had hired that he felt it was important to meet with Dana Beach, director of the SCCCL. His intention was not to further antagonize Beach, but to discover what the group thought was wrong with the proposed sewer

The development team for Dewees Island® successfully argued that pervious roads would restore the aquifer by using a natural sand base. Residents get around the island on foot or in electric-powered golf carts on the unpaved roads. *(Reprinted with permission from the Island Preservation Partnership.)*

system—and fix it. Through a series of meetings, Knott convinced Beach that he was genuinely concerned. He paid for improvements recommended by the group. The appeal was dropped.

Beach brought in Bobby Carlysle, a leading national expert on wastewater treatment, who designed a system in which Beach had complete confidence. The only problem was the high cost. "To John Knott's credit," Beach told *Charleston Magazine,* "they did not try to negotiate the system. Unlike every other situation we've been in, this was no nickel-and-dime process...their board agreed to everything." While Beach is still opposed to certain aspects of the project, such as the land plan and number of homesites, he does not like to criticize developers who go beyond established standards, which he believes Dewees Island has done.

According to Knott, the issue is about trust—"Doing what you say and doing more than what you say." Knott's recommendation to developers is elegantly simple: "Don't promise more than you can deliver, and deliver more than you promise." This is what builds trust, he believes.

Knott's team tried to bring local government officials into their planning process, but had little success. Much of the resistance came in the area of infrastructure. Public health and water agencies resisted innovative wastewater treatment systems; and the utility company balked at the idea of using alternative power-generation technologies. Charleston County's public works department was adamantly opposed to using pervious roads rather than asphalt. As a result, Island Preservation Partnership had to resort to appealing for variances project by project, item by item. Ultimately, they won most of their variances by arguing that Dewees Island's development methods would result in reduced toxicity, lower pollution, energy and water savings, and habitat enhancement. Although the Partnership spent more time than usual with officials and consultants, the approvals they secured saved a lot of money in direct infrastructure costs.

Knott suggests that codes are often based on prescriptive standards whose origins are long-forgotten and no longer applicable. Often, all that remains is the standard. For example, the wide radius required for cul-de-sacs exists because in the early days, fire engines needed much more space to maneuver than do modern fire trucks.

Knott's strategy in the face of opposition was first to understand what effects the existing codes were intended to achieve, then to show that the codes were outdated and that there were other—better—ways to satisfy the goals. The development team had to research and understand what the standards behind the codes were aiming for, then develop performance standards that provided some way of measuring the desired effects in terms of benefits. Finally, the development team had to get agreement from the code officials that their proposals would achieve the same or better results than the existing prescriptive codes.

Knott's advice to developers is to avoid being adversarial in the approvals process. First, ask the right questions. Then ask, "If I can come back with a solution that meets performance standards but isn't to code, will you grant a variance?" For example, he went around and around with public works regulations over the issue of pervious roads. His team finally prevailed by arguing that pervious roads would restore the aquifer by using a natural sand base. From the developer's standpoint, they are less costly to install and maintain than importing man-made materials, and they obviate the need for storm drains.

Green development projects may also have to deal creatively with health and security codes. Dewees Island developers encountered standards that required lighting around commercial pools. They wanted to use trees instead of light stanchions to hold the lights up at their community pool. The trees would look more natural, save money, and last a lot longer. After a protracted discussion, Knott finally succeeded in getting the code official to agree that, yes, trees would last longer than light stanchions.

Knott also wanted to use table salt instead of a more toxic chlorine treatment for the community pool. He convinced the officials by arguing the following points: table salt provides a more natural chlorinating process; it leaves no residue; it is less expensive; it is more healthful, and swimmers feel better in the pool. Unfortunately, this process of obtaining variances does not make it any easier for future developments to get approvals (i.e., it does not change the code), but it does establish a precedent that developers of future projects can point to.

Knott and other green developers are frustrated with a system that limits the possibilities of new approaches that achieve better results. Knott's incentive to invest so much time and effort in gaining these variances was the opportunity to be creative and demonstrate a better way, but the extra time required can be a very real disincentive. Given the current barriers, those who want to create environmentally sound developments must be willing to invest that extra time, according to Knott. "Most of us in building and development have this idea—we've got to dig this hole, cut this lumber…I'm better off spending my time in planning and research *before* putting the hole in the ground. I find that when I put that extra time in, I usually end up with systems and approaches that are generally more cost-effective when incorporated on the front end, which reduces capital risk, because we need to put less capital out. If it makes sense, it usually costs less to operate and maintain."

Dewees Island's community pool is treated with table salt, a more natural process than the conventional toxic chlorine treatment. This solution is less expensive for the developer and more healthful for the swimmers. *(Reprinted with permission from the Island Preservation Partnership.)*

Getting Beyond Resistance

Passive solar buildings are often required to include conventional backup heating systems, because building officials do not trust that the passive system will work. For example, the Sony Pictures Daycare Center, one of several new buildings at the Sony studio in Culver City, California, was designed to be highly energy efficient. It exceeds California's Title 24 energy standards by 35 percent. Yet building officials still required a small backup air-conditioning system "just in case" — even though the building is so efficient that it should never need to use the system. These additional expenses required of developers or owners may eliminate the cost advantages of the energy-saving features. The situation may begin to change, however, as energy-conserving designs and technologies become better understood and as more developments incorporate them.

At the University of British Columbia's C. K. Choi Building, existing codes presented problems, but the project consultants worked hard to inform and suggest equivalencies to the building inspectors. Although the composting toilets were the

How Specs Live Forever

The following example may be apocryphal, but is nevertheless an amusing tale that highlights the fact that building and product specifications, like rules of thumb, often linger long after their original rationale has vanished.

The U.S. standard railroad gauge (distance between the rails) is 4 feet, 8.5 inches. That's an exceedingly odd number. Why is that gauge used? Because that's the way they built them in England, and the U.S. railroads were built by English expatriates.

Why did the English people build them like that? Because the first rail lines were built by the same people who built the pre-railroad tramways, and that's the gauge they used.

Why did they use that gauge then? Because the people who built the tramways used the same jigs and tools that were used for building wagons, which used that wheel spacing.

Okay! Why did the wagons use that odd wheel spacing? Well, if they tried to use any other spacing the wagons would break on some of the old long distance roads, because that's the spacing of the old wheel ruts.

So where did these old rutted roads come from? The first long-distance roads in Europe were built by Imperial Rome for the benefit of their legions. The roads have been used ever since. And the ruts? The initial ruts, which everyone else had to match for fear of destroying their wagons, were first made by Roman war chariots. Since the chariots were made for or by Imperial Rome, they were all alike in the matter of wheel spacing.

Thus, we have the answer to the original question. The United States standard railroad gauge of 4 feet, 8.5 inches derives from the original specification for Imperial Roman army war chariots. Specs and bureaucracies live forever. So the next time you are handed a specification and wonder what horse's ass came up with it, you may be exactly right—because the Imperial Roman chariots were made to be just wide enough to accommodate the back-ends of two war horses.

Source: Found drifting on the Internet, source unknown.

most difficult feature to get approved, the mechanical engineer for the project succeeded in securing early approval from the local health department. One of the biggest obstacles, it turned out, was the concern that a small child might fall down the toilet "chutes" three stories to the tanks located in the basement. Although they finally convinced Vancouver code officials that this system would work and be safe, they still had to build a sewer connection to Vancouver's system "just in case." The University's own operations and maintenance employees proved to be the greatest barriers, refusing to believe there could be another, more efficient way to handle waste. They were won over after the project team took them on a field trip to see other composting toilets in the area and a graduate student did a cost/benefit study to demonstrate the economic benefits. The team also had to commit to installing a monitoring system to regularly test liquid effluent (graywater from sinks and liquid from the composting toilets), which is treated in a subsurface-flow constructed wetland system along the edge of the building and used for irrigation.

Rocky Mountain Institute was able to construct its main building without a furnace (at 7,100 feet altitude) by demonstrating that the code requirement for maintaining comfortable operating temperatures could be achieved using passive solar energy. It helped, however, that they had two of the nation's leading energy experts to make the case.

Build In Flexibility

When current regulations or codes preclude a designer or developer from implementing all of the intended green measures, it sometimes makes sense to design flexibility into the project so that as regulations do change, minor tuning can achieve the original environmental goals. Bob Berkebile, architect of an expansion at the Kansas City Zoo, wanted to use a constructed wetland to treat wastewater from the African exhibit. Such a system was prohibited when the zoo was built, but changes in the regulations were expected in a few years. So Berkebile incorporated a "dual head" on the wastewater plumbing. Until the regulations are modified, wastewater will go into the normal sewers. Once the new standards take effect, a valve will be turned and the wastewater will be diverted to the natural wetlands for water purification.

For the same reason, engineer Marc Rosenbaum, P.E., of Meriden, New Hampshire, regularly specifies separate graywater plumbing in new houses. The effluent pipes come together before exiting the house to a septic system, but can easily be adapted for separate use of the graywater component if and when regulations are changed.

Rocky Mountain Institute's headquarters in Colorado is proof of the effectiveness of passive solar heating. The building has a wide array of lush tropical plants and one of the highest-altitude banana trees in the world in its greenhouse. *(Reprinted with permission, © Robert Millman.)*

Progressive Codes, Zoning Mechanisms, and Municipal Programs

More sustainable development can be encouraged in many ways. Citizens and elected officials can change municipal plans, adopt creative zoning ordinances, strengthen energy codes, and use innovative tax incentives to protect open space. Some of these strategies encourage voluntary actions through incentives, such as a streamlined approvals process for those who incorporate certain features. Others rely on such mandates as building codes and zoning ordinances. One of the most effective ways to encourage change is to offer technical assistance and education for municipal planning officials. Developers can also be proactive in their local communities, getting involved on commissions and planning boards and encouraging government leaders to adopt measures that are being used successfully elsewhere.

Reworking codes and regulations is an incredibly time-consuming process, nearly always opposed by those who think that they will lose something in the process. For example, Michael O'Brien, mayor of Forest Grove, Oregon, found that in his town, "like most places, the resistance to higher landscaping standards also comes from realtors, developers, builders, and banks as well as public-safety departments. The fear, of course, is that higher standards will increase the costs of development and reduce profit margins."

The city of Los Angeles, which has for decades been the epitome of poorly planned sprawl development, plans to turn over a new leaf. It is now promoting high-density, transit-oriented, mixed-use development and community-responsive planning. The city's General Plan as well as the Metropolitan Transit Authority's (MTA) new policies both call for high-intensity commercial and mixed-use facili-

---

LA's Bold Steps to Change Development Patterns

Los Angeles's first step will be to focus on the Alameda District Plan, covering the area near the city's historic Union Station. The plan seeks to create a livable, high-density community in an area that is currently occupied by rail yards, parking lots, vacant lots, and low-density commercial uses. It calls for up to 11 million square feet of mixed-use, pedestrian-oriented development linked to the hub of the region's public transit system through the adaptive reuse of Union Station. The key provisions that will guide this plan include the following:

- Restrictions on land uses that do not support transit ridership.
- Reduced parking spaces (two per 1,000 square feet rather than the existing three per 1,000 square feet).
- Establishing a new zone that permits mixed use by right rather than as a conditional use.
- Land-use guidelines that encourage a mix of employment, retail, restaurants, and entertainment within close proximity.
- Current zoning requirements allow a floor/area ratio (FAR) of 1.5. The proposed plan will allow an overall average FAR of 4.2, with no limit for individual parcels.

In February 1996 the city's Planning Commission approved the overall project and granted other necessary building approvals.

Source: Adapted with permission from *Urban Ecologist* 1(1996).

ties to be located in centers near transit stations. The policy provides guidelines for Transit-Oriented Districts (TODs) that lie within a half-mile of transit stations, with both minimum and maximum densities specified (see "LA's Bold Steps to Change Development Patterns" on page 218 for more information).

The successful Green Builder Program created by the city of Austin, Texas, links voluntary actions by builders to the city's long-range planning goals. Program reach and participation are increasing every year. It has gained international attention and has served as a model for other programs nationwide. Such cities as Santa Monica, California, and Tucson, Arizona, are looking into setting up similar programs. The Green Builder Program was created by the city to encourage construction of energy-efficient, environmentally responsible buildings. Founded in 1991 to introduce sustainable construction practices into the mainstream, the program uses a "push-and-pull" strategy, giving the building industry the training and tools it needs while marketing the benefits to consumers as well as construction professionals.

By mid-1996, Austin's program was dealing more extensively with volume builders, and close to 10 percent of houses being built were certified Green Builder homes. More than 6,000 homes have been built as part of the program. The program's residential component offers a rating system of one to four stars, depending on the extent to which a builder addresses various criteria relating to the environmental characteristics of the house (for example, energy efficiency, water efficiency, indoor air quality, and resource-efficient materials). Austin's commercial building component also assists design teams in incorporating sustainable concepts into the design and construction of commercial buildings.

A number of innovative building practices and technologies have been introduced through the Green Builder Program. For example, higher performance standards for ductwork will be tested on a number of Green Builder homes. Once proven, such measures will likely become standard requirements in Austin. According to Austin Green Builder Program staff, developers proposing green projects rarely experience problems with approvals as long as any new products being used have been independently tested and meet code requirements.

City planning staff in both Austin and San Jose, California, stress the importance of testing ideas and technologies before making them part of municipal codes. San Jose often uses its own facilities to test various standards under consideration. For example, the city tried using sand filters to treat parking lot runoff by separating oil and water. Unfortunately, the system did not meet performance expectations. Rob Burkhart, of San Jose's Environmental Services Department, explained that the department would much rather test concepts than mandate them and hope that they work. Before establishing a requirement to use vegetative swales in development projects, the city tested the concept at one of its fire stations.

Burkhart also found that developers are willing to abide by more stringent guidelines *if* the municipality's requirements are explicitly defined and explained early in the approvals process. Developers are constantly pushing to keep up with their tight schedules, being highly aware of the time value of money and the optimal time to bring their product onto the market. Developer Jonathan Rose concurs: "I don't mind regulation and strict design guidelines as long as I can develop by right…and not spend years in the approvals process. Zoning should reflect a community's values—when it doesn't, it leads to a long process of wrangling, which often weakens the product."

Ashland, Oregon, a city of 17,000 located 15 miles north of the California border, has gone further than perhaps any other municipality to encourage sustainability. With strong support from residents, Ashland's city government and the local utility company have made energy conservation and more responsible growth high priorities. In 1980 the town enacted a solar access ordinance. Since 1981 housing density bonuses have been offered as an incentive for energy and water efficiency. Ashland also has a Model Energy Code that promotes energy-conserving construction in new facilities. The local utility, Bonneville Power Administration (BPA), offers commercial building auditing and design assistance through the Energy Smart program.

Ashland's density bonus program for residential development works like this: During the preliminary review process, developers present their basic plans (placement of water and sewer lines, etc.) and state their commitment to the efficiency program. Their preliminary plans are circulated among the various department heads for review and comment. Before a building permit is issued, each developer's commitment to the efficiency program is verified to check that it meets Ashland's guidelines. A point system enables developers to pick from different categories to meet the standards. The number of points awarded for each energy- and water-efficiency measure and the number of points needed to increase permitted building densities are listed in tables within the ordinance. This method has proven to be an effective way to encourage energy-efficient building.

City government and staff are working to expand the scope and "greenness" of Ashland's program to include sustainable materials, embodied energy, composting, and pedestrian access issues. While the energy- and water-efficiency program

Developers of the Tolman Creek Shopping Center in Ashland, Oregon, had to modify their plans to address the city's concern about the loss of the old-growth oak trees and the project's impact on the creek running through the site. *(Reprinted with permission from Doug Child.)*

for density bonuses addresses only residential development, the city also takes a strong stand on commercial projects and expects them to meet Ashland's Model Energy Code.

To facilitate greater consistency and coordination, Ashland has established a Division of Community Development that contains the Planning, Conservation, and Building Departments. This structure fosters teamwork and gives staff more ability to influence developers' designs early in the process. Department staff are able to give developers the necessary information up-front—a procedure that is unlike the more typical experience in so many municipalities in which the developer submits final plans satisfying one department's requirements, only to have another department come up with more hoops to jump through. In Ashland, developers know what to expect from the beginning.

Why does Ashland go to such lengths to promote green development? Conservation officer Dick Wanderscheid observes that Ashland's population is well educated; many have chosen to live in the area because of the cultural and environmental amenities that Ashland offers. "People are also starting to realize they need to be more sustainable and that we can't just go on wasting resources. This caring is becoming much more mainstream, and is reflected in their life-styles." Ashland also has well-informed elected officials who support these initiatives. Says Wanderscheid, "It becomes a team effort: the citizens and the public officials working together to make change. Finally, it stems from the heart—if you live your life in this sustainable manner, then you want your city to reflect those values too."

Watson and Associates, developers of the Tolman Creek Shopping Center in Ashland, would have saved themselves a lot of time and money had their initial proposal addressed the city's priorities. They planned to build a standard, 94,000-square-foot shopping plaza containing four building complexes: one occupied by Albertson's (a supermarket chain), another occupied by Payless Drugs, and two occupied by smaller retail and commercial businesses.

Their original plans called for removal of all existing vegetation—including several large oak trees—and culverting the stream that runs through the site, so that the new shopping plaza would perch neatly on the property. Concerned about the loss of the old-growth oak trees and the project's impact on the creek, the city refused to approve the project until the layout was modified to accommodate the oak trees and the stream. The developers were also required to meet the town's energy standards and to minimize parking impacts.

To comply with the city, the site was completely redesigned, with decks and raised walkways bridging the stream. Today this outdoor area is one of the most important amenities of the Tolman Creek Shopping Center, and people often take

---

Information Sources for Government Officials

Increasing numbers of municipalities around North America are taking significant steps to adopt more progressive regulations and incentives for green development. Government leaders and planning officials should be made aware of these successful models. There are many sources of information for both government officials and developers who want to know what has been done in other places. One such source is the U.S. Department of Energy's Center of Excellence for Sustainable Development. The Center's web site points users toward sustainable community codes and ordinances that include solar access, guidelines for innovative construction systems, and charters of sustainability.

a break from shopping to sit outside and enjoy a glass of iced tea as they listen to birds in the grove of oaks.

Within the mall, Ashland's Model Energy Code also influenced building design. When the architects and engineers for Albertson's and Payless Drugs presented their stock designs for chain stores, the city asked them to upgrade the buildings to meet Ashland's code and introduced them to the free consulting services offered by BPA. BPA consultants revised the plans, which resulted in significant energy savings, including roughly $40,000 in annual savings to Albertson's alone. While the energy performance of the buildings significantly exceeds code, it is hardly leading-edge. Even greater energy savings, as well as lower capital costs, could have been realized if energy-efficiency measures had been introduced at the initial design phase rather than as revisions to stock designs.

City regulations also ensured below-normal traffic impacts of the new mall. An Ashland city ordinance permits just three parking spaces per 1,000 square feet. Typical malls provide eight spaces per 1,000 square feet. (This provision has had the effect of keeping big box discount retailers out of Ashland.) The developer of Tolman Creek had to make sure this restriction would not keep business away, so features were included that encourage bicycle, pedestrian, and public transit access.

The environmental considerations were entirely new both for the Tolman Creek developers and for the chain stores that located there. The city planning director indicated that this retail development could be much better, but that compared with a standard strip mall with large anchor stores, it is "light years ahead" in terms of design—blending with the existing landscape, providing pedestrian access, and exhibiting a high level of energy efficiency. Financially, the mall is performing well. While the local community tends to oppose large chain stores, the revised, more environmentally friendly design led to acceptance of the project because people saw Albertson's and Payless as trying to fit into the community rather than inflicting a generic shopping center on the town.

Permitting Better Communities

Any town-planning text prior to 1935 has references to social issues, to technical issues, to aesthetic issues. But after the war, specialists and bean counters took over. It was as if America had suffered a stroke: we lost language, we lost the ability to think complexly.

Andres Duany, Newsweek, *May 15, 1995*

Many existing zoning regulations limit community-sensitive planning and design on the macro scale. Neotraditional or New Urbanist principles, as discussed in Chapter 3, offer many advantages when applied to communities, including reduced automobile dependence, improved neighborhood interaction, and the designation of publicly owned open space. But permitting these developments can be very difficult. Well-known neotraditional planners Andres Duany and Elizabeth Plater-Zyberk of Duany Plater-Zyberk (DPZ) were quick to discover the limitations of conventional zoning when they set out to recreate projects based on traditional neighborhood forms.

Tired of repeated struggles with existing municipal ordinances, DPZ created a whole-systems approach to planning. The firm developed a model ordinance, referred to as a "traditional neighborhood development" (TND) ordinance, to streamline the zoning process. Instead of trying to push through individual variances to the existing codes, the firm typically presents a totally new package of codes and design elements to the approvals board. This "overlay" ordinance deals with such issues as street width and layout, building setbacks, alleys, lighting, and signage. The firm tries to obtain one variance for the entire project, in effect replacing the existing zoning as it relates to that project site with their overlay zoning. Communities in several states have recognized the benefits of such overlay ordinances, which can be tailored to each community's specific needs, and have incorporated them into their local zoning laws (see "Applying Traditional Neighborhood Development Ordinances" on page 225 for more information).

Another leading practitioner of new town development, Peter Calthorpe, of Calthorpe Associates in Berkeley, California, has also frequently run into obstacles to securing approvals. Calthorpe was asked to redesign Laguna West, a master planned community in Sacramento, into a "pedestrian pocket," and his plan became one of his earliest neotraditional projects to be built. Calthorpe's design was intended to foster community by relating buildings to one another and to the larger development, while mixing more than 3,000 units of housing with parks, lakes, commercial space, retail stores, and industry. Pedestrian-oriented features included homes that are sited on narrow tree-lined streets with wide sidewalks, with front porches and garages tucked behind. River West Development, the project's developers, first tried using legal arguments to get the street width variance called for in Calthorpe's design, with no success. To satisfy these concerns, Calthorpe and River West decided on a novel demonstration. They blocked off a street to the proposed width, parked cars along it, and spent $5,000 to rent a fire engine, an ambulance, and a garbage

Applying Traditional Neighborhood Development Ordinances

Many people believe that neotraditional planning is mostly about design aesthetics. But Duany and Plater-Zyberk know otherwise. According to William Lennertz, who contributed an essay to the book *Towns and Town-Making Principles* describing DPZ's work, "Regulatory codes lie at the heart of Duany and Plater-Zyberk's work. Early in their work they realized that existing zoning ordinances—more than economics or planning and design philosophies—were impediments to achieving more urbane communities. Conventional zoning frequently works to segregate activities. Duany and Plater-Zyberk set out to reform zoning to do the opposite—to connect, to aggregate, and to unify."

DPZ's code package has become standardized over time, while still adaptable to specific local needs. The codes usually consist of five documents:

- *Regulating Plan.* A more technical rendering of information presented through the master plan. Identifies street types and public spaces reserved for civic buildings, squares, and parks. Shows platting of private building tracts and assigns building types to each.

- *Urban Regulations.* Regulates aspects of private building types that affect public spaces, usually through prescriptive standards such as requirements for front porches or percentages of street facades on a common frontage line. Sometimes accompanied by illustrations that include a summary of standard building types and a plan for a composite block.

- *Architectural Regulations.* A matrix that regulates building configurations, materials, and construction techniques.

- *Street Sections.* Drawings specifying the character of public spaces that are intended to make pedestrians feel safe, while allowing acceptable automobile movement. Includes details on travel and parking lanes, sidewalk widths, etc.

- *Landscape Regulations.* Specifies planting types for streets, squares, and parks. Intention is to achieve "a naturalistic reforestation" of the town, using species that are drought-tolerant and provide good habitat for local fauna.

Duany and Plater-Zyberk's codes can also be applied to the more complex conditions in existing communities. For example, Trenton, New Jersey, adopted a code that, according to Lennertz, "addresses the architectural and urban issues of a dense downtown. And the Traditional Neighborhood Development Ordinance is a comprehensive code for municipalities whose existing bylaws preclude the creation of traditional neighborhoods."

Source: William Lennertz, *Towns and Town-Making Principles* (New York: Rizzoli International Publications, 1991).

Laguna West, a master planned community in Sacramento, is one of architect and planner Peter Calthorpe's earliest neotraditional projects. *(Reprinted with permission from William D. Browning, Rocky Mountain Institute.)*

truck with drivers to drive up and down the street, passing each other. They video-taped the simulation, showed it to code officials—and got their variance.

Infill development (discussed in Chapter 3) is one way to use land more efficiently, reduce sprawl-related auto dependency, and enhance community character. Planning departments in such cities as Portland, Orlando, and Sacramento are actively encouraging infill development. Nancy Pappas, who reported on Traditional Neighborhood Developments for *Consumer Reports* in May 1996, observed that planning staffs in those cities complain that they cannot get developers interested in this style of building because it deviates from standard suburban subdivision patterns. Portland has sought to create a development pattern focused on compact urban forms revolving around centers and transit corridors, with a clearly defined growth boundary. The tight boundaries have forced an increase in infill development and conversion of older neighborhoods into mixed-use centers, opening up new employment opportunities.

Accessory Units

Accessory units, also called carriage units or granny flats, provide one of the quickest, easiest ways to raise densities in urban North America while increasing the supply of affordable rental housing. Many existing single-family homes have underutilized space that can be converted into accessory units. New cottages can be built on existing lots or above garages. These apartments can provide opportunities for affordable housing for students, elderly relatives, single people, or young couples. They also provide a source of income for home owners, or the chance to exchange services (gardening, child care, computer assistance, etc.) for rent reductions.

Despite their many benefits, zoning laws often prohibit accessory units. There is a strong push for changes in these laws in many areas. This has happened in such U.S. cities as Boulder, Seattle, and Greenwich, Connecticut. Orlando amended its code to permit accessory garage apartments as well as front porches that extend beyond the front yard setback.

In municipalities that are struggling to provide affordable housing, permitting accessory units is a good way to turn things around. Washington, D.C.–based planning consultant Patrick Hare calculated that building just one accessory unit per 1,000 single family homes in the United States each year would produce an additional 48,000 rental units annually. This would represent a very substantial increase of about 14 percent in the annual production of affordable rental housing. Best of all, the increase would be created through simple zoning changes rather than expensive public housing programs or regulatory measures.

Accessory units, such as this one in Laguna West, California, increase densities and the number of affordable housing units in a development. *(Reprinted with permission from William D. Browning, Rocky Mountain Institute.)*

Tougher Energy and Water Codes

Energy codes have been introduced in cities around the country to improve the energy performance of new buildings. Energy codes can specify actual energy performance or offer prescriptive requirements for insulation, window glazings, and other building components that affect energy performance. Some codes offer both approaches as optional paths to compliance. The performance approach is more complicated than the prescriptive approach, but offers greater flexibility to the designer (allowing the use of passive solar design, for example, instead of high R-value walls, with the same net effect on energy costs).

To aid municipalities and states considering such codes, a Model Energy Code was developed with support from the U.S. Department of Energy. According to the Alliance to Save Energy in Washington, D.C., if the 1991 Model Energy Code were adopted for residential construction nationwide, it would save the average household $150 in annual utility bills. Yet many states still do not have even minimum energy codes. Communities whose building codes date before 1980 would be wise to revise those codes, given the improvements in efficient building technologies.

Although California's Code of Regulations Title 24 is the strictest energy code in the country, Santa Barbara County's Planning and Development Department knows that energy-efficient building design can exceed these standards. The department has created the Innovative Building Review Committee, which offers free consulting on energy-efficient design. The impetus for this project was the department's finding that those in the development/building industries who wish to incorporate efficiency measures in their designs often experience prolonged review when proposing new or different technologies. The committee will remove this impediment by speeding up the review process while helping applicants exceed Title 24 by 15 percent or more for residential development, and 25 percent or more for commercial and industrial development, if the consulting services are applied early enough in the design process.

Codes and Design Standards for Water Conservation

Many communities have found that legal mandates are necessary to promote water-efficient landscapes — incentives just do not make enough impact. From a water utility's perspective, design requirements are a relatively inexpensive method of ensuring that new landscapes are as water-efficient as possible. Meeting these requirements can save customers money both on initial landscape installations and on future maintenance costs. Such regulations are usually incorporated into building permit approval processes and include limits on turf area, limits on overall water budgets, and prohibitions against certain kinds of plants. The Global Cities Project has shown that regulations covering landscaping for new construction can reduce projected water use by up to 50 percent in dry regions.

California's Water Conservation in Landscaping Act, enacted in 1993, requires cities and counties to implement landscape conservation requirements for new and existing commercial, industrial, governmental, institutional, and multifamily developments. If a municipality has not adopted its own ordinance or demonstrated that no ordinance is necessary, the state's model ordinance must be used. California's Goleta Water District developed and implemented landscape requirements for all new construction, including single-family homes. Former Goleta Water Conservation coordinator Larry Farwell estimated that this single act led to a 50 percent reduction in water use for landscaping. Richard Bennett of California's East Bay Municipal Utilities District (EBMUD) estimates that landscape standards will reduce water use in new construction by approximately 25 percent over conventional landscapes. Tests conducted by EBMUD on landscape retrofits actually saved 90 percent of landscape water.

GRAYWATER

Graywater systems that divert wastewater from showers, sinks, and washing machines for use in subsurface irrigation constitute a special case of water conservation. When major droughts in California in the 1980s and 1990s resulted in widespread bans on watering lawns, pressure mounted for the legislature to relax prohibitions on the use of graywater for landscape irrigation. In a typical household, graywater can provide roughly 50 gallons per day for reuse. Following the lead of Santa Barbara, Goleta, and other California communities, in 1994 California's legislature passed statewide guidelines for the safe use of graywater for subsurface irrigation. The law carefully prescribes exactly what can be considered graywater and exactly how it can be used for subsurface irrigation — the water cannot come within four inches of the ground surface and cannot be used on food crops, for example. After several years of study, *Graywater Systems for Single-family Dwellings* was added to the California Plumbing Code. This is an adaptation of a graywater standard incorporated into the Uniform Plumbing Code of the International Association of Plumbing and Mechanical Officials (IAPMO) in 1992.

In California, permitting graywater is usually up to county health officials. Their stance varies widely from having never heard of it, to opposing it, to finding it acceptable. Approvals have been easier, however, since publication of a year-long study of eight graywater subsurface irrigation system installations by the City of Los Angeles Water Reclamation Office, which found that graywater use would not create significant health risks for users or the community.

BIOLOGICAL WASTEWATER TREATMENT SYSTEMS

Using natural cycles of plant and animal life to process wastewater, rather than chemicals and mechanical systems, diverges greatly from the conservative civil engineering profession's thinking. Yet sometimes precedents set in one jurisdiction allow progress to move forward in another. The Solar Aquatics System developed by John Todd was certified by the Commonwealth of Massachusetts for use in Harwich, Massachusetts. This certification by Massachusetts eased approvals for such a system in Providence, Rhode Island.

Once municipalities are aware of the benefits of biological wastewater treatment systems, the approvals process may get easier. Neighbors should find them less offensive than conventional wastewater treatment systems, and they can be situated in populated areas because their operations are odor-free. If done well, they can also be aesthetically pleasing. The ability to integrate such systems into the landscape means they can be well suited for industrial and food processing sites. *Environmental Building News* reported that M&M/Mars Company's "positive experience with living machines in Henderson, Nevada, and Waco, Texas, has spurred them to order three additional systems for plants in other parts of the world. These advantages should help living machines attain significant market penetration."

WATER-EFFICIENT PLUMBING FIXTURES

Since the enactment of nationwide standards for water-efficient plumbing fixtures (toilets, shower heads, faucet aerators) the need for local regulations has been greatly reduced. In areas with water shortages or potential shortages, however, some municipalities have required developers to carry out existing-building retrofit programs to generate comparable water savings so that the new development will not increase total water use or sewage treatment plant impacts in the community. The city of Morro Bay, on California's central coast, used to offer developers and builders two options. They could pay the standard hookup fee (used in part to replace the city's leaky water mains), or they could retrofit existing buildings until they had saved more than enough to match their new use and avoid the hookup fee. As a result, builders retrofitted—with replacement toilets, shower heads, and kitchen and bathroom faucet aerators—40 percent of all Morro Bay homes in the first four years of the program, at a cost of about $350 per retrofitted home. By 1996 the regulations had tightened: a developer's only option was to retrofit existing buildings, at a ratio of two to one (twice as much water saved through retrofits as consumed by the new project) for residential, and three to one for commercial development.

Conclusion

The approvals process can sometimes be an obstacle to green development, because local planning bodies and the community may not be familiar with the ideas being proposed or aware of the benefits to be realized. At the same time, however, the ease with which some green developments sail through the approvals process can be an important driver for the green elements of a development. By creating open space, minimizing traffic impacts, and generally reducing environmental impacts on infrastructure, green developments are inherently more palatable to most communities and will generate less opposition throughout the approvals process.

Green developers often find themselves playing an educational role, teaching the community about what is proposed and why it will be beneficial. On the other hand, communities like Austin have taken a leadership role in educating local builders and developers. Drawing from the experiences of other developments, when available, can help this process, but local projects may not exist. Imagination, creativity, skills, and commitment are often required to present a project so that it will be clearly understood and approved in a timely manner.

Communities that want to foster better development practices should determine how they can encourage the kind of development that will benefit the community over the long term. They should examine existing zoning bylaws or ordinances, as well as other plans and policies that influence development. They should create mechanisms to reward developers who are "doing the right thing" instead of penalizing them with an approvals process so onerous that only the bravest and most patient can surmount it.

As more green developments come to fruition around the country and as communities begin to see the direct and indirect benefits of these projects, the approvals process should become easier. Today's pioneers have to work harder, but they will also be able to reap the rewards and recognition bestowed on industry trendsetters.

At Second Street Studios in Santa Fe, high vaulted open space provides a pleasant working environment in this print shop. *(Reprinted with permission from Wayne Nichols.)*

CHAPTER **8**

Financing

DEVELOPER JONATHAN ROSE AND HIS PARTNERS, Wayne and Susan Nichols and Peter Calthorpe, knew there was an untapped real estate market among Santa Fe's artists and start-up businesses in the late 1980s. They formed ASA Group (Artists Studios Associates) to develop affordable "live/work" units for this market niche. Research revealed that many of Santa Fe's artists were illegally working out of spaces not zoned for commercial activities, because they could not afford to rent studio space while also paying rent for their homes. ASA's brainchild, Second Street Studios, provides combined living and studio space for artists, craftspeople, and small businesses. Phase One consisted of 35 live/work units—the beginning of a multiphased project that has breathed new life into this part of Santa Fe, sandwiched between an old blue-collar barrio and an industrial area two miles southwest of the city's historic Plaza.

The challenge the developers faced for this innovative project was obtaining the necessary financing. At the time, no one else had developed live/work space, so there were no comparables. Local banks viewed the project as too risky, since the market was not proven. Although the project had a residential component, it did not fit residential loan criteria that would qualify it to be sold on the secondary market with credit enhancement by the Federal Housing Authority (FHA), Freddie Mac, Fannie Mae, or the state Housing Authority, as can usually be done with residential loans—lenders typically categorize loans as residential, commercial, or industrial, but not a combination of these types.

Rose finally secured construction financing for the first phase of development from Banker's Trust in New York City, based on his successful track record and past banking relationships. After spending many years trying to find a permanent loan, the developers eventually secured financing from one of the first securitized commercial lending pools of the 1990s. By opening day in January 1990, 50 percent of Second Street Studios was leased—with very little marketing—and the rest was leased within two months.

The next phase of Second Street Studios was easier to finance. Charter Southwest, a local bank that had funded an artists' studio complex built by Rose and Sim Van der Ryn several years earlier, had confidence in the project based on the success of the first phase. Phase Two was the Santa Fe Arts Building, a renovation of an 18,000-square-foot warehouse into a graphic arts building with commercial studio space. Says Rose, "The building configuration was not appropriate for live/work space. As a purely commercial building, it was easiest to obtain a construction loan from the bank and a permanent mortgage from Standard Insurance Company." With the success of these two phases, Rose and the Nicholses again returned to live/work development on the property, this time with both construction and permanent loans from Charter Southwest.

Investors in Second Street Studios have been receiving approximately 20 percent return on investment (ROI) annually. Rental revenues have easily covered operating costs and construction debt service. Indexed with the consumer price index (CPI), rents have been rising at 2.5 to 3.0 percent a year, although in early years they rose at a higher rate because of the high demand for live/work space in Santa Fe. Second Street Studios has nurtured almost 100 small businesses and has been fully leased since it opened.

Jonathan Rose is one of the few developers to successfully create environmentally responsive, mixed-use developments. Rose maintains that his success as a developer is contingent on two critical facts: he maintains a good relationship with bankers, and he has never defaulted on a loan. The reason is that his projects are well thought out in advance. And while his project types are innovative, the fundamental financial aspects remain quite conservative, which allows lenders to trust him.

Says Rose, "I have forged relationships with my bankers and I maintain those relationships so they feel secure. I let them know that if they stick with me, I'll stick with them." Bankers with whom Rose works are able to share any concerns they may have, rather than simply turning down a loan because it does not fit their mold. This is unusual in an age when local banks are being bought up by national banking institutions whose financing decisions are based on spreadsheets and pro formas instead of strong customer relationships and connections to the community.

Rose has found that projects with a diversity of uses and building types have a harder time with financing becasue of ingrained lending practices. "Lending institutions prefer to lend to projects that have one large tenant rather than many small tenants. Time and again we see large, single-use buildings in bankruptcy because IBM or Wal-Mart moved out and no one moved in. Projects that are flexible enough to serve a wide variety of users have much higher lifetime occupancy rates."

This chapter examines some of the challenges in financing innovative green developments and reviews a few of the approaches that have been successfully used to surmount these hurdles.

The Uphill Battle to Finance Green Developments

Someday lenders will look back with retrospective wisdom and wonder why they had been so reluctant to finance the sort of environmentally responsible and community-sensitive projects profiled in this book. Green developments, after all, are providing less expensive places to live in and operate; they are providing more attractive, more popular communities; they are producing healthier, more productive and profitable workplaces; and they are often less expensive to build as a result of the whole-systems approach used in the planning and design.

But today green development projects frequently do have a hard time when it comes to financing. Their products are unfamiliar to lenders and investors, and until comparable projects exist there is a natural reluctance by a conservative industry to enter the unknown. Success will depend on hard work, creative planning, and the use of some innovative financing mechanisms. In some cases it may be necessary to gloss over the green or innovative features of a project and emphasize instead the financial merits, the applicability to the market, or the avoidance of risks.

In addition to encountering a long approvals process, developers Michael and Judy Corbett had a difficult time financing Village Homes in Davis, California, in the early 1970s. Banks were reluctant to lend money for a development they viewed as unconventional and to a developer without large-scale experience. It was also a tough time in the real estate lending cycle to borrow money.

In 1973 the Corbetts bought an option on a 10-acre site by putting down $10,000. They raised $120,000 from 13 investors to begin predevelopment activities and to get bank support. They were able to get the land owner to finance the full 70-acre land sale, which they purchased in increments over five years, at $6,000 an acre.

Finding a construction lender for such an unconventional development was a problem. Michael Corbett met with failure when he tried to sell banks on the merits of his concept. One bank turned him down, he said, "not because the management doubted the financial feasibility of the project, but simply because it did not like what I was trying to do." In early meetings with bankers, Corbett promoted the energy savings and other anticipated benefits of Village Homes, but

Developer Michael Corbett found that bankers were skeptical when he discussed such features as edible landscaping and natural drainage. Today community members enjoy these features. *(Reprinted with permission from William D. Browning, Rocky Mountain Institute.)*

that just made the bankers more skeptical. He found that "eyes rolled back" when he discussed features like edible landscaping and natural drainage.

After modifying his approach to focus on the number of lots sold and other conventional measures of a real estate investment, Corbett obtained infrastructure financing from Sacramento Savings and Loan. The first loan, for $170,000, provided the limited partnership with enough working capital to put streets and utilities in the first phase of 10 acres.

Construction began in October 1975. The Corbetts eventually built more than half of the 240 homes in the subdivision, and they subjected all homes and landscaping to strict architectural review. The project was built-out in 1981, and, despite the initial lack of enthusiasm from the real estate community, each of Village Homes' five phases sold out quickly. The houses were designed for a moderate market, with prices ranging from $40,000 to $60,000. A sweat-equity program allowed several low-income construction workers to buy homes, while the majority of the homes were sold to young professional families.

Despite initial skepticism from financing institutions, Village Homes has been a dramatic success, both from an environmental/community perspective and financially, with investors achieving returns of approximately 30 percent per year. Michael Corbett believes that the industry has become more accepting of innovative projects over the past two decades. Still, he says, the ability to obtain funds remains largely a matter of track record, and he advises green developers, "Keep the concept as simple as possible when you go to the bank."

Developers Jim Chaffin and Jim Light faced somewhat different obstacles when they sought financing for Spring Island. The development team had years of experience and a strong track record, but lenders questioned why in the world they would take the risk of reducing the number of homes on the island to a tenth of the permitted number, without increasing each lot's price accordingly. Their inability to sell the financial community on their environmentally inspired concepts, coupled with their belief that an overall cultural and psychological shift was occurring in which people wanted to be associated with environmental values, caused the developers to take a different tack.

Chaffin got a one-year option on the island, moved to the area, and spent that year figuring out how to make their concept work. He got approvals for the master plan and for the bridge connecting the island to the mainland (via another island). The development company also set up the Spring Island Trust to preserve 1,000 acres of land on the island. Once the master plan was approved, Chaffin brought small boatloads of people to the island to experience its beauty, while trying to

The development company set up the Spring Island Trust to preserve 1,000 acres of land on the island, called the Chechessee Nature Preserve. *(Reprinted with permission from Skip Meachen.)*

presell lots. Over lobster bakes, he shared his dream, attracting 36 early buyers at $300,000 per lot, raising $10 million before actually closing on the land deal.

Part of that $10 million financed construction of the bridge and other infrastructure. The success of the presales convinced NationsBank to lend another $17 million to the project. About six months later, a Japanese firm, Nippon Landic, provided another $20 million in venture capital as an equity partner. By late 1996, 90 percent of the debt had been paid off, with Chaffin reporting a "very strong absorption rate and at a high price." The partners anticipate that the future investments of another $13 million needed for infrastructure will be carried by cash flow without requiring additional financing. ROI is running 23 percent annually after debt service, over a 10-year period.

The bank was uneasy about the idea of removing the Spring Island Trust acreage from future development, in case it was forced to foreclose on the property, so it kept a mortgage on the Trust's acreage until a specified amount of debt had been repaid. The developers did not like this provision, because it reduced the level of protection on this pristine land, but they went along with it. After the debt level was reduced, the Trust's preservation was assured.

Bankers were also leery about Spring Island's unusually strong covenants on site protection, including an undisturbed "nature curtain" where only the driveway can be seen from the road. They questioned whether people would spend a substantial sum for a lot where their house could not be seen. The developers' belief that those restrictive covenants would actually be viewed by some as an inducement to buy proved correct. The bank thought they were "nuts" to ask $300,000 for two acres without beach frontage, yet Chaffin found it was these covenants that ultimately created the lots' high value. Establishing covenants and ensuring land preservation are among the cheapest ways to create value for a development, because they require no infrastructure investment or ongoing operating expenses. After a year of looking at how many lots had sold as well as who was buying—which included prominent members of both the business and the environmental communities—the bank was finally convinced that, indeed, there was a market for this kind of development.

Although Chaffin and Light had worked with NationsBank for many years prior to the Spring Island project, it took the bank several years to trust the developers' market assumptions. Chaffin, like Jonathan Rose, believes that in the end, their track record in always paying the bank back, as well as their past banking relationships, is probably what got them their financing.

Recognizing a Premium Product

Another financing problem that green developers may face results from higher costs. Although green developments do not have to cost more than conventional projects, some do. Even if the market is willing to pay the premium price, lenders may not be willing to provide more financing. This was a problem the developers of Prairie Crossing faced.

In 1987 an equity partnership financed the $5.2 million to acquire the land on which Prairie Crossing, near Chicago, now sits. When applying for bank loans, which financed all other costs, Prairie Crossing's development team laid their vision out up-front. Lenders were perplexed by the unconventional site plan, which included preservation of open land and a working farm along with the new

The unique components of the Prairie Crossing site plan, such as preservation of open land and a working farm, perplexed lenders. *(Reprinted with permission from William D. Browning, Rocky Mountain Institute.)*

home development. They were also skeptical that homes could be sold at the price predicted by the pro forma. In Grayslake, Illinois, where the project is located, typical home prices run from $175,000 to $225,000. Yet in 1996, Prairie Crossing's average home price was approximately $300,000. The higher selling prices were necessary because the development cost more—because open space, including a working farm, was being preserved.

Ultimately, debt financing was secured using publicly held stock, rather than real estate, as collateral. The fact that the bank did not hold a mortgage on the land gave the developers freer rein and worked to their benefit in the appraisals process. Frank Martin, president of Shaw Homes, Inc., explained, "There will be a bias against anything you do different than a conventional subdivision if it adds to the cost. But the fact that the bank does not hold a mortgage on the land has given us flexibility, which is really important for us, considering the unique components of Prairie Crossing, such as additional community amenities, energy saving construction, and more standard features than usual in individual homes."

As it turned out, the gamble worked. Homes sold successfully at the higher prices, because enough people value what they are getting. Martin believes that the Prairie Crossing developers have created real value through what they have done. "Although there is an additional cost," he said, "people are recognizing the value in our homes and the community environment and are willing to pay for it. The reality is, the market can be very humbling. You might have the most wonderful thing in the world, but if nobody perceives value and buys, it doesn't mean a thing."

While many green developers have faced serious challenges in financing their projects, it is important to note that this is not always the case. Some financiers have been impressed by a project's attention to environmental and community issues. Inn of the Anasazi developer Robert Zimmer obtained his initial construction loan (a three-year construction/mini-permanent loan) from the Bank of America based on his track record and the bank's belief that Santa Fe represented a viable investment. In late 1994, though, when the developers refinanced their permanent loan through ITT Real Estate Financial Services, ITT's vice president noted that ITT wanted to be associated with this project because of its authentic commitment to environment and community, as well as the developer's track record.

The Bank of America was impressed by the Inn of the Anasazi's attention to environmental and community issues. *(Reprinted with permission from Inn of the Anasazi.)*

General Approaches to Financing

There are no simple rules about obtaining financing for a green development. Every project will be different, at least in the early years of this specialized type of real estate development. Before getting into specifics about financing strategies and sources, it makes sense to examine the general approaches to financing.

Debt Versus Equity Considerations

Based on his experience with Spring Island, Jim Chaffin believes that a green developer's best bet is either to get an option on a property and prove that a market exists through presales, or to locate substantial equity investment (in which the investors own a percentage of the project above what is financed by debt). He explains that with debt, banks never lend 100 percent of project costs, and that "releases will be pretty stiff." (A release is the percentage of a lot's sale price that lenders require be put toward repayment of the loan; the larger the release percentage, the more difficult it will be for a developer to meet loan repayment requirements while also paying up-front costs of marketing, sales, capital improvements, etc.) Chaffin cautions that sustainable development still has a way to go before banks or equity partners will be fully comfortable with it. "If you're going to do green development, it is important to have enough equity to address the fact that absorption is not going to be predictable, because you have to educate your market." He suggests that green developers need to be even more conservative than conventional developers in their pro forma estimates for the first couple of years, because it will take time for the market to catch on to the benefits of such projects.

Although it may be easier to take out loans than to raise money, equity financing buys more time to work out a plan that everybody will be satisfied with, and it generally keeps greater control in the developer's hands. There is usually uncertainty about how long any new or unusual type of project will take to get approvals, and the compound interest on debt could limit future options.

Developer John Knott has particularly strong feelings about the advantages of equity over debt. To ensure that the long-range objectives for Dewees Island® would be met without compromising the commitment to environmental responsibility, the Island Preservation Partnership (IPP) was structured as an equity-based project. Knott remarked, "Our financing advantage is that without debt, we do not

By early 1997, 60 lots had been sold on Dewees Island®, completing the first phase of development and a portion of the second. Lot prices have gone up significantly since 1992, and net profits were exceeding pro forma targets by about 90 percent. *(Reprinted with permission from the Island Preservation Partnership.)*

have the monster of interest demand on our backs. This allows a more patient approach to development—no one can take the project away." The new partners invested equity capital and development expertise, while the original landowners provided land and a preexisting $5 million note on the property—the only debt carried by the project. This note was assumed by the partnership as part of the land contribution in exchange for a 50 percent interest in the joint venture. Before the IPP was formed, a significant amount of the island's Phase One infrastructure had already been developed (including roads, power, water, and phones), which decreased both development costs and the developer's up-front risk exposure.

As of January 1997 about $1 million in debt remained, with gross income projected at $44 million. Current profit projections are nearly double pro forma estimations—net income originally projected to reach $12 million is now estimated to reach $23 to $24 million. Break-even occurred with the sale of the 40th lot. ROI is expected to average between 30 and 35 percent annually. ROI is this high in part because cost savings for infrastructure (resulting from environmental features) reduced equity needs. Revenues will continue to be reinvested until the island's infrastructure is completed.

In 1996 the original Dewees Island land partners were bought out by a New York and Charleston-based investment group that included some Dewees Island residents. The new investors paid $6 million to buy the 50 percent interest in the project, giving the original owners a return halfway through the project equal to that projected upon total completion of the project.

SPEAKING THE LANGUAGE OF FINANCIERS

Developers proposing innovative projects stand a better chance of success in their quest for financing if they talk in terms bankers understand. Lenders are often presented with concepts they neither understand nor care about—they have heard too many oddball ideas and have seen too many architectural renderings. What they want to know about are the projected cash flows, revenues, and expenses.

Lenders will better understand the benefits of resource efficiency if they see how it will reduce operating costs and affect net operating income, cash flow, and debt service. Those trying to get financing for green developments often miss the mark by failing to get financiers to understand the benefits of these projects in the financiers' own terms—not sustainability, diversity, or ecology, but return on investment, bottom line, and cash flow.

In general, the financial industry does not yet include the long-term economic implications of energy-saving design and other sustainability measures in its definition of fiduciary responsibility. Energy is fairly easy to quantify, but such advantages as productivity and health are more difficult to put into dollar terms. In time, it is likely that financial tools will be developed that better account for life-cycle costs, resource depletion as a form of capital depletion, and the many benefits of green development that are described throughout this book. But for now, most green developers will have to pitch their arguments in ways that lenders relate to.

SPECIAL CHALLENGES WITH MIXED-USE AND OTHER INNOVATIVE DEVELOPMENT PATTERNS

In a risk-averse financial industry, the various participants, from bankers to insurers to appraisers, are slow to innovate and resistant to ideas that are not well established. Lenders also may fear that "green" limits the market, although this is increasingly being shown to be a false assumption. In fact, green developments that include site plans based on concepts such as New Urbanism, transit-oriented planning, mixed-use, clustered design, and land preservation include features that should make them inherently more attractive to financiers.

One of the beauties of mixed-use projects, such as Second Street Studios, is that they are able to evolve with the market. The spaces in these projects can often be used not only for industrial, office, retail, and residential purposes, but also for various combinations of these. Thus, mixed-use projects are able to respond to a very broad range of markets and economic conditions. For example, when rental apartments in Santa Fe were in great demand and rental rates climbed appreciably, Second Street Studios had a higher residential occupancy. In 1996, when there was a glut of all project types in Santa Fe, with commercial vacancies at 10 percent, Second Street Studios remained full, thanks to its unique character, flexibility, and good value. The tenant mix is always changing.

Leland Consulting Group of Portland surveyed lenders to identify obstacles to the execution of the state of Oregon's "smart growth" program. They found that lenders unequivocally believed that innovative projects required clear limits on the risk that the lender could accept. While placing importance on such factors as pre-leasing and on-site management, lenders strongly preferred to work with a developer who had a track record, financial capability, and experience in the product type.

Real estate lending is also historically a cyclical process, based on boom and bust cycles. In times when money is readily available, it is easy to develop junk. When money is tight, it is difficult to develop anything, which often sends people looking for better products. Many of the projects profiled here struggled to get financing, while some other green development proposals were altogether unsuccessful, in part because they sought financing in a "bust" time of the cycle—the late 1980s and early 1990s. Others did not pass muster because of the inexperience of their would-be developers.

One of the great barriers to financing mixed-use projects is the lack of support from the secondary mortgage market. FHA lending programs were set up to assist in the development of housing—not communities. Thus FHA loan requirements allow only very limited forms of mixed-use development. Only 20 percent of a multifamily project can be commercial space. Although residential loans are often sold to the secondary mortgage market—FHA, Fannie Mae, Freddie Mac—this does not protect the lender from the risk of defaulted loans. Thanks to Fannie

Mae's "pass through" requirement, the primary bank is financially responsible for the project through foreclosure of the asset. Because banks do not enjoy being in the business of owning real estate, innovative projects proposed by developers who do not have strong track records cause anxiety that is not allayed by securitization through the secondary mortgage market.

Creative Financing Strategies for Green Development

While some current aspects of green developments are perceived by lenders as negatives (lack of comps, untested markets, costs associated with land protection, etc.), other features can be advantages in seeking financing. Some of these advantages accrue to the future occupants, helping to ensure strong demand, others reduce project costs or reduce the likelihood of lawsuits—but all serve to reduce the overall risk to lenders and investors. They should be explained to lenders in this way.

REDUCED CAPITAL COSTS

Lower capital costs mean that the developer does not need to borrow as much money, which means lower exposure for the lender and less risk of default. There are many ways in which environmentally responsible planning, design, and construction can lead to lower capital costs. One of the most obvious is that higher density, narrower streets, and alternatives to storm sewers that rely on natural infiltration of storm water require less infrastructure and fewer engineering expenditures. Careful energy design can permit downsizing—or even elimination —of mechanical equipment. Construction costs can be reduced through clustering of buildings, more efficient use of materials, and waste minimization. And cost savings can accrue from more rapid construction schedules, which can result from careful front-end planning.

Although Prairie Crossing cost more to develop than conventional subdivisions in Grayslake, the developers were able to save almost $1.4 million, or $4,400 per lot, because the measures to reduce environmental impacts also reduced infrastructure costs (see "Prairie Crossing's Infrastructure Savings" on page 247). These savings were put back into the budget for amenities and enhancing common open space, thus creating making a more visually appealing community.

Prairie Crossing's Infrastructure Savings

Decreased road width (8–12 feet narrower than traditional subdivision streets)	$178,000
Elimination of paved sidewalk (except for Village area)	$648,000
Elimination of curb and gutter (except for Village area)	$339,000
Decreased storm sewer (due to natural storm water management)	$210,000
Total savings	**$1,375,000**

Source: Personal correspondence with Frank Martin of Shaw Homes, Inc., September 1996.

REDUCED OPERATING COSTS

Energy, water, maintenance, and disposal costs can all be dramatically reduced by using green design strategies. Not only will this benefit occupants, but the savings can flow directly to the bottom line by providing more net operating income for the developer/owner and leading to higher building valuation. How this can work is described in "Capturing the Value of Energy Efficiency" on page 248. This can provide one of the strongest financial arguments for green development.

A building's value relates to financing, because the building is used as collateral by the lenders. When operating costs drop, the value increases. Since loans are based on a percentage of a building's value, a building that is worth more should be able to receive a higher loan amount. While a larger loan means higher payments, these higher payments will be more than offset by the income increase resulting from efficiency improvements. If lenders refuse to recognize this fact and give a borrower less money than desired, at least the owner will have a higher cash flow to direct back to the building.

In undertaking energy retrofits on large commercial spaces, Kevork Derderian of Continental Offices Ltd. (COL) has found that the idea of increased building valuation has received scant attention when energy efficiency is discussed. While owners and developers often discuss the higher up-front costs for energy-efficient equipment, they tend to overlook the fact that their building can increase in value by a substantial amount. Both owners and tenants have to be convinced and

Capturing the Value of Energy Efficiency:
It's All in How You Calculate It

Eric Hafter, president of ELH Development Services in Sacramento, California, has spent years marketing energy efficiency to both the public and private sectors, for both new and existing buildings. Hafter considers investing in energy efficiency "one of the best decisions around." Yet while most companies that market energy investments use "payback calculations" as the selling point, Hafter argues that payback is the wrong focus. Rather, he suggests that investing in energy efficiency is a financial question that should be presented in financial terms. "Financiers look for things they can understand," he says.

Hafter reasons that since an asset's value is determined by using the prevailing cap rates (the rate —expressed as a percentage—at which a future income flow is converted into a present-value figure) and the building's cash flow, savings from energy efficiency have an immediate impact, not just after the payback period. The cash flow from a project, along with the cap rate, determine the building's value through the following formula:

$$\text{Building value} = \frac{\text{net operating income}}{\text{cap rate (\%)}}$$

For example, assume a cap rate of 10 percent. If a building's annual net operating income (NOI) is $100,000 (net of expenses but before taxes and loan payments), the capital value of the building is $1 million ($100,000/ 0.10). Assume further that a $40,000 energy retrofit will save $10,000 per year in operating costs. Simple payback calculations suggest a four-year payback (often beyond the threshold of facility managers). The $10,000-per-year savings, however, starts the first year and continues far beyond the "payback period." Assuming all other items (rent and nonenergy expenses) stay the same, the building's annual income jumps to $110,000. At the same 10 percent cap rate, this changes the building's value to $1,100,000—an increase of $100,000. The change itself can be calculated:

$$\frac{\text{Change in NOI}}{\text{cap rate.}} = \frac{10,000}{10} = \$100,000 \text{ increase in value}$$

By increasing the building's value by $100,000, this $40,000 investment provides a 250 percent return on investment! Further, if the retrofit is financed over seven years at 11 percent, the owners will increase their net cash flow by $1,500. Hafter says that the only risk is that you lose the tenants and have to shut the building down. "In this case, you have bigger problems than energy efficiency to deal with."

Source: Personal correspondence with Eric Hafter, ELH Development Services, December 1996.

guaranteed that energy-efficiency measures will indeed positively affect building value and cash flow.

When COL, as project manager for the MERITT Alliance, undertook energy improvements at the Continental Office Plaza in Chicago, they convinced a local bank to lend money for the energy-efficient equipment based on the projected energy savings. This 25-year-old, 130,000-square-foot building desperately needed an overhaul. It had leaky windows, used too much electric lighting, and needed new chillers. A standard energy retrofit—replacing the aging chillers and retro-fitting the lighting—was estimated to cost $419,930, or $3.29 per square foot, and to save $.47 per square foot. In comparison, the more extensive retrofit carried out by the MERITT Alliance, which included installing better mechanical equipment with variable-speed motors and an automated energy control system, cost $453,405, or $3.56 per square foot—$.27 more per square foot—but was estimated to save $.84 per square foot. The MERITT retrofit was projected to save $96,000 in annual energy costs, but actually ended up saving $110,000 annually.

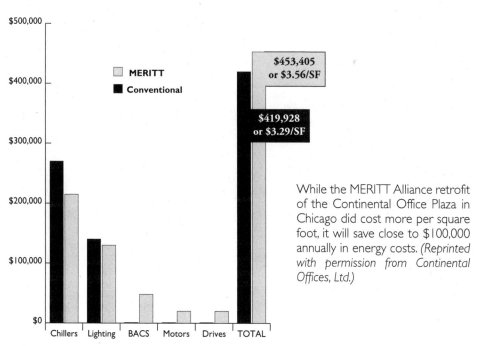

Cost Comparison
MERITT vs. Conventional

While the MERITT Alliance retrofit of the Continental Office Plaza in Chicago did cost more per square foot, it will save close to $100,000 annually in energy costs. *(Reprinted with permission from Continental Offices, Ltd.)*

The cost of the new equipment was financed by a seven-year operating lease from Northern Trust, a Chicago bank. (An operating lease means that the energy-efficient equipment becomes an operating expense, rather than a capital expenditure.) After the operating lease is paid off from the energy savings at the end of year seven, the annual energy savings of $110,000 can be applied to cash flow, as it will no longer have to be used to service the equipment lease debt. In other words, when capitalized, these savings will increase the building's value by more than one million dollars, while costing the developer nothing. And, with lower operating expenses, once the new leases are rolled over, the owner will be able to charge a higher net rent in the marketplace. With the same total occupancy costs, more money will end up in the owner's pocket.

Continental Towers IV is a 320,000-square-foot, 10-story building soon to be built by the MERITT Alliance. Integrated front-end teamwork produced a highly energy-efficient building design, for which construction cost will run less than one dollar per square foot higher than conventional construction. However, the anchor tenant was skeptical that it would actually see the reduced operating costs, which

The 10-story Continental Towers IV building, soon to be built by the MERITT Alliance, is designed to be highly energy efficient. Its construction cost will run less than one dollar per square foot higher than conventional construction, and much lower operating expenses are expected. *(Reprinted with permission from Continental Offices, Ltd.)*

were projected by COL to be 70 cents per square foot per year less than typical energy costs for comparable buildings. COL backed its projections with a stiff financial commitment, guaranteeing that the building will achieve at least half the projected savings—35 cents per square foot per year. If the building meets its projected operating savings, the tenant's total occupancy will remain as anticipated. If the building's actual savings in energy costs come in at less than 35 cents per square foot relative to comparable buildings, COL will pay the difference to the tenant. And any savings over 35 cents per square foot will be split 50/50 with the tenant.

This arrangement benefits the tenants, who get not only the operating savings, but also associated benefits such as improved occupant comfort and potential productivity increases, while paying no more than competitive market rates. Because the tenants have a triple-net lease (whereby they pay a net rent, with all operating costs and real estate taxes passed through to them as well), the building owner can charge higher than market net rent by showing tenants that their overall costs will remain the same—thus increasing the owner's cash flow and the building value.

COL's Derderian observes that saving 35 cents per square foot per year in energy costs sounds like small potatoes, but when applied to 120,000 square feet of office space, it will result in more than $40,000 in annual savings. When capitalized, this adds an additional $400,000 in value should the building be sold or refinanced.

PREFERENTIAL LEASES AND HIGHER OCCUPANCY RATES

One way to appeal to financiers is to show them how green developments can capture a market advantage or cost benefit through green design and construction. For example, in a tight market, owners/developers can charge more for space with lower operating costs. In a softer market, they can gain a market advantage by passing savings on to tenants. To date, green developments in the commercial arena have generally enjoyed higher occupancy and absorption rates because of this competitive advantage. Residential green developments have, to date, achieved acceptable absorption rates, while often garnering price premiums.

For example, 2211 West Fourth, in Vancouver, successfully charges premiums on rents, because tenants save money on utility bills thanks to the attention to energy efficiency during design and construction and the free hot water from ground-source heat pumps. Denver Dry Goods' residential component is completely rented, with a waiting list for both market-rate and affordable units. The project's success has gotten the Colorado Housing Finance Authority interested in pursuing other downtown housing projects and has inspired another 18 mixed-

use projects in downtown Denver—all financed and at full occupancy, adding 2,000 residents to this revitalizing area.

When Norm Thompson Outfitters went looking for a headquarters building in Hillsboro, Oregon, it ended up with a new building that was not only cost-effective, but also energy efficient and environmentally friendly. But the company doesn't own it; it signed a 10-year lease on a two-story, 54,000-square foot build-to-suit developed by Trammell Crow. In this case, despite the fact that Norm Thompson was driving the project, the developer was not willing to take the risk incurred through the additional capital cost for efficiency measures. The developer worked out a lease structure with its client whereby Norm Thompson will pay back the extra capital costs through higher lease rates, expecting to realize operating savings that will bring overall costs in line with other buildings in the market—at less cost to the environment.

While the building integrates many green features, Norm Thompson staff remained conscious of development costs, not wanting lease rates pushed too high. They specified that the incremental capital outlay for environmentally responsive features must pay for itself within eight years. The University of Oregon's Director of Energy Studies, G. Z. "Charlie" Brown, analyzed 20 energy-efficiency measures in four categories: lighting, HVAC, glazing, and insulation (including reflective coatings). For each, he calculated the incremental project costs, annual energy cost savings, and simple payback period. After factoring in rebates from Portland General Electric and tax credits from the state's Department of Energy, Brown found that 8 of the 20 proposed measures to reduce energy and resource use would pay for themselves within 8 years—and some as little as 4.1 years. These 8 measures were integrated into the project. Capital and operational savings were realized mainly from downsizing mechanical equipment. The project team found that the costs of using recycled materials and incorporating a native landscape were comparable to those of a standard design, but the low irrigation needs of the native landscape resulted in almost 50 percent savings, as compared with conventional practice.

Trammell Crow has benefited from its involvement with this project in many ways, according to marketing coordinator Steve Wells. Accommodating the needs of a strong tenant without putting itself at financial risk was one benefit. The company has garnered a great deal of publicity for its efforts: "Not many have yet done this, or know the issues. We have now been through a process where we had to clean the slate on old rules of thumb and learn how to do things in a different way. For example, we had to decide if a certain light is what we really wanted to use, or whether another kind of light would better meet the client's goals, instead of just assuming something would be fine. So, we successfully gained experience with energy conservation and other environmental issues by working with a high-demand client, which can only help us in the future."

REDUCED LIABILITY

Lenders do not like risky projects, yet there are many faces of risk in the building industry. These include not only projects that may seem financially shaky, but also those that involve people's health, safety, and welfare. The current litigious climate has financiers increasingly concerned, yet they have generally failed to make the connection that green developments are less risky developments because they pay closer attention to such issues as environmental protection, occupant health, and building and materials quality.

Researchers at Lawrence Berkeley National Laboratory (LBNL) have identified improperly performing heating and cooling systems as a major cause of litigation and contractor call-backs. A process called building commissioning (discussed in Chapter 9) aims to increase quality control through post-construction inspections and to put mechanical equipment in optimal working order, thus maximizing energy performance and minimizing health and safety risks. Insurers and legal experts have cited commissioning as one way to decrease the likelihood of professional liability claims.

Evaluation of residential building code compliance has shown that performance targets established by building codes are often not met in the field. Liability resulting from safety- and performance-related noncompliance is an increasing concern in the building industry. Green developers, whose products often exceed code minimums significantly, are much less likely to have liability concerns in this area.

An LBNL analysis of top-floor apartments in typical Chicago apartment buildings showed that reflective roofs, insulated attics, and natural ventilation would have greatly reduced temperatures and health risk during the intense heat waves of 1995, in which more than 700 Cook County residents died in just over five days.

As described in Chapter 1, developers and building owners have been found liable for "sick building syndrome" (SBS), which can result from pollutant emissions from building materials, mold growth caused by improperly functioning mechanical equipment, and many other (poorly understood) problems. Highly publicized lawsuits over SBS at two courthouses and a U.S. Environmental Protection Agency office building have demonstrated that this is a real concern.

The world's $1.4 trillion insurance industry is becoming increasingly concerned over the threat that climate change poses to its financial health. According to the Reinsurance Association of America, almost 50 percent of the insured losses from natural disasters over the past 40 years have occurred since 1990, including Hurricane Andrew, with insurance losses of nearly $16 billion. Other natural disasters that may stem from climate change and increase financial risk to this industry include mud slides, flooding, wildfires, urban heat waves, and agricultural damage. This possibility is gradually making the financial industry more keenly attuned to the impact of human behavior on the built and natural environment.

Selling lenders on features that decrease liability risks may strengthen chances of securing financing. Lawsuits and workers' compensation payments put financial stress on building owners that can "trickle up" to the lenders. No financier wants to be left holding the purse strings on projects in which the developer's or builder's inattention created a high-risk project down the line.

Sources of Financing

In general, green developers go after the same sources of financing as conventional developers: bank loans, venture capital, private investment, and the like. A difference, however, is that by virtue of their environmental and socially responsible features, some green developments have other opportunities available to them, ranging from whole-project financing to financing for only a portion of a project, such as energy-efficiency measures.

PUBLIC PRIVATE PARTNERSHIPS

Increasingly, partnerships between multiple players are being used to finance development and redevelopment projects that breathe life into depressed or decaying urban areas. Public-sector sources often provide financing assistance for projects that will result in some public benefit. Not-for-profit groups can also become partners and provide financing for projects that address their environmental or community-oriented values, through tax-avoidance vehicles, donations, and infrastructure assistance.

Jonathan Rose's Affordable Housing Development Corporation (AHDC) teamed up with the Denver Urban Renewal Authority (DURA) to renovate the historic Denver Dry Goods building in downtown Denver. The city had purchased the century-old building, hoping to renovate and sell it, but it had difficulty securing financing. Meanwhile, DURA was offering financial assistance to boost downtown retail, and the city was planning to locate affordable housing in Denver's suburbs. Jonathan Rose pointed out that encouraging *downtown* housing would naturally lead to more retail activity. At first, Rose was looking for infill sites rather than renovation possibilities, because of concern over potentially high remediation costs resulting from the presence of lead paint and asbestos. However, he also believed that if a renovation project was attractively located, the market would make up for those additional costs. The Denver Dry Goods building, situated in a prime downtown location, might be ideal. The partnership between AHDC and DURA to renovate the Denver Dry Goods building into a mixed-use project was born.

Prior to this project's being approved, no lending in downtown Denver had occurred in 10 years. A downtown housing task force, comprised of lenders, developers, and planners, was created to examine downtown Denver's needs and

Developer Jonathan Rose showed the city of Denver that encouraging downtown housing would naturally boost retail activity. His Denver Dry Goods renovation introduced a mixed-use project and has paved the way for several other such projects in the downtown area. *(Reprinted with permission from Hooman Aryan.)*

existing strengths. This task force paved the way for collaboration throughout the project. Together, its members created an impressive mixed-use project with three floors of retail and offices and three floors of housing that is 80 percent affordable and 20 percent market-rate.

The project developers, AHDC and DURA, divided the $35 million project into four pieces, each with a $7 to $9 million package of loans, grants, and other types of funding. The project used 23 different sources of funding, including historic and low-income tax credits and a state bond issue. Because the 23 sources of financing involved 40 attorneys and a tight time frame, Rose gave one portion of the financing document to each attorney to write up, with the understanding that each package would be reviewed by the other 39 attorneys. This emphasis on cooperation for the good of the whole expedited the paperwork, according to Rose, and resulted in each attorney's becoming invested in the vision of an affordable, mixed-use project downtown. "People got out of an antagonistic position and put aside their own interests," he said. "The process built a sense of community, because as the momentum grew, people became committed to getting the project done rather than breaking the deal."

The new headquarters of the American Association for the Advancement of the Science (AAAS) is a green building exemplary for its attention to energy efficiency, natural daylighting, avoidance of ozone-depleting refrigerants in chillers, and extensive IAQ measures. It is also one of the few new buildings to be erected in Washington, D.C., in recent years. While numerous organizations have fled the city for the booming suburbs of Maryland and Virginia, AAAS chose to stay in Washington, believing the city to be a more fitting home for this national organization. The organization's need for financial assistance resulted in a mutually beneficial partnership. Washington's city council voted to help pay for the $69 million construction project by making available to AAAS the proceeds of the sale of $52 million in low-interest, tax-exempt bonds (this is pass-through financing that does not come out of the city's regular budget). In return, AAAS hired minority contractors, offered D.C.-based firms the first shot at construction contracts, and kept more than 300 jobs within the city. Washington's Economic Development Office estimated that the city's financing assistance will save AAAS about $40 million in interest over the first 30 years of occupancy.

In Tucson, Arizona, the Civano project is building a new sustainable urban village of 2,500 homes in four neighborhoods. One goal of Civano is to demonstrate the marketability of a large-scale development blending resource efficiency and neotraditional design elements at affordable prices. In July 1996 the develop-

The energy-efficient American Association for the Advancement of Science building in Washington, D.C., obtained city financing assistance, which will save AAAS about $40 million in interest over the first 30 years of occupancy. *(Reprinted with permission, © Maxwell MacKenzie 1996.)*

ers—initially a joint venture between Case Enterprises and the British Columbia–based Trust for Sustainable Development (until Case bought out the Trust's share)—purchased the land at a state auction for the minimum bid of $2.3 million. One advantage to the developers was that 118 acres of the 916 developable acres already had approvals in place. Site development (infrastructure and landscaping) will cost about $30 million, with vertical construction costs estimated at $400 million.

Because the developers were not sure they could build resource-efficient homes, offices, stores, and community centers without pricing themselves out of the market, the city agreed to share some of the risk and is a financial partner in this privately owned development. The city recognized that Tucson could either continue its current sprawl development patterns, with the city inevitably facing higher future costs in infrastructure and services, or it could proactively direct growth into high-density, clustered development in areas where growth is already occurring.

As a financial partner, Tucson agreed to finance infrastructure costs of up to $38 million through municipal bonds. The city will also spend $3 million in city funds for off-site infrastructure improvements and the construction of Civano's primary boulevard and will direct up to $4 million in future general obligation bonds toward constructing a community center and park. Having the city as a lender means that the developers do not need to educate the banks on the benefits of compact, environmentally responsive mixed-use development. The project will also get a lower interest rate on tax-exempt financing—banks would charge a premium for the risk—while the city still gets a respectable interest rate on its loan.

In exchange, the city plans to recoup some of its investment through reduced costs for long-term water treatment, road maintenance, trash disposal, and pollution abatement. The city estimates that it will save approximately $500,000 annually in avoided costs of infrastructure by affecting demand as well as supply. Thus, if Civano works, the city's $7 million investment ($3 million for infrastructure and $4 million for community center and park) will be repaid within eight years, and the city hopes to receive an estimated annual increase in revenue of $1 million, net of operating expenses. Says project manager John Laswick, "Three million dollars sounds like a lot of money, but it can defer major political problems surrounding infrastructure, so it's worth a try." Increasing numbers of cities and counties are facing capacity shortages with water supply, sewage treatment, roads, and solid waste. For example, Pima County recently imposed an

This Tucson, Arizona, site will soon be developed as Civano, where homes are expected to sell for a premium of about $10,000 more than similar homes. *(Reprinted with permission from Community Design Associates.)*

impact fee on development on the other side of Tucson because of undercapacity of roads. To meet growing demand for water, Tucson just tapped into water from the Central Arizona Project, despite great public resistance.

Meanwhile, Civano's developers are seeking equity partners because they want the flexibility that comes with this financing. They plan to pay the first $5 million with their own funds and to seek equity partners to finance the rest on a "last in, first out" basis in which later investors can recoup their investments first. Conservative absorption schedules by third-party appraisers estimated an ROI of 30 percent.

Civano homes are expected to sell for a premium of about $10,000 over similar homes. Since the project is being financed in part through city municipal bonds, half the premium will be amortized over 25 years (through a special tax assessment paid back to the city by Civano residents), with the other half passed along to the buyer as part of the purchase price. Kevin Kelly, president of Case Enterprises, believes people will be willing to pay for the benefits that will come attached to Civano. "We've opted to sell quality homes and quality of life," he says, "so people aren't just buying a certain number of rooms, they are buying a well-designed, well-appraised house within the context of a well-designed and amenitized community. We are selling the whole community, not just the house. The best real estate and communities around the country have always been so because of how they are integrated with the rest of the community. Buyers understand that all those factors will affect the value."

Looking ahead, Kelly believes that Civano will set the standard for future development in Tucson. "When we start to show the market what is achievable at similar price points to what is available today," he said, "the consumer will start to demand this as a standard. Once that happens, other developers will be forced to build this way as it will become the expectation. I think market demand is shifting this way.... We happen to be ahead of the curve, but in three to five years we'll become the standard for Tucson."

Infrastructure construction is planned to begin in spring of 1997. Civano's grand opening, including 12 model homes and a neighborhood center, should happen late in 1997. Because Case Enterprises committed to making job creation an integral part of this sustainable community, the first actual construction happened in the environmental technology park, which broke ground in December 1996. The first client is a manufacturer of solar electric (photovoltaic) panels—a joint venture between Tucson Electric Power and a Denver R and D firm. The second commercial project will be a garden center and landscape firm, which will salvage native plants from construction sites and set up a center to teach the public about desert vegetation.

Pension Funds

Pension funds represent a huge pool of investment money and today are often the dominant equity partners in real estate ventures. A recent issue of Equitable Real Estate Investment Management's annual publication, *Emerging Trends in Real Estate 1996,* forecast that pension funds "can be expected to step up activity and focus on small- to medium-sized deals. But mortgages don't hold as much interest." While the average pension fund's share of money invested in real estate was about 4 percent in 1996, total pension fund assets in the United States totaled over $2.5 trillion, meaning that $100 billion of pension money is currently invested in real estate. Like insurance companies and investment firms, most pension funds have professional investment managers who are both extremely cautious and diversified in carrying out their fiduciary responsibility to minimize risk and maximize returns for their investors. They tend to view anything out of the ordinary as high-risk. Some pension funds, however, are influenced by their members and are more willing to venture into new territory. In general, these are locally controlled and self-directed, usually embracing the view that the overall long-term health of society falls within their fiduciary responsibility. They want their investments to benefit future generations. Such locally controlled funds are a good source of financing for green developments.

Pension funds can have a tremendous impact on the built environment once their managers recognize the financial benefits of environmentally responsible development. Bamberton, a green development on Vancouver Island in British Columbia that has undergone a long, drawn-out planning and approvals process, is being financed by $30 million (as of late 1996) from four British Columbia pension funds representing 250,000 Canadian workers. The project, initiated by the Trust for Sustainable Development (one of the original development partners in Civano), was recently sold to a development company owned by 29 pension funds. As investors and owners, these pension funds recognize that environmentally and socially responsive communities are easier to approve and will be beneficial to investors as well as to society—and thus are defensible within their fiduciary responsibility.

The 1996 book *Financing Change: The Financial Community, Eco-efficiency and Sustainable Development,* by Stephan Schmidheiny and Federico Zorraquín, reported: "Some pension funds...appear willing to stretch their interpretation of prudence to enable them to practice what has become known as economically targeted investing. These funds allocate a small portion of their portfolio to socially important areas thought too risky by others: mortgage-pools for low-cost housing,

Bamberton, a mixed-use redevelopment of an industrial site on Vancouver Island in British Columbia, is being financed by $30 million from four British Columbia pension funds. *(Reprinted with permission from William D. Browning, Rocky Mountain Institute.)*

small business loans, and so on. By September 1993 more than $23 billion had been allocated to such efforts by the 20 biggest pension funds in the United States."

DEEP POCKETS WITH SHARED VALUES

Wealthy individuals, foundations, and privately owned companies have often sought to put their money where their values are, whether by donating to causes that support such values or investing in projects that are reasonably risky but echo their beliefs.

John Clark's vision of Haymount led him to a partnership with investors who share his commitment. The W. C. and A. N. Miller Company of Washington, D.C., a third-generation family business, is well respected for building and completing high-quality communities in Virginia and Maryland since 1912. Edward J. Miller Jr., president of the Miller Company, commented in a June 1996 *Washington Post* article by Christine Mayer that Clark's "unchecked enthusiasm and dedication to his cause" helped convince his company to join the project. "He articulated it very well," recalled Miller, while adding that the deal also made a great deal of sense. "It was not the typical '80s deal—all cash, a quick settlement, and then flipping it for a lot more money. A lot of developers went out of business because of that kind of approach to the land. This opportunity was well priced."

Thus the Haymount Limited Partnership is a partnership of the John A. Clark Company and the W. C. and A. N. Miller Company. The Miller Company also found Haymount attractive because Clark was able to package the deal based on the 1,650-acre property's current $5 million value rather than its future value. Clark was able to get the land at that price by convincing George Fisher, the landowner, that Fisher could either charge more for the property at the time of sale or become a limited partner and—should the project meet or exceed its pro forma—make a great deal more money in the long run. The Miller Company realized the strength of the deal: it could purchase the land for $5 million, invest several million more in the predevelopment and approvals process, and should the project fail to get approvals, still have a viable exit strategy. If necessary, it could sell the improved land under existing zoning and still make money on the deal.

Haymount developer John Clark was able to obtain the 1,650-acre property for $5 million by convincing the landowner that he could either charge more for the property at the time of sale or become a limited partner with the potential to make a great deal more money in the long run if the project met or exceeded its pro forma. *(Reprinted with permission from William D. Browning, Rocky Mountain Institute.)*

The MacArthur Foundation, as a minority (35 percent) partner in Abacoa, a new 2,050-acre community under construction in Florida, not only provided start-up funding but also got involved in the development process in order to create a new model of environmentally sensitive development, as reflected in its land-use patterns, habitat protection, and homes intended to meet the EPA's Energy Star criteria.

Abacoa was conceived in 1993, when the MacArthur Foundation was approached by the city of Palm Beach with a proposal that they work together to produce a comprehensive development on 2,000 acres owned by the Foundation, part of 45,000 acres bequested to it as part of John D. MacArthur's $3 billion dollar endowment. This land is strategically located for future development—within Florida's growth corridor. The Foundation's initial goal was to form a team to plan the project through the approvals stage. After the project received its permits and approvals in June 1995, the Foundation had to consider whether it wanted to participate in development activity as well as being the landowner. It decided to partner with a development company that, with a two-thirds voting interest, would orchestrate the process and capture the margin, while the Foundation, with a 35 percent voting interest, would continue to safeguard the project's adherence to environmental goals, including the protection of key habitat areas.

The Trust for Sustainable Development, described earlier, which initiated both Bamberton and Civano, is thinking about going public to raise funds for environmentally responsible development. It has found that many people—ranging from wealthy individuals to average working people—want to direct their investments toward financially sound, environmentally and socially responsible projects, but lack viable alternatives. Most of the existing socially responsible investment funds today are labeled "socially responsible" because of what they *avoid,* not because of what they proactively seek out. The Trust for Sustainable Development hopes to give investors an option to put their money into something positive, helping to create a built environment that is more environmentally and socially responsible.

Appraisals—An Integral Part of the Financing Equation

Appraisals play an important role in financing. The developer depends on an appraisal high enough to finance the project adequately. Green developments today are at a disadvantage in this regard. The conventional appraisals process can pose a barrier when some of the project's benefits are not understood. Financial consultant Jean Driscoll believes that the appraisal process is "inherently biased toward the conventional." According to Driscoll, "If a property is unconventional or unusual, it is very unlikely that there will be comparables. It is thus likely that the appraisal will be discounted because the property is different, and will not capture the value of its being unconventional." Calculations for traditional loan qualifications rarely take into account differences in operating costs resulting from energy features or savings in transportation costs because of access to public transit.

Standard appraisals usually focus on the product without accounting for the economic value produced by pedestrian amenities, nearby services, higher-quality infrastructure, and other benefits currently viewed as externalities. For example, by comparing only individual housing units, appraisers give them the value they would have in conventional subdivisions without the amenities. In general, when there is a departure from the conventional subdivision plan, there will be a bias against the development if anything unconventional adds to the costs.

Sometimes, though, the appraisals process can work in favor of environmentally or community-responsive features, showing enhanced project value. One example is the neotraditional development Laguna West in Sacramento, California. Although the addition of trees, lakes, paths, and other features that architect Peter Calthorpe incorporated into the redesigned plan added $1,500 to the cost of each lot, as compared with the original plan, it also boosted each lot's appraised value by $15,000.

The Real Goods Solar Living Center in Hopland, California, is a unique building and site. Luckily, it had a sympathetic appraiser, Dean Strupp, as well as a regional lender, National Bank of the Redwoods, which had been the CEO's banker for many years. Because the building was unusual, Strupp appraised it differently than he would have a standard building and site. He did not think the usual appraisal approach was appropriate to this particular project, because it is a unique demonstration facility whose educational aspects should give it a premium value. He chose to appraise the project using the "value-in-use" model, whereby the building serves a special purpose that is applicable to a specific user, rather than the more typical "income-and-sales" approach.

Strupp thought it helped Real Goods' appraisal that the company owned the land free and clear and spent a lot of its own money developing the site, which had been purchased inexpensively with equity. Real Goods developed access to the site, upgraded it, and rezoned it from unusable commercial property sitting in a floodway and floodplain to a buildable site with only parking in the floodway (which

The appraiser for the unique Real Goods Solar Living Center in Hopland, California, chose to appraise the project using a model whereby the building serves a special purpose for a specific user, rather than using the more typical "income-and-sales" approach. *(Reprinted with permission from Jeff Oldham.)*

was permitted, if the lot remained unsurfaced). Before construction even began, Real Goods had made a large investment in the project, including lots of landscaping, which enhanced the value of the land. Although Real Goods invested about one million dollars in site development, Strupp valued it at $720,000 because he believed the creative and elegant landscaping might not be as highly valued by the next tenant.

The appraisals report avoided detailing innovative measures. In regard to innovative construction methods, alternative materials, and site development techniques, Strupp says, "The trick is to gloss over it rather than emphasize it." For example, the report did not cover the fact that Real Goods was restoring wetlands on the property. Instead, the report emphasized the company's efforts in floodplain management and avoidance of flood hazard. Strupp was also careful not to call undue attention to the straw-bale construction system employed in the building. He found out from Mendocino County's planning department that straw-bale had been approved twice before in the county. In the appraisals report, he simply described the construction method and concluded that the exterior walls would provide good protection and insulation. Rather than discussing it as an innovative, alternative building material, the report simply said that straw-bale construction is a technique that has previously been used and is permitted under Section 105 of the Uniform Building Code, which addresses alternative materials.

In appraising the building's value, Strupp characterized it as a "trophy-style retail building due to its unusual architecture." He guessed that if Real Goods were to move out, the building would be most appealing to another company that wanted a "high-profile, sexy building." For comparables, he looked at other high-end local buildings, as well as retail properties that were not highly comparable but "the best I could come up with," he said. "I just built a case for it and hoped they would buy it."

When the land on which the new community of Civano will sit was appraised, the appraisers felt that they could not accurately establish a value for land with the parameters of the Civano plan—a village with resource conservation features— because no comparables yet existed. Thus, the land was appraised at a rather low value, which reflected the view of those in Tucson's development community that developing this property was not feasible, given its location "in a relatively undeveloped section of metropolitan Tucson and the current supply of available inventory within established master-planned projects in the region." The valuation concluded that the highest and best use at the time was as an investment, to be held for later commercial and residential development. Yet after reviewing demographic and development trends, the city concluded that the combination of a nearby growing commercial market and the scarcity of developable land will enable Civano to benefit from both its location and its unique product and price range. The city observed: "The appraisal acknowledges the uncertainties involved in bringing such a new product to the market. As such, the relatively low initial valuation counterbalances these risks with a modest land cost....As with any major development project, Civano's success will call for substantial creativity, adequate financial capacity, and effective marketing."

As more green developments are built, there will be more comparables on which to base valuation for buildings that are more efficient in their use of resources or otherwise responsive to environmental and community concerns.

CREATIVE MORTGAGES THAT REWARD EFFICIENCY

There are various creative financing strategies that modify the terms of loans and can thereby help to make green building projects more feasible. While relatively new and quickly evolving, most of these opportunities are currently available to building purchasers or owners, rather than developers, but their net results can be to the developer's advantage.

ENERGY-EFFICIENT MORTGAGES

One problem with most existing mortgage programs is that they do not account for deviations from standard formulas. Because lenders want to ensure that home buyers do not borrow more money than can be repaid, they make standard assumptions about the cost of living. The maximum amount a bank will loan for a mortgage is usually determined by a formula based on salary level, assuming that a certain percentage of the home owner's salary will be needed for paying utility bills, costs of car ownership, and so on.

In recent years, however, those basic assumptions have been challenged through the "energy-efficient mortgage" (EEM), which some lenders now offer for energy-efficient homes. Lenders who offer EEMs realize that money saved on home energy costs will be available to pay a higher monthly mortgage. Thus, EEMs allow home owners to afford more expensive homes. They also provide a larger pool of qualified buyers for homes of a given value. EEMs allow banks to "stretch" prospective home buyers' qualifying debt-to-income ratio by two to four percentage points on a conventional mortgage. In real dollars, this means that if a home buyer's annual household income is $50,000, he or she can borrow an extra $11,357 on an 8% conventional mortgage (see "Understanding an Energy-Efficient Mortgage (EEM)" on page 269).

The state of Colorado's E-Star™ program is serving as a model for the nation's first market-based energy-efficient mortgage, rating, and finance program. Freddie Mac and Fannie Mae agreed to meet the Colorado Energy Mortgage Pilot Program guidelines. Both the Department of Housing and Urban Development (HUD) and the FHA, which helped develop Colorado's guidelines, agreed to underwrite loan procedures nationally. Through this program, home buyers who meet prescribed energy efficiency thresholds for new and existing homes become eligible for increased debt-to-income ratio stretches of 2 percent. Program goals include encouraging the market to use energy ratings and EEMs and ensuring that this information is conveyed to area multilisting services and appraisal data banks so appraisers will be able to use traditional comparison sales analyses in the future. Colorado's program is also encouraging realtors to urge lenders to offer EEMs. The E-Star program argues that realtors can make more money on such listings, and that lenders can gain a larger pool of qualified buyers and a competitive edge, at least until EEMs are offered more widely.

GMAC Mortgage Company, a subsidiary of General Motors Corporation and one of the largest mortgage companies in the United States, has added an E-Star incentive program to its stable of loan programs. GMAC offers various incentives to encourage participation, including ½ percent off the standard 1 percent origination fee and a free appraisal for home buyers whose new or existing homes have received an E-Star home energy rating. Loan Officer Jill Griffin explained: "From a mortgage lending perspective, E-Star is phenomenal.... We can assist our clients in qualifying for a larger home or a residence with more options and upgrades through a 2 percent EEM ratio stretch. Perhaps the biggest benefit is the fact that home owners receive an energy-efficient home which is comfortable year-round, with lower annual operating and utility costs."*

Energy-efficient mortgages support residential developers by expanding the market base for homes. This is particularly important with lower-cost housing, because the "stretch" they provide in the lender's qualifying ratio is most valuable for the first $100,000 to $150,000 of the cost. Recently built Habitat for Humanity homes in the Chicago area qualified for EEMs, which significantly increased their affordability at the lowest end of the home-buying market.

In Austin, Texas, a hotbed of green building, thanks to the Austin Green Builder Program, production builder Legend Communities, Inc., is building an affordable community called The Meadows of Walnut Creek, which will consist of 94 homes rated "three stars" out of five by the Austin Green Builder Program. Because these homes will be economical to maintain, principal Haythem Dawlett told *Urban Land,* "We even convinced lenders to allow a greater debt-to-income ratio for buyers, since their monthly utility bill will be so low."

LOCATION-EFFICIENT MORTGAGES

A study sponsored by the Natural Resources Defense Council (NRDC) found that people who live near their place of employment can realize substantial savings in transportation costs. Such savings could be applied to their housing needs, just as energy savings are through EEMs. For example, the study suggests that households near urban centers in the San Francisco Bay Area save $350 to $450 per month. If this saving was fully and reliably recognized in home mortgage underwriting as a valid equivalent to increased income, it could amortize as much as an additional $50,000 in home ownership borrowing.

The "location-efficient mortgage" (LEM), currently under development, provides one way of doing this. The LEM is designed to encourage and facilitate

---

*Reprinted with permission from *E-Star Times* (winter 1996/1997).

Understanding an Energy-Efficient Mortgage (EEM)

Here is how an EEM works for borrowers purchasing a home with a sales price of $104,000:

	EEM	Standard Loan
Lesser of Sales Price or Appraised Value	$104,000	$104,000
Mortgage Loan Amount @ 95%	$98,800	$98,800
Principal and Interest @ 8%	$725	$725
Private Mortgage Insurance	$65	$65
Taxes and Insurance	$150	$150
Total Principle, Interest, Taxes, and Insurance (PITI)	$940	$940
Maximum Qualifying Debt-to-Income Ratio	30%	28%
Qualifying Income	**$37,600**	**$40,286**

(For an FHA loan, the standard ratio would be 29% instead of 28%, and the EEM stretch ratio would become 31% instead of 30%. The mortgage loan amount would be 97% instead of 95%.)

Here's how an EEM would benefit a potential buyer, whose annual salary is $35,000, in purchasing a home with a 30 year loan at an 8% interest rate:

	EEM	Standard Loan
Allowable monthly payment	$875	$816
Maximum loan amount	**$119,248**	**$111,207**

Source: Reprinted with permission from *Energy Rated Homes of Colorado,* December 1996.

home ownership in transit-accessible inner-city and denser suburban neighborhoods. As areas increase in density and become transit accessible, they become more "location efficient," enabling people to drive less and to own fewer or no cars.

A partnership including the Surface Transportation Policy Project, the Center for Neighborhood Technology, and NRDC is fine-tuning an analytical model that correlates household geographical location with transportation efficiency and household transportation expenditures relative to other locations within a given metro area. The partnership is seeking to stir interest among primary and secondary mortgage market lenders in demonstrating the location-efficient mortgage. It is hoped that Fannie Mae will agree to participate as part of its announced desire to underwrite affordable mortgages.

FINANCING ENERGY EFFICIENCY

Many utility- and government-sponsored programs offer some form of financing assistance to encourage energy savings. This runs the gamut from design assistance to rebates for installing energy-efficiency measures. Some programs focus on residential sectors of the real estate industry, while others support green commercial buildings. A recent survey by the Energy Manager's Multisite Assistant On-line Service (EMMA) found that more than 170 electric, gas, and combination utilities offer some type of incentive or rebate program for their commercial customers. When considering building green, developers and architects should check with government agencies and utilities to find out what sort of incentives may be available.

THIRD-PARTY COMPANIES

Energy Service Companies (ESCOs) provide a one-stop-shopping approach to energy efficiency for existing commercial buildings. ESCOs perform energy audits, provide financing, select and install energy-saving measures, and monitor, measure, and verify energy savings. Often, they will pay the up-front costs of a retrofit and then bill the customer in installments, based on the energy savings. These payments are often guaranteed to be less than the amounts the customer would normally be paying for monthly energy bills.

The smaller ESCOs combined are currently doing about $700 million in efficiency retrofits per year, while industry giants Honeywell and Johnson Controls together carry out another billion dollars' worth of energy-efficiency work annually. A number of businesses as well as federal and state agencies also provide some funding for retrofits. But taken together, these amounts are still a drop in the bucket when compared with the money that could be spent cost-effectively, which is believed by the U.S. Department of Energy (DOE) to be $15 to $20 billion annually.

Financing is a big obstacle facing businesses and institutions in need of energy-efficient retrofits. The expected payback of these investments may not meet the required thresholds for investments (especially with publicly owned companies.) And lenders have been reluctant to provide loans for such projects because the quality of retrofits has historically been variable and the savings can be unreliable. Although the DOE estimates that there is currently a need for about $100 billion in capital to conduct cost-effective energy retrofits in the public- and commercial-building sectors, the actual funding level is only enough to retrofit about 5 percent of the buildings a year.

However, this situation may change. Under the Clinton Administration, DOE is working to create a secondary market for energy efficiency in partnership with a number of public and private entities. Such a market would allow anyone with a potential stream of energy savings—whether a utility, hospital, corporation, or government agency—to recover its investment in energy improvements immediately, freeing up capital for other reinvestment purposes while enjoying the many benefits that efficiency can provide.

This market would work like the secondary market for home mortgages. In that market, millions of dollars of individual mortgages are aggregated. An average default rate is assigned to the loans, and the portfolio can then be sold to a secondary market. Working with large financing volume and standardizing the procedures will control risk, which is important in allaying fears in the financial markets about the quality and reliability of efficiency retrofits. To address market uneasiness with buying back streams of savings and reselling them, DOE has launched a national monitoring and verification protocol involving the major national organizations that represent utilities, public utility commissions, state energy offices, government agencies, and energy professionals. Already widely adopted, the North American Measurement and Verification Protocol creates consensus among building owners, contractors, and lenders about how energy-efficient equipment should be installed and maintained and how its performance should be monitored.

By summer 1996, this protocol had been enthusiastically received by Wall Street financial institutions and major bond credit-rating agencies, which see its potential for expanding their business into the thousands of buildings currently requiring retrofits. The World Bank used the protocol as an important component of two energy-efficiency loans to Russia totaling $350 million, and the Chicago Board of Education is issuing $870 million in city-backed general obligation bonds to build or retrofit city schools and will use the protocol to help ensure high and reliable levels of savings. The DOE hopes to encourage and foster a secondary market for energy and water efficiency with an initial minimum contract size of $20 to $30 million and to build on the enthusiasm of major financial institutions to obtain an initial market volume in 1998 of perhaps a half-billion dollars, increasing to $5 billion annually by the turn of the century.

Greg Kats of DOE notes: "The particularly compelling thing about energy efficiency is that in the public and commercial sectors alone there is over $100 billion worth of potential efficiency investments with internal rates of return on the order of 20 to 25 percent. The fact that those investments are not being made is one of the largest market failures of our economy. You're talking a net of about 40,000 jobs per year and 6,000 permanent jobs per billion dollars put into energy efficiency! The point is that lack of funding for energy efficiency represents a huge market failure. The secondary market mechanism would help answer this problem by providing a large and relatively low-cost source of funds for energy efficiency."*

Some wonder whether this system might limit creativity and whole-systems thinking by prescribing fixed solutions to energy efficiency needs. DOE staff do not feel that this is a concern. Reducing the cost of efficiency, they suggest, will encourage new and better technologies by establishing industry consensus on "best practices" regarding options for implementing energy-efficiency measures. Creativity should not be stifled. And this type of program demonstrates that creating reliable market-based mechanisms for funding efficiency is a high priority for the federal government.

UTILITY COMPANIES AND ENERGY FINANCING

Utility companies have played a very active role in financing energy improvements through a wide range of *demand-side management* (DSM) programs. The basic reasoning behind DSM is that it is more cost-effective for both utility companies and their customers if these companies invest in energy conservation instead of having to build new generation capacity. At a peak in the early 1990s, utilities were spending as much as $3 billion per year on residential and commercial DSM projects, though many of those programs have been eliminated or downsized with deregulation of utility companies and more competitive pricing structures. DSM programs in some areas still offer developers an opportunity to finance either additional front-end design work or incremental costs of installing the highest-efficiency equipment.

B.C. Hydro, one of Canada's largest utility companies, shifted to an aggressive DSM focus after citizens expressed strong disapproval of a proposed huge new dam. The company's Power Smart division has used a variety of incentive and customer education programs to help the utility reach its goal of avoiding the need to build the planned dam while ensuring that customers have adequate services. In

*Reprinted with permission from the U.S. Department of Energy.

addition to a mix of appliance rebates and assistance with energy-efficiency improvements in residential retrofits, B.C. Hydro has reached out to the building industry—architects, developers, builders, and commercial building owners. The utility offers design consultation and building simulation services to help improve the energy design of commercial and industrial buildings. If a developer (or owner) agrees to employ some or all of B.C. Hydro's recommended strategies to reduce a building's energy load, the utility will award rebates or make incentive payments. For example, a $42,000 (Canadian) rebate was paid to the University of British Columbia for energy-efficiency measures included at the C. K. Choi Building. And the Crestwood Corporate Centre received $207,560 for design assistance and additional efficiency measures at its Building No. 8 in Richmond, British Columbia.

Financing Open Space Protection and Stewardship

Throughout much of the country, large parcels of farmland, woodland, and other open space are being turned into subdivisions, either because farming is just too hard or the profits from selling out are too attractive. Protecting some of the nation's remaining open space, important habitats, and wildlife corridors is a key priority of many green developments. Fortunately, there are many strategies being used successfully to finance the protection of some of these lands.

In fiscally difficult times, funding of open space becomes more problematic for government and charitable organizations. However, some interesting tools have emerged that make this easier, including conservation easements and the establishment of open-space acquisition funds based on transfer taxes, sales taxes, or bond issues. On Martha's Vineyard, a real estate transfer tax has provided the Land Bank with more than $20 million to buy and protect open space. Collaborative efforts between conservation organizations, businesses, and government entities can be very effective in protecting large and ecologically significant lands while also benefiting investors, landowners, and neighbors.

Spring Island's 1,000-acre nonprofit Trust is supported by a 1.5 percent fee on the initial sale of each lot and 1.0 percent on each subsequent resale. Unfortunately, in their haste to create the Trust, the developers set it up as a 501(C)(4) rather than a 501(C)(3). This means that the Trust itself can get tax

Crestwood Corporate Centre Building No. 8 received $207,560 from British Columbia Hydro for design assistance and additional efficiency measures. *(Reprinted with permission from Teresa Coady, Bunting Coady Architects.)*

breaks, but not those who donate to it. Although Spring Island sales are strong, this condition could prove problematic, as people are less likely to donate additional funds when they do not receive tax breaks.

As environmentally sensitive lands have become more scarce, a number of environmental organizations have begun pursuing partnerships with developers. Land protection accomplished through limited development is increasingly recognized as a mutually beneficial means of safeguarding important lands. The Nature Conservancy, the Conservation Fund, and the Trust for Public Lands have all played major roles in creatively engineering agreements that preserve open space and sensitive habitat, while also practicing sound business strategy.

The Nature Conservancy (TNC), established in 1951, is one of the premier real estate companies in the country—a *conservation* real estate company. It often uses a joint venture strategy or acts as a broker, purchasing critical land and holding it until a concerned constituency, ranging from local citizen groups or municipalities to the U.S. National Park Service, can come up with the purchase capital. TNC has protected more than nine million acres since its establishment and manages three million acres in its preserves, the largest private conservation holding in the United States.

TNC's Conservation Buyer Program matches conservation-minded people with appealing, ecologically valuable land in western states. It offers an opportunity to acquire and retain land ownership while working in partnership with the Conservancy to preserve the property in perpetuity. Conservancy scientists work with real estate brokers and willing sellers to identify properties that have high ecological value. The properties are placed in a Conservation Buyer Property Database, which lists TNC's portfolio of properties throughout the West. Buyers of these properties agree to protect the land by entering into a permanent conservation easement that limits development and specifies uses of the property that are compatible with mutually agreed-upon conservation objectives.

Sometimes this program can lead to land protection beyond property lines by encouraging the protection of neighboring properties. For example, a Conservation buyer's purchase of a 3,600-acre Wyoming ranch was the catalyst for permanent protection of four adjoining properties covering 5,000 acres. Conservation buyer transactions can be structured in many different ways, some of which may generate significant tax benefits.

The Nature Conservancy is delving deeper into the limited development concept in the Davis Mountains, in west Texas. TNC has obtained an option on 33,000 acres of the McIvor Ranch. The McIvors, who have owned this ecologically unique ranch for more than 110 years, have practiced "exceptional land management" (according to TNC) and have offered to sell the majority of their 40,000-acre ranch to TNC. The Conservancy sees this as an "incredible opportunity to leverage the ranch's protection into a landscape-scale private conservation initiative, turning the tide from subdivision of ranch land and disruption of key ecological process toward supporting and enhancing the existing strong land ethic of ranchers in West Texas."

The McIvor Ranch encompasses part of a 1,400-square-mile mountain island area, which provides critical habitat for almost 100 plant and animal species that are endangered, threatened, rare, or sensitive. To protect a core 10,000 acres of critical, high-elevation habitat, TNC is marketing six contiguous 3,000-acre lots to Conservation buyers. These lots come with a predetermined building envelope and restrictions, as well as conservation easements that will provide a buffer around the preserve. Selling these lots will cover TNC's purchase of the McIvor Ranch ($10.3 million) and establish a $1.3 million endowment for perpetual stewardship. In addition, the owners of the six tracts will, through a Landowners Association consisting of TNC and themselves, have an ownership interest in a 4,075-acre common area.

Environmental organizations are also working to protect open space and affordable housing. The Conservation Fund, based in Alexandria, Virginia, was established with the purpose of bringing pragmatic solutions to the landscape by balancing conservation values with economic returns. The Fund worked hard on Aspen Village, near Aspen, Colorado, not only to preserve open space on the bulk of an 879-acre tract, but also to preserve a 150-unit mobile home park as affordable housing for local residents in one of the highest-priced land markets in the country. Landowners Armand and Celeste Bartos wanted to sell their mobile home park to its residents, who had been renting for many years, and to preserve the rest of their land as open space and ranching land. By partnering with the Conservation Fund, they were able to make their dream come true, as well as the dreams of the many new home owners of Aspen Village.

The Fund first purchased the property at a deep discount, thanks to the Bartos's vision for the land and its people, and created a conservation plan for it. Two years of work followed with project partners including Pitkin County, wildlife experts, the Aspen Valley Land Trust, and the Aspen Village Homeowners Association. The 33.7-acre trailer park was subdivided into 150 individual mobile home pads, and the subdivision was then sold to the Homeowners Association. Pads were then resold to residents through transactions approved by the local housing authority to protect affordability while also raising money to fund the Homeowners' Association. The vast majority of the property was downzoned, at the Fund's request, from an already-approved 14-unit subdivision, to a permit for just one residence within a small building envelope. That will better protect the landscape as well as deer and elk migration corridors. An endowed conservation easement, which guaranteed open space and wildlife protection on 828 acres and preserved existing agricultural uses, was then conveyed to the local Aspen Valley Land Trust.

This was another win-win situation. The Bartoses benefited from the tax advantage, as well as from the assistance they received in taking the project through the approvals process and developing creative land conservation strategies that addressed their values and vision. The Conservation Fund got its money back upon the resale of the land and also made some money, which went back into its revolving fund to purchase more projects in the future. And the mobile home park residents, as well as the resident deer and elk population, have a permanent place to call home.

The Trust for Public Lands (TPL) is another key player in land conservation, generally moving land from private to public ownership. It specializes in offering landowners conservation easements and other means of land conservation. TPL is involved with the Santa Lucia Community Preserve being developed by the Rancho San Carlos Partnership. The project's developers plan to donate 90 percent of its 20,000 acres to the Santa Lucia Conservancy, a TPL affiliate. Will Rogers, vice president of TPL, calls the project's vision "a model for private sector land development."

Along with these nationally recognized organizations are some 900 local, regional, and statewide land trusts that are protecting farmland, woodlands, and open space throughout the United States. The Vermont Land Trust (VLT), for example, has protected more than 100,000 acres of land since its founding in 1977—more than 2 percent of that small state. While some of these lands have been purchased outright, most have been protected through the donation or purchase of development rights. In some cases deals are worked out with developers for the VLT to acquire development rights on a significant portion of a given parcel, while still permitting low-impact development to proceed on a portion of it. Once development rights are sold or donated to VLT, that land will always remain as open space or farmland.

Conclusion

Even the best, lowest-impact development ideas are just that—ideas—unless they can be turned into successful projects. That usually necessitates obtaining financing. Financing remains one of the biggest challenges to green developments today. Green developers have to work with the same financial institutions that are working with conventional developers. They have to play by the same rules of pro formas, return on investment, and risk avoidance.

Despite these challenges, green development is moving ahead as a growing sector in the real estate industry. Developers like Jonathan Rose and Harold Kalke are proving that development projects can be good for the environment, good for the community, and good for the bottom line, all at the same time. Over time, green development will change from being something different that takes more effort to finance, to being the norm. In fact, many of the elements of green development featured in this book may soon become *requirements* for financing, because they help to assure the long-term financial viability of a project. Perhaps one day it will be the "conventional" developments that struggle to secure financing, while the green developers drive around in limousines—albeit renewably fueled, super-efficient limos!

Turner Construction built the 44,572-square-foot Southern California Gas Company's Energy Resource Center in Downey. Turner was part of the team from the beginning of the process, offering help in considering the end use of the project and minimizing the costs. *(Reprinted with permission, © Milroy/McAleer.)*

CHAPTER 9

Construction

TURNER CONSTRUCTION IS A 90-YEAR-OLD COMPANY with a brand new mission: "To be the recognized industry leader in sustainable construction." The single largest building contractor in the United States, Turner is employing cutting-edge strategies on its wide-ranging, primarily commercial-scale projects to improve overall energy performance, reduce natural resource consumption, and lessen impacts on the environment.

At Turner, teamwork is key to achieving these goals. The company encourages developers and owners to form a team with its staff early in the development process, so that ideas for ecologically responsible building practices can be shared and a whole-systems approach to design and construction can be taken. By getting involved early in project planning, Turner can help the design team consider the end use of the project and minimize the costs and impacts of the building's location on the site. For example, the company submits ideas for minimizing earth moving and disturbance of the vegetation and topography.

Turner offers design and preconstruction services in order to help the design team source and evaluate green building materials, select energy-efficient building and mechanical systems, and conduct life-cycle assessment of products and technology choices. With annual construction projects worth about $2.8 billion, Turner also has the leverage to influence building product manufacturers and distributors to increase the availability of green products.

During construction, Turner requires subcontractors to sign contracts agreeing to carry out job-site recycling of waste. Turner's project supervisors ensure that all subcontractors comply with their agreements. According to Ian Campbell, Turner's Director of Sustainable Construction, waste management represents only a small percentage of project costs, but a well-managed recycling program will save money without costing any more. Says Campbell, "It's small, but every penny counts because profit margins are so narrow in the construction industry."

In addition to hundreds of thousands of dollars in savings through job-site recycling, Turner has reaped the benefits of widespread media attention for its environmental initiatives. "The bottom line for the company is we make money by differentiating ourselves in the market," asserts Campbell. The new focus on sustainable construction practices is an opportunity to tap a growing demand for green development. While in some cases Turner has taken the initiative to promote environmentally responsible design and construction to developers, on other projects, clients interested in green development have been drawn to Turner because of its reputation. Beyond making money, says Campbell, "it's the right thing to do." Campbell and many other Turner employees and senior management bring their "passion and values" to their new mission. Campbell is working with staff in all of Turner's 36 offices across the United States to educate and encourage both top-down and bottom-up investment in greener building practices. On a corporate level, the company is committed to providing quality service and quality products, and it believes that offering greater energy efficiency and improved indoor air quality are key to delivering quality buildings.

Campbell describes Turner's green construction approach as a learning experience. Project by project, Turner is strengthening its commitment to environmentally responsible construction, says Campbell. While it continues to forward these goals within its own company, Turner also believes it is its responsibility to lead the industry. Ed diTomas, the company's chief engineer, has stated, "We'll set the standards, because right now, there are no standards."

Construction is the stage in which all the visions, planning, and designs for a development are brought to fruition. Buildings that existed only on paper or in computer come into being. This is an exciting, but also high-risk, stage of development, and "doing it green" can be seen as adding one more element of risk or challenge. Even the best-laid plans of a green designer can fail if construction is done in an uninformed or irresponsible manner. While Turner is setting a good example in the construction industry, most of the rest of this $800-billion-a-year industry often lacks the knowledge, skills, or incentives to practice environmentally responsible development.

This chapter provides an overview of environmentally responsible construction practices. By the time a project gets to the construction stage, most of the environmental impacts are largely determined. Nonetheless, there are numerous opportunities during construction to help make a project more environmentally responsible and safer for its builders and future occupants. Areas to consider include purchasing of materials, minimizing site disturbance, ensuring workers' and occupants' health, using materials and resources efficiently during construction, minimizing and carefully managing construction waste, and making sure buildings perform as designed and built.

Construction Team Management

Experience has shown that successful green developments exhibit a combination of demonstrated leadership, emphasis on teamwork, and detailed verbal and written guidelines during the construction phase of development.

The project driver, as always, has a key role during this stage. He or she may also be the overall driver of the project (the owner, developer, or project architect) or may be someone delegated to manage construction, such as the owner's representative. This role requires frequent and clear communication with key players (including subcontractors and consultants) and conscientious supervision of construction practices and materials substitutions. A project may not succeed without the full cooperation of construction team members.

COMMUNICATION

If construction workers are made aware of how their piece of the puzzle fits into the whole project scope—especially green aspects of it—they will tend to work more cooperatively. Otherwise, they may resolve problems with an eye only on meeting schedules and containing costs, but not helping to fulfill the overall vision.

Tom Hoyt, president of McStain Enterprises, one of Denver's top production home builders, discovered that architects and owners may not be aware of problems that can arise during construction as a result of their designs or materials choices. On one of his projects in Boulder, subcontractors were required to use a drywall product selected for its environmental features. However, those who specified the product did not realize that it had an inadequate distribution network and was hard to install, leading to costly delays.

For these reasons, Jonathan Rose, developer of Denver Dry Goods and Second Street Studios, recommends including contractors as early as possible in the development process. He tells of one meeting at which the architect was reviewing preliminary design ideas, when a contractor suggested that simply altering the room dimensions slightly would eliminate the need for trimming framing lumber and drywall, thus saving time and money and reducing waste.

Design/build teams, like those Rose uses, make it easy to include contractors in the goal-setting and design process. The public bidding process adds more complications, but there are still ways to bring contractors in early. On public bid projects, Rose invites selected contractors to participate in meetings before contracts are awarded. These contractors will understand the project better, and so may stand a better chance of being awarded the contract. Rose has also paid contractors a fee to participate in the prebid design process. Even if they do not win the bid, they will benefit by gaining a better understanding of green development, and the team will benefit from the contractor's knowledge and insight.

Whether or not contractors are included in the early stages, they must be made aware of the vision for the whole project and the requirements of the design. On a bid project, it is unlikely that the construction team will have been involved in the design stages, so a kickoff meeting is advised, bringing the general contractor and all subcontractors together to explain the project's goals and guidelines before ground is broken. At the Audubon Headquarters renovation in New York City, the design team hosted several informal preconstruction meetings to educate contractors and solicit their support in making the project a model of sustainability.

Through clear communication and training, workers can be initiated into the hows and whys of green construction practices. At the new San Francisco Main Library, project architect Anthony Bernheim participated in weekly meetings with the contractor, consultants, and subcontractors to identify upcoming construction issues, paying particular attention to indoor air quality. He believes it is crucial to hold such meetings frequently to ensure the integrity of a building's whole design —and it seems to have worked. The library opened on April 18, 1996, at 11:00 A.M.

Cooperation Instead of Competition

In master planned developments and subdivisions, individual builders or contractors often compete on the same price points within each stage of the development. This may work well within a conventional project, but does not further the goals of a green development, because it may set up the project's builders as direct competitors, rather than as competitors with builders in other developments. Developer John Clark is pursuing a two-pronged strategy to foster "collaboration within—competition without." Clark believes that marketing dollars are better spent creating a cohesive marketing strategy for the entire community rather than having individual builders differentiate themselves within the development. Haymount's development company provides centralized marketing to give home buyers a feeling for the entire community. At the same time, builders do not compete on the same price points in any given phase. Rather, each rotates the types of homes they build so that they will never be building the same product at the same time as another builder. Each will have a chance to build at different price points over time.

At 11:30 a librarian approached Bernheim and remarked, "The staff was skeptical about indoor air quality, but the air in our space is wonderful!" When she saw him 10 days later, she was quick to tell him that librarians were still pleased with the air quality.

If the construction team members understand why certain materials and techniques are being used and if they have a grasp of the whole design, they are more likely to work actively toward improving the end product. When Turner Construction was hired by Southern California Gas Company to build its new Energy Resource Center, Turner clearly bought into the vision. The construction company went beyond compliance with a Memorandum of Understanding that put in writing its commitment to helping make this a green project. Turner found opportunities to make the project even greener while gutting the existing building for renovation. It reused existing electrical conduit, as well as wood that was salvaged from a building destroyed by the 1989 San Francisco earthquake. Although these ideas required change orders, they were acclaimed as improvements to the project.

By recycling its office building, the Energy Resource Center saved $3.2 million over conventional construction. *(Reprinted with permission, © Mike Marshall, Southern California Gas Company Energy Resource Center.)*

TRAINING

On Dewees Island®, developer John Knott requires potential builders to undergo 40 hours of education on green construction in general, as well as on the Dewees Island Architectural and Environmental Design Guidelines, which established a wide range of required procedures. Builders who complete the seminars are placed on Dewees Island's Preferred Builder List, which home owners are encouraged to use (see "Dewees Island Builder Program" on page 286).

The most notable and wide-ranging example of a training program in green construction is the Austin Green Builder Program in Texas. Participating builders can apply the Austin Green Builder rating system (which awards one to four stars) to their houses and use that information in marketing. Associate members, including architects, engineers, tradespeople, suppliers, and consultants, can also attend training programs.

Members of the Austin program receive two books: the *Green Building Guide,* which describes specific options for various green building techniques and strategies keyed to the program's point system, and the *Sustainable Building Sourcebook*, which offers practical guidance and information, including extensive resource listings for materials, specialized services, and professionals. The Green Builder Program sponsors regular conferences and seminars, including a monthly series offered by a spin-off group called the Sustainable Building Coalition.

Although a considerable investment of time is needed to learn new techniques, contractors who are involved with green building projects stand to benefit greatly by developing skills that differentiate them from competitors. Says manager Doug Seiter, "Clearly builders see the marketing potential for green homes in Austin—a testament to the program's ability to get beyond the custom home market and to tap into the area's production builders."

SUPERVISION

Many designers never see the small, but often significant, differences between blueprints and a completed building. Some modifications that are not visible once the building is completed can have a big impact. Moreover, once the walls are sealed, it may be impossible to tell whether specified construction procedures were followed—for example, whether proper damp-proofing and drainage were provided on foundation walls, insulation was installed and sealed properly, or windows were properly sealed before trim was installed. All too often, haste or ignorance leads contractors to cut corners or misunderstand instructions. That is why on-site supervision is so important.

The Sustainable Building Technical Manual, produced by Public Technology, Inc. (PTI), suggests that while meetings should be held with all subcontractors before they begin work, it is also critically important to carry out regular monitoring, inspection, and supervision throughout the construction process.

Tom Hoyt of McStain Enterprises finds that combining supervision with demonstration gets results. He once discovered that the HVAC contractor was not sealing joints in ductwork, arguing that it made no difference to performance. Hoyt ran tests on the system to demonstrate that the resulting leaks would compromise both energy efficiency and air quality. Once the installer understood the importance, all the joints were sealed.

Ideally, all projects should have an on-site construction manager or owner's representative who ensures that the owner's and designers' vision is carried out. The construction manager's tasks include making sure that the right people are

Dewees Island Builder Program

On Dewees Island, developer John Knott and his team have taken a proactive approach to educating builders and architects. Those interested in building on Dewees are required to attend an education seminar to learn how to design and build in a more environmentally responsive way. Training does not stop there; before a construction crew begins work on a new home on the island, Knott arranges an on-site lunch to introduce them to Dewees' approach to minimizing the impacts of construction.

(Photograph reprinted with permission from the Island Preservation Partnership.)

Beyond green construction techniques, Knott shares the broad environmental and social impacts of construction. "Teach principles," says Knott. "Teach the why—empower people to use their inherent values and wisdom to innovate and bring new ways to others." Knott has found that once the people doing the building understand and buy into the goals, they will take more responsibility and pride in the outcome—"You get a great response."

While inspiration and education are key, detailed restrictions and guidelines for Dewees Island mandate numerous strategies and policies for environmental protection. Trees that have to be removed from a building site, for example, must be transplanted rather than cut. The permanent impact arena (house, building footprint, and driveway) is limited to 7,500 square feet. Areas temporarily disturbed during construction must be reclaimed. Construction waste must be separated for recycling. (Reuse of construction waste has provided numerous free resources for building and landscaping projects.) All cleaning and maintenance of construction machinery and other polluting activities must take place at the Public Works washdown/containment area on the island.

Contractors are required to put up a $5,000 cash bond or letter of credit to assure protection of the island's environment and wildlife from impacts of equipment, improper waste storage, and accidents. A representative of the island's Architectural Resources Board inspects building sites weekly and levies fines for infractions on the construction site.

While ensuring that the environmental goals of Dewees Island are honored, the development team has also been proactive in establishing strong relationships between suppliers, architects, and builders—both to educate and to influence broader change.

on-site with the proper resources to do the job, and inspecting construction quality. To do this the manager must understand the building's design features, particularly any that are integrated or unconventional. Jonathan Rose comments that the owner's manager is key. "Someone needs to be watching," he says. "All one has to do is to open up a wall built by someone else to find gaps. An owner's rep would ensure it was well insulated."

While supervision and inspection of work may seem burdensome or costly for the contractor, managers usually save more money than they cost by preventing the need for corrections and repairs at the end of the job. As Anthony Bernheim says, "You pay for it at the beginning, or you pay for it at the end." For the owner, it assures quality—you get what you pay for—and helps avoid delays that could result from corrections down the line.

Putting It in Writing

Good verbal communication and visual inspection, while extremely important, are not substitutes for clear, detailed written instructions. It is rare that a contractor actively seeks initiatives to improve a project's performance (despite the notable exceptions described in this chapter). The typical contractor's goal is to maximize profit by building to the requirements set forth in the construction guidelines and specifications in the minimum time and at the minimum cost possible. One of the best ways to encourage contractor participation in improving building performance is through the profit motive, using "carrots" such as bonuses and performance-linked payments. The other approach, using penalty clauses and performance bonds, is also effective and more commonly used.

Guidelines and Contracts

Voluntary or mandatory guidelines for green construction may be written for an individual building, a development, a town, or a larger region. They can cover a wide range of issues. The guidelines for the Southern California Gas Company's Energy Resource Center (ERC) project defined the responsibilities of all members of the project team, including the owner, the designers, and the contractors. Malcolm Lewis, P.E., a vice president of the company overseeing the final check of the building, recommends that guidelines for the construction team's responsibilities should include understanding the design intent, selecting qualified subcontractors, making a commitment to sustainability, cooperating with commissioning (described later in this chapter), and complying with codes. The guidelines for the ERC included intermediate targets and goals and were accompanied by a description of the plan to monitor the process.

The benefit of guidelines is that they do not necessarily have to specify to the letter what must be done. Creative solutions to problems should be encouraged as long as these do not compromise overall performance.

Guidelines may be incorporated into the specifications or into the construction contracts. In planning their own office renovation, architects and planners Veazey Parrott & Shoulders wrote project guidelines into the foreword of the specs document. The guidelines described the approach to green building that the firm advocates. The guidelines and the green features of the building were well publicized in the advertisement for bids. This is unusual, but it helped bring contractors to the project who were willing to take the project's goals to heart. Mike Shoulders, a partner in the firm, says that the architects also kept a careful eye on the construction work to make sure the contractors had the right idea, particularly since this was the building they were going to work in.

To ensure that all principles adopted during the design process were respected during construction and operation, the team for the Crestwood Corporate Centre in Richmond, British Columbia, developed a set of Quality Assurance Guidelines. Each member of the team developed guidelines for his or her own portion of the work. These covered site issues, building envelope elements, and installation of mechanical and electrical equipment. The guidelines applied to both the construction and operational phases of the project.

More specific instructions can also be written into contracts. At a project in King County, Washington, the general contractor, Turner Construction Company, wrote waste separation requirements into each subcontractor's agreement. When metal and other garbage contaminated a bin for drywall waste, the site superintendent was able to require those responsible to sort this refuse out again. The workers learned to recycle.

SPECIFICATIONS

Specifications (specs) prescribe a project's standards in such matters as selection and quality of materials, installation procedures, administrative protocols, and site controls. When a project includes unusual or innovative practices or requirements, it is especially important to have well-defined specs.

Specs can cover such issues as product choices, procedures for product substitutions and design changes, waste management requirements, protection of plants and wildlife on-site, clearing of the site during construction, dust and erosion control, handling of materials, and on-site cleaning and maintenance procedures.

As discussed later in this chapter, substitutions are sometimes unavoidable, but inappropriate changes can seriously compromise building performance and environmental characteristics. It is very important to know ahead of time exactly what is acceptable and what is not. The product options section of the specs should clearly outline criteria for substitutions. Wood can be required to come from a certified well-managed source, materials can be required to be nontoxic and/or zero-VOC emitting, and so on. Vague terms like "low-emissivity glazings" can mean anything from a double-glazed window with an low-e film and an R-

Development of the Veazey Parrott & Shoulders building involved detailed specs covering, for example, the use of low-VOC paints and carpets. A partner's office featured here has undyed natural wool carpeting, installed using the no-VOC Shaw Advantage system. *(Reprinted with permission, © Fred Reaves, Light and Ink.)*

value of less than 3 to an R-10 center-of-glass superwindow. In specs, one often sees the words "or equal." This phrase needs particular scrutiny to prevent unacceptable choices.

The specs used for the Veazey Parrott & Shoulders building were very detailed, covering, for instance, the use of low-VOC paints and carpets, countertops with nontoxic adhesives, high-performance heating and air-handling systems, high-efficiency lighting systems with motion sensors, a rooftop ice-storage system for off-peak electric cooling, and the separation, recycling, and reuse of materials.

CHANGE ORDERS

Projects that fall short on front-end planning may find themselves paying for it later through change orders that result from design flaws or the unavailability of specified materials.

When E SOURCE, an energy-efficiency information firm that is a subsidiary of Rocky Mountain Institute, decided to move into new office space in Boulder, Colorado, the staff worked with the building owner to make certain that their new offices would reflect the firm's mission. When E SOURCE came on the scene, the building under way was a typical speculative office project whose design was 90 percent complete. E SOURCE signed a seven-year lease as the anchor tenant on condition that the development team would work with E SOURCE staff to increase the building's energy efficiency. While total energy consumption was successfully reduced by more than one-third from original projections, the new owner also paid a premium price for upgrades that were implemented as change orders. According to E SOURCE, the cost of change orders was the biggest impediment to improving the project's resource efficiency late in the design process. Change orders resulted from doing the redesign *after* the contract for the core and shell had been awarded. Actual costs exceeded change-order estimates by about 50 percent as a result of complications in procurement and installation.

On the other side of the coin, thoughtful planning can often, though not always, head off the need for change orders. Developer Harold Kalke claims that his mixed-use project at 2211 West Fourth Avenue, in Vancouver, had fewer change orders than usual because the preconstruction work on specs and designs was so thorough.

The Real Goods Solar Living Center in Hopland, California, incurred a greater-than-average number of change orders because of subcontractors' lack of understanding about the innovative straw-bale and passive-solar design of the building. Continual refinement by the owner and architect also contributed to changes. Project manager Jeff Oldham offers this advice to minimize the need for change orders: "Write clear specs, have an on-site project manager 'with a whip,' constantly monitor progress, and train your contractors."

Sensitive Construction Practices

Issues of site preservation and indoor air quality (IAQ) are usually addressed in the planning and design phases of a development. But construction activities can have a significant impact on the site and the building. Poorly planned or managed construction procedures can result in damaged vegetation, polluted groundwater, and IAQ problems. Conscientious construction practices help avoid such problems.

SITE PROTECTION

Careful site management is vital for protecting existing trees, other vegetation, and soils—all very important considerations for a green development. During construction such practices can also result in significant cost savings to the contractor by avoiding the need to repair erosion damage and reducing the amount of after-the-fact landscaping required. In protecting vegetation, soil compaction is a very important concern; compacting the ground around trees can injure or kill the trees even if the trunks are not touched.

Strategies for protecting trees and the immediate area during site work include the following: careful selection of excavation contractors who will be attentive to these concerns; providing excavation contractors with clear specifications on protective measures (including penalty and/or incentive clauses); identifying construction vehicle parking and staging areas away from trees and other fragile areas; conducting an inventory of trees on the site prior to site work and selecting those to be protected; erecting fencing around the "drip-lines" of selected trees to keep construction equipment away from the ground under those trees, as well as away from the trunks; minimizing changes in grade on the building site; and terracing when grade changes are unavoidable. A more complete checklist of protective measures is provided in Appendix D.

The design for United Parcel Service's (UPS) new corporate headquarters on a wooded site in Atlanta called for existing trees to brush right up to the building's windows. This meant using a construction approach that would minimize disturbance to the vegetation. The construction team assembled much of the building off-site and used only a narrow staging area around the building footprint. While this approach required some redesign of the roof beams to enable large cranes to be mounted on them, the resulting increase in construction costs (3 to 5 percent) was more than made up in avoided landscaping costs. The extremely tight work site made it necessary for subcontractors to bring their equipment and materials to the work area from an off-site parking area and use cranes, elevators, and wheelbarrows to move them within the staging area. The contractor suggested this policy may have increased worker efficiency as a result of fewer trips back and forth to their trucks for supplies. The project was completed on schedule and under budget.

El Henry of Beers Construction, the general contractors for the project, commented, "UPS saved money on landscaping costs because you don't have to

Much of the United Parcel Service building was assembled off-site, and thus only a narrow staging area around the building footprint was necessary. Some redesign of the roof beams was necessary to allow large cranes to be mounted on them. (Reprinted with permission, © Brian Gassel, Thompson, Ventulett, Stainback & Associates.)

landscape what you didn't destroy." Site-sensitive construction practices were ensured by careful planning of such construction logistics as material storage and equipment access, as well as by implementing a tree-protection program that carried financial penalties for damage. The rules were violated only once; a loss of two trees resulted in fines of about $5,000 to the contractors.

Special techniques for site-sensitive construction may have to be developed in order to minimize the impact of heavy machinery. The green home-building firm Bigelow Homes has designed a special tree-removing "spatula" that minimizes damage to trees during transplanting so that large trees can be moved more successfully. The company also uses a crane to lower roofs into place when working on heavily wooded sites.

United Parcel Service's corporate headquarters saved money on landscaping costs because of the company's site-sensitive construction practices. *(Reprinted with permission, © Brian Gassel, Thompson, Ventulett, Stainback & Associates.)*

INDOOR AIR QUALITY

Construction processes create potential IAQ problems from a host of sources. These can affect the health and comfort of construction workers as well as the health of future occupants. The Occupational Safety and Health Administration (OSHA) dictates standards and practices to protect construction workers from exposure to air contaminants and respiratory irritants. However, with the exception of prohibitions against lead-containing paints and asbestos, there are few requirements for protecting building occupants from materials or construction activities that may endanger their health and comfort. Whether or not OSHA standards apply, avoiding the use of toxic or dangerous materials is almost always advantageous for workers, occupants, and everybody else.

Many aspects of construction can have IAQ impacts. Workers' health can be affected by dust and other particulates generated from carpentry, drywalling, and other construction activities. Glues, paints, and solvents emit volatile organic compounds (VOCs) into the air. Welders and gasoline or diesel generators emit combustion gases. Some of these contaminants can be eliminated by careful materials choices; others can be minimized through careful construction practices.

Architect Teresa Coady prides herself on the attention paid to IAQ issues at Building No. 8 at the Crestwood Corporate Centre in Richmond, British Columbia. Coady's specs avoided materials that would produce toxic fumes. She designed the building's HVAC system for a higher-than-normal rate of air exchange. The construction documents also guided the crews in specific practices to protect the building's air quality for future occupants.

During her weekly site visits, Coady inspected the project for potential IAQ problems. She made sure that ductwork was sealed to keep out the airborne dust

Architect Teresa Coady kept a close eye on the construction of Building No. 8 at the Crestwood Corporate Centre in Richmond, British Columbia, to ensure that indoor air quality was not compromised. *(Reprinted with permission from Teresa Coady, Bunting Coady Architects.)*

and VOCs generated during construction. She made sure polyethylene vapor retarders were installed before drywall installation began, so as to avoid potential moisture problems in the building and contain dust. The American Lung Association cites mold and mildew resulting from indoor moisture as one of the most significant causes of IAQ problems and "sick building syndrome." One benefit of fiberglass insulation is that it does not absorb water. However, it does attract dust. If drywalling begins before a vapor retarder is installed, dust from the drywall will adhere to fiberglass insulation, readily absorbing moisture. In a wet climate like that of the Pacific Northwest, it is especially important to avoid materials that may trap moisture in the walls of buildings.

The Sustainable Building Technical Manual suggests sequencing construction activities to minimize contaminant "sinks." Whenever possible, materials that absorb VOCs, such as fabric panels, carpets, ceiling tiles, furniture, and moveable partitions systems, should be installed *after* VOC-releasing products such as paints, adhesives, and sealants have had time to air out. "Sequencing these construction activities is critical to protecting the building's air quality," notes Coady, "and doesn't cost any more—it just requires that we schedule the subs [subcontractors] accordingly." Occupant comfort and safety, as well as reduction of the potential liability caused by exposure to construction pollutants, are among the reasons that Bentall Corporation, Inc., the developer of Crestwood, has supported Coady's efforts.

Protecting occupants' health from airborne contamination is particularly important during renovation projects. In addition to blocking ducts, there are a number of effective strategies to keep dust, gases, and other potential hazards from migrating to parts of the building not under renovation, or to nearby buildings. These include installation of plastic sheeting around the construction area and depressurizing the work area to help prohibit the escape of contaminants. Conversely, pressurizing the *occupied* areas with fans can inhibit the influx of airborne contaminants from the construction area. The American Society of Heating, Refrigeration and Air Conditioning Engineers (ASHRAE) and OSHA are developing ventilation standards and requirements for IAQ controls during construction in renovation projects.

Some IAQ experts recommend that a new building's central ventilation system should *not* be operated during construction. Running the system can allow dust, as well as VOCs emitted from the paint or carpet, to adsorb into the ductwork and air-handling equipment, from which the dust and VOCs can later be released into

To prevent the adsorption of dust and VOCs (emitted from paint or carpeting) into the ductwork, some indoor air quality experts advise against operating a new building's central ventilation system during construction. *(Reprinted with permission, © Milroy/McAleer.)*

the building interior. Instead, separate, portable fans can be operated during construction to exhaust contaminated air from the building and ensure adequate fresh air delivery for workers.

Materials

The proper selection of materials has a major influence on the success or failure of a green building. Material selection is also often one of the most visible and attention-getting green aspects of a project. Most decisions about materials are made as a part of the building design process, but as quite a few green builders have discovered, *choosing* products and actually *getting them* can be quite different issues. The new, specialized, or limited-production products often specified for green projects may be difficult to actually get to the job site in a timely manner, so contractors often have to go to a little extra effort in tracking down these materials or must be ready to suggest substitutions. Planning ahead and providing plenty of time in the project schedule for procurement are very important.

THE DEVIL IS IN THE DETAILS

There may be higher costs associated with using unusual or green materials, including higher prices and the extra time it takes to seek them out. Moreover, as Tom Hoyt of McStain Enterprises has found, specifying green materials requires a lot of attention to detail. Avoiding VOCs in the construction of a house, for example, means not only contending with limited supply networks for some low- or zero-VOC products, but also making decisions about numerous small, unforeseen appli-

Tom Hoyt of McStain Enterprises specifies green materials to avoid VOCs in the construction of his residential developments. *(Reprinted with permission from David Johnston.)*

cations of adhesives, varnishes, sealants, and other materials—products that may not be clearly specified by the designers. By taking a responsible attitude toward the use of potentially hazardous substances, installation contractors can greatly improve the quality of a building's air, both for the workers and for the final occupants.

SOURCING AND SUBSTITUTIONS

Architects and designers are often unaware of problems that can arise during construction as a result of their materials choices. Some of the newer water-based acrylic exterior paints, for example, have a narrower temperature range within which they can be applied, as compared with solvent-based paints. Specifying acrylic paints for a project nearing completion in the autumn in Minnesota can cause problems. Specifying 20 percent fly ash in the concrete for foundation walls is not practical if fly ash is not available to ready-mix concrete suppliers in that area. Specifying wood from certified well-managed forests is a great idea, but supplies of such products are still limited and distribution networks do not exist in many areas. Contractors for green building projects have to be ready for these problems and must be able to come up with acceptable substitutes.

Planning ahead is essential. Designers of National Public Radio's Washington, D.C., offices and studio focused considerable attention on selecting materials that were safe from an IAQ standpoint and had other environmental advantages. But it was clear that these priorities would have an impact on construction. The project manager made sure that contractors were aware of potentially longer lead times for sourcing these materials so that the entire project could stay on schedule.

When a specified material simply is not available, product substitution is necessary. Purchasers may need guidance in selecting appropriate substitutions for green products. When substitutions must be made because of high costs or long lead times, it is important to ensure that they meet the needs and satisfy the goals of the design. At the Town and Country grocery store in Poulsbo, Washington, some of the specified products, such as recycled-content tile, were beyond the project budget and more conventional materials had to be substituted. The project architect signed off on all necessary and appropriate substitutions.

As green building becomes more common, appropriate materials are becoming easier to obtain. For such products as high-recycled-content drywall and low-VOC sealants and paints, price premiums that once were quite significant have either disappeared or are coming down as more manufacturers and products compete in the green market.

To help make appropriate product substitutions, contractors should gain some familiarity with trends and developments in the green building product area. Generic "green specifications" are now available, and information on thousands of green products is available in several green building product directories—in both paper and electronic versions (see Chapter 6 for more on environmentally responsible building materials).

It is possible to reduce a project's use of resources substantially by reusing materials salvaged from existing buildings, particularly in renovation projects. Compared with new materials, salvaged materials require very small inputs of energy to make them usable. Reusing materials that would otherwise have been discarded can save money twice: first, by avoiding the purchase of equivalent new materials; and second, by avoiding the cost of disposal. Some salvaged materials, however, will cost the same as, or even more than, new materials. Salvaged timbers, for example, after cleanup and remilling, may cost significantly more than new timbers (though the quality is often better, because the old-growth trees commonly used for the salvaged timbers are less available today.) Typically, the issue of salvaged material use is addressed during the design phase (see Chapter 6), but there may still be opportunities during construction to use additional salvaged materials or to identify opportunities that the designers were not aware of, as occurred at the C. K. Choi Building at the University of British Columbia.

Construction and Waste

Construction consumes a lot of resources and generates a large amount of waste. According to Worldwatch Institute, three billion tons of raw materials are used to construct buildings each year. Depending on the region, between 15 and 40 percent of a landfill in the United States may be comprised of construction waste. In Worldwatch Institute's booklet *A Building Revolution*, the authors note that the construction of a typical 1,800-square-foot, 150-ton home in the United States generates approximately seven tons of solid waste. Furthermore, one house or apartment is demolished for every six that are built. The energy consumed during the construction of a highly energy-efficient building, according to *Environmental Building News*, can be more than that building will consume for heating and cooling over 50 years of operation.

Cut Waste, Save Money

Traditionally, the construction industry has paid very little to dispose of waste; most communities have provided plentiful landfill sites with low tipping fees. Recently, however, overflowing dumps and more stringent environmental regulations have resulted in rising costs for waste disposal. According to the National Solid Waste Management Association, tipping fees nearly quadrupled in all regions of the United States over the years 1985 to 1995, and they continue to rise. This economic pressure has stimulated waste reduction, salvage, and recycling.

The construction industry is also experiencing growing regulatory pressure, at both the national and local level, to reduce waste. The Canadian cities of Toronto and Vancouver, like a number of municipalities in the United States, have placed restrictions on the kinds of materials that can be put in landfills. Toronto has banned cardboard, fine paper, clean wood, concrete, rubble, and scrap metal—all materials with potential for recycling or reuse—as well as drywall. Other cities have implemented extensive waste reduction programs. Portland, Oregon, which has tipping fees of $28 to $35 per ton, has gone further than most cities by establishing a goal of recycling 60 percent of all waste by 1997 and requiring recycling of wood, metals, and cardboard for all construction projects over $25,000 in size.

In 1994, Pizzagalli Construction, Vermont's largest construction company, was hired to convert an IBM office complex in Essex Junction into a warehouse. As described in the March/April 1995 issue of *Environmental Building News*, the project entailed removal of 5,500 sheets of 4' × 10' demountable drywall. Landfilling the drywall, at $74 per ton, would have cost about $20,000. Gary Parkinson of Pizzagalli figured that there must be a better option. He had heard about the Vermont Business Materials Exchange, a network through which companies can buy, sell, or trade materials not useful to their companies but possibly useful to others. He contacted Bob Lawson, the man who manages the exchange. While it was too late to advertise the availability of salvaged drywall in the network's newsletter and still meet the company's remodeling schedule, Lawson suggested that Parkinson send a press release to the *Burlington Free Press*, the local newspaper, offering the drywall free to anyone who would pick it up in 20-sheet-minimum lots.

By the afternoon of the day the article ran, all of the drywall was spoken for. "As fast as we could take it down, it was gone," said Parkinson. Pizzagalli used care in removing the drywall and salvaged about 75 percent of it. Even with some added labor for careful removal, Pizzagalli saved about $15,000 in avoided landfill

Reducing Waste and Saving Money
Through Building Reuse

When the Southern California Gas Company decided to develop a resource-efficient building, the Energy Resource Center, the team suggested recycling an existing building. Doing so saved $3.2 million in infrastructure and land costs and kept 350 tons of material out of the waste stream (concrete, roofing, drywall and metals). Eighty percent of building materials used in the renovation were themselves of recycled content. The cost savings realized by the Gas Company by reusing this older building are listed in the following chart.

Recycled vs. New Construction Cost Comparison for the
Southern California Gas Energy Resource Center

Project Comparison 44,000 SF Facility	Recycled Building— Energy Resource Center	Conventional Construction
Item Description	Cost	Cost
General Conditions	$889,290	$1,223,200
Site Work	452,757	1,046,320
Concrete	316,384	616,000
Masonry	31,000	231,000
Metals	1,029,375	1,591,000
Carpentry	94,914	316,800
Thermal/Moisture Protection	388,590	389,840
Doors, Windows, Glass	318,604	356,400
Finishes	1,021,494	1,179,200
Specialties	78,148	127,600
Equipment	75,270	92,840
Conveying Systems	31,500	79,200
Mechanical and Plumbing	810,982	1,073,160
Electrical	1,220,316	1,420,320
Total Construction Costs	**$6,758,624**	**$9,742,920**

costs (not including the avoided cost of trucking). People coming for drywall also hauled off about 50,000 square feet of carpeting, saving the company a few thousand dollars more in avoided landfilling. This was a win-win situation for everyone involved, and it happened because someone at the construction company had his eyes open and his mind working.

Regulations in some areas are helping to spur recycling. For example, wallboard is banned at Vancouver-area landfills because it can generate the toxic gas hydrogen sulfide under wet, oxygen-starved conditions. A drywall remanufacturing plant is capitalizing on this opportunity and handles most of the scrap wallboard from renovations and new construction.

When The Body Shop refurbished a building in Wake Forest, North Carolina, for its new headquarters, the project team donated salvaged materials to the nonprofit builders of Habitat for Humanity in Wake County for resale or use on affordable housing projects. By so doing, The Body Shop not only received a tax benefit for the donation, but avoided tipping fees as well.

The demolition of the Okalla Prison in British Columbia, south of Vancouver, was put to bid. Each contractor submitting a bid was requested to provide two contract prices: one for a straight demolition and one that maximized reuse or recycling of demolished materials. The winning contractor submitted a bid in which the cost without recycling was 35 percent greater than it was with recycling. The savings came from both the sale of salvaged materials and the avoided tipping fees. The recycling program took one and a half months longer, but salaries for this period were offset by the income derived from selling the salvaged materials and the contractor was glad to have the extra work. The local community benefited too: 1,590 concrete blocks were donated to a local boys' club, which cleaned them for reuse, and local residents were invited to a "garage sale" on the site to salvage lights, wood, and miscellaneous items.

Builders typically spend about 2 to 5 percent of their overall construction budget disposing of job-site waste. The primary barrier to recycling is a reluctance to spend time and money to sort and separate waste, as is usually required. Valley Resource Management, a regional nonprofit organization in western Colorado, works with construction companies to encourage recycling by helping them recognize its cost-effectiveness. At a 30-home construction site in Snowmass Village, Colorado, the group offered to pay Shaw Construction Company up to $4,000 to cover any additional labor or other costs from a recycling program. Little employee training was needed. Even without the financial aid, Shaw saved more than $8,000 in tipping fees and diverted 54 percent of the waste stream from the landfill.

Okalla Prison Building Demolition

Material	Status Quo Demolition (estimated)		Pilot Project	
	Recycled Materials (cu yds)	To Landfill (cu yds)	Recycled Materials (cu yds)	To Landfill (cu yds)
Wood	0	1,860	1,800	60
Concrete	220	650	870	0
Scrap Metal	0	60	60	0
Tar and Gravel Roofing	0	96	16	80
Drywall	15	0	15	0
Total	235 (8%)	2,666 (92%)	2,761 (95%)	140 (5%)

Source: British Columbia Building Corporation, *A Case Study of Disposal Alternatives in the Demolition of a Public Institution* (1995). Reprinted with permission from British Columbia Building Corporation, Canada.

WASTE AVOIDANCE

Managing and recycling waste once it has been produced can be profitable; so can not producing it in the first place. As explained in Chapter 6, material-efficient design, careful construction detailing, and careful selection of materials can all help reduce waste. World Watch Institute's booklet, *A Building Revolution,* describes an advanced approach to construction waste avoidance taken by Shimizu Corporation in Japan, one of the world's five largest construction companies. Shimizu has a Global Environmental Charter, in which it pledges to incorporate environmental concerns in all its work. In keeping with this commitment, Shimizu has developed an advanced robotics system to construct high-rise buildings, combined with just-in-time delivery of precut materials to the job site each day. This eliminates the need for on-site storage and reduces packaging and construction waste by as much as 70 percent on some projects.

Design strategies that consider the building's disassembly before it is even built can greatly reduce demolition and renovation costs. Avoiding the use of adhesives and making mechanical fasteners accessible and obvious are ways that today's construction can help tomorrow's demolition.

Other types of waste can also be reduced at the job site. *The Sustainable Building Technical Manual* recommends giving contractors an incentive to conserve energy and water. Contractors will reduce energy and water consumption during construction, the manual suggests, if they are made financially responsible for all energy and water permits and consumption charges required during construction. Monitoring energy and water use can also help identify areas of waste. Further recommendations for achieving on-site energy and material savings include using the conduit system for temporary lighting during construction and making sure that the lighting can be turned off during nonconstruction hours. The manual contains numerous other suggestions for efficient use of energy, water, and materials.

Waste Management Plans

More and more developers, owners, and architects are requiring that contractors implement a waste management plan to avoid high disposal costs and facilitate recycling. The waste management plan specifies procedures for determining what wastes will be generated, explains how those wastes are to be managed on the job site, clarifies responsibilities regarding waste management, and either specifies where recyclable materials are to be taken or prescribes the research needed to determine the recycling options. (A waste management plan outline developed by the NAHB Research Center is shown in "Developing a Residential Waste Management Plan" on page 306.) A job-site recycling coordinator with the authority to train and supervise workers can help to ensure that such a plan is carried out thoroughly. Opportunities for recycling vary by project and depend on the following:

- The composition and quantities of waste generated on a project;
- Local, regional, state, and federal regulations, landfill costs, and capacities;
- The total cost of disposal (handling, containers, transportation, and tipping, or other disposal fees);
- Local and regional options for recycling and salvage; and
- Potential income from the sale of recyclable materials.

A consideration to bear in mind is the highest and best use of recycled material. For example, *reuse* of scrap wood is the most resource-efficient strategy, whereas sending scraps to be remanufactured into wall materials maintains its high value but consumes more resources during remanufacturing. Chipping the wood and using it for either composting or hog fuel (waste wood used for producing heat and/or electricity) is a lower-grade use of the wood resource, but certainly better than sending it to a landfill.

Wood (and paper) waste, which often constitutes 65 to 80 percent of total construction waste by volume, is difficult to extract after it is mixed with other construction wastes, so on-site separation is important. Yet space constraints on construction sites have encouraged a trend toward single-bin disposal. This causes wastes to be commingled (mixed together), making reuse, salvage, or recycling more difficult. Turner Construction Company uses a compartmentalized single bin to allow on-site separation.

In some areas, construction waste services will pick up commingled waste and separate it at their own materials recovery facilities (MRFs). The builder or contractor pays for waste hauling, though sometimes at a somewhat lower rate than charged by a conventional waste hauler. While this arrangement may be simpler for the contractor, commingling the waste generally means that the profit from waste recycling goes to the hauler, not the contractor.

There are growing opportunities to salvage or recycle construction wastes through waste exchanges (local, regional, and national) and recycling services. Those making competitive bids would do well to find out ahead of time who will accept what. Many cities have listings of haulers, MRFs, private recycling companies, and salvage dealers.

Opportunities exist for other businesses to make money while supporting recycling and salvage efforts. When the Oregon Arena Corporation was planning the Rose Garden, a new $146 million arena for the Portland Trail Blazers, a small local firm called River City Resources Group suggested to the owners that they establish recycling requirements for the project. The owners hired River City to design the bid specifications. Turner Construction Company, the general contractor, implemented an extensive recycling program that reduced construction waste 95 percent by volume. Turner saved $190,000 on construction costs by rerouting 45,000 tons of concrete, steel, gypsum, paper, and other construction waste to recyclers. Partly as a result of the success with waste management on this project, Turner now develops detailed waste management plans for all large projects.

Developing a Residential Waste Management Plan

Step 1. Identify components of waste stream and learn conventional costs.

Step 2. Understand conditions affecting waste management decisions.

Step 3. Establish a plan.

Waste reduction: Identify and implement efficient framing techniques.

Contract structure: Require subcontractors to haul their own wastes.

Waste recycling

Separation by builder/subcontractor

Self-haul

Haul by others

Separation by others

Job site cleanup service

Commingled recovery

New ideas: Wood/gypsum uses and take-back policies

Source: Residential Construction Waste Management: A Builder's Field Guide, NAHB Research Center, 400 Prince George's Boulevard, Upper Marlboro, MD 20774; (301) 249-4000. Reprinted with permission from National Association of Home Builders Research Center.

Cleaning Up

There are a number of important green considerations in the postconstruction phase, when a building is being cleaned and prepared for occupancy.

As mentioned earlier in this chapter, materials for the new National Public Radio headquarters in Washington, D.C., were carefully chosen to avoid toxic emissions. However, it is practically impossible to construct a building without any harmful VOCs. So, to ensure good indoor air quality, the HVAC system was run at full capacity for 10 days between the end of construction and the time the occupants moved in. This flushed most remaining airborne toxins out of the building. Some IAQ experts recommend carrying out this sort of flushing activity with separate fans that are not part of the permanent HVAC system so that contaminants do not become lodged in the building ducts and air-handling equipment.

Upon postconstruction inspection of the San Francisco Main Library, construction dust and dirt were found in numerous locations. This would have compromised the IAQ of the building. The project manager, Anthony Bernheim, suggests that as well as requiring inspections and cleanup, requirements such as cleaning air filters at building start-up should be written into the specs to ensure that the contractor leaves no dirt or debris behind.

Occupant health can also be jeopardized during the postconstruction phase by ill-conceived or poorly carried out cleaning activities. The specifications for the Benedict Commons housing complex in Aspen, Colorado, called for no glues to be used in carpets and for low-VOC paints to be used throughout. However, while inspecting the project, developer Jonathan Rose detected toxic fumes. It turned out that the postconstruction cleanup crews had used heavy-duty cleaners that left remaining fumes. Attention must to be paid to every stage of a green development.

While inspecting Benedict Commons, an affordable housing project in Aspen, Colorado, developer Jonathan Rose discovered that post-construction crews had used toxic cleaners, tainting the indoor air quality. *(Reprinted with permission from Gunnar Hubbard, Rocky Mountain Institute.)*

Commissioning

In most construction projects, the tasks given the highest priority at the end of the construction stage include finishing the final punch list, obtaining building inspector signatures, getting the occupants into the building as quickly as possible, and getting out. Design flaws, construction errors, unforeseen interactions between systems, and inadequate control systems often surface at this stage, but a shortage of time and tight budgets often result in failure to deal adequately with this "fine-tuning." The result is less-than-optimal energy performance of the building, occupant discomfort, and a host of annoying call-back problems. The best way to avoid such problems is to carry out a thorough "commissioning" program.

Commissioning is the process of ensuring that a building and its systems are functioning in conformity with the design intent and the occupants' operational needs. Commissioning is a relatively new focus of attention—virtually unheard of before the 1990s. Now it is the subject of major conferences and workshops nationwide. Although commissioning is often considered to be a postconstruction activity, it properly begins during the predesign phase and continues through the training of the operation and maintenance staff and the occupation of the building.

The scope and time frame of commissioning varies from project to project. Mechanical systems and energy management control systems are a key focus of commissioning. In large buildings with extensive use of such features as daylighting, passive ventilation, and passive solar heating, commissioning can be quite complex, requiring the tuning of mechanical systems and controls to optimally benefit from natural energy and airflows. The required scope of commissioning may dictate who is selected for the task: an architect, an engineer, or another trade professional such as an HVAC installer. Some developers hire a specialized commissioning agent. Typically, the commissioning agent is brought in during or after construction, but sometimes this individual may join the team even before construction begins. At the San Francisco Main Library, a third-party commissioning agent was brought on board to inspect and review the successful completion of the construction phase.

Performance expectations for the building should be laid out in contracts and specifications. Commissioning will evaluate performance to determine whether the structure meets those expectations. Commissioning is especially useful in ensuring that optimal energy-efficiency performance—as per design—is achieved. It can also address air quality and thermal comfort.

COSTS AND BENEFITS OF COMMISSIONING

It makes economic sense to commission every building, although it is rarely done. The costs of commissioning are a very small fraction of the typical construction budget. For example, commissioning the new $100 million San Francisco Main Library cost about 0.06 percent of the project's budget. The city actually wanted to skip commissioning, but project architect Anthony Bernheim convinced city officials that it would be less expensive than bringing in specialists later on if something went wrong. He argued that costs to fix mistakes would appear sooner or later.

The benefits of commissioning can be tremendous. During construction of the Capital Circle Office Center in Florida, the commissioning agent discovered beam openings in upper air plenums of the buildings that would have lost half the

---

Getting More Information on Commissioning and Recommissioning

The leading organizations involved with commissioning and recommissioning (discussed in Chapter 11) information are listed here, along with other recommendations for building owners and managers. Refer to Appendix C for addresses and phone numbers.

- American Society of Heating, Refrigerating and Air Conditioning Engineers (ASHRAE).
- American Council for an Energy-Efficient Economy (ACEEE).
- U.S. Environmental Protection Agency's (EPA) Energy Star Showcase Building Program.
- U.S. Department of Energy (DOE) Building Measurement and Verification Protocol, 1996.
- Local utility companies may offer commissioning programs or other resources to assist building owners.
- The annual Building Commissioning/Recommissioning Conference is currently the most complete one-stop source of information. For information, call Portland Energy Conservation, Inc. at (503) 248-4636.

conditioned air through the top of each building. The additional HVAC capacity to make up for these losses would have cost $250,000 per building in "first cost" and resulted in $30,000 of wasted energy per building per year.

According to Lawrence Berkeley National Laboratory, commissioning can save as much as 40 percent of a building's utility bills for heating, cooling, and ventilation. ASHRAE reports that owners have been known to pay $8 per square foot per year in additional operating costs because of faulty design or installation of HVAC systems. ASHRAE has also found that the cost of commissioning a mechanical system generally is between 2 and 5 percent of the installed equipment price, and that the cost to operate a commissioned building should be 8 to 20 percent less than for an equivalent building that was not commissioned.

Southern California Edison examined seven buildings, ranging from small offices and stores to larger retail and office buildings, to determine the costs and benefits of commissioning. The study found that commissioning cost an average of

During the commissioning of Capital Circle Office Center in Florida, the commissioning agent discovered places where half of the conditioned air would have been lost through the top of each building. *(John Owen, photographer. Reprinted with permission.)*

$0.28 per square foot and realized annual energy savings of between 0.3 and 3.4 kilowatt-hours (kWh) per square foot (see "Energy Savings Resulting from Deficiency Repairs" on page 312). This meant thousands of dollars of savings per year for many of these buildings. Other, non-energy-related, benefits were not calculated.

This study points out that problems can be quite different from one building to another and that single, rather simple, problems can have profound effects on energy consumption in a building.

Some of the benefits of commissioning are neither immediate nor easily measured, but are nonetheless very important. Commissioning increases the equipment reliability and life span of mechanical systems, because there is less wear and tear on mechanical systems that are installed and functioning properly. Over time, this should reduce maintenance costs.

Another long-term benefit of commissioning is improved occupant comfort and IAQ. As discussed in previous chapters, better IAQ may improve worker productivity and reduce absenteeism; it can also reduce the likelihood of litigation by occupants. Carl Lawson, of the ASHRAE technical committee that handles commissioning issues, noted in his article, "The Price of Commissioning Equals Cost Savings," that the average cost of a litigative claim for a building is $85,000. More than 70 percent of such claims could have been avoided if the buildings in question had been commissioned.

Finally, commissioning provides an excellent opportunity to transmit knowledge about the building to its occupants. In fact, this training function is one of the most important benefits of commissioning. Commissioning documents are essentially operating manuals for a building. They provide information about the building's expected performance, how it was designed, and how it should be operated. At Farson's Brewery in Malta, the brewery's operators were brought into the commissioning process so that they could better understand how this energy-efficient, passive-solar facility worked and how it should be operated. The result was improved energy performance.

THE SPREAD OF COMMISSIONING

If commissioning makes so much sense, why is it done so rarely? There is a widespread lack of awareness about it. Owners who do know of it often think they are already getting it as part of the standard construction services. Inspection teams are seldom knowledgeable about—or rewarded for—the final performance of a

Energy Savings Resulting from Deficiency Repairs

Note: These savings are energy estimates. A DOE-2 energy simulation using actual metered end-use data is under way by Edison Envest to refine these energy saving numbers.

Building Type	Deficiency Repairs	Energy Savings kWh/y	Building Total Annual kWh Savings	kWh Savings per SF	Percent Energy Savings
Retail (Clothing)	Evaporative cooler maintenance	224,379	224,379	1.5	7.4%
Large Office	Fix economizer control	128,450	128,450	0.8	5.2%
Retail (Clothing)	Fix two economizers	359,829			
	Fix four enthalpy controllers	71,966	431,795	2.5	11.2%
Small Office	Repair one economizer	153,961			
	Calibrate thermostats	8,200	162,161	3.4	27.0%
Small Office	Fix CHW pump control	29,324			
	Repair two economizers	81,273	110,597	2.2	12.2%
Small Office	Replace receiver controller	41,724	41,724	0.3	2.4%
Retail (Grocery)	Energy savings—not quantified				

Source: C. Kjellman, Deborah Dodds, and Tudi Haas, *A Building Commissioning Study in the Home Stretch* (Third National Conference on Building Commissioning, 1995.) Reprinted with permission from Christie Kjellman for Southern California Edison, a division of Edison International.

project. If problems are encountered, the quickest and easiest solutions are typically employed. Commissioning takes time, and the owner or developer often wants to get occupants into a building as quickly as possible so as to avoid delay penalties, to get early-completion incentives, or to begin earning revenues.

Owners who are carrying heavy financing burdens sometimes prefer to put off any expenses they can, even if doing so means paying higher operating costs or paying for early repairs. Unfortunately, when renters will be paying energy costs, the incentives for properly commissioning a building and fixing problems before occupancy are even lower.

Despite these pressures, commissioning is gradually becoming more common. In some areas, utilities offer commissioning services or—as New England Electric and Seattle City Light do—offer owners incentives for commissioning. Some local and state governments have also instituted building commissioning programs. Montgomery County, Maryland, has developed a commissioning manual and sample specs that must be followed for all of its new building projects. The state of Florida is saving millions of dollars on its new buildings by coupling high-performance design with commissioning. To date, the state's commissioning costs have been repaid quickly in each case through corrections to building integrity, not even counting the savings from energy improvements. The U.S. federal government has also now mandated a commissioning policy for federal buildings and has developed a model plan and specifications.

In the private sector, some companies and institutions, including Westin Hotels, Boeing, and a number of universities, have instituted commissioning programs for all new buildings. Typically, an independent third-party commissioning agent or commissioning authority is hired, who reports to the owner. The commissioning agent may work directly for the owner or be under contract to the general contractor or construction manager. Some architects are also now starting to include commissioning as part of their services.

Conclusion

Communication, leadership, and training can all help build an effective construction team. The activities of the team members on-site, as well as the products of their work, affect the success with which the green development vision is brought to life during the construction phase. Without adequate attention to construction details, indoor air quality, and mechanical equipment installation and tuning, a building will fail to achieve its potential. See Appendix D for a checklist on green construction strategies.

Located north of Denver, Greenlee Park features 170 units of environmentally sensitive housing that includes town houses, small carriage houses, and attached units. (*Reprinted with permission from David Johnston.*)

CHAPTER 10

Marketing

COMPETITION WAS FIERCE in the Denver home building market when McStain Enterprises began developing Greenlee Park, in Lafayette, north of Denver. Developers Tom and Caroline Hoyt knew that a market existed for environmentally sound homes, and they knew that there was a demand for affordable and flexible housing arrangements. So they built Greenlee Park—170 units of environmentally sensitive housing that includes town houses with two master bedrooms, small carriage houses, and attached units with the appearance of large manor homes. The Hoyts also knew that the product they were creating was different; the challenge would be to market it effectively.

Tom Hoyt identifies point-of-sale as the key to getting people in the door and selling them on the features. It is a challenge, according to Hoyt, to make environmental building experts out of his own sales staff and the real estate agents with whom they work. The McStain team worked with their green product suppliers and manufacturers, who helped pay for an attractive point-of-sale piece—a three-fold brochure that highlights environmental features of the homes, the developers' guiding philosophy, and the benefits to buyers of this building approach.

The Hoyts, along with environmental building consultant David Johnston of What's Working, recognized that green features would help differentiate their homes in the Denver market while allowing buyers to feel good about the broader implications of the purchase they were considering. The strategy McStain Enterprises took in marketing was to educate prospective home buyers about the advantages of the environmental features found in the homes. McStain's literature addresses energy efficiency, indoor air quality, and efficient use of resources and building materials, and describes the environmental benefits of such features as

A model home at Greenlee Park displays some of the environmental features and demonstrates their benefits. *(Reprinted with permission from David Johnston.)*

heat-recovery ventilators, cellulose insulation, carpeting and patio flooring made from recycled materials, superwindows, and finger-jointed studs, which are produced from scraps of wood otherwise discarded. A model home displays some of these features and explains their benefits.

McStain Enterprises' marketing strategy involved an aggressive public relations campaign. The Boulder County Chamber of Commerce held an open house at McStain's model home. Local real estate journalists jumped at the chance to cover the development, because it differed so markedly from surrounding subdivisions. Said Hoyt, "To my knowledge, nobody else in the Denver area is doing this in the production mode, so we've gotten a lot of press." Feature stories about McStain Enterprises in the *Rocky Mountain News* and *Denver Post* emphasized the environmental features. This free marketing generated a lot of traffic. By the June 1996 opening day, McStain had presold more than 75 percent of the 48 homes in Phase One of Greenlee Park.

McStain's Greenlee Park is a successful green development not only because of the cutting-edge environmental building features integrated into the homes, but also because it has succeeded in the marketplace. Effective marketing made this happen. The most exciting green features mean nothing if potential buyers do not understand their benefits and if the project does not succeed financially. The need to market effectively applies to all real estate development — whether conventional or green.

By their very nature, though, environmentally sensitive developments have some inherent advantages when it comes to extracting the greatest value out of tight marketing budgets. As companies work to stretch scarce marketing dollars, public image can play an important role. Green developments are favorably placed to reap the benefits that accrue to projects with positive public images. This chapter tells a number of stories illustrating how and why green developments have done so well in attracting buyers or lessors. It examines conventional marketing strategies as well as some creative new strategies for bringing sales prospects to the door and then closing the sale.

Getting Attention: The Power of Free Press

The money we spent in going beyond code requirements has been repaid in free press, and that kind of coverage brings people to my sales center. When people come out and experience the open spaces and the wildlife, they're sold. It sells itself.

Joseph Fraser, developer of Summerfield, an environmentally sensitive golf course in Stuart, Florida, in Builder, *February 1995*

Green real estate development is new. It is exciting. It is newsworthy. The most market-savvy green developers are taking advantage of the current interest, relying on free media coverage for a significant part of their marketing efforts. Some projects have received many thousands of dollars' worth of coverage in the press at little cost to them.

Green developers have often been able to drastically lower advertising budgets by putting more effort or money into public relations. Media coverage is different from advertising, because the information generally is not coming from the beneficiary of that coverage, at least not directly. But this does not mean that such coverage is always free. Generating positive media coverage usually means investing in public relations efforts—for example, calling up editors with news or story ideas, sending out press releases, and inviting writers to visit a project and effectively hosting them. A well-thought-out plan and an exciting story can add up to highly cost-effective marketing.

Stanley Selengut is a master of soliciting free press coverage. While the typical resort spends 10 to 15 percent of gross revenues in marketing, Selengut spends almost nothing, relying instead on the media to carry his message. In the mid-1970s, when he started his modest Maho Bay resort with just 18 rustic "tent-cabins," he managed to pique the curiosity of a *New York Times* writer, who visited the resort. Recognizing the resort's uniqueness, he wrote a front-page story for the Sunday Travel Section, which generated a remarkable 3,000 inquiries. Maho Bay was on its way to financial success. "You didn't have to be a genius," notes Selengut, "to figure out that if you did something right and got this kind of support, you were onto something." Along with coverage in the *New York Times,* Selengut's projects have been written up in such publications as *Gourmet, Vogue,* and the *Los Angeles Times.* His second project, Harmony, won *Popular Science*'s 1994 "Best of What's New" grand award for environmental technology, as well as an eco-tourism award from Condé Nast.

Developer Stanley Selengut spends almost nothing on marketing his eco-resorts, such as Estate Concordia on St. John, relying instead on press coverage to generate interest. *(Reprinted with permission from Maho Bay Camps, Inc.)*

Selengut prefers to spend his money on product innovation rather than on marketing. Effective use of the press has allowed Selengut to spend more on enhancing the environmental features of his resorts. This innovation ensures that Selengut will continue to create newsworthy projects that will, in turn, attract press coverage. Just as Maho Bay and Harmony were ground-breaking projects that generated extensive press coverage, his newest project, Estate Concordia, is on the cutting edge as well.

His media strategy is validated by the bottom line. Says Selengut, "I do know we make a huge amount of money—our net profit is almost 25 percent of our gross—and nobody does this!" Maho Bay tents are consistently booked; even Selengut has a hard time getting in.

The Boston Park Plaza Hotel is another green project that used the press to create a national identity for itself—and generate sales. In the late 1980s, the 977-room hotel, owned by the Saunders Hotel Group (a family business), was marketed on its rate (then about $89 a night). In 1990 the owners carried out a landmark retrofit, integrating resource efficiency and environmental goals. They installed 1,686 insulated-glass windows—operable but blocking most outside noise—saving the hotel about $75 per room in annual energy costs, with a 10-year payback. A comprehensive recycling program set up for the hotel directly benefits employees, who decide how deposit money from collected beverage containers is to be spent. In bathrooms, individual shampoo bottles were replaced with dispensers for top-quality shampoo. High-efficiency shower heads and low-flow toilets replaced standard models. Guests can choose whether or not they want

Boston Park Plaza's rise in value between 1990 and 1996 is attributed to the national attention it received for its environmental initiatives. *(Reprinted with permission from William D. Browning, Rocky Mountain Institute.)*

their towels and linens changed daily. The hotel reuses fabrics, restores older furniture, and donates goods to shelters and nursing homes when no longer suitable for hotel rooms.

In January 1996, the Plaza was bought by a partnership, comprised of the Donald Saunders family and the Starwood Lodging Trust, for $100 million, which was more than its appraised value. But by this time it had developed a special identity as "Boston's hotel," the place where the action is. Rates were running at $140 to $160 per night, which is slightly lower than competitors' rates because the Plaza does not have to fund the overhead associated with a chain hotel.

Marketing director Todd Hoffman attributes the rise in the hotel's value between 1990 and 1996 to the national attention it received for its environmental initiatives. In 1993 the hotel hired a market research team to do random samplings of tourists visiting Fanueil Hall. Respondents' awareness of the Boston Park Plaza ranked with that of the national chains—Westin, Marriott, and Sheraton. Hoffman credits extensive national media coverage as the reason for the hotel's widespread public recognition.

Boston Park Plaza never directly advertised the company's green initiatives. Instead, it let third parties tout its environmental leadership in the hotel industry through coverage by CBS, CNN, the *New York Times, USA Today, Fortune,* and numerous industry publications. In fact, the media recognition garnered by the hotel for its trail-blazing environmental program earned it the Golden Bell Public Relations Award.

The marketing staff effectively leveraged annual expenditures of less than $500,000 on advertising and marketing (as compared with the millions spent each year by competitors) to establish this local and national recognition. Because of its environmental programs, the Boston Park Plaza Hotel was one of nine recipients of the Environment and Conservation Challenge Award in 1992 from the President's Council on Environmental Quality, which further boosted public visibility.

While it is difficult to quantify the amount of business, both conference and individual, that has resulted from the hotel's environmental policies, the marketing staff is sure that such issues have been a closing factor for many clients. In 1993, the Saunders Hotel Group conservatively estimated that $1.5 million dollars in new group business had been brought in since the hotel found its green market niche.

Word of Mouth and Referrals

As almost any business expert will affirm, satisfied customers are the most effective salespeople. With a relatively new product that does not yet have much market penetration, word of mouth and referrals are particularly important. Not surprisingly, this has become an important component of the marketing efforts for many green developments.

In the Vancouver market, developers typically spend about 4 percent of gross revenues on advertising, including brochures, sales commissions, and sales centers. Harold Kalke's 2211 West Fourth project did not need to. By typical standards, the advertising budget to sell the 78 condominium units would have been about $650,000 (Canadian). Instead of putting so much money into advertising, Kalke and his company let the project sell itself.

He found that the development's location was its most powerful selling point. A high-quality, 16' by 16' sign on-site informed passersby that the development would be a street-oriented community project with residential, retail, and office components. The sign listed some of the development's unique features: geothermal heating, rainscreen walls (a double exterior wall system that achieves outstanding thermal, acoustic, and moisture performance), energy efficiency, filtered water, timeless architecture (rather than a particular trendy style) — features not typically included in such buildings. The apartments had a community-oriented layout and provided comfort, resource efficiency, environmental sensitivity, and lower operating costs. The signage piqued curiosity and helped attract local media coverage. Although the location brought people in, the features sold it once people realized they were looking at something special.

Kalke and his staff used friendly, personalized marketing to sell and lease space. He has found that while such personalized marketing is much more time- and energy-intensive, it is also more dynamic. People are often inundated, he says, with "slick marketing campaigns that build up hype through sales centers and brochures." Salt Lick Productions, Kalke's development company, saved $850,000 on real estate agents' leasing and sales fees by selling and leasing most space directly, which was possible only because of the company's success in capitalizing on free media coverage and market differentiation.

Of course, developments do not sell themselves without a helping hand. Kalke carefully selected a mixture of neighborhood-serving businesses that he believed would best "fit" at 2211 West Fourth's location. He then used the presence of desirable retail tenants to help sell potential residents on the benefits of mixed-use —residents could go downstairs to pick up some milk, browse new titles at the bookstore, or get a cappuccino.

Kalke estimated retail space premiums of $6 to $8 per square foot per year higher than the market at that time. Office space leases were signed at about $16 per square foot in an area where office space is usually leased at $8 per square foot. Kalke also believes that the long-term outlook is very good. "The type and quality of the tenants assures us of a quality income stream with strong potential for rate increases upon renewal of the initial five-year lease terms," he said.

Potential home buyers always ask about price and square footage. Kalke's apartments are smaller than most in the area, making the price per apartment ($169,000 to $179,000) competitive, but the price per square foot higher. He tells potential buyers that this is irrelevant—what is important is the use of space, not the volume, and these apartments are designed to maximize space use. (He has

While his 2211 West Fourth apartments are smaller than most in the area, Harold Kalke argues that what is important is the *use* of the space, not the volume, and that these apartments are designed to maximize space use. *(Reprinted with permission, © Rob Melnychuk.)*

found that while the public clearly understands the concept of the use of space, the building industry is still married to such "bigness" issues such as floor-area ratio, gross-to-net, and square footage.) He asks tenants, "Do you ask the square footage of a car before purchasing? No. Instead, you are concerned about comfort and functionality—and you climb into the car to check out how the space works." Kalke gives tours to emphasize how functional the spaces are. His marketing style has paid off. Eighty-five percent of both retail and residential spaces were under contract by the time construction ended, with a full 100 percent under contract within three months of completion, thereby keeping carrying costs down.

When developer John Knott sought to fulfill his vision of creating an environmentally responsible development on Dewees Island® off the South Carolina coast, he found that many of the ecological features of this project would be viewed as negative attributes in the traditional recreation markets: no golf club, no marina, no vehicles except for electric golf carts, no pavement, no conventional lawns, no irrigation except by using collected rainwater. When he narrowed his target market to a subgroup of this recreation market, however—to people with strong environmental values—he found that these same environmental features became *positive* attributes, rather than negatives.

Market research told Knott that this subgroup valued such ideas as "interaction with the natural world" and a retreat for an "intergenerational community." In developing their marketing strategy, the Dewees Island team saw their challenge as very simple: "We don't have to go after 2 percent of the entire population, we're going after 2 percent of a very selective group." By defining quite clearly who their potential buyers were, they were able to target their promotional materials specifically to that group.

An initial conference between Dewees Island team members included a brainstorming session to identify key selling points. Out of this emerged a positioning statement. The list was then cross-referenced to the market research report, and several key selling points were agreed upon: beach, environmental preservation, proximity to Charleston, limited access, exclusive retreat, learning, intergenerational, and legacy. The positioning statement that emerged emphasized four of the island's key selling points: "Dewees Island—a private, oceanfront retreat dedicated to environmental preservation."

An important part of the approach to marketing Dewees Island was to build support for the project within the regional community. The marketing strategy called for participating in environmental awards programs, developing a public relations program to win over influential people within the Charleston community, directly communicating with Isle of Palms residents (where Dewees Island's marina is located), and securing endorsements from regional wildlife and environmental groups.

A key part of this effort was making sure that the development really did meet its lofty environmental goals so that it could win such third-party endorsements. The Dewees team recognized this in their marketing strategy, noting, "Although what we are doing must be understated, the quality of everything we do (including the facilities) must be first class." They have succeeded admirably: Dewees Island has won a number of prestigious awards, including the 1995 Keep America Beautiful National Award in the Local Business/Industry category, and the 1993 South Carolina Land Development Stewardship Award.

To emphasize the development's character as an exclusive retreat, the marketing strategy focused primarily on networking through personal referral rather than advertising. "Third-party testimonials of what you are affirms your uniqueness and builds trust in prospects and pride in your owners," says Knott. More than 50 percent of Dewees Island sales result from owner referrals—a telling example of owners' enthusiasm, especially in the early stages of a development project.

Dewees Island uses a monthly newsletter, the Dewees Island Chronicles, to communicate with owners, friends, and potential buyers. (Reprinted with permission of the Island Preservation Partnership.)

Dewees Island's emphasis on networking and public relations resulted in smaller than average advertising expenditures. By June 1996 the development had received an estimated $5 million dollars in free media coverage. Certainly the environmental features have generated extensive press attention, but Knott also attributes coverage to the project's efforts in education, community partnership, and outreach. Participation in regional education initiatives has been an important part of the project's public relations endeavors.

Dewees also uses a monthly newsletter to communicate with owners, friends, and potential buyers. While many developments publish newsletters, the *Dewees Island Chronicles* goes beyond most, covering environmental activities, unique wildlife sightings, and educational programs, as well as progress in new home construction and lot sales. Even though the newsletter is a marketing publication, it also serves as a communication vehicle for

Dewees Island's marketing strategy focused primarily on networking through personal referral, rather than advertising, to emphasize the project's character as an exclusive retreat. *(Reprinted with permission from the Island Preservation Partnership.)*

residents, conveying to potential buyers that a tight community is developing on the island.

By taking what could appear as negative attributes and presenting them as positive features to the appropriate market segment, Knott found interested buyers willing to pay a premium for a community that does not cater to golfers and boaters, but is a small, quiet neighborhood of homes nestled within the natural beauty of Dewees Island.

Affiliation with Energy and Environmental Programs

Marketing efforts can get a significant boost if builders and developers affiliate with one of the dozens of voluntary programs throughout North America promoting energy-efficient, environmentally responsive, and healthy buildings. Unlike building codes, which mandate a certain level of performance, voluntary programs encourage builders to improve design, construction, and, in some cases, material selection, and they generally "aim a lot higher" than codes. These programs can help attract press coverage and positive name recognition.

Some of these programs were developed and sponsored by electric utility companies wanting to reduce electric demand to avoid the need for building expensive new power plants (a strategy called demand-side management). Other programs are sponsored by such government agencies, building associations, or nonprofit organizations that promote various environmental or health-related causes. Sponsors of these programs benefit from the end result (lower electricity use for utility companies, pollution reductions for the Environmental Protection Agency, etc.). The builder or developer benefits through marketing support, including independent third-party endorsements of their projects. In some cases the marketing benefit is improved public visibility; in others, the program office conducts active marketing—including advertising—and passes on sales leads to participants. Most, but not all, such programs have some costs associated with participation, such as a membership fee, training costs, and the like.

R-2000

The Natural Resources Canada R-2000 Program is an example of a voluntary program that has gone far beyond improving the performance and salability of individual houses to change Canada's entire housing industry. In the 1970s, Canadian home builders were not known for innovation or quality. Most houses were poorly insulated, drafty, potentially dangerous (because of the presence of combustion gases), and prone to moisture problems. To address these concerns and deal with rapidly increasing energy costs, energy experts in the Canadian government developed the R-2000 program.

The program developed standards to greatly improve energy efficiency, eliminate moisture problems, and, more recently, to promote health and environmental features. It offered training programs and a construction manual to teach builders how to meet the stringent R-2000 standards. Not only did several thousand builders across Canada join the program, but energy and quality standards throughout the Canadian housing industry improved dramatically. With greater public awareness of the benefits of energy-efficient houses resulting from the R-2000 outreach efforts, buyers began to demand better houses. Even those builders who did not join the program found that buyers expected homes built to R-2000 standards were inquiring about such features as high-performance windows, airtight construction, and heat-recovery ventilators. Within the short span of about a decade, Canada turned around the image of its housing, which had been poor-to-mediocre, to top-quality, state-of-the-art.

Modeled after the R-2000 program, the C-2000 Program for Advanced Commercial Buildings was later introduced, setting aggressive targets for reducing energy use as well as requiring design teams to develop strategies for achieving high performance in other areas, such as indoor air quality, lighting quality, adaptability, environmental quality, and ease of operations and maintenance.

Austin Green Builder Program

The Austin, Texas, Green Builder Program is not only an education program, it is also a tremendous marketing tool for environmentally sensitive builders and developers, because it increases awareness of—and demand for—green buildings.

Member builders can promote themselves as part of the Austin Green Builder Program. The program's staff offers marketing assistance to builders through advertising, assistance in developing marketing plans, and public relations campaigns. The program's marketing director, Jill Mayfield, writes an informational newspaper column directed at consumers. She focuses on getting the word out to the public that "green building is very doable."

Unlike Tom Hoyt of McStain Enterprises, Mayfield suggests promoting the benefits of green homes, such as durability, comfort and health, rather than focusing on specific green features. She has found that home buyers often do not understand how houses can address environmental issues, but they are almost always concerned about their family's health. Mayfield offers the following tips:

- Use the phrase "environmentally sound" rather than "green."
- Stay away from technical information until getting prospective buyers into the house, at which point they will be more interested in details.
- Get them to look at the house by talking in emotional terms and taking it down to the family level. Families are looking for safe, comfortable places to live. Don't talk about killing the planet—keep it positive. Focus on the positive effects on families; explain that you are providing a healthier home for them and their family, thanks to nontoxic materials. Show them that using recycled materials and energy and water conservation is the right thing to do, emphasizing that by choosing to live this way, they'll make a difference.
- Be sure to use the usual marketing strategies: press releases, ads, open houses, and giveaways, but also don't be afraid to spend money on something a bit more unusual. Promotions, such as water-saving kits from hardware stores, are cheap and easy. Hire a freelance writer to write an article about your building and send it to the paper.
- Be bold. Call a media person—if not, nobody will ever know what you are doing.*

Mayfield believes that high-profile promotions such as a builder show, a "green" parade of homes, and newspaper columns get better results than ads. The ads she places are specific and generally targeted toward consumers through the Sunday Home Section of the local paper. Five years into the program, she believes that while the Texas public is supportive of environmental concepts, people remain undereducated about the benefits green building can offer when they buy a new home or remodel an existing home.

EPA Green Lights and Energy Star Programs

Developers can cash in on free marketing through the EPA Green Lights Program and several other programs under the Energy Star banner. Like the R-2000 program to the north, these are voluntary, nonregulatory programs geared to promoting energy efficiency and reducing pollution by encouraging businesses, manufacturers, organizations, and individuals to invest in energy-efficient lighting and office equipment and to raise energy standards in new buildings.

---

*Source: Personal communication with Jill Mayfield, June 1995.

The Green Lights Program was the first of these EPA programs promoting energy efficiency, and it remains a good model. Largely geared toward businesses and commercial building owners, the program promotes the idea that companies can save money while creating a cleaner environment. To meet the requirements of the program, a prescribed level of lighting energy efficiency must be achieved. Green Lights participants typically cut their lighting bills in half while enhancing their environmental image, maintaining or improving lighting quality, and increasing employee productivity.

As of June 1995, Green Lights partners included 40 percent of the nation's Fortune 500 companies, as well as thousands of smaller businesses. Green Lights "allies" included electric utilities, lighting manufacturers, and distributors. The allies are an integral part of Green Lights, ensuring a lasting future demand for energy-efficient products by increasing the share of the market dominated by such goods.

The EPA's Energy Star Buildings Program builds on the Green Lights Program to focus on the opportunities available in most commercial buildings to achieve additional energy savings while lowering capital expenditures. A residential component of this program has also been launched. Companies, called "partners," that join the Energy Star Buildings Program sign a memorandum of understanding that outlines both the partner's and EPA's responsibilities throughout a five-stage implementation plan, with the Green Lights Program as the first stage. The EPA asserts that partners can expect to reduce total building energy consumption by 30 percent, on average, by following its strategy. EPA publicizes participation in the Energy Star Buildings Program through public service announcements, magazine articles, awards programs, and profile cards highlighting participants' initiatives.

Being a part of the Energy Star Program leads to great cross-promotional opportunities for both allies and partners. The *Green Lights & Energy Star Update* is mailed monthly to a readership of more than 40,000. An October 1995 issue showcased retail partners Target, Longs Drug Stores, Safeway, and Home Depot, which were upgrading their facilities' energy efficiency or meeting Green Lights criteria in new construction. Some businesses also publicize their efforts to their customers. Home Depot, for example, hangs "We Care About the Environment" banners in its 400 stores, highlighting the company's involvement with Green Lights, recycling programs, and other measures.

LEED RATING FOR COMMERCIAL BUILDINGS

Both Great Britain and Canada have reported early success with their voluntary rating systems for commercial buildings (BREEAM and BEPAC). In the United States, the U.S. Green Building Council has also been developing a rating system called the Leadership in Energy and Environmental Design (LEED™) Building Rating System. The LEED program is notable for its consensus-based, market-driven approach to encouraging green commercial buildings. The development of the system has received extensive input from the Council's membership, which represents many facets of the building industry, including manufacturers, architects, developers, and environmental organizations. At least three drafts of the rating system have been voted on by members through a thorough balloting process that required clear explanation from members on points of disagreement, and then required the committee developing the system to respond, either making recommended changes or disputing them and working toward resolution.

The LEED system is designed to rate new and substantially renovated commercial office buildings. Credits will be awarded for meeting green criteria. The system is intended to be comprehensive in scope yet simple in operation. Certification will rest with a licensed architect or engineer, who will review and verify compliance with the criteria. Participants then submit documentation along with a certification fee. In exchange, their buildings will receive a plaque of certification and national recognition through an aggressive marketing program.

The U.S. Green Building Council anticipates that participation will offer a clear way for developers and owners of commercial buildings to distinguish themselves in the marketplace. Once the standards have been finalized, building owners and developers will have clear goals to shoot for. The system is designed as a tool to edge the marketplace toward greener development. Over time, the standards for green buildings will become more stringent, as participants become more experienced in green building.

Working with Real Estate Professionals

When Michael Corbett began developing Village Homes in the 1970s, there was nothing else like it. The 240-unit subdivision, with clustered passive-solar homes, lots of public parks, and preservation of organic farming areas, was so unlike other

Coldwell Banker Residential identifies Village Homes as "Davis's most desirable subdivision." Featured here is the neighborhood's community center. *(Reprinted with permission from William D. Browning, Rocky Mountain Institute.)*

developments that real estate agents did not want to have anything to do with it. As a result, the Corbetts had to rely on word of mouth and referrals to find their first buyers. "Initially," Corbett recalled, "local realtors discouraged people from looking at Village Homes. After about six months and rapid sales of units, the realtors turned around." Today, a leading local and national real estate firm, Coldwell Banker Residential, not only carries Village Homes listings, but identifies Village Homes as "Davis's most desirable subdivision," and touts the "wonderful Village Homes ambiance."

An often overlooked strategy for marketing green developments is to work closely with local real estate agents. This oversight is not very surprising, given that real estate professionals have not always been receptive to new ideas. Jill Mayfield, of the Austin Green Builder Program, believes that real estate agents may be the least educated segment of the building industry regarding green building. One goal of Austin's marketing strategy is to increase realtor understanding and acceptance of the Green Builder Program and its rated homes by demonstrating that promoting such homes is good for business. The features these homes offer, Mayfield argues, provide realtors with an important marketing edge.

Mayfield joined the local Board of Realtors to influence the Austin market. She is a member of the committee that chooses speakers for monthly meetings, contributes to its newsletter, and helped formulate a course on selling environmentally sensitive homes. Program staff at the Austin Green Builder Program are also trying to increase awareness among realtors by sending brokers their newsletter, keeping the local real estate community up to date on green building events and news, and recruiting a realtor to serve on the Green Builder Advisory Board.

At Dewees Island, the inclusion of real estate agents in initial charrettes and planning sessions for the development ensured that the realtors would be enthusiastic about the unique concepts expressed by this island development. That effort has paid off through strong sales.

Marketing the Benefits of Energy Savings

Bringing potential customers to the door is one component of marketing; closing the sale is another. A wide range of strategies has been employed by green developers to persuade potential buyers, lessors, or renters of innovative projects to sign on the dotted line. Many of these strategies involve promoting the benefits of energy savings—a key component of environmentally responsible buildings, whether commercial or residential.

Convincing buyers or renters of the benefits of energy efficiency is not always easy. People tend to focus only on first cost, neglecting the operating cost. They will buy a 75¢ light bulb, for example, rather than a $15 compact fluorescent light, even though over its lifetime the compact fluorescent will save two or three times its cost in electricity and it will last 10 times as long. Green developers have used various strategies to convince potential buyers that their homes or buildings are better than the competition because they will use a lot less energy. A few examples are profiled in the following paragraphs.

Philip Russell is a Florida home builder who builds quality, energy-efficient structures. Besides founding Russell Home Builders, Russell is also president of Energy Smart Corporation (ESC), which promotes the use of energy-efficient designs, practices, and materials in the home building industry. ESC promotes energy-efficiency as a key marketing strategy. Once customers understand the economic benefits of green measures, he feels, they will be willing to buy such homes. ESC has used a number of strategies to educate customers and to demonstrate green features.

Russell knows that "customers are not mind readers." Since more than half of what goes into a home is hidden, he suggests that builders devote considerable effort to telling customers about the features, products, and materials that make houses energy efficient. "Demonstrate the things they can't see, such as insulation, the air barrier, and the ventilation system. Don't forget to sell the benefits of things they can't put an immediate price tag on — healthy air, low levels of dust, even temperatures from floor to ceiling," he says. Like Jill Mayfield of Austin's Green Builder Program, Russell believes strongly that energy efficiency, health, and comfort are strong selling points, especially if the message is put across in a clear, simple, and entertaining manner.

He launched a demonstration home program featuring a "behind the walls" exposition that gives buyers a chance to see the inner workings of a home before it is finished. Visitors have an opportunity to see how products work and why such features as house wrap, foam sealant around penetrations, and radiant foil in the roof were installed

When Russell founded ESC in 1990, his initial strategy was to create demonstration homes as a focal point for local educational efforts. ESC licenses builders to create demonstration homes that are open to the public for four months before being put on the market. Corporate allies donate materials and appliances for the homes, including recycled products, insulation, and energy-efficient appliances. ESC promotes the homes heavily to get traffic, anticipating that 10,000–12,000 people will pass through each home. Many of the corporation's promotions are actually joint promotions with its sponsors and other interested parties. For example:

- Each demo home is affiliated with a charity, which is able to hold functions there.
- Sponsors can hold practical, educational seminars in the homes. Some teach dealers and subcontractors how to design and install new products. Other seminars are less technical, focusing on the consumer. For example, Sears — an Energy Smart sponsor — gives cooking classes on the energy-efficient ranges.

- Banks hold seminars on energy-efficient mortgages.
- Utilities, with whom ECS also establishes partnerships, sponsor a variety of programs.

Russell finds energy efficiency alone to be a hard sell. Homes also have to offer the life-style features buyers want. So his homes include lots of daylight, high-tech electronic entertainment and communications systems, and space for exercise equipment. Energy Smart homes sell for 5 to 7 percent more than conventional houses, but Russell has found that buyers are quite receptive to green homes once they understand the technologies and products used to achieve good energy performance.

Perry Bigelow, a builder of affordable, energy-efficient tract housing in the Chicago area, offers a remarkable guarantee with his homes: the seasonal heating bill will be less than $200, or Bigelow Homes will pay the difference. While he does not believe this guarantee alone sells many homes, it differentiates him from the competition and brings swarms of interested buyers to his model homes. "All our advertisements point out the $200-a-year heating cost. It almost makes people say they owe it to themselves to come to our products and take a look."

Bigelow Homes has received numerous awards and tremendous media attention by proving that resource-efficient housing can be delivered at any price. Yet Bigelow does not tell his sales staff to emphasize the energy-efficient characteristics or construction techniques of the homes. Formerly a design-oriented custom home builder, Bigelow believes that what motivates the buyer is not the technical performance of a home, but how people see themselves cooking in the kitchen or playing with the kids in the living room. The company places strong emphasis on such features as sun rooms and vaulted ceilings that make the houses "live bigger." They also create outdoor "rooms," common spaces where neighbors can interact. The only role that energy efficiency plays in the actual sale of homes is its impact on comfort—no drafts in the living room, a cozier bedroom, and warmer toilet seats.

Bigelow has had to make good on his guarantee only twice, thanks to super-insulation and a whole-systems approach to developing cost-effective energy-efficiency measures. An added bonus to his home buyers is that the lower operating costs resulting from the energy-efficient features also help buyers qualify for loans with a higher lending limit under the Federal Housing Administration's Energy Efficient Mortgage lending guidelines.

Toolbox: How to Make a Truth Wall

A "truth wall" provides an excellent way to show how and why a building is different from the competitors'. A truth wall in a model home is a cutaway sample of a wall that shows customers the building before it is drywalled or otherwise finished. Customers get to see exactly how the insulation and air barrier are installed, for example. This teaches potential buyers about building in general, and why the house is better than its competition. If the customer later asks questions of other builders about their homes that they cannot answer, the green builder will have a unique selling point.

Method 1. When constructing the wall section, leave off the sheathing material to expose the inner layers of construction material.

Method 2. For masonry construction: At the end of an interior wall that terminates in the middle of a room, refrain from capping or otherwise finishing the end section. The exposed section of wall can serve to illustrate how the wall was constructed and with what materials.

Builders who do not use model homes can construct portable cutaway samples to illustrate construction details on-site. The effect will be even greater if they place it alongside a cutaway sample of a wall built to minimum code requirements.

(Photo by Kathleen Mink, Rocky Mountain Institute.)

Marketing Energy-Efficient Mortgages and Energy-Improvement Mortgages

In many areas developers and builders of energy-efficient homes can now benefit from energy-efficient mortgages (EEMs). While probably too complex to use in broad marketing campaigns, EEMs can be useful in closing sales. The basic idea, as described in Chapter 8, is that because home owners will spend less of their monthly budget on energy bills, they can afford a higher mortgage. Lending institutions that offer EEMs allow buyers to spend a higher percent of their monthly income on mortgage payments, thus raising the price ceiling for a home purchase. This opens up the market to people who otherwise could not afford to buy their homes and allows buyers to purchase larger homes than would otherwise be possible.

Local branches of banks may not be aware that they offer EEMs. In Colorado's Roaring Fork Valley, home to Rocky Mountain Institute, local builder Mark Thomas, a representative of Normerica Custom Homes, brought to the attention of his local Chase Manhattan Bank branch that the bank's policy was to offer EEMs. Once Thomas's banker became aware of this program, she began working with him to spread the word. Soon after, advertisements began appearing in local papers touting the benefits of homes eligible for energy-efficient mortgages. Not only did Thomas's company benefit, but other builders of energy-efficient homes profited from expanded consumer awareness. A subsequent seminar on EEMs sponsored by Energy Rated Homes of Colorado attracted an encouraging number of lenders and realtors who were eager to learn more about this new tool.

Although many lending institutions now offer EEMs, most consumers are not yet aware of their existence or benefits, and few developers are actively promoting this opportunity. Green developers and builders can use their homes' eligibility (they must pass certification tests) for such mortgages as yet another means of market differentiation.

Energy-improvement mortgages (EIMs) are similar to EEMs but applied to energy-efficient retrofits of existing homes either at the time of sale or when a home owner plans improvements. John Wendt, a Century 21 realtor in Delta, Colorado, uses EIMs to create a current and future competitive advantage for himself, while creating increased value and comfort for his residential clients. Before listing a residential property coming onto the market, Wendt pays out-of-pocket the $100 to get the home rated for an EIM, so that he can list it as an already rated property. He is therefore well prepared when people inquire about utility costs, as well as potential problems should they decide against making improvements to their prospective home. Wendt argues that "'typical' utility costs are a myth…utility costs are a function of individual life-styles." EIMs provide the opportunity to make energy-efficiency improvements, and Wendt explains to clients how the mortgage ratio "stretch" enables them to afford the needed improvements. He works closely with a local lender who will split the energy rating cost with him if the loan is carried through her company. This lender also works with an appraiser who knows the ropes and helps rated projects move through the appraisals process.

And that's not all. Wendt also calls his previous clients to explain how improving their home energy efficiency through an EIM will help them to keep up with the market and live in a better, more comfortable house. "I put my money where my mouth is," he says. "I pay for the energy audits to get the home rated. I'm creating my own inventory of homes I'll sell in the future."

MARKETING ENERGY SAVINGS IN THE COMMERCIAL ARENA

The MERITT Signature Development Alliance, coordinated by Continental Offices Ltd., recognizes the marketing benefits of lower energy use and improved comfort in the commercial office space market. As described in Chapter 4, the MERITT Alliance has identified a tremendous market for environmentally responsive commercial office renovations. It estimates that most of the three billion square feet of office space built in the 1980s has a 20-year useful life and will soon need renovation.

Given this market, MERITT figures it can capitalize on product differentiation by providing commercial space that offers lower operating costs and greater comfort, which in turn can improve worker productivity. The MERITT Alliance is marketing its services to chief financial officers of companies, people who will clearly understand the economic benefits. Continental Offices believes this marketing angle will strongly differentiate MERITT from the competitors, many of whom are ignoring the potential to upgrade Class B or C (lower-grade) buildings and increase their value and income stream.

Continental Offices is one of many real estate development companies that has gone on-line, marketing via a web site (or home page) on the Internet. Its joint web site with MERITT has "hot-links" to the web sites of other organizations—business partners General Electric and Herman Miller, suppliers such as Carrier Corporation, and environmental organizations including Rocky Mountain Institute. A simple keystroke instantly takes a browser to these other pages. Through such linkages, the Continental Offices web site turns up in lots of places and can be found through any number of word or category searches.

Free press and third-party endorsements can work wonders, but many green projects still need to recruit potential clients. John Baxter of Compass Associates, Inc., who is MERITT's outside marketing consultant, believes that development can be a profoundly positive social and economic activity, if done with integrity. He emphasizes that marketing strategies for environmentally sensitive developments must be targeted, specific, professionally done, and carefully researched. "It takes more time and is more expensive, but the hit ratio and opportunities for success are far higher than with conventional development. It's not a short-term deal, and it's not for somebody who is looking to make a quick buck. If you don't believe it, don't think it's the 'flavor of the month' and go out and try to sell it, because it won't work. Doing so does a real disservice to the idea that we have one environment, that we aren't merely bystanders or observers."

Baxter believes that mass marketing green commercial developments is a waste of time. He recommends carefully determining the types of clients desired, then marketing to them by name, using video, direct mail, or personal appointments. Any free publicity—in trade publications and the general press—will be of great benefit. He suggests targeting promotional mailings for prospective clients, lessees, or tenants toward anybody within an identified radius who is involved with environmental values.

In targeting potential corporate clients, Baxter emphasizes that green buildings have to be marketed very carefully by developers to emphasize economic return. "If it cannot be proven that it will provide a significant return above the IRR [internal rate of return] or hurdle rate for the prospective client," says Baxter, "the proposal won't be heard." In addition, the presentation must be heard by the senior executive or decision maker within the client organization; if it does not reach this person or the next key influencer, it will most likely be a waste of time and money. He suggests showing the financial viability and return on capital, then, once the presenter gets the person's attention, talking about reduced operating costs, payback periods, and residual value, as well as the idea that the building can be a vehicle for the client to enjoy the additional bonuses of positive image within the client's industry and recognition for his or her actions toward the environment.

BUILDINGS THAT REFLECT CORPORATE VALUES

Buildings can also reflect corporate values and, by doing so, help attract like-minded tenants. In early 1996, the American Association for the Advancement of the Science (AAAS) moved into its new headquarters building in Washington,

The environmental features reflect the values of the American Association for the Advancement of Science and are strongly emphasized in its marketing strategy. *(Reprinted with permission, ©Maxwell MacKenzie, 1996.)*

D.C. Besides serving as the AAAS headquarters, the building is about one-fourth leasable space. The terms of the bond that financed the building confined lessees to like-minded, scientifically oriented nonprofit organizations. These terms made targeting potential lessees easy, yet it also meant an extremely limited target market.

AAAS's marketing strategy strongly emphasized the building's environmental features, which include natural lighting, non-ozone-depleting chillers, and healthful indoor air. Within two months of opening, three-fourths of the space had been leased or was spoken for by such organizations as the Natural Resources Defense Council, the Association for Women in Science, and the American University Research Association, indicating that these groups were eager to work in an innovative building that paid attention to employee comfort and environmental stewardship.

BUILDING CORPORATE IMAGE BY MARKETING THE GREEN MESSAGE

A building can be a powerful marketing tool for companies that lease or sell space. It can also be a marketing tool for companies not involved in real estate. Some environmentally responsible corporations are quietly — or not so quietly — asking that their buildings reflect their corporate values or mission statements.

Real Goods considers the Solar Living Center's landscaping to be an important part of its marketing efforts. The landscaping's dramatic sculptural aspects entice people to pull over and visit the site, drawing visitors from the more than six million cars that pass the site annually, simply to tour the grounds. The Center's landscaping was carried out in the first phase of construction and greatly helped in establishing the site's character. While the landscaping at most commercial projects is more a cosmetic afterthought, the Solar Living Center has extensive gardens and edible landscaping, features that reinforce the energy-efficiency message.

The Real Goods Corporation markets itself as "green" — no holds barred — and markets its new Solar Living Center as the embodiment of that greenness. It views its marketing efforts as a benefit not just to product sales, but "for life on Earth" by helping to publicize green building and living. The Center's highly visible environmental features have played a key role in Real Goods receiving extensive free publicity, worth hundreds of thousands of dollars. Its new building and grounds demonstrate to customers that Real Goods practices what it preaches, and that should help the company's bottom line.

Felissimo is a high-end retail boutique in Manhattan that carries a unique array of attractive and environmentally friendly products, everything from furniture to clothing and household items. A renovation of its century-old, five-story building incorporated numerous environmental features and proved that a green development can be elegant. Working with several artists, Clodagh Design created a design for Felissimo that appeals to all the senses; two small fountains add a soothing note. Wood came from sustainable sources, and some furniture was made from fallen cherry trees. All finishes were nontoxic and water based.

The Energy Resource Center's building is itself a teaching tool. *(Reprinted with permission, © Milroy/McAleer.)*

Felissimo serves as a good example of a retail store that has integrally linked its space with its products' theme. The building also acts as a positive internal marketing tool. Because workers love the space, employee retention is high and the company never has trouble finding new employees.

When the Southern California Gas Company originally conceived of a demonstration building to help its customers become more competitive through energy-efficient practices, it did not realize that the building itself would prove to be a powerful marketing tool. The Energy Resource Center (ERC) was built to house seminars advising clients on a range of energy problems, including design measures that affect energy consumption. But the management team soon realized that they could use the building itself as a teaching tool in carrying out its two major functions: as a venue for conducting seminars on the efficient use of natural gas products and as a conference exhibit facility that rents out meeting space, including an 8,000-square-foot exhibit hall and a dozen specialty rooms for meetings and workshops. Each of the 12 meeting rooms has a theme, highlighting, for example, indoor air quality issues, new residential construction practices, natural gas vehicles, and climate control. The rooms also demonstrate green technologies, which offers opportunities for cross-marketing with such manufacturers as Carrier Corporation and Interface Carpet. Reuse of products and materials is also emphasized; examples range from the recycled building itself to a staircase from a movie set, a reception area countertop made from crushed glass, and reprocessed wood from a Banana Republic warehouse condemned in the Lomo Prieta earthquake. Environment-sensitive features are identified by plaques throughout the building. Thus, customers simply looking for meeting space may find themselves learning about resource efficiency as well, which may help to broaden the Gas Company's client base.

The Gas Company identified the ERC's potential audience as its 215,000 commercial and industrial gas customers. The marketing strategy was shaped by a limited budget that maximized exposure to targeted audiences (energy decision makers) mainly through publicity, direct mail, and special advertising in the trade media. The ERC's performance has given the company extensive free press for its leadership in energy, environmental, and building industry trade journals. Manufacturers of green products used throughout the ERC also include the name of the ERC in marketing their products, which gives additional exposure to Southern California Gas Company. ERC staff believe that the building's main selling point is the fact that it is 80 percent recycled. It sends the message to corporate America that companies can make a conscious decision to help the environment. And the ERC can help them do so.

Marketing Savings During Leasing Negotiations

Leases vary by building type, regional practices, and market conditions. But prevailing leasing structures all too often marginalize efforts to promote resource efficiency. Owners lack incentives to improve efficiency when their tenants will benefit from the savings but do not have to bear the capital costs. Even worse, some landlords profit from tenant energy bills through markups, which creates a disincentive to initiate energy conservation measures—the building owner makes more money when the tenant uses more energy.

Whatever the leasing structure, at the time of lease negotiation potential tenants can be educated about the benefits of green buildings. Operating cost savings offer developers and owners more flexibility in lease negotiations. By sharing these savings and providing added project amenities derived from green features, building owners can reduce tenant turnover. Utility savings can pave the way for lower occupancy costs—a clear advantage in retaining key tenants. And consciously providing and promoting healthful indoor environments can increase occupant productivity and comfort while reducing absenteeism—both of which can also increase tenant satisfaction and retention and, thus, owner profitability.

Any savings passed along to tenants will improve a building's competitive advantage. More attractive lease rates lead to faster absorption rates and lower vacancy rates. John Cordonier of Bentall Properties Ltd., which developed the Crestwood Corporate Centre in British Columbia, finds tenant retention a powerful incentive for investments in energy efficiency. "If you don't retain a tenant, your $25-per-square-foot tenant improvement investment is obsolete, and you must invest that money again. Part of the payback is having tenants who are happy with lighting, ventilation, landscaping, and indoor air quality."

When using leases that pass all costs—including utilities—on to tenants, green developers can benefit by emphasizing the differences in operating costs between their buildings and their competitors' buildings. When marketing residential units at 2211 West Fourth, Harold Kalke emphasizes the utility savings that tenants will realize, including free hot water from the retail tenants' ground-source heat pumps. Since his commercial and retail tenants have triple-net leases, the energy savings from the ground-source heat pump are passed along to them. But Kalke believes that over the long term, lower operating costs will result in higher profit margins to the landlord as well, because, he says, "Healthy, prosperous tenants result in healthy, prosperous landlords."

Keeping an Eye on the Big Picture

Developers and owners who make claims about the "greenness" of their projects will find that they receive criticism if users do not perceive that those claims are being satisfied. The Post Ranch Inn sits delicately in its surroundings in California's breathtaking Big Sur. As described in Chapter 7, careful attention to siting so as to minimize environmental, traffic, and construction impacts in this fragile environment won the 30-unit resort approvals after a long, arduous permitting process. But customers attracted to the Inn because of its environmental image were disappointed by the Inn's lack of attention to environmentally sensitive operations—they did not believe it was enough to be site-sensitive. The Inn responded to customer feedback by bringing the facility and operations in line with its image, including a graywater irrigation system, lighting improvements, and numerous energy improvements.

Marketing is a key priority for any business venture, whether it produces clothes pins or real estate developments. Environmentally responsive development is just as dependent on well thought out marketing as any other real estate product, but by virtue of innovative design features and association with environmental values, green developments have some unique advantages and opportunities when it comes to attracting customers. Green developers are recognizing these benefits. Indeed, the fact that green developments are easier to market has begun to attract mainstream developers to the field.

A few of the many innovative marketing strategies that have been used by green developers have been described in this chapter. Yet this is just a snapshot. Many other approaches have been used, and new ideas are emerging all the time. Creativity is very much a part of marketing green developments.

Customers attracted to the Post Ranch Inn because of its environmental image were disappointed by the Inn's lack of attention to environmentally sensitive operations—they did not believe it was enough to be site-sensitive. This encouraged the Inn to develop other ways to promote sustainability. *(Reprinted with permission from William D. Browning, Rocky Mountain Institute.)*

New Village Homes has blossomed into a much loved community for the richness and diversity it offers residents. *(Reprinted with permission from William D. Browning, Rocky Mountain Institute.)*

CHAPTER 11

Sustaining the Green Development

THE SATISFACTION AND PRIDE IN THEIR COMMUNITY felt by residents of Village Homes more than a decade after completion of the development is not coincidental. Village Homes thrives today because it was planned, designed, and built with deliberate attention to creating a community.

Completed in 1981, the Davis, California, project is one of the first modern developments that can be considered "green." Its success—first as a real estate development and now as a community—can be traced back to its designers' and developers' whole-systems approach that considered end-use/least-cost issues. Over time, Village Homes has become a dearly loved neighborhood, with lower utility and food costs and a strong community fabric, because it was designed to endure. The turnover rate in Village Homes is very low, with residents often opting to remodel and add on, rather than move to a larger home. When homes do go on the market, they sell at a premium price and faster than homes in nearby subdivisions.

The 240 homes are clustered in groups of eight surrounded by common space and are connected by pedestrian walkways. The subdivision was laid out so that the small passive-solar homes would have good solar exposure. The original residents were able to decide how their common areas would be landscaped—whether with grass, gardens, tot lots, or barbecue pits—creating diversity among shared spaces.

Village Homes is successful in large part because of developers Michael and Judy Corbett's foresight as to how a livable community should be designed and managed to make it successful. The Corbetts knew that to get residents invested in the development, they would have to be involved in decision making as the project evolved over time. The community members would then be responsible for what happened in their own neighborhood, instead of leaving it in the hands of a property manager or absentee developer. The Homeowners Association at Village Homes owns the household commons, the greenbelt commons, the agricultural lands (orchards and vineyards), and the community center. The Association makes management and financial decisions on such issues as maintenance of open space and recreation facilities, harvesting and distribution of produce, and allocation of revenue from some office space and rental units. The Corbetts believe that this model helps develop social participation skills for residents and leads to the development of a healthy, neighborhood-based community.

A network of pathways and houses around common areas ensures that people get to know their neighbors, which has kept the crime rate extremely low (about one-tenth that of the surrounding town of Davis). The compact, pedestrian-oriented design encourages residents to walk to meet their daily needs; the average walk to the grocery store is just 10 minutes. Village Homes is also located close to the largest employer in the area, the University of California at Davis, so many residents can walk to work. The average number of cars per household is only 1.8 in Village Homes, as compared with 2.1 in a standard development.

Residents enjoy much lower energy bills thanks to homes designed to incorporate passive solar technologies in a wide range of architectural styles. Annual household energy bills range from one-third to one-half of those in surrounding neighborhoods as a result of passive heating, natural cooling, solar hot water systems, and reduced amount of pavement (which keeps ambient air temperatures lower during Davis's hot summers).

Village Home residents pick fruit for breakfast from the thriving trees along the meandering paths. This edible landscape produces oranges, almonds, apricots, pears, grapes, persimmons, peaches, cherries, and plums. Community gardens, located on the west side of the development, give residents the opportunity to get out and grow together. A portion of this garden is used for commercial organic farming; much of the delicious produce is sold to local restaurants and markets. Frequent harvest festivals and other gatherings bring residents together and ensure that the strong sense of community will be maintained at Village Homes.

The developers of Village Homes created a neighborhood that they believe helps to promote social participation and a strong community. *(Reprinted with permission from William D. Browning, Rocky Mountain Institute.)*

All too often, little attention is paid to how real estate developments will function after opening day. But that is what really counts. One of the characteristics that sets green developments apart is that these projects' effects on occupants, on the larger community, and on the environment over a very long time horizon is carefully considered as the development is designed and built. Green development is not just about buildings; it is also about what those structures create. Increasingly, designers and developers are realizing that developments can play an important role in teaching and encouraging a more sustainable way of life, both for occupants and for people in the broader community. Developer John Knott asks, "What value is there in creating a physical sustainable community if you don't have a way to ensure that the people in it will continue to create sustainability?"

This chapter examines what happens *after* the green development is occupied —and how decisions made during initial planning and design can help to ensure that the development's operation will aid in moving society in the direction of sustainability. Some of these impacts are direct and easy to quantify: low energy use, eliminating the need for harmful pesticide treatments, and making it easy for occupants to recycle wastes, for example. Others are more subtle and less quantifiable, such as reducing automobile dependence through the creation of bicycle and pedestrian trails and generating sustainable economic development in the region.

Operating a development in a manner that moves us toward sustainability does not just happen. It requires attention to education. It may require the creation of operating guidelines for a building that specify cleaning procedures, maintenance practices, and other provisions relating to operation. And it almost always requires a willingness on the part of the developer to consider the big picture—a whole-systems approach to development with a clear sense of what the project can accomplish.

Reducing Direct Environmental and Health Impacts of Operation

The operation of buildings and building grounds carries a heavy environmental burden. All such operations use energy and water, generate waste, and emit pollutants through cleaning and maintenance. Earlier chapters, particularly Chapters 5 and 6, have addressed how these impacts can be minimized through design features that affect operation. But it is important that buildings are operated to ensure that the benefits envisioned during design will be realized over the long term.

BUILDING MAINTENANCE

> No maintenance, no building—every building is potentially immortal, but very few last half the life of a human.
>
> *Stewart Brand,* How Buildings Learn, *1994*

One of the most obvious, yet often forgotten, truths about a green building is that it will remain a green building only if it continues to function in the resource-efficient manner it was designed and built for. Often, projected energy savings are not achieved because of inadequate building operation and management practices. Careful ongoing maintenance is required to ensure that this does not happen.

Environmentally responsible maintenance includes such measures as keeping solar and other systems working, maintaining the efficiency of mechanical systems, controlling moisture problems, maintaining healthful indoor air quality, and using environment-friendly cleaning products.

One stakeholder concerned about the quality of a development's upkeep is the property manager. Property management has evolved to include much more than just collecting rents and carrying out standard building maintenance. Property managers face intense financial pressures to cut costs, maintain tenant comfort and health, manage properties to enhance value, and demonstrate fiscal responsibility. With the pressure to reduce operating costs and liability, property managers constitute a prime market for those ready to instruct them on the benefits of green development.

Helping Companies Improve Their Environmental Performance—BREEAM

The United Kingdom's Building Research Establishment Environmental Assessment Method (BREEAM) was first introduced in England in 1993 to help building managers understand and improve the environmental performance of their buildings. The procedure, which also became available for commercial office buildings in Canada in late 1996, examines and evaluates all aspects of office operations that have an environmental impact and recommends areas of improvement. In addition to such direct impacts as energy, water, paper usage, indoor air quality, and waste management, the program also addresses such issues as commuting, business travel, and working at home. The process takes just a few days (five days for a 150-person office) and can offer significant savings for both the company and the environment. In Canada, BREEAM is administered by the environmental consulting firm ECD Energy and Environment Canada, Ltd. For information, contact:

ECD Energy and Environment Canada, Ltd.
165 Kenilworth Avenue
Toronto, Ontario M4L 3S7
(416) 699-6671; (416) 699-9250 (fax)

CLEANING PROCEDURES

Barney Burroughs, an indoor air quality consultant with Building Wellness Consultancy in Atlanta, offers a warning: "Poor housekeeping maintenance can negate the finest designs and construction efforts with regard to air quality. Cleaning chemicals, vacuuming techniques, and other purposeful practices such as pest control should be scrutinized to make sure that they are all lowering and not aggravating contaminant levels." To address such concerns while meeting their goal of providing an attractive, healthful, comfortable, pleasant sales environment for their customers and employees, the Gap Corporation's Banana Republic store on Santa Monica's Third Street Promenade specified that only nontoxic, biodegradable cleaning products be used in cleaning the building.

A major cause of ill health can be the spraying of pesticides. VeriFone, who manufactures the key pad for credit card verification equipment, implemented a Safe Pest Control Policy, which prohibits the use of known toxins and defines safe, acceptable methods for pest control in the company's green building in Costa Mesa, California. Pest control is handled in a way that does not require spraying pesticides within the building. During construction, for example, a "safe" drying powder was applied inside the walls to kill insects that might penetrate the building's shell, thus avoiding the need for most postoccupancy treatments. Since the building serves as a model for VeriFone facilities worldwide, it was important to develop clear and easily transferable guidelines for cleaning and maintenance. Corporate architect Scott Churchill noted that this "ensures that all the work that went into this green building effort will pay off by providing [the company's] people a safe place to work, not just a less smelly new building which is then polluted." Chemicals used to maintain the facility have been carefully reviewed and selected for employee safety.

ENSURING HEALTHFUL INDOOR AIR QUALITY

> I love coming here to work every day. I love knowing that I'm not breathing crud. In other buildings I'd look up and see the air vents were always full of grime. Maintenance people were in here just yesterday cleaning the vents. I like to see that.
>
> *Elizabeth Hax, Membership Department,National Audubon Society,*
> Audubon House, *1994*

Maintaining healthful IAQ is a key aspect of green building maintenance. IAQ is not a simple, easily defined concept. The indoor environment in any building is

Environmentally Sound Cleaning and Housekeeping Practices

1. Commit to the continual education of building occupants and custodial staff.

2. Clean to protect health as well as appearance.

3. Clean and maintain the building in an integrated manner. Cleaning and maintenance in one area of the building can have major impacts on other areas.

4. Schedule routine housekeeping and custodial services. Frequent, thorough, regularly scheduled housekeeping and custodial services provide the most efficient and effective means to achieve high building performance.

5. Develop procedures to address accidents—air contamination caused by noxious chemical reactions, spills, and water leaks.

6. Minimize human exposure to harmful contaminants and cleaning residues.

7. Minimize chemical and moisture residue when cleaning.

8. Ensure the safety of workers and building occupants at all times.

9. Minimize the pollutants that enter the building. Dilution of chemicals does not eliminate contamination; control at the source is recommended.

10. Dispose of cleaning waste in environmentally safe ways.

Source: Stephen Ashkin, for Public Technology, Inc.'s *Sustainable Building Technical Manual: Green Building Design, Construction and Operations.* (See Appendix B for order information.) (Reprinted with permission from Public Technology, Inc., the nonprofit R&D organization of the National League of Cities, the National Association of Counties, and the International City/County Management Association.)

influenced by the site, climate, outdoor air, building systems, construction techniques, contaminant sources, and building occupants. To ensure good IAQ, the designers of the National Audubon Society's headquarters (a renovated 100-year-old building in New York City) considered not only how the building would be renovated and what materials would go into it, but also how it would be operated. Croxton Collaborative Architects, the project architects, developed purchasing guidelines for cleaning supplies and plant care in the building. They went so far as

Indoor Air Quality Tool Kit

The EPA's Indoor Environment Management Branch developed a useful publication to help building managers prevent IAQ problems and resolve such problems if they do come up. *Building Air Quality : A Guide for Building Owners and Facility Managers* is divided into four sections: (1) The Basics: Factors Affecting IAQ and Effective Communication, (2) Preventing IAQ Problems: Developing an IAQ Profile and Managing Buildings for Good IAQ, (3) Resolving IAQ Problems: Diagnosing and Mitigating IAQ Problems, and (4) Hiring Professional Assistance to Solve IAQ Problems. Extensive appendices contain valuable information on moisture and mildew problems, asbestos, radon, HVAC-related problems, and measurement of indoor air quality.

(See Appendix C for contact information.)

Sample Form
Incident Log

File Number	Date	Problem Location	Investigation Record (check the forms that were used)									Outcome / Comments	Log Entry By (initials)
			Complaint Form	Occupant Interview	Occupant Daily	Log of Activities	Zone/Room Record	HVAC Checklist	Pollutant Pathway	Source Inventory	Hypothesis Form		

to develop their own specialized procedures for cleaning the natural wool carpeting. And, because this was New York City, they also carefully researched nontoxic chemicals for removing graffiti.

It is important to establish a means of tracking occupant complaints about IAQ and implementing a procedure for follow-up. Prompt response may prevent the problem from growing into a major one. Using an "incident log," described and illustrated in "Indooor Air Quality Tool Kit" on page 354, is one way to accomplish this.

Regular maintenance of the HVAC system is important to prevent IAQ problems. Keeping HVAC systems in proper running order not only reduces energy costs, but can also prevent serious IAQ problems from cropping up. Maintenance tasks include cleaning out air intake plenums, cleaning or replacing filters, and—as necessary—cleaning ducts, louvers, screens, and dampers.

IAQ experts are increasingly targeting mold and other biological contaminants, along with the biological VOCs they can emit, as leading causes of IAQ problems. Therefore, maintenance inspections should focus on basements, crawl spaces, and HVAC ducts, all of which can host biological contaminants. Such problems as leaky pipes, standing water, insect infestations, piles of debris, and rotten wood should be promptly dealt with to reduce the risk of problems.

As discussed earlier, cleaning compounds should be carefully selected, and procedures for proper usage should be specified. Potentially dangerous or toxic chemicals such as fuels, solvents, and pesticides should be stored outside occupied spaces.

Landscape Care

Maintenance procedures outside the building are also important. Improper landscaping procedures can waste energy and water and pollute ecosystems. Planting native, low-water-use grasses can eliminate the need for irrigation, mowing, and pesticides and, in the process, save money for owners. Using graywater for subsurface irrigation can reduce or eliminate the need to use potable water.

Andropogon Associates Ltd., an ecological planning and design firm in Philadelphia, believes that it is crucial to develop a monitored landscape maintenance program "to ensure that policies and management fulfill long-term goals and are informed by real science." The firm further advises, "A key objective is to ensure that the most effective strategies are applied and to ensure that chronic problems are not exacerbated by routine maintenance operations." Andropogon also recommends creating and regularly updating a site data base that can be used to make future decisions on landscape management. Through learning from past experience, the costs and impacts of future landscaping practices can be reduced.

Landscape architect Stephen Goetz, who consulted on Boeing's Longacres Park project outside Seattle, advises that achieving ecologically sensitive landscape maintenance requires training contractors in appropriate methods. He has found

Planting native, low-water-use grasses such as those used in this prairie landscape near Chicago can eliminate the need for irrigation, mowing, and pesticides, saving money for years to come. *(Reprinted with permission from William D. Browning, Rocky Mountain Institute.)*

that many people do not understand the complex issues involved in landscape maintenance. For example, Goetz stated that there is only about a 5 to 10 percent success rate—on the high side—in mitigation wetlands (new wetlands created to mitigate destruction of natural wetlands during development), as a result of design and maintenance problems. "People just don't understand the complexity of creating an ecosystem," he says. "Designers hope their landscape is going to be better than it is. And this keeps happening over and over, because no one is looking at what went before." This perpetuation results in a huge amount of wasted money and time. Goetz notes that the current process does not allow the design team to learn; they are not paid to come back and assess how they did their work. When they are used, such "feedback loops" can be a tremendous asset to developers, designers, and landscape managers.

Integrated Pest Management (IPM) is an element of environmentally responsible landscape maintenance. IPM is a coordinated approach to pest control that uses only the amount of pesticide necessary to prevent unacceptable levels of pests while causing the least possible harm to people, property, and the environment. It discourages undesirable insects and plants by optimizing horticultural and biological controls, including cultivation, watering and fertilization practices, use of pest-resistant plants and crops, introduction of natural predators and parasites of pest species, and strategic placement of beneficial insect habitats. Pest populations are carefully monitored, and small amounts of damage below an "economic threshold" are tolerated. This method can save costs and increase profits. An increasing number of golf course managers include IPM in their maintenance plans, as do some groundskeepers at corporate campuses.

The developers of Spring Island, in partnership with David Wilhelm of Vail, Colorado, are developing the Roaring Fork Club, a Jack Nicklaus golf course in Basalt, Colorado. The developers hired permaculturist Jerome Ostenkowski to help design biological "islands" throughout the course that will include native plants to attract birds and other biological controls for unwanted pests. This is quite different from the conventional golf course design approach that relies on heavy chemical usage. Ostenkowski hopes to take this golf course even further to include edible landscaping along the greens, with vineyards, fruit trees, and berry bushes.

HELPING OCCUPANTS PRACTICE ENVIRONMENTALISM THROUGH RECYCLING

With the average office worker generating more than 100 pounds of waste paper each year, recycling paper and other resources is an important part of environmental responsibility. At the National Audubon Society's headquarters in New York City, staff set an ambitious goal of recycling 80 percent of all waste from the building to save some 42 tons of paper a year. To accomplish this, Audubon first assessed its existing waste stream to determine exactly what was being thrown away. It worked with Waste Management, Inc. to design the actual recycling system. In addition to furnishing each desk with a specially designed three-slot basket for recycling, the system called for four building-high chutes that gave employees means for convenient separation and disposal. Each chute is dedicated to a particular recyclable product: paper, aluminum, plastics, and glass. The chutes empty into a basement recycling center where waste is processed for shipping to a recycling outlet. The capital cost of installing this system was $185,000. Ken Hamilton, the facility manager at Audubon, reports that the chute system is working well; currently, the headquarters is recycling about 70 percent of its trash. (An initial goal of composting food waste proved problematic in an eight-story building.) In the future, should regulations requiring sorting of recyclable materials come into play, Audubon estimates that it could save more than $12,000 per year in hauling fees.

High-Rise Recycling Corporation has estimated that a standard 20-floor building can save $27,200 annually in labor costs by handling recycling with a chute system instead of floor-by-floor recycling. The potential savings realized from reduced trash hauling fees is $4,800 annually. Thus, a total annual savings of $32,000 is possible. When offset by installation costs, the company claims an increase in cash flow of $8,000 a year. Low-tech recycling systems, as a part of standard daily or weekly maintenance, is another option for large buildings.

INDUSTRIAL FACILITIES — SPECIAL CONSIDERATIONS

Operating a manufacturing facility in a more sustainable fashion may require examining how a company produces its products. Responsibly developing industrial facilities, therefore, means examining the manufacturing process and looking for opportunities to improve environmental performance and complement the company's green vision.

Ecover is a Netherlands-based manufacturer of eco-friendly cleaning products. In 1990 the company decided to create a building that would serve as the symbol of its commitment to the environment and distinguish it from the other large corporations producing soaps and detergents. Ecover built an ecologically sensitive plant that minimized waste in the manufacturing process and eliminated toxic by-products. Through analyzing the soap production process itself, the company found that energy could be saved by recovering heat from the soap drying process. A special water purification system was designed around the soap manufacturing process. Ecover saves almost $10,000 yearly through the use of these efficient systems.

Ecover employees enjoy their work environment and are committed, cheerful, and motivated, in part because of the attention received from the plant's many visitors. Ecover hopes this factory will be considered an experiment, a first try at an ecological factory, and that other companies will examine and learn from its whole-systems approach.

Office furniture manufacturer Herman Miller is another company on the leading edge of environmentally responsible manufacturing. Environmental measures have been integrated into the design and construction of its new Simple Quality Affordable (SQA) facility in Zeeland, Michigan, as profiled in Chapters 5 and 6, and the company's environmental ethic extends throughout the corporate structure, as evidenced by its Environmental Awareness Statement:*

As a corporate steward in our communities, through continuous improvement we will:

- Minimize waste by following the priority order of reduce, reuse, recycle, compost, incinerate, landfill.
- Implement technologies to efficiently use energy resources.
- Strive to surpass conformance to the law. Compliance will be a minimum standard by which we rate our performance.
- Use compact resources to promote environmental knowledge and awareness to those involved in our business, including our employees, customers, regulators, suppliers, neighbors, and competitors.
- Review and improve the environmental impact of materials in use in our products and processes.

In putting these principles into practice, Herman Miller has dramatically reduced both the use of harmful chemicals and the amount of waste generated. The company has developed an Environmental Quality Action Team, a multidisciplinary group whose members include communications staff, marketing staff, and packaging engineers, among others. This team assists in coordination and policy development regarding environmental initiatives. Environmental Affairs manager Paul Murray says, "Sixty to 70 percent of environmental suggestions come from the production floor."

The company is working toward a corporate goal of zero landfill use. A comprehensive reusable packaging program has begun. Reducing landfill waste has resulted in major savings for Herman Miller through less trucking of waste, lower tipping fees, and revenue from waste recycling. Herman Miller has also made significant progress in cutting air pollutant emissions. In the company's wood finish line, more than 95 percent of its solvents are now captured and destroyed.

---

*Reprinted with permission from Herman Miller, Inc.

In addition to having a green facility, VeriFone has modeled environmental responsibility in its operations and manufacturing processes. *(J. R. Anderson, photographer. Reprinted with permission.)*

In addition to renovating an existing building for one of its new manufacturing facilities, electronic equipment manufacturer VeriFone has incorporated environmental responsibility into its operations. The company studies the impact of each action taken and devises solutions to reduce or eliminate negative impacts. Even while reducing costs and becoming more competitive, VeriFone has retooled its manufacturing processes to eliminate CFCs, invested in energy improvements, reduced water waste, dramatically reduced solid waste production, implemented programs to provide a healthy work environment for all employees, and worked to protect endangered species around the world. The company's whole-systems approach takes into account "everything from the components that go into our products, from the environmental practices of our vendors, to how much energy we use in our buildings."

Improving the Green Development

Once a green development is completed, a process is needed to evaluate how it is working and how it—and future projects—can be improved. A carefully planned feedback loop can provide this information. Amory Lovins is well known for saying that "any system without a feedback system is stupid. It will continue to make the same dumb mistakes rather than making interesting new ones." Conscientious green developers have to review their projects and assess how they are functioning.

THE DEVELOPER'S CHECKUP

Many of the green developers featured in this book keep close tabs on their projects to learn what worked and did not work. Harold Kalke's offices are situated in his own mixed-use project at 2211 West Fourth Avenue in Vancouver. Jim Chaffin's primary residence is on Spring Island, and Michael and Judy Corbett live in Village Homes. However, in lieu of living or working within one's own development, visiting the building(s) regularly, conducting postoccupancy reviews, and collecting and analyzing performance data, such as energy use, can inform developers' future projects.

A key part of environmental architect William McDonough's design process is his postoccupancy walk-through. Once a building is completed and operational, he asks workers how they like their space and whether they understand the various features that make the building green. He keeps a log of this feedback so that he can learn from it and apply the lessons in future designs.

Developer Jonathan Rose of Affordable Housing Development Corporation takes this step even further. After a project is complete, he talks to every one of the tenants to discover what they like and do not like and to gather other facts specific to the project. With the Denver Dry Goods Building, for example, he wanted to find out what percentage of tenants did not own a car, since the project is accessible by public transit. Rose also observes how people interact on the site. He learned this from his great uncle, a high-rise developer in New York City. By interviewing tenants in the high-rise housing projects, his great uncle learned that families typically put babies in the dining room to sleep. With the limited room layout in these buildings, a window could either be in the kitchen or in the dining room; when he learned the dining room would be used as a bedroom, he decided that it should have the window.

RECOMMISSIONING

> This little noticed, un-glamorous "back-end" of the process is at least as important as the previous stages, because an inefficient system well run will often work better than an efficient system run poorly.
>
> *Amory Lovins, "Energy Efficient Buildings:*
> *Institutional Barriers and Opportunities," 1992*

A building is a lot like a car: it needs to be tuned up periodically to make sure it is operating the way its designer intended—and maybe even a little better. This process, sometimes referred to as "recommissioning," is similar to the commissioning process described in Chapter 9. During recommissioning, all aspects of building operation are examined with an eye toward improvements in energy performance, comfort, and indoor air quality. At the same time, such building design elements as exterior shade systems can also be examined and adjusted as needed.

The dramatically increasing number of papers presented at conferences sponsored by ASHRAE and the American Council for an Energy Efficient Economy (ACEEE), as well as the emergence of an annual conference devoted entirely to commissioning and recommissioning, give testament to the significance of this procedure. Fortunately, the economics of recommissioning are typically very attractive, with reduced energy use giving a quick payback on the investment. The other benefits can be icing on the cake.

Recommissioning is typically carried out by a team comprised of facilities engineers and operators, energy auditors, energy management and building system commissioning experts, and indoor air quality specialists who aim to optimize the performance of building systems and equipment. They seek to make improvements in such areas as HVAC systems, refrigeration, controls, lighting, and building envelopes. This process typically involves collecting temperature, pressure, and humidity data throughout the building and in mechanical systems, and then identifying opportunities for improvement. With mechanical systems, equipment is often tuned up as part of recommissioning, which can involve such actions as balancing airflows, cleaning and adjusting burner nozzles, and adjusting controls. A complete floor-by-floor audit of a facility may examine office equipment, other plug loads, and building occupancy patterns. Interviews with key building operations personnel are typically conducted. Sophisticated hourly energy simulation models of the building may be produced. With all this data accumulated, a strategy session is then conducted by the recommissioning team to create an implementation plan.

The recommissioning process may include periodic monitoring and diagnosis of equipment and components to identify potential future failures. *(Reprinted with permission, © Milroy/McAleer.)*

Some industry professionals call for "condition monitoring" or "predictive maintenance." This means conducting periodic monitoring and diagnosis of equipment and components to identify potential future failures. The procedure improves the overall "health" of mechanical systems to extend their useful life. High-quality, well-calibrated sensors are vital for accurately monitoring a building's performance.

A paper presented at the 1995 Building Commissioning Conference by Helen Kessler and colleagues examined the recommissioning of One First National Plaza, a 1960s-era office tower in Chicago. The owners wanted to achieve a longer life for the building's systems while reducing energy costs. During recommissioning, the team found that the air volume was oversized for the building during most periods of the year, and that the most significant improvement would be to reduce the number of supply fan motors from two to one in most air handling units This relatively simple modification led to savings of more than $200,000 per year.

While recommissioning is not yet routine, as more green buildings enter the market it will become an increasingly common strategy to ensure their longevity and effectiveness. For information and resources on recommissioning, see the discussion on commissioning in Chapter 9.

Influencing Attitude, Productivity, and Performance

> We shape our buildings and then our buildings shape our lives.
>
> *Winston Churchill*

Well-designed green buildings and landscapes will have a long-term positive impact on people's attitudes, productivity, and performance. In fact, achieving a high-quality living or work environment can be one of the strongest drivers of green development, especially in the work environment where greater occupant satisfaction can translate into higher productivity.

At The Way Station, a mental health facility in Maryland, patients and employees relish the quality of the space and how comfortable and pleasant it is to be there. In a July 1994 *Solar Today* article, chief operating officer Tena Meadows observed, "It makes a tremendous difference for our patients with depression and mental disorders to be in a building that embraces the natural world and feels expansive and sunny." Open design with no corners, exposed natural wood beams, spaces bathed in daylight, and trees growing up through the interior greenhouse provide a sense of comfort and security for patients. The directors and staff affectionately refer to their building as a "clubhouse" and have noted that Way Station patients make faster progress in treatment than in their former facility.

Employee productivity and reductions in absenteeism, noted elsewhere in this book, are important benefits of green development. To date, anecdotal evidence, including that collected by Rocky Mountain Institute, suggests that green buildings improve worker productivity and health. Scientific studies are now under way to verify such claims. What is not clear is *why* green buildings have such impacts. Which aspects of green design matter most? What types of work and what health characteristics are most likely to be affected?

The U.S. Department of Energy (DOE) is beginning to supply answers through various research efforts. A 1994 DOE-funded study by the Center for Building Performance and Diagnostics at Carnegie Mellon University, *The Intelligent Workplace Retrofit Initiative,* found that occupants close to windows reported fewer health symptoms than occupants near the middle of an office space or in the interior core of a building. An ongoing DOE-funded Green Building Benefits Study is developing a scientifically based protocol to assess the relation-

The Way Station features open design, a lack of corners, exposed natural wood beams, spaces bathed in daylight, and an interior greenhouse, all of which provide a sense of comfort and security for patients. *(Reprinted with permission from William D. Browning, Rocky Mountain Institute.)*

ship between green buildings and human outcomes. Program administrators at DOE believe that if worker health and productivity claims are shown to be true, the potential economic payoffs to organizations are great and will certainly warrant increased investment in green buildings.

This Green Building Benefits Study, led by Pacific Northwest National Laboratory, is currently examining two Herman Miller buildings in Zeeland, Michigan, the older Phoenix Design building and the new SQA building. These buildings were selected because they enabled the research team to conduct "before" and "after" assessments. The older Phoenix Design building provided baseline data against which worker responses and outcomes in the new building can be compared. Herman Miller is committed to full collaboration in the research effort and is providing researchers with data. Researchers have a full year

The Green Buildings Benefit Study, led by Pacific Northwest National Laboratory, is examining two Herman Miller buildings in western Michigan to determine why buildings that incorporate natural processes and features have a positive effect on people. The daylit corridor of the Herman Miller SQA building is shown here. *(Don Van Essen, photographer. Reprinted with permission.)*

of preassessment data on the old building and will gather two years of data on the new building and its employees.

The study uses the "Biophilia Hypothesis" as its framework. This idea, put forth by Harvard scientist E. O. Wilson and others, suggests that humans are innately attracted to—and prefer—nature and natural processes because of our long evolution in natural landscapes. The Green Buildings Benefit Study is based on the idea that buildings can be thought of as modern-day habitats and that green buildings can have positive impacts on people if the buildings incorporate natural processes and features. Biophilia features as applied to green buildings include viewscapes, daylight, sensory retreats, opportunities for active and passive contact with nature, sensory change, variability across time and space, and the incorporation of natural themes, archetypes, analogs, and materials into the built environment. Whether this particular study will answer the question of why natural features seem to improve worker health and productivity is unknown, but this research direction is extremely exciting.

Education: A Key Component of Green Development

Education plays an important role in any green development, but in two very different ways. First, building owners and/or occupants must be educated or trained to ensure optimal functioning of the buildings and grounds. Second, education can be incorporated into a development's ongoing operation to extend positive environmental and social impacts beyond its borders.

EDUCATING THE OCCUPANTS

If occupants understand the vision of the development as well as the specifics of how it works, they will more likely be willing participants in sustaining the project's intent and the project will be more successful at expressing that vision. It is unlikely that most green developments will achieve their full potential without educating occupants in some way.

To ensure a lasting and successful project, it is vital for developers, owners, and architects to inform and train occupants and/or building managers about how the building works and how to operate it for optimal performance, even if it requires an initial investment. According to the EPA's Air Pollution and Control Division, the payoff derived from higher performance levels and reduced liability risk should be well worth the initial investment. If a building operates differently from conventional buildings—for example, if it relies on passive solar heating or natural cooling—the training may have to be quite specialized.

By being integrally involved in operating or managing a building, occupants can become better tuned in to the building's connections with the seasons, the local climate, and the relationship between building operation and occupant health. When the San Francisco Main Library was completed, for example, the design team explained the green aspects of the building to the librarians, particularly in regard to indoor air quality, a primary concern of the librarians. By fully understanding the various healthful-building features, library staff became strong advocates for the entire green agenda. Project architect Anthony Bernheim suggests that builders hold seminars with videos to train and prepare occupants in how to successfully occupy a green building.

In addition to training, providing a written operations and maintenance manual for a building is highly recommended. *The Sustainable Building Technical Manual* suggests developing written policies and procedures for the facility staff. Such an operations and maintenance manual should address inspection, preventative maintenance, cleaning, and repair of equipment. Providing Material Safety Data Sheets (MSDS) and information on cleaning and pest control methods should also be part of these procedures. An easily accessible written manual will help ensure that the investment in training is not lost with staff turnover.

What can happen if operational procedures are *not* followed was described in Chapter 2 with the example of Malsapino College in British Columbia. This carefully designed passively ventilated building did not work as intended, because neither the occupants nor maintenance staff were taught how to use the building's operable vents. They did not understand that the vents had to be opened and closed each morning and night. Consequently, offices and classrooms overheated, particularly on the building's south side. Unfortunately, the college's solution was to install a conventional air-conditioning system instead of teaching the building managers how to correctly operate the passive ventilation system.

Another example of problems resulting from improper education occurred at the Boyne River Ecology Center in Ontario, a 6,000-square-foot environmental demonstration center for children founded by the Toronto Board of Education and the Ontario Ministry of Energy and Environment. Because the Center's staff did not understand the whole-systems nature of the center's design and approached it using old habits of thought, they compromised several aspects of the building's original intent. Architect Doug Pollard observed, "The lesson is that although the children get it intuitively, the adult world of educational institutions is not up for attuning to unfamiliar music."

The building was designed to have "near zero impact" on the environment. It was powered entirely by photovoltaic cell banks, a hydroelectric generator, and a wind turbine. Reliance on natural ventilation was an additional strategy for energy independence. Interior partitions were stopped short of the ceiling to allow air movement through the spaces and up to the cupola for venting. Unfortunately, the acoustic baffles the architect specified were never installed, as a result of cost cuts, so the noise transfer between rooms became a problem. To solve this, the Board of Education's maintenance staff decided to block off the space from the top of the partitions to the ceiling by glassing them in. This simple but narrowly focused solution negated the natural ventilation strategy.

The installation of a conventional heating system further disrupted the design's original intent. The building is largely underground and has a well-insulated shell, so heating and cooling loads are extremely small. Instead of putting in a traditional furnace, a fireplace was installed in the center of the building to provide a bit of extra heat when necessary. The construction crew substituted lower-cost, tempered glass for the infrared-transparent and thermally safe glass around the fireplace that had been specified by the architect and approved by authorities. When a very large fire was set over Christmas break, the glass imploded. Resulting lawsuits uncovered the unauthorized glass substitution. But the focus of attention was shifted by attacking the appropriateness of using a fireplace as a central heating system. The architect tried to explain how the system worked, but was broadsided by another individual who insisted that the facility install a furnace, which resulted in forcing a hookup to the electric grid.

In contrast, consider the experience of the Vista Hotel in New York City. Damaged by the World Trade Center bombing in 1993, it was closed for renovations. During this time some of the staff raised concerns about the wastefulness and pollution caused by hotel operations. The hotel management took the opportunity to develop an environmental strategy and, in the process, became the first chain-owned hotel (then Hilton International) to become certified as an "Eco Hotel" by HVS Eco Service. HVS is a private firm that rates hotels' commitment to various environmental criteria, including solid waste management, energy efficiency, water conservation, legislative compliance, and employee education and training. Vista recognized the market opportunity offered by becoming the first certified Eco Hotel and helping to launch a trend toward proactive, voluntary compliance driven by the private sector rather than by government. Since then, the hotel industry has recognized the significance of embracing environmental issues, with some hotels striving to become certified and others undertaking various environmentally responsible practices.

HVS presented Vista with an extensive list of recommendations, many of which were acted on after consideration of capital costs, expected payback, and staff preferences. Staff training was a key component of this transition to an Eco Hotel. HVS created an employee handbook for Vista that spelled out green standards, starting with solid waste management, energy conservation, and water conservation. For example, the hotel began buying shampoo in bulk instead of giving guests individual throw-away bottles and started using paper shoulder covers rather than plastic for laundry—resulting in a huge cost savings for the hotel. Existing staff were brought up to speed on the new standards, and HVS came in every month to train new staff.

Staff quickly became enthusiastic participants in "green teams," which maintained the building and constantly sought ways to improve environmental performance. These teams included everyone from the 18-year-old kitchen help to upper management. They were able to discuss their concerns freely because a problem-solving atmosphere was established. Incentive programs were developed to further educate and motivate employees, including the "Eco-employee of the Month" program. Staff enthusiasm ran high. Dinner parties were held for the departments that showed the greatest improvement. When he visited Vista, Chris Balshe of HVS Eco-Services noted that employees were very proud of the green initiatives the hotel had undertaken: "It gave them personal satisfaction and set them apart from all of the other hotels in the area and gave them motivation and pride in their company." Employee retention was much higher, and even in the food service department not a single employee left during the two years after the renovation — a remarkable statistic in the city's hotel industry. The media and the guests were also overwhelmingly positive. When Vista distributed a questionnaire to its guests, 86 percent commended the hotel on its environmental initiatives.

Unfortunately for employees and the environment, when the hotel changed management from Hilton International to Marriott International, the green operational measures were generally suspended as part of a huge employee turnover, including up to 75 percent of upper management. Consequently, the hotel lost both its HVS certification and the opportunity for employees to feel invested in resource efficiency through their deeds — which had been shown to benefit the hotel's business operations.

Miraval, a luxury resort in Catalina, Arizona, has also worked with HVS Eco Services to get guests and staff excited about green initiatives. In 1995 the hotel was the first to receive the highest possible Eco-Tel certification of five "globes." Like the Vista Hotel, Miraval changed ownership to the Ritz-Carlton after receiving the certification. Employees were nervous at first that the new management might eliminate the green programs. But this did not happen.

When the new management came in, one of the first things it did was call a staff meeting of all the employees. The head manager asked, "What is this place really about?" The staff replied that the environmental initiatives had become an integral part of the atmosphere at the hotel. The new managers were excited by this concept and willing to learn more about what it meant to operate responsibly, believing that it really was a part of this resort's experience.

To unify the understanding of the hotel's vision, management, staff, and HVS representatives developed an Environmental Mission Statement: "Miraval is dedicated to fostering an environmental awareness among its guests, educating its employees, and operating in an environmentally responsible manner to establish a harmony with the community." The goals of this mission include minimizing Miraval's impact on the environment, creating a unique guest experience through environmental responsibility, establishing Miraval as a contributing member of the community, creating a safe and healthful workplace, and reducing operating costs.

Miraval's policy is not to be blatantly forward about its green initiatives, but to offer opportunities for guests to probe deeper if they are interested. For example, certain highlighted items on the menu are organically grown or locally produced. If guests ask, the staff will describe other hotel initiatives and even provide tours of green features. To reduce water and energy used to wash towels and sheets every day, the resort places an environmental directory in each room informing guests that if they are willing to have their linens washed less frequently than every day, they should turn over a special stone to alert the maid. This stone has Miraval's environmental message engraved on one side. Chris Balshe of HVS reports that a very high percentage of guests participate in the program.

Education is also important within residential communities. The marketing staff at Dewees Island® make a point of explaining to prospective home owners up-front that the island is focused on environmental sensitivity. "We work to educate home owners on the unique needs of the environment and encourage them to integrate themselves into their surroundings," says developer John Knott.

Knott believes that if people understand the reasoning behind environmental regulations or initiatives, they will become more invested in the outcome and may come up with new ideas to further those objectives. He illustrates this idea with the well-known parable: If you give a man a fish, he eats for a day; if you teach a man *how* to fish, he eats for a lifetime. Residents of Dewees are able to use their own values and wisdom to innovate and bring forward new ideas to improve the development. To further environmental education on the island, the development also employs a full-time environmental educator and a full-time landscape ecologist.

An interesting program on Dewees Island that teaches children about the environment is the Biodiversity Swap Shop located in the Education Center. Kids under 18 can choose to develop a brochure or write a report about anything on the island —plant, animal, or whatever they like. They create the art, the research, and the

On Dewees Island® a number of interesting programs have been created to teach children about the environment. *(Reprinted with permission from the Island Preservation Partnership.)*

writing. Once a project is accepted by the education director, the child is awarded "bio bucks," which they can use to buy such things as aquariums, backpacks, books, and nature CDs at the Biodiversity Swap Shop (much of the inventory is donated). The report material becomes a resource base on which every child can leave his or her mark. The program teaches children how to do research and write a report, promotes artistic talent, and conveys economic concepts through the purchase power of bio bucks. Kids also learn about their particular aspect of the Dewees Island environment. Knott says this program institutionalizes sustainability and makes it *intuitive* for children; he calls this "building institutional memory."

These activities help residents change their life-styles to become stewards of the island. Knott hopes that within 10 years he will see "a community at Dewees where residents' intuitive connection and respect for natural systems is restored." Other activities also further residents' understanding of *why* they should care about these issues. Instead of establishing principles and regulations that people are mandated to follow, these programs help residents understand the basis for regulations and empower them to push the system further—to take responsibility and feel ownership.

EDUCATION BEYOND THE DEVELOPMENT'S BORDERS

A green development can effect change far beyond its borders, helping to make environmental practitioners out of visitors, guests, and the surrounding community. The development can continue this educational role long after the media events surrounding the project's ground breaking or grand opening.

Since opening in October 1993, the Caribbean eco-resort Harmony has offered guests an opportunity to participate in operating their solar-powered cottages overlooking Maho Bay. Developer and owner Stanley Selengut spent $80,000 per unit to construct cabins using such recycled building materials as crushed-glass roofing tiles, wood-plastic composite decking, and recycled newspaper subfloors. Rainwater for guests' use is collected on the roofs and stored in cisterns beneath the cabins, and power is supplied by solar panels and small wind turbines.

Guests participate in the research aspect of Harmony by tapping into a personal computer that reports their current energy "budget" before and after they shower, microwave, or flip on the ceiling fans. The visitor experience is an environmental education as well as a vacation. In fact, Selengut says—only half jokingly—that he charges *tuition* rather than rental fees for the units. Visitor responses are being gathered in a data base to be used for developing more efficient and innovative products.

The Real Goods Solar Living Center in Hopland, California, makes numerous educational activities available to visitors. Visitors can tour the property to learn of the guiding principles of sustainable living and come to appreciate the beauty that lies in the details of the project. An automated education system is being planned that will offer videos on sustainable building practices, including those used at the Center.

The project has incorporated a number of fun activities to encourage learning about efficiency and sustainable issues. Visitors can see photovoltaics, solar water pumping, and wind power demonstrated. A "truth window" is provided by a cutaway through the plaster showing the straw-bale walls, so that visitors can see and touch how this alternative structure was built. A glass wall allows close-up viewing of the stand-alone (not connected to the utility grid) electrical system.

During summer months, visitors can also test the shading capabilities of the manually adjustable hemp awnings. Mark Winkler, director of the Center, describes one of the playful water features. "A sand and water area for children of any age has been designed, in which a solar-powered pump will provide a water source that can then be channeled, diverted, dammed, and flooded through whatever sandy topography the kids have created. Block the sun reaching the solar panel and you stop the flow of water—a great place to learn both engineering and social skills."

The landscaping is a special treat for visitors. In place of a conventional turf landscape, Real Goods features an array of orchards and elaborate water-efficient gardens. Visitors will be able to see and even take part in restoration efforts on the site, planting native species on this reclaimed Department of Transportation dump site and restoring a riparian canopy along a creek. A visitor walking through one of the unique vine arbors will experience the cooling provided by the shade of these plants. More distant visitors can tour the Real Goods Solar Living Center by making a "cyber stop" at Real Good's web site.

Employee education is also addressed through the building's design. Real Goods has provided staff with an operator's manual to teach them how to properly tune the building for comfort and when to open and close clerestory windows. Although this system could have been automated, the designers chose to let the staff interact with the building to give them a chance to understand how the building responds to its environment.

The Shenoa Retreat Center in Philo, California, is home to seminars on ecology, personal growth, and sustainable living. Shenoa creates an opportunity for staff, members, and guests to learn about and experience sustainable life-style choices. Volunteers cultivate heritage seeds to help preserve the diversity of plants once found in this region of California. This enterprise is of particular importance, because the nation's increasingly centralized seed distribution network and the use of hybrid varieties are causing a massive loss of plant genetic diversity. Shenoa's colorful, thriving one-acre organic garden helps further the education mission by teaching sustainable agriculture to staff and visitors. Excess produce from gardens goes to nearby homeless shelters, senior centers, and food banks. Guests are invited to take food back to their own local food shelters as well. Shenoa also sponsors workshops to demonstrate the final step in creating a self-sufficient garden—saving and storing seeds for the following year.

Probably no commercial development goes further with education beyond its borders than Dewees Island. The development sponsors an annual green building

Children in the Real Goods Solar Living Center's play area choose the hand pump or the solar pump to draw water, then divert it through aqueducts made of PVC scraps to make streams and sand castles. *(Reprinted with permission from Jeff Oldham.)*

trade show and educational workshop to teach green issues to architects and builders involved with projects on the island. The event is now regional, with other sponsors, advancing sustainable design ideas to building professionals throughout the Southeast.

Dewees Island has created partnerships with schools in three surrounding counties, sponsoring environmental programs that include class instruction and a field trip to the island. Kindergarten through 12th grade classes visit the island regularly throughout the school year to learn about the coastal environment. "We're not only teaching about native ecosystems," says Knott, "but teaching how to live with natural ecosystems." Some visiting classes actually spend time planning how they would build their own developments on the island, then review their ideas with the island's full-time environmental educator.

The Center for Regenerative Studies, at California State Polytechnic University, Pomona, provides a university-based setting for education, demonstration, and research in regenerative technologies—technologies that turn self-

At the center for Regenerative Studies (at California State Polytechnic University), residents grow a variety of crops in a sustainable, "closed-loop" agricultural system. *(Architect: Dougherty & Dougherty; photographer: Milroy/McAleer; owner: California State Polytechnic University, Pomona. Reprinted with permission.)*

renewing resources and wastes into usable food, water, and energy. The Center's facilities demonstrate its integrated approach to issues of food, shelter, water, energy, and materials, showing how the physical needs of a community can be met in a sustainable fashion while minimizing negative impacts on the surroundings.

The first phase of the Center opened in 1994 after a comprehensive planning period of 20 years. Ultimately, the Center will be a community with about 90 students, faculty members from a wide range of disciplines, and visiting experts who participate in the Center's research. Buildings are located on a hillside with their longer facades facing south and are surrounded by native deciduous vegetation. Two dormitory buildings were designed and built to test two approaches to climate-responsive, passive solar design. One is light and airy, built on stilts; the other is massive and bermed into the ground. The performance of these two buildings has been monitored, and the information is being incorporated into future projects at the Center. Energy needs are met by passive and active solar technologies and a biomass heat-storage facility (in which waste materials are broken down through biological processes to provide bio-gas fuels). In addition, the Center experiments with producing ethanol from crop residues. Residents grow a diverse range of crops in a sustainable, "closed-loop" agricultural system that is integrated with the buildings and their wastes.

The Center also strives to address the interrelationships among humans. To help foster a community atmosphere for the students living at the Center, evening meals are shared and weekly meetings discuss the Center's operations. Students are asked to log the amount of time they spend doing tasks for the Center to keep the systems working. The Center was designed as an open-ended development so that as new technologies and interests arise they can be incorporated.

Supporting Responsible Agriculture Through Green Development

At Village Homes agriculture is integrated throughout the development, with commercial fruit and nut orchards, a commercial organic produce farm, smaller "home-scale" garden plots, and edible landscaping along pathways and roads. Since the project was built on productive farmland (a former tomato field), developer Michael Corbett wanted to make agriculture an integral part of the resulting community. Today, Village Homes remains one of the best examples of integrating agriculture and development.

As Village Homes demonstrates, integrating agriculture into a development project can be very attractive. It is also becoming increasingly important as more and more farmland is consumed by population pressures and sprawling development practices. Open space, farmland, wildlife habitat, and wetlands are disappearing at a rate of more than 2 million acres every year in the United States—an area more than twice the size of Rhode Island. Many states have lost a huge percentage of their farms over the last 50 years. In Connecticut, for example, there were 22,240 farms in 1944 and just 3,500 by 1987—a decrease of 83 percent. According to the U.S. Department of Agriculture, between 1982 and 1992

Agriculture can be integrated in a variety of ways throughout a development; possibilities include fruit and nut orchards, organic produce farms, garden plots, and edible landscaping. *(Reprinted with permission from William D. Browning, Rocky Mountain Institute.)*

developed land in the United States increased by 14 million acres, having been converted from pastureland, rangeland, cropland, and forest land.

One solution people are turning to is Community Supported Agriculture (CSA), a type of "subscription farming" in which buyers contract for a certain amount of fresh produce each week from the farmer. CSAs are becoming a popular means of linking local producers with local consumers. Farmers are assured of markets for their produce and usually receive payment up-front, which helps them meet the cash-flow problems that are prevalent in the farming community. This arrangement encourages local, sustainable farming practices and provides members with healthful, usually organically grown, produce. CSAs first came to North America from Europe in 1986 and since then have taken root. In 1996 there were more than 500 CSAs throughout the United States.

Integrating CSA operations into real estate development can yield many benefits: making homes more attractive to potential buyers, speeding the approvals process with regulatory bodies concerned about loss of agricultural land, providing home owners with healthful food, keeping some of the land undeveloped, and strengthening the larger community. The developers of Prairie Crossing, the mixed-use development being built on rural farmland northwest of Chicago, have gone to great lengths to ensure that farming will not disappear from the land. Half of the development's 667 acres will remain as open space with prairies, meadows, wetlands, and a 150-acre working farm, including a 10-acre CSA. Inclusion of the CSA encourages residents to consume locally produced organic food, thus supporting the resident farmers. Goals of the program include protecting the long-term health and productivity of the soil and helping the larger community to directly support ecologically sound farming through subscriptions to the CSA. Each of Prairie Crossing's CSA members receives approximately 10 pounds of produce per week throughout the 20-week growing season.

The greater the density of humans, the more challenging agriculture becomes. An apparent oxymoron, "urban agriculture" has strong proponents nationwide. It offers an opportunity to convert organic wastes into resources while revitalizing underutilized urban areas for productive purposes. Enterprising individuals, organizations, and companies, from Harlem to Seattle, are converting abandoned lots and rooftops into productive gardens. Commercial urban agriculture operations find customers right around the corner. Any time locally grown produce can displace food shipped across the country, dramatic savings will be realized in transportation energy use.

In the early 1900s, Charles Weeks, a successful poultry farmer from Indiana, purchased 300 acres of land by the San Francisco Bay in what is now East Palo Alto. He divided the land into individual parcels for farmers, promising "One acre and independence in California." Today the land is known as the Weeks neighbor-

---

Want to Learn More About Urban Agriculture?

The Urban Agriculture Network is a global resource center working to promote agricultural production in urban areas. For information, contact:

Urban Agriculture Network
1711 Lamont Street N.W.
Washington, DC 20010
(202) 483-8130

hood, and despite its location in a run-down urban environment beset by drug-related crime and unemployment, the neighborhood remains a sort of oasis of open space where vestiges of agriculture can still be found.

Residents see the Weeks neighborhood for the potential it holds and are concerned about the threat of unfettered development. They are working with the nonprofit organization Urban Ecology and the National Parks Service to develop a neighborhood plan that promotes thoughtful growth (through infill and high-density development) coupled with protection and support of urban agriculture. The plan specifically calls for preservation of the area's farmland, which was identified by residents as the key to conserving its cultural history. The plan reserves large lots for agriculture and related businesses, linking environmental goals to economic revitalization. The goal is to strengthen the local economy through diversification, keeping locally generated money circulating within the neighborhood, to foster a more cohesive sense of community.

Another way that green developers can support local agriculture is to set aside places within developments in which weekly farmers markets can be located. In Philip Langdon's book *Urban Excellence,* Robert Sommer observes, "A farmers market is a community event. It is a place where people congregate and exchange ideas and talk 'neighborhood' and politics. By contrast, the supermarket is a sterile and desocializing environment."

If all goes according to plan, organic farming at the new town of Haymount in Virginia will replace the conventional pattern of chemical agriculture that has existed on the land for the past 40 years. A scheme has been devised to allow an organic farmer to lease a large block of farmland for $1 a year for 30 years. The farm will provide produce for restaurants, grocery stores, and a farmers market in the town where Haymount residents, as well as others from the area, will be able to purchase produce and support local sustainable agriculture.

Developments can incorporate another aspect of agriculture and restoration by promoting the cultivation of native seeds, with ecological benefits potentially extending far beyond the development. Restoration expert Jim Patchett of the Conservation Design Forum in Naperville, Illinois, has found that tall-grass prairie seed production can be tremendously lucrative, as seeds typically sell for far more than other field crops. Depending on whom a farmer sells to, and for what purpose, $10 to $30 per pound can be earned from native seed production. During the first years of production, when there is less root competition, a farmer can get 50 pounds per acre—at a minimum of $10 per pound, 50 pounds makes seed production very competitive with typical soybean and corn crops. If the demand for native seed continues to increase, profits could also rise significantly.

At Rancho San Carlos near Monterey, California, a native plant nursery has been established to help restore areas of the 20,000-acre site, which was degraded by decades of ranching and other human activities. Various native plants and seedlings are being cultivated at the nursery. The nursery operation should grow as the development proceeds, because it is supported by an educational foundation that is, in turn, funded by transfer fees from lot sales. The nursery will supply seeds of native seeds not only to the 20,000-acre Rancho San Carlos development, but also throughout the region. EarthBound Farms, an organic farming company, also leases farmland on the property.

The Community Within

One of the most exciting aspects of a green development is its potential to form a strong community among its residents. The word "community" derives from the Latin *communis,* or "common," from which "communicate" also derives. As used here, "community" draws from this sister word to encompass the idea of a group of people in communication with one another, both directly and indirectly. Creating community means establishing a framework in which residents get to know their neighbors and interact on a frequent and healthful basis. The establishment of a community fabric is crucial if people are to work together to protect their shared environment.

How a development can inspire the establishment of strong communities is important to understand. Beyond simply leasing or selling houses or commercial space, developers should examine how people live, work, and interact within these spaces so that the development can support community building.

Dewees Island presents a rich example of how a development can create a community among its residents. Donald Lesh, a member of the President's Council on Sustainable Development, lauds the project: "Dewees Island truly sets an international model for sustainability. I have not seen any development in my range of experience that so completely articulates sustainable practice." Community development is an intricate aspect of the project—a fundamental element. Developer John

Knott said he bases this on no more than the basic principles of building community: initiative, involvement, understanding, and education. A sense of community permeates every activity on the island and influences the lives it touches.

A building block of the Dewees Island community is a common vision for the island's future and a unique respect for its heritage. To build this heritage, each new resident of Dewees receives a Life Document, a thick binder with every article (positive or negative) that has appeared about the island. The document is updated every two months. The property owners have their own board with 17 committees, one of which is an archive committee with information on the island dating back to A.D. 1560. This committee also captures history through the Dewees Island collective photo album, recording island events, including all family reunions, weddings, and funerals. Thus, in 50 years residents will be able to look back through the archive and understand how their personal lives are interwoven with the community's history.

Respecting the region's cultural heritage, Dewees Island has helped resurrect a local indigenous industry in basket weaving using the island's native sweetgrass. It

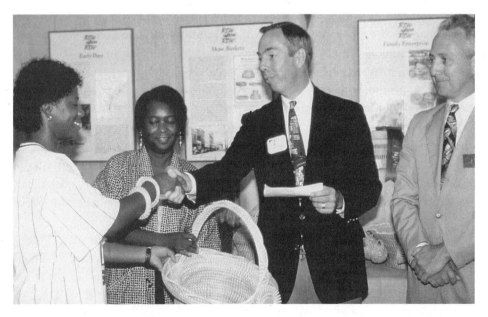

On Dewees Island, the award-winning Mt. Pleasant Sweetgrass Basket Makers are presented their awards by developer John Knotts. *(Reprinted with permission from the Island Preservation Partnership.)*

Spring Island provides information to residents on the island's natural resources, such as this magnificent live oak forest, said to be the largest on the East Coast. *(Reprinted with permission from Betsy Chaffin.)*

established a partnership with the Mt. Pleasant Sweetgrass Basket Makers Association. This organization has had trouble in the last several years finding sweetgrass, so Dewees Island provided them with harvesting rights in the wildlife refuge. In exchange for this privilege, the artisans give demonstrations in weaving and offer classes for the island's educational programs. An annual Sweetgrass Design Competition is held on the island to celebrate this traditional art form.

Not far away, another South Carolina island has also identified community as an important priority. When developing Spring Island and recruiting potential home buyers, developer Jim Chaffin and his partners kept asking themselves, "What do we want Spring Island to look like 50 years from now?" This long-term focus has led them to establish a number of activities to ensure that the development maintains its green focus. The first step in the process is educating the residents. Each member of Spring Island is given a *Spring Island Handbook*. This book provides information on the island's natural resources, helps residents understand how their properties fit into the island's ecosystem, explains the

Planning for Pedestrians

Incorporating pedestrian-oriented design is another way to help residents live in a more environmentally sensitive manner. Elitch Gardens is an urban infill mixed-use project being planned on a 30-acre site in north Denver, Colorado. Located in a densely populated area, the project lends itself to pedestrian-based design, because many commercial and retail ventures are within walking distance. This project will create a larger economic base for these businesses while also benefiting Elitch Gardens residents. Affordable Housing Development Corporation, the project's developer, created a design for Elitch Gardens that focuses on pedestrians and links the community with the surrounding neighborhood. Traffic-calming techniques, such as on-street parking, will create an environment that encourages people to walk. Live/work opportunities will eliminate the need of some residents to drive. Senior housing will be located near the project's park, plaza, and theater, so residents can easily access them without needing to drive.

Live/work opportunities will be woven into the development around the wonderful mature landscaping on the site of the old Elitch Gardens amusement park in Denver. *(Reprinted with permission from the Affordable Housing Development Company.)*

island's land management plan, and describes the Spring Island Trust. The *Spring Island Handbook* provides guidance to members on how to manage their own landscape so that the "mystique of Spring Island" is maintained.

By understanding the island and their relationship to it, residents will do their part in keeping the island operating at its fullest potential while minimizing human impact. Betsy Chaffin, the Trust's executive director, believes that the land stewardship exhibited on each individual home site will be a big part of the answer to the question, "What will Spring Island look like for future generations?"

A newsletter keeps residents up to date on what is happening around Spring Island and what they can do to help with Spring Island Trust projects. A visiting artists program offers artists, writers, historians, philosophers, poets, and musicians a retreat area and an opportunity to carry forward cultural creativity on the island. Members can attend the artists' presentations and exhibits. The community also offers guided nature tours and ocean kayaking to educate residents and visitors about Spring Island's unique ecosystem.

COHOUSING

Cohousing is an innovative form of housing that creates a strong sense of community through both physical design and social structure. Pioneered in Denmark, this cooperative housing structure was brought to the United States by architects Kathryn McCamant and Charles Durrett. They coined the term *cohousing* to refer to a preplanned community of individual, self-sufficient private residences, with extensive common facilities designed to make life easier and friendlier for all community members.

The common facilities in a cohousing development usually include a community kitchen and dining hall, a child care area, gardens, workshops, and guest rooms. In addition, the community may own some equipment cooperatively, such as lawn mowers, laundry equipment, a truck for hauling furniture or firewood, a van for transporting groups of residents, and various tools. Community members typically eat most meals in their own residences but dine together several evenings each week in the common house, with residents taking turns preparing meals, cleaning up, and simply enjoying dinner with their neighbors and friends. The shared facilities provide social and practical benefits not found in a typical neighborhood.

Cohousing and the Developer

How is cohousing relevant to developers? For one thing, it offers the ability to penetrate a market niche that is dissatisfied with current speculative housing options—home buyers who want not only a house, but also a tight-knit community. Moreover, cohousing communities usually need a professional to guide them through the development process. Several savvy developers have discovered that cohousing is an underserved market segment.

When the process is handled correctly, developers can make as much profit from cohousing as from conventional subdivisions. In essence, their projects can be presold, with an identified and committed customer base—before breaking ground. Jim Leach, president of Wonderland Homes Development Company in Boulder, has developed custom homes for many years and has now found a profitable new market niche in developing cohousing communities as joint ventures with cohousing groups. Leach has developed at least five cohousing projects in the area, including Nyland. He has found that cohousing offers great advantages to developers who approach the process carefully. Leach requires 70 percent of his homes to be presold before breaking ground. This gives him sufficient capital to cover predevelopment costs and to raise potential additional investor capital from outside sources to secure a development loan for site development and common facilities.

Cohousing projects can be categorized on a continuum ranging from projects initiated and controlled by the cohousing group, to projects initiated and controlled by a developer. In between are various "joint ventures" in which project risk and control are shared between a cohousing group and a for-profit or nonprofit developer. The Doyle Street project in Emeryville, California, is one example of a developer-driven joint venture. The Nyland community was a group-initiated joint venture, in which the residents worked with Jim Leach of Boulder's Wonderland Homes.

The developer-initiated joint venture means that the developer finds a site, maintains site control, and at some point assembles a group to complete the project as a joint venture. The challenge is to recruit the group and go through some of the same processes that are employed in group-initiated projects, but within a much shorter time frame.

Those experienced in cohousing suggest a joint venture between developer and home owners as a preferred solution because the predevelopment investment is shared, which reduces the risk (as well as the up-side profit potential). Another solution is to pursue bridge loans to cover the period while home owners transfer equity from their old homes (if they own them) to the new cohousing homes. While cohousing is not a solution for everybody, there is a large enough pool of people interested in this form of community to make it a worthwhile specialty for progressive developers.

For more information on cohousing:

- The CoHousing Company

    1250 Addison Street #113
    Berkeley, CA 94702
    (510) 549-9980

- *CoHousing: A New Approach to Housing Ourselves,* by Kathryn McCamant and Charles Durrett. Ten Speed Press, 1994

- *The Cohousing Handbook,* by Chris Hanson. Hartley & Marks, 1996

- *CoHousing: Contemporary Approaches to Housing Ourselves,* a quarterly journal published by:

    The CoHousing Network
    P.O. Box 2584
    Berkeley, CA 94702
    (510) 526-6124

- *Rebuilding Community in America: Housing for Ecological Living, Personal Empowerment, and the New Extended Family,* by Ken Norwood, AICP, and Kathleen Smith. Shared Living Resource Center, 1995. This book explores cohousing as well as other forms of community-oriented living.

The Doyle Street Cohousing Community in Emeryville, California, transformed an industrial urban environment into a safe and comfortable neighborhood. *(Reprinted with permission of the CoHousing Company.)*

McCamant and Durrett's book, *CoHousing: A Contemporary Approach to Housing Ourselves,* describes why this housing arrangement is proving attractive: "People speak of their frustration with the isolation of current housing options, their desire for more contact with people of different ages and for a spontaneous social life that doesn't require making appointments with friends, and their need for a better place to raise children." By combining individual units with common areas for community-focused activities, cohousing offers both privacy and the advantages of living in a tight-knit community. By late 1996 there were more than two dozen completed cohousing projects in the United States and more than 150 groups in various stages of development, ranging from site identification to construction. Cohousing communities are located in rural areas, suburbs, and, increasingly, cities.

In Emeryville, California, a group of strangers came together and transformed an industrial urban environment into a community of neighbors, a safe and comfortable home called Doyle Street Cohousing Community. A developer converted an abandoned brick warehouse into 12 loft-style units with high ceilings and large windows. Prices for these 780- to 1,600-square-foot units are comparable to those for similar housing in the area. But residents of the Doyle Street development get something extra for their money—common areas that include a sitting area with a wood stove, a kitchen and dining room for shared dinners, a children's playroom, a workshop/rec room, a storage area, laundry facilities, and a hot tub. The residents of Doyle Street run the gamut from young married couples with children, to middle-aged singles, and an elderly widow.

The residents of the Southside Park cohousing project in Sacramento used creativity and innovation in transforming a rundown site in a deteriorated neighborhood into a community of 25 households. Interested future residents gathered in programming groups to envision the design for the project. The groups required that up to 40 percent of the housing be affordable units. Another key principle was to create an environment that encouraged interaction with the surrounding neighborhoods—to act as "a bridge to build community."

Some cohousing groups have integrated green elements—a natural fit for residents who tend to be sensitive to environmental issues as well as community building. The Nyland community in Colorado, completed in 1993, is the largest U.S. cohousing community to date. Forty-two homes are clustered on six acres, with the rest of the 43-acre site left undeveloped (and 13 acres deeded to the city of Lafayette for public use). Nyland lies within commuting distance of Denver and Boulder, yet has a rural feeling. Duplex and triplex units, as well as a 6,500-square-foot common house, line a circular pedestrian pathway. Other shared elements include a combination wood shop and auto shop, a greenhouse, a barn with stable, a large vegetable garden, a playing field, an orchard, and a wilderness area. From the beginning, Nyland residents identified energy efficiency as a high priority. Residents incorporated innovative energy-saving designs, building techniques, and fixtures into their community to minimize operating costs and improve environmental performance. Nyland exhibits one of the highest levels of energy efficiency in Colorado, with monthly energy bills projected to average between $15 and $20 for each home.

Reaching Out to Strengthen the Larger Community

Educational outreach programs offered by a few green developments were described earlier in this chapter. But education is not the only way a green development can positively affect surrounding communities. Larger, mixed-use projects can have a powerful influence on the surrounding area and at the same time strengthen their own performance. A number of exciting projects are helping to revitalize entire regions, fostering economic prosperity in previously depressed areas or reclaiming polluted wastelands.

In the 1970s, Granville Island, a peninsula in Vancouver, British Columbia, was a run-down, polluted industrial waterfront that had been largely abandoned as a lost cause. Rehabilitation of the 36-acre site began with the transfer of ownership from the Province of British Columbia to the city. It has been turned into a vibrant mixed-use community replete with markets, art galleries, shops, affordable office spaces converted from abandoned warehouses, and newer mixed-used buildings. High-density, low-rise condominiums, an elementary school, and an art college are connected by bicycle and foot paths, and residents enjoy playgrounds, tennis courts, green spaces, and local pubs. Built from an industrial wasteland, Granville Island today is a community-building success story that has helped to generate economic prosperity for this part of the city. The development was the driver of this renewal.

The Island Preservation Partnership, developers of Dewees Island, has gone so far as to establish a nonprofit organization to benefit the Charleston area, near Dewees Island. The Harmony Project was founded in 1992 by John Knott and Mel Goodwin, a former South Carolina Sea Grant Marine Extension director. John Knott explained that this project is a "nonprofit partnership dedicated to implementing sustainable communities and practices at all levels of the region's economy and culture." It primarily works in promoting sustainability, resource protection, and environmental responsibility to low- to middle-income people, charities, the business community, schools, and government.

One aspect of the project is the Harmony Warehouse, where salvaged building materials that would otherwise have been disposed of are stockpiled in a warehouse for affordable building projects. The goal is to provide, within five years, more than 5 percent of the building materials for the area's affordable housing projects. Another endeavor is the community greening program in which kids from youth centers, neighborhood groups, and schools help to restore abandoned lots in downtown Charleston. They plant flowers that are sold at the farmers market, the money from this effort going back to help fund other community-based improvement projects. The long-term goals of the Harmony Project include implementing community-supported rural agriculture, using a downtown farmers market as the vehicle to do so, helping with sustainable land planning for large tracts of rural land, creating an eco-industrial park development, and promoting job creation based on using resources efficiently.

The operations of the Inn of the Anasazi in Santa Fe shows sensitivity to existing Native American and other cultures and to the local community on many levels. *(Reprinted with permission from the Inn of the Anasazi.)*

Hotel developer Robert Zimmer believes that a tourist-oriented development should support local customs, traditions, rituals, and mythologies. Operations at the Inn of the Anasazi in Santa Fe, which he developed, demonstrate sensitivity to the city's existing cultures and the local community on many levels. The restaurant buys produce and meat from local farmers. Most of this is organically produced and comes from a network of multigeneration land-grant Hispanic families. This buying decision helps to keep the land in agricultural production and in the hands of the families. Excess food from the restaurant goes to homeless shelters. Kitchen scraps are donated to organic pig farms. Most of the Inn's furniture is locally made and reflects the Santa Fe aesthetic, helping the hotel cement its connection to the culture. Artwork throughout the hotel is representative of Santa Fe's three cultures — Hispanic, Native American, and Anglo. Hotel toiletries are produced by a local company using such Native American ingredients as incense cedar. No harmful

Artwork by the sons and daughters of famous Hispanic artists are exibited at a festival at the Inn of the Anasazi. *(Reprinted with permission from the Inn of the Anasazi.)*

chemicals are used in the process. These products are also sold through the hotel, further supporting local suppliers.

Inn of the Anasazi employees are able to put in as much as two hours a week volunteering for local nonprofits as part of their hotel work. Staff can choose to sign a "Right Livelihood" agreement that empowers employees to undertake ecologically responsible efforts in the name of the hotel. All of these activities not only benefit the Santa Fe community; they benefit the hotel as well. Staff turnover is very low, and the management has fielded requests from other hotels in the area to offer seminars on employee retention. The hotel also makes space available for community events on holidays. Unique programs include Native American storytelling, videos on stereotyping, a seminar in Spanish and English on HIV awareness, and discussions of ethnicity. The staff at the Inn is representative of the three cultures. At a seasonal festival, the Inn exhibited artwork by the sons and daughters of famous Hispanic artists of the area. The exposure it created for these young people has led to work in creating several murals in Santa Fe.

Because hotels and other tourist facilities reach a wide customer base, they have potential for broad impact. Guests are on vacation, relaxed, and in a "teachable moment"; they can take ideas they pick up on environmental practices back home with them. Developer Robert Zimmer says, "International tourism, travel, and the hospitality industry can be empowered to act as dynamic waves in the tide of global consciousness toward world peace, understanding, and sustainability, but it is ultimately the developer who must choose a course for the future."

What is the vision for the future of green development? Developers have an opportunity to direct change that will benefit not only themselves, but also society and the environment. *(Reprinted with permission from Curt Carpenter.)*

CHAPTER 12

What's Ahead for Green Development

IT IS A LATE APRIL MORNING IN THE YEAR 2050. A bright blue sky dotted with a few puffy white clouds graces the Cleveland skyline. The young trees—some of them now 30 feet tall—are just beginning to come into leaf in the new city arboretum. The arboretum is intermingled with the latest major real estate development, a large series of curving, interconnected towers with lower floors occupied by retail and office space, and upper floors by residential units. The mix of apartment types and sizes assures a wide diversity of household types and income levels among the residents.

Even though the city is full of activity this morning, it is quiet. The few vehicles to be seen on the streets are electric-powered, mostly by silent, zero-emission hydrogen fuel cells. Most of the people get around on foot or via the comfortable, efficient mass transit system. Although Cleveland's light-rail system has grown modestly from the few lines that snaked through the city decades ago, modern, clean, articulated buses now serve as the primary means of public transit. Efficient, simple entry platforms at floor level function like subway platforms and streamline the loading and unloading of passengers, but at just a fraction of the investment required for subways. Because cars are few, these fuel cell–powered buses deliver passengers quickly and conveniently to their destinations.

But the destinations this morning for most Cleveland workers are far different from what they might have been at the turn of the century. Workplaces are dispersed throughout the city and intermingled with residential developments. Many people work out of their homes or within a block or two from home, across one of the many small parks that grace the city and provide a pleasant walk to work. Today is sunny and warm, so many of the commuters who travel across town are doing so by bicycle rather than bus or rail. Some stop by one of several farmers markets nestled within the city parks to buy locally grown produce. The many bicycle pathways through restored woodlands and the absence of congestion on the streets make bicycling a far different activity than it was in the late twentieth century. Many of the less fit bicyclists are riding light-weight carbon fiber hybrid-electric bicycles, allowing them only as much exercise as they can handle.

Cleveland is strong and healthy. While crime still exists, it has dropped off considerably in recent decades because of the gradual reduction in stress, the improved economy, and the stronger community support networks in the city. Children grow up today knowing their neighbors and being an important part of the hundreds of cohesive neighborhood-scale communities that exist throughout the city. When problems come up, residents pull together and support one another—whether Asian, Hispanic, African-American, or Caucasian.

There is to be a big celebration this afternoon at the North-Central Square, a large public park along the Cuyahoga River. A new outdoor concert hall is being dedicated to developer and local hero Elden Carrol. Now retired, Carrol helped to transform Cleveland into the vibrant and healthy place it is today. He grew up in a Cleveland public housing project and saw many of his African-American friends die as teenagers. He had even been a gang member himself, briefly, as a youngster. But Carrol became inspired by a new movement that was just beginning to sweep the nation in the early twenty-first century—a Green Development movement that recognized that social good could be achieved through responsible real estate development and that development could help to protect the dwindling natural environment while still being profitable.

His involvement in development was gradual at first. In his early twenties, he fixed up tenement houses, focusing on the neighborhood where he had grown up. With full support from the city and various lending institutions eager to help him with his dream, Carrol began transforming run-down slums into strong communities. He remembered all the things he had longed for as a kid growing up in Cleveland—like a place to play basketball late at night and a place where poor kids could explore the Internet—and he incorporated these features into the communities he built.

Carrol's success grew, and with it, his stature. He was elected to the Cleveland City Council in his thirties and served for a decade, helping to establish policies that would bring about the kind of widespread change that he now knew was possible. He recognized that maximum benefit would be achieved if different disciplines worked together from the onset, whether to redesign a city street to better meet pedestrian needs or to establish proactive operations to fight crime. One of his goals was to encourage more people like him to get involved in this restorative development. A favorite initiative of his on the city council had been the establishment of the city's constructed wetland wastewater treatment system. The project, which also provided much-needed wetland habitat and recreational opportunities, paid for itself in just three years and has continued to save taxpayers millions of dollars annually ever since.

He eventually returned to the private sector, where his heart was, and continued his development work. Once scoffed at, his ongoing emphasis on energy efficiency had become widely respected and, indeed, the standard in this post-petroleum age. While Carrol understood the energy benefits, he always emphasized the people benefits—the creation of spaces that were more comfortable, for example. Building energy codes had been converted to performance codes to allow innovators greater flexibility, and some had disappeared altogether, unnecessary in the market-driven building industry. Developers who competed for better energy performance were rewarded by the market, helped along by feebates (rebates for efficiency choices) for electric, gas, water, and sewer hookups. Anyone trying to sell a building today without the newest generation of photovoltaic-integrated R-12 superwindows, passive solar heating, natural cooling, and at least R-40 walls would be laughed at.

Back in the private sector, Carrol could also pursue his long-held goal of bringing nature back to Cleveland. His work in establishing several wildlife preserves along the Lake Erie shoreline and restoring marshland along the Rocky River near the old airport gave him great satisfaction. Many of these accomplishments were done as part of his extensive redevelopment projects. Through his ecosystem restoration work, he became active with the local Audubon chapter and eventually was elected president of the state chapter—the first African-American to hold that position. In that role, Carrol helped to mend past divisions between environmentalists and developers and established a strong political coalition of conservationists, developers, ordinary citizens, and government officials. This coalition pushed through some key legislation that protected large tracts of open space beyond Ohio's urban growth boundaries and enabled the reestablishment of elk and bison in Ohio, even while permitting the kind of environmentally responsible development for which Carrol had become famous.

Carrol also helped to transform Ohio's industry. His election to the board of Central Telecomm resulted in dramatic transformations to that company—one of the nation's largest manufacturers of satellite telecommunications equipment—and throughout the entire industry. Carrol helped to institute a new way of looking at manufacturing at Central Telecomm. Waste became unacceptable; it represented lost resources. The life cycles of all materials were studied, and all opportunities for avoiding environmental impact and reducing the consumption of raw materials were implemented. Carrol helped to put in place a cutting-edge industrial facility on a long-abandoned industrial site, where more than a dozen industries and agricultural enterprises now work together in Cleveland's inner city. The waste from one process is the raw material for another. Everybody is a winner.

Meanwhile, the way of thinking embodied by Elden Carrol and hundreds of leaders like him across the country has eventually become a firmly established part of modern educational institutions. Architecture school curricula, for example, emphasize integration, teamwork, and whole-systems thinking. Ecosystem studies have become an important element of engineering curricula. Economics courses include major segments on the ideas of natural resources as capital, green accounting, and the significance of end-use/least-cost opportunities in economic decision making. These paradigms have spilled over into corporate America and have become standard ways of doing business.

By the time of the unveiling of Elden Carrol's statue—carved from regionally quarried granite—this afternoon, the breeze will carry the wonderful spring scent of the hundreds of cherry trees in bloom as birds sing from the fringe of native woodland bordering the river.

Cleveland may not look like this in 50 years, but it will certainly be different than it is today. Change is a certainty in any community. Just as developers in the post–World War II decade largely defined the built environment that exists at the end of the twentieth century, so too will today's developers make a major mark on society in the mid-twenty-first century. Developers have an opportunity to direct that change in a way that will benefit not only their pocketbooks, but also society and the ecosystems that we are all part of. The real estate industry is on the brink of a tremendous period of change that will, in large part, determine what our places of work and living will be like in 50 years.

Developers can follow the path of least resistance, which, for a few more years, may include conventional subdivision developments and office towers that are built without respect for the needs and health of their occupants. Or developers can be leaders in the transformation to a new paradigm, a new way of approaching development that respects and enhances the surrounding natural systems and social fabric.

This book has profiled a few of the developers who today are choosing the latter path, and who are leading the industry—with heads held high—into the twenty-first century. Achieving the vision of Cleveland described earlier, or any vision like it, will not be easy. Indeed, it will be tremendously challenging, with numerous obstacles along the way. But it is possible. This chapter takes a look at some of the ways in which such a transition can occur and, indeed, is beginning to happen. It is happening on many different levels and from many different directions. Government programs are encouraging green development through regulations and incentive programs. Manufacturers are arriving there through realization of bottom-line benefits. Educators are instilling new ways of thinking in their students. And community groups are pulling together to take hold of their future.

Cities—Establishing a Framework for Green Development

Achieving the ultimate green development will require support at many levels. It will require developers who are willing to risk money on the expectation that such projects can succeed. It will require a public that understands what is different about green development and asks for it. And it will require municipalities that are willing to put in place incentives to encourage this sort of innovation. This will happen as city and town planners and elected officials begin to recognize that a development reaches far beyond its immediate boundaries, affecting surrounding communities, economies, and ecosystems. A number of cities today are making strides in developing a comprehensive framework within which a green developer can weave projects that both support community and make a profit.

Oregon and several of its cities have been leaders in proactive land-use planning, largely because of sprawling development that at one time was consuming 30,000 acres of agricultural land each year. In 1979, Oregon became the first state to enable legislation for Urban Growth Boundaries (UGBs). A UGB prohibits development beyond an established boundary, encourages increased density within the urban environment, and leaves an undeveloped "green ring" outside the city as agricultural land or open space. Because of this UGB legislation and other statewide efforts to deal with sprawl, by 1996 the amount of Oregon's agricultural land lost annually had dropped to 2,000 acres.

The Portland Metro program was developed in response to the sprawling development on the farmland and forests surrounding Portland. The region's UGB includes 364 square miles around Portland, including 24 cities and urban portions of three counties. Portland Metro is working to maintain this UGB (which was set as a boundary only until the year 2000) in the face of pressures from the region's population explosion. According to a *Newsweek* article in May 1995, planners in Portland believe that by 2040 the population will increase 77 percent, but they are committed to increasing residential land use only 6 percent during the same period. In 1992 growth management became the number-one focus of Metro. The program started work on a Regional Framework Plan that local governments had to comply with and that was enforced. This plan took a comprehensive look at how all of the issues related to growth management inter-relate: transportation, land use, local government, and social issues.

With the UGB and regional plan regulations in place, developers must abide by them. John Fregonese of Metro's Growth and Management Services says that many Portland developers are coming forward with innovative solutions— "Developers are really bringing the residential projects into the city." Fregonese notes that there are thousands of units about to be developed in mixed-use settings. There are many fix-up projects under way, he says, such as conversion of abandoned brownfield sites into mixed-use communities.

Currently, 6.2 million people live in the San Francisco Bay Area, and much of the region's 4.5 million acres is still open space. However, it has been estimated that over the next 30 years the urban area could double if the present development pattern of new towns appearing and old suburbs expanding continues.

Blueprint for a Sustainable Bay Area was initiated by Urban Ecology, an Oakland-based nonprofit focused on rebuilding cities in harmony with nature. The goal of the *Blueprint* is to help the community spell out its vision and to steer

Portland is one of the many cities across the country making strides in developing a comprehensive framework into which a green developer can weave projects. The photograph at the top shows Pioneer Square as a parking lot in 1965 before revitalization. The second photograph shows the revitalized area during a festival. This area also has light-rail train access. *(Reprinted with permission from Metro.)*

the Bay Area on a more responsible path for various categories of land use, ranging from compact urban neighborhoods to wild ecosystems. "It is designed to educate, invigorate, and create a sense of hope that sustainability can result from a combination of dedicated individual action and wise regional decision making and coordination," explained Wood Turner in a 1996 *Urban Ecologist* article.

The action items in the *Blueprint*, which were arrived at through a participatory process involving hundreds of local individuals, call for construction of infill housing, creation of secondary units on single-family lots, and development of residential units above downtown shops. The *Blueprint* includes ideas for densifying industrial districts to levels at which mass transit could be supported and for redeveloping vast parking lots into new urban centers. It also calls for fostering closed-loop production. The government will actively recruit businesses that create closed-loop industrial systems. San Francisco has embraced the *Blueprint* and is already taking such steps as relaxing zoning restrictions for the purpose of increasing housing densities, making local transportation less auto-dependent, restoring natural areas, and developing a Growth Limitation Plan.

There are glimmers of hope around San Francisco that, if duplicated throughout the region, would create a more sustainable community overall. Some ideas were spawned by natural disasters. After the 1989 earthquake weakened the struc-

---

A Test of a Pilot Process

In early 1997, the Florida House Foundation gathered a panel of experts in sustainable community design to test a pilot process for redefining the "highest and best use" of a 1,000-acre parcel near Sarasota, Florida. The process was proactive instead of reactive. Rather than waiting for the landowner's proposal, the community analyzed the site's potential according to its own demographic, ecological, fiscal, and other criteria. From the analysis is emerging a list of possible uses for the land, which are being run through a filter for community desirability and will be refined into the proposed site plan.

Since the process is just being tested, it will take time to see whether it actually works. But if all goes well, the community will get a project more in keeping with its needs. A more intelligent and efficient pattern of development will be established. The developer will win, too, by being spared much of the expense and time of the traditional adversarial approvals process.

Public transportation is offered free of charge to the Chattanooga public by way of a four-mile CARTA electric bus route through the city. *(Reprinted with permission from the Chattanooga News Bureau.)*

tural integrity of the Embarcadero Freeway, new possibilities opened up for waterfront activities and the city's historic Embarcadero piers again saw the sun after years of being overshadowed by the freeway. A $62 million revitalization project is being built to restore this whole area.

Chattanooga, Tennessee, has a long history of heavy industry, which has left its environment seriously degraded. There are stories of people driving around in the middle of the day with their headlights on because the smog was so thick. But the city is reviving itself both economically and environmentally. Chattanooga has been working hard to solve its environmental problems since the early 1970s, originally spurred to action when it was named the most polluted city in 1969. The city spent $40 million on air pollution control equipment to make the downtown suitable for responsible development. This generated a total investment of $739 million, 1,300 new permanent jobs, and more than 7,000 construction jobs. Chattanooga made a commitment to broad-based local participation and a balancing of environmental and economic health. A project called Vision 2000 was launched under the leadership of a nonprofit organization, Chattanooga Venture, to help build consensus among the citizens of Chattanooga. It brought some 1,700 participants together to brainstorm how to create a cleaner, greener, safer city with rehabilitated housing and non-polluting jobs. Some 223 projects came out of the sessions, along with a list of 34 goals to be achieved by the year 2000.

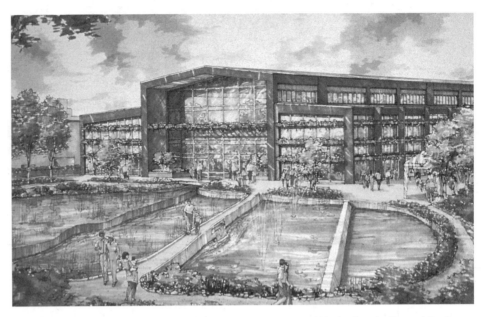

Chattanooga's zero-emissions commercial and industrial park in its South Central Business District will use a Living Machine™ to treat sewage, wastewater, and polluted soils. *(Reprinted with permission from the Chattanooga News Bureau.)*

Chattanooga's accomplishments to date are impressive: an extensive network of pedestrian and biking paths, noticeably cleaner air, and a restored river. Free public transportation is provided via a four-mile electric bus route through the city. The city has invested $60 million in affordable housing programs through the Chattanooga Neighborhood Enterprise. The city has won numerous awards for these and other accomplishments, and it continues moving forward.

Currently, Chattanooga is planning a zero-emissions commercial and industrial park known as the South Central Business District. Working with Peter Calthorpe, William McDonough, and other designers, the community came up with a plan to redevelop this abandoned area that had left a legacy of soil contamination and urban decay. City leaders from the public and private sectors have created partnerships among city, county, state, and federal agencies, corporations, private businesses, local and national organizations, clubs, and individuals. They have all come together to make a better place to live. John Todd's Living Machine™ biological wastewater system will be used to treat sewage and polluted soils. The plan is to turn the area into a center for environmentally responsive businesses to operate in a closed-loop manner (see further discussion of closed-loop manufacturing in the following section). Also in the plans are improved pedestrian and transit connections to the site and the encouragement of diverse uses in a surrounding pedestrian-scaled neighborhood.

The United States is far from alone in its examination of how to achieve more livable cities; there are many lessons to be learned from around the world. One of the most exciting urban initiatives is happening in Curitiba, known as the ecological capital of Brazil. The city is building efficient mass transit systems as an alternative to private car use, minimizing pollution and waste, encouraging the efficient use of resources, and implementing numerous social programs.

Planning and land-use management have been key to the success of Curitiba. During the rapid urbanization of the city in the 1960s, city leaders recognized the need for an overall plan. The first plan submitted called for widening main streets to better provide for automobiles. But this would have destroyed the fabric of the city, because many historic buildings would then have been torn down. Architect Jaime Lerner, the mayor at the time, was very vocal about his opposition to this plan. He stressed the importance of designing in a manner that meets people's needs, and he suggested other ways of addressing automobile traffic. The decision was made to emphasize mass transit as part of an overall integrated planning effort. Because the city made this decision, Curitibans now save 27 million car trips every year and use 25 percent less fuel per capita than other Brazilians.

Curitiba's public transit system includes color-coded buses and numerous frequently scheduled routes to provide an attractive and efficient bus service. An efficient payment and loading system modeled after those of subways was developed. (Subways were too expensive an option for the city.) A loading tube, which is at the same level as the bus aisle, with an attendant in the tube to collect the fare, makes pick-up and drop-off far more efficient than with most bus systems. This innovation, along with the idea of extra-long buses (three times the length of normal buses) with hinges to round corners, was the brainchild of Jaime Lerner. Five doors on these buses open and close at each stop. In his book *Hope, Human, and Wild: True Stories of Living Lightly on the Earth* (1995), Bill McKibben noted that during rush hour traffic, 20,000 bus passengers an hour can move in one direction. While carrying four times the passengers, the system cost just 0.5 percent per kilometer as much as Rio de Janeiro's subway system. More than 65 percent of Curitibans use the bus system every day. The city owns the tubes, worth $4.5 million, and private companies own the buses, worth $45 million.

The city needed industry to support the economy, so it purchased land along bus corridors and earmarked it for denser, high-rise development. Stringent regulations were established on preserving green space and maintaining water and air quality. Jaime Lerner, now governor of the Brazilian state of Paraná, says, "Curitiba is not a model but a reference—more important as a reservoir of direction and hope."

Curitiba, Chattanooga, San Francisco, Portland, and other progressive cities offer increasing opportunity to green developers. A framework is being created that developers can fit into—providing their products to receptive markets and, quite likely, being able to benefit from various incentives that will begin to reward, rather than penalize, forward-thinking developers.

Closing the Loop with Manufacturing

There are many players in the development industry, including manufacturers. A veritable revolution is occurring within some leading-edge corporations that recognize the need for sustainability. Manufacturing practices are being redesigned not just to minimize, but to actually eliminate waste, to convert to closed-loop manufacturing in which no polluting effluents are produced, and to plan for the eventual reuse of their industrial buildings and design them accordingly.

In Germany, the Recycling and Waste Management Act of 1996 requires manufacturers to be responsible for the whole life cycle of a product, from the mining of materials, to manufacturing, to disposal or recycling at the end of its useful life. The Act is helping move the country toward a closed-loop economy. In a 1996 *EcoNews* article, Guy Duancey said that this new law "gives priority to waste avoidance by requiring the use of low-waste product designs and closed-loop approaches to waste management and by promoting customer behavior oriented to the purchase of low-waste and low-pollution products."

Hamburg chemist Michael Braungart and architect William McDonough have been developing the Intelligent Products System™ since the early 1990s (and through their company, McDonough Braungart Design Chemistry, since 1996). This system defines three levels of products: consumables, products of service, and unsaleables. *Consumables* are organic products that are eaten or will biodegrade without any harmful effects. These products would be designed for decomposition rather than recycling. *Products of service* are durable items like TVs and cars, which would not be sold but would instead be licensed to people by the original manufacturer. As author and environmental entrepreneur Paul Hawken describes the idea, "If a company knows that its products will come back someday, and that it cannot throw anything away when they do, it creates a very different approach to design and materials." *Unsaleables* are toxic materials. These are items that can never be thrown away and cannot serve as food. They will always belong to the original maker and will be stored in protective containers until a safe method of detoxification can be found. This system makes manufacturers responsible for the long-term effects of the products they produce.

In the United States, Interface Carpet is taking this concept to heart with its Evergreen Lease program. Carpeting is leased rather than sold to a client and is taken back at the end of its useful life. The company never relinquishes ownership of the product, so it maintains responsibility for its entire life cycle. This makes sense, as the user wants only the service of the carpeting, not responsibility for its disposal. In addition, Interface primarily sells carpet tile. The company points out that just 20 percent of a typical carpeting gets 80 percent of the wear. Most carpet owners tear up and throw out entire floors of carpeting when only the worn-out parts need replacement. Carpet tiles allow the carpet owner, Interface, to provide the user the same quality of "carpet service" with far fewer materials and vastly less waste. Ultimately, Interface will convert its linear manufacturing process into a cyclical, semiclosed-loop process in which old carpeting is recycled into new.

Interface CEO Ray Anderson has made a remarkable commitment to the environment, pledging that his company, which has 40 percent of the world's carpet tile market, worth $1 billion a year in sales, will actually become a net producer of energy. Reading Paul Hawken's *Ecology of Commerce* changed Anderson's life, giving him "a vision and a powerful sense of urgency." In the keynote address to an Interface task force that had been organized to look at the company's environmental position, he presented Hawken's ideas and brought forward the idea, "Interface, the first name in industrial ecology worldwide." He wanted the participants to consider converting Interface into a restorative enterprise. "The economic viability of the Evergreen Lease for us," said Anderson, "depends on our ability to recycle used face fiber into new face fiber and used carpet tile backing into new carpet tile backing." The company has not yet achieved this goal economically, but it continues to move toward it.

Other companies are working on this concept too. Carrier Corporation, one of the world's largest manufacturers of HVAC equipment, is developing a leasing program to provide and sell the *service of comfort*, rather than selling just the equipment. One such lease is currently being negotiated with the Sands Hotel in Atlantic City. As companies begin taking ownership of their products throughout the life cycle, they will increasingly move toward closed-loop manufacturing processes.

A classic example of closed-loop manufacturing and industrial ecology can be seen in Kalundborg, Denmark. A network of private companies, energy producers, and agricultural enterprises use one another's waste products as resources, turning unwanted by-products and waste into valuable inputs. A coal-fired power plant generates waste heat that is used by an aquaculture facility that raises 200 tons of turbot and trout annually. Gypsum produced from the pollution-control equipment on the power plant's smokestack (sulfur emissions convert calcium carbonate into calcium sulfate, or gypsum) is used by a drywall manufacturing plant in place of virgin (mineral) gypsum. The waste steam from the power plant is used by an oil refinery and a pharmaceutical plant. Wastewater from the oil refinery is used by the power plant. A pharmaceutical company is processing sludge from its fermentation process with chalk-lime to make fertilizer for local farming operations. A cement plant and a chemical manufacturer are also part of this interconnected system in which all operations benefit from their association with the others, saving the costs of waste disposal as well as raw material acquisition.

The industrial ecology approach used at Kalundborg saves $12 to $15 million annually, along with 19,000 tons of oil, 30,000 tons of coal, and 600,000 cubic meters of water a year. This synergy did not happen overnight; it took 25 years for the network to evolve. It is particularly impressive because it was industry driven, without government regulation or laws, although some of the pollution-control laws requiring lower pollution levels from smokestacks and effluent helped encourage the process. The earliest agreements were based on economic savings of avoided wastes and the financial benefit of selling wastes for raw materials. More recent initiatives have been driven largely by environmental concerns, which can also be strong economic motivators.

Building on Kalundborg's experience, there are several initiatives in the United States to implement this type of industrial ecology synergy. Some of these efforts are being discussed as part of larger mixed-use developments that will include residential components, which are not a part of the Kalundborg project.

The preferential use of green building materials by the construction industry can help to drive more responsible manufacturing practices. At least one U.S.

drywall manufacturer, for example, now promotes the fact that a significant portion of its gypsum is "synthetic" flue-gas desulfurization gypsum. In green developments, specifying new carpeting that was recycled from old carpeting, foam insulation produced from packaging foam, and steel studs made from recycled automobiles can help promote a shift of the manufacturing industry in this direction.

Montana State University's planned 100,000-square-foot National ReSource Center will incorporate a wide range of innovative yet practical environmental materials, as well as designs, construction techniques, and operation procedures, that will minimize environmental impact. It will be a privately owned and operated educational facility that will function as an interface between the Montana State University programs and various non-university constituencies, including individuals, government agencies, businesses, and industry in Montana.

Designers of the National ReSource Center are creating new products out of waste material from local industry and generating opportunities for sustainable business. For example, the design team researched the use of mine tailings from a local gold mine as the aggregate in concrete block construction. There are huge quantities of mine tailings in Montana, so a new market could open up for this

Montana State University's National ReSource Center will incorporate a wide range of innovative designs, environmental materials, and construction techniques that will minimize environmental impacts. *(Rendering by Place Architects. Reprinted with permission.)*

waste material. Fly ash, a by-product of coal-fired power plants, was also recommended to replace a significant portion of cement in the building's concrete.

The textile industry is also working toward reducing wastes and ultimately reaching a closed-loop system. Green architect William McDonough was asked by Design-Tex, Inc., a manufacturer of commercial office furniture fabric and a subsidiary of Steelcase Corporation, to design an environmentally sensitive upholstery fabric. He agreed, on the condition that he could design not only the fabric, but also its manufacturing process. McDonough specified that at each step of this process, no toxic chemicals be used and no air pollutants be emitted. The fabric that resulted is biodegradable and made entirely of free-range sheep wool and organically grown ramie. Chemical giant Ciba-Geigy took the challenge to work with McDonough and chemist Michael Braungart to find pigments that are made without the release of carcinogens, heavy metals, mutagens, endocrine disrupters, or other chemicals that can build up in the human body. Starting with some 8,000 chemicals, they narrowed these down to just 38 that they considered acceptable for fabric production. The resulting textile looks and feels better, while costing less to make. The Swiss mill that produces the fabric sells all the scrap material to local strawberry farmers, who use it as composting ground cover instead of plastic, whereas conventional fabric trimmings are treated as toxic waste. McDonough comments, "We need to take filters out of the pipes and put them in designers' heads where they belong." Innovative thinking like this in other related areas of the building industry can help "close the loop" and lead to a more sustainable, less wasteful future.

Looking Ahead to the Next Generation: The Importance of Learning Institutions

Education is absolutely critical to the widespread implementation of green development. University curricula in architecture, engineering, and building trades do a very poor job in teaching the benefits of whole-systems thinking and integration. Civil engineers, for example, may not learn about natural infiltration solutions to storm water runoff concerns, focusing instead on calculations of the fluid dynamics of flows through storm sewers that are designed to carry water off a site as quickly as possible. Architecture students are rarely advised to assemble multidisciplinary teams early in the design stages for a project—a practice that is necessary to fully capture end-use/least-cost opportunities.

A few schools and other educational programs are finally beginning to realize these shortcomings. Several dozen university building projects throughout North America, including the University of Montana project described earlier, are incorporating green design features and green materials. These projects are serving a very important function by demonstrating what is possible with leading-edge building practices and providing others—including developers—with an opportunity to learn from their experiences. But just as important is the integration of curricula with the role of these buildings as demonstrations.

The Environmental Studies Center at Oberlin College in Ohio is a 10,000-square-foot building designed by an interdisciplinary team of William McDonough + Partners, Andropogon Associates, Inc., John Lyle of the design firm Living Technologies, Lev Zetlin Associates Engineering Services, Hammond Construction, Rocky Mountain Institute staff, David Orr (head of the School of Environmental Studies at Oberlin), plus students and staff from the college. The building design includes state-of-the-art energy- and water-efficiency measures, renewable energy technologies, innovative green materials, biological wastewater treatment, and ecological landscaping.

More important than the building itself, however, are the educational aspects of its creation. Orr is a leader in pushing people to think beyond conventional boundaries. He notes that we are currently in a crisis of value, ideas, perception, and design. If you get the design wrong, he says, "the problems ripple out like water in a pond when a stone is thrown." He stresses that we need to think in the larger context while reducing problems to a manageable scale.

For the Oberlin Environmental Studies building, Orr and his team sought to produce new solutions by asking such questions as these:

- How can my project not only consume as little energy as possible, but go beyond to actually generate energy (to be a net exporter of energy)?
- What can my project do to heal the environment (and not just limit its impact)?
- How can the water discharge from my project be cleaner than the water that came into it?

Asking different questions resulted in a different project than is found on a typical university campus today, and played an important educational role. The concept

The Center for Regenerative Studies demonstrates its integrated approach to dealing with issues of food, shelter, water, energy, and materials, showing how the physical needs of a community can be met in a sustainable way while minimizing negative impacts on the surroundings. *(Architect: Dougherty & Dougherty; photographer: Milroy/McAleer; owner: California State Polytechnic University, Pomona. Reprinted with permission.)*

document called for full-cost accounting for all materials, labor, resources, technologies, and systems. And the program specified that the building be a net exporter of energy and produce zero harmful emissions. The resulting design allows the building and landscape to function as a single system and to be a living learning tool.

Orr points out that there are more than 3,700 colleges and universities in the United States with $70 to $90 billion a year to invest in building and renovation projects. What a great opportunity for green developers to bring to other campuses throughout the United States the kind of example David Orr has brought to his Ohio campus. Through his Environmental Studies Center, Orr has also sponsored environmental design conferences targeted toward educators nationwide. In addition to providing information on sustainable design, these programs have sought to inspire other educators to incorporate integrated environmental studies into their curricula.

The Center for Regenerative Studies at California State Polytechnic University in Pomona, described in Chapter 11, has students living in a setting that teaches about energy and integrated environmental design. Their residential buildings are living laboratories, complete with agricultural enterprises in which they grow their own food. Two phases of the project were completed by 1996, and a third phase was being designed by students.

The Transition from Pioneer to Mainstream in the Development Industry

There are two primary drivers that will bring mainstream developers into the world of green development. The first is an increasing awareness that we all need to do our part in ensuring that our children and grandchildren will have a safe, healthful, and enjoyable place to live. Many of the pioneering green developers came to the field through this sort of altruistic awareness and caring for the environment. The second driver, which will increasingly pull mainstream developers into the fold, is an economic one. They will turn to green development, because that is where the profits will be found.

One could try to make value judgments about these two motivations—that the altruistic reasons are somehow better—but the distinctions are increasingly blurring. Profit-seeking developers will appreciate this as they begin to see what their green developments achieve and how they benefit both communities and nature. If green development also makes them feel good—even subtly—their commitment will be reinforced. On the other hand, as altruistic developers "do the right thing," they will probably make a lot of money, as many are beginning to discover.

Green developer John Clark initially built projects that he looks back on with some regret for their lack of long-range vision. His Haymount development in Virginia will be far different, establishing the leading edge of environmentally responsible mixed-use development. But the project is not different from his early projects in regard to the profit motive. Clark does not hide the fact that he and his partners stand to make a lot of money in Haymount, and he argues that green developers should maximize their profits: "Don't leave money on the table. Every time a dollar goes around, part of it should stick to you. The opportunities are limited only by your imagination."

As the master developer of Haymount, Clark has thought of many ways to keep income streams flowing his way over the long term. The phasing of the project is in chunks—350 to 400 housing units and 80,000 to 120,000 square feet of commercial and retail space for Phase One. The first building to be constructed (in which Clark has a financial stake) will be an inn with two restaurants and a European spa. The restaurant will allow the organic gardens to start production and then to have a steady market. A bakery and a butcher shop are next on the list for opening.

The eventual size of Haymount (9,500 residents plus 2,200 employees of industrial and commercial components) offers numerous opportunities to capture future markets. Clark plans to initiate multiple joint ventures to provide residents and businesses with services—everything from cable and security to waste management and recycling. For example, the plan is to collaborate with farmers on agricultural activities and strike up a partnership with a concert promoter for construction of an outdoor entertainment center. While ensuring long-term income streams for the Haymount Company, Clark will also be bringing a solid clientele to his partners, who will sell their goods or services to Haymount's future citizens.

Kevork Derderian, president of Continental Offices Limited (COL), has developed commercial office space in the Chicago area for more than 25 years. He became interested in green development after hearing Amory Lovins describe the financial benefits of integrated HVAC design. He invited Lovins to speak to an assembled team of companies with which COL works, and became intrigued by the broader issues and benefits of green design (particularly the indoor air quality benefits).

While Derderian is strongly supportive of the underlying social and environmental values inherent in green development, he remains just as influenced by the bottom line as he ever was. He feels that it is just good business to know each of his tenants and their secretaries by name. They are individuals with individual needs and desires, not just numbers or statistics. As a result, he saves time and dollars, thanks to high tenant retention. He does not have to spend a lot of money on marketing, tenant improvements for new tenants, rental space left vacant, or similar items.

Restoring the Physical and Natural Environment

Many environmentalists continue to think of developers as enemies of the environment. Many examples can be found in which development has had a devastating impact on natural ecosystems and destroyed open space, but developers need not carry forward this reputation. Some of today's leading green developers are winning environmental awards for their efforts to protect natural areas, even while making money. Developers control billions of dollars spent annually on land and building; they have the financial power—and, increasingly, the philosophical will—to help ensure that future generations will also have open space to use and enjoy.

Much, indeed most, of our urban and suburban land has been significantly degraded through decades or centuries of use. Even many "wild" open spaces are in desperate need of ecological restoration to bring back diverse and healthy ecosystems. Restoration and revitalization of the natural environment will likely become an even greater focus of green development. Wild and productive areas can exist in the backyards of large mixed-use developments, and these can both help nature and enhance project values.

As one of the largest infill projects in the country, the Stapleton Redevelopment Project presents a great example of how an urban community can adapt and revitalize. It will serve to strengthen the neighborhood that has grown up around Denver's old Stapleton Airport. Throughout the project development process more than 100 community meetings took place to encourage community-wide participation. Some meetings were even broadcast on television. The first action items involved many environmental remediation activities on the site, including digging up and recycling airfield paving.

With the help of a partnership between the city and county of Denver and the citizens advisory board, the Stapleton Redevelopment Foundation's plan integrates jobs, environment, and community. Comprising 4,700 acres of publicly owned land within the heart of the city, this is the largest urban redevelopment opportunity in the history of Denver and will take 30 to 40 years to fully complete.

This project, in conjunction with the reworking of the Rocky Mountain Arsenal and along with Lowery Air Force Base, will provide a major wildlife refuge. It will evolve into a mixed-use community offering integrated commercial space, housing, and recreation, all with access to public transit. A third of the property will be

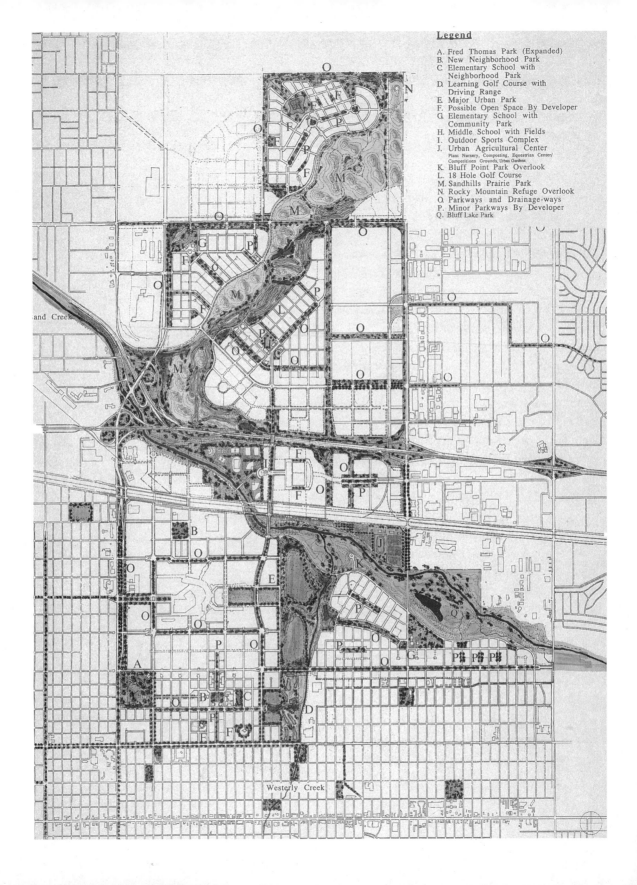

restored as parks, recreation areas, and open space. The design calls for the creation of eight districts, each containing an identifiable center and integrated walkable spaces. The Stapleton Redevelopment report states, "The open space system serves a major role in unifying the eight districts, making effective regional connections and restoring the ecological health and natural systems on and off the site."

The plan stresses compact, high-density development. It strives to reduce infrastructure costs by requiring water reuse, energy and water efficiency, a renewable energy supply, and innovative storm water management. Designers are working toward a zero net contribution to landfills, in part by setting up a "resource recovery village" to promote recycling and reuse. This might include matching leftover building materials from one project with someone who needs such materials for another building endeavor. One portion of the plan includes an urban agriculture element, featuring farms, equestrian facilities, composting yards, and a nursery. This area will also provide opportunity for educational experiences.

Funding sources for project infrastructure are very diversified and include infrastructure fees, local tax and assessment districts, private capital, state and federal transportation funding, private foundation grants, general municipal revenues, tax increment financing, airport system revenues, and connection fees.

The remarkable capacity of natural systems to recover from ecological devastation is well known. In *Hope, Human and Wild,* Bill McKibben describes how nature can recover itself, if allowed to, using the example of reforestation that has occurred in the Northern Forest—an ecosystem "that hit rock bottom" but has been making a remarkable recovery. Most of the forests of the northeast were chopped down within 100 years of European settlement. When settlers moved farther west, however, the eastern forests recovered and long-extirpated animal species, including moose, cougars, and perhaps even wolves, have begun moving back.

Similar levels of restoration have been occurring in once-dead rivers and lakes throughout the eastern United States, including the infamous Cuyahoga River in Cleveland, which caught fire in 1969. At one time the Connecticut River served as an open sewer for much of New England, while today it is widely used for recreation.

In another type of restoration, Bernadette Cozart is bringing vibrant color and food production to one of New York City's most depressed areas. The Greening of

◄— The 4,700 acres of publicly owned land for the Stapleton Redevelopment project in the heart of Denver is the largest urban development opportunity in the history of the city. The redevelopment plan illustrates how an urban community can adapt and revitalize itself. *(Reprinted with permission from Stapleton Redevelopment Foundation 1995; Cooper Robertson and Partners; Civitas; BRW; Andropogon Associates; Harold Massop and Associates.)*

The Stapleton Redevelopment plan features such elements as urban agriculture, with farms, equestrian facilities, composting yards, and a nursery. *(Reprinted with permission from the Stapleton Development Corporation.)*

Harlem, as the project is known, was created by Cozart to provide local children with satisfying activities to help keep them away from gangs and drugs. The loosely knit community organization is turning abandoned lots, often crack-cocaine hangouts, into beautiful urban gardens, play areas, and cultural treasures. Cozart works extensively with the Harlem schools and with community groups in this effort. There are lessons that developers can learn from this example, especially the tremendous good that a few individuals can do to improve their surroundings.

The L.A. Eco-Village Demonstration project in Los Angeles is part of an international sustainable neighborhood group that seeks to model healthier ways of living based on environmental sustainability and social and economic justice. Robert Gilman of Context Institute explains: "An Ecovillage is a human-scale, full-featured settlement which harmlessly integrates human activities into the natural world in a way that is supportive of healthy human development and can be successfully continued into the indefinite future." The L.A. Eco-Village Demonstration project works with surrounding neighborhoods and the city to bring a whole-systems perspective to urban planning and community development activities. Lois Arkin, director of the L.A. Eco-Village, explains that "by creating a practical demonstration of healthy urban life in the village, the intent is to manifest a different way of being in the city, a way in which the social, economic, and physical web of life are deeply felt and experienced."

At first the group wanted to build a new village on a clean site, but then realized that working with an existing neighborhood was more environmentally responsible. In one of the areas most severely affected by civil unrest and the Los Angeles riots of 1992, the ideal site was found. The project includes an existing two-block, 500-person mixed-income, multi-ethnic, intergenerational working class neighborhood three miles from downtown Los Angeles. Currently, there are only a handful of the total number of residents in the area working on the eco-village project, but interest is high.

Projects within the eco-village include car sharing (including use of electric vehicles), traffic calming, tree plantings, community gardens and orchards, eco-business planning, composting, a cooperative farmers market, an ethnic conflict resolution center, energy-efficient and affordable housing, and economic development activities.

In Chicago, developer John Podmajersky has integrated this sort of community participation into his work (see Chapter 5). His projects have been inspired by the needs of the local neighborhood, and they have, in turn, strengthened those communities. In many cities and neighborhoods there are residents who are

The L.A. Eco-Village Demonstration project, working with surrounding neighborhoods and the city, provides a whole-systems approach to urban planning and community development. This photograph illustrates a community tree planting event. *(Reprinted with permission from the CRSP/L.A. Eco-Village.)*

These "before" and "after" photographs illustrate how developer John Podmajersky has revitalized his Chicago area community. *(Reprinted with permission from John Podmajersky Management, Inc.)*

working to inspire better, stronger communities. To ensure that their products will do well and do good, wise developers will seek out such people and make use of their wisdom and skills at community building.

Ever Forward

The development world is going through a period of rapid change; that much is clear. The projects described in this book—and many others throughout North America and the rest of the world—can no longer be considered only aberrations to the status quo. These projects represent the beginning of an industrywide shift that will grow exponentially over the coming years. Developers who are leading this transition, individuals like Michael and Judy Corbett, Jim Chaffin, John Clark, Kevork Derderian, John Knott, Jonathan Rose, and Robert Zimmer are playing an invaluable role as the innovators—the explorers venturing into new territory. The rest of the development community is watching closely, well aware that the success or failure of these cutting-edge projects will probably establish the course of real estate development for the next generation.

If these projects do succeed, and if the ideas they embody catch on widely among developers and other players in the real estate and building industries, we can expect to see a dramatic turnaround in the way developers are perceived by environmental groups and society at large. In 50 years, the next generation of developers, like the fictional Elden Carrol, could emerge as the heroes of the twenty-first century, the leaders who not only salvaged our decaying inner cities, but also provided for future generations by ensuring that our natural heritage will be here to inspire and enrich us.

Along the way, these green developers will prosper financially. They will do so because their products make sense and will be in demand. Corporations will come to appreciate the productivity benefits and enhanced profits that carefully designed and built (or renovated) office buildings can provide. Home owners will come to appreciate—and demand—communities that enrich their lives and living spaces that are comfortable, convenient, and affordable to operate. The period of time during which green development can be called *new* or *untried* or *risky* will be very short. Soon, green development will not even need the moniker "green." The elements that today define a development as green will be conventional practice. Standard development in the early twenty-first century will exceed even the green features described in this book.

Project Profiles and Contacts

Green Development Case Study Profiles

The information for each of these profiles was acquired from the project's developer or owner. Certain financial information could not be attained. The projects are grouped by real estate type.

Note: Contact names are listed with the profiled projects. Addresses and phone numbers of contacts are listed at the end of this appendix.

Residential

Project Name: Dewees Island®

Location: Barrier island near Charleston, South Carolina

Developer: Island Preservation Partnership (IPP)

Contact: John Knott Jr., CEO, IPP

Date Completed: Phase I: Begun August 1992. First home constructed September 1993. By first quarter 1997, 60 home sites in Phase I had been sold and 20 homes had been built. In Phase II, 18 lots were available.

Project Size

    Site (gross land area): 1,200-acre island

    Building: 420 buildable acres (But will disturb less than 5 percent of the land. Impact is restricted to 7,500 SF per lot.)

Project Description: Resort/residential community with build-out of 150 single-family residential homes; 40 percent of buyers are permanent residents. Project includes a marina, a nature center, a guest lodge, and interactive nature trails.

Hard Costs

> **Site Acquisition Costs:** The IPP formed as an equity-based partnership. New partners invested equity capital and development expertise, and land partners provided land and $5 million in debt. Each group received a 50 percent interest.
>
> **Site Development Costs:** $2.2 million
>
> **Building Construction Costs:** $3.1 million

Soft Costs

> **Development and Administration:** $3.1 million
>
> **Marketing/Leasing:** $4 million
>
> **Architectural/Engineering:** $1 million
>
> **Environmental Reserve:** $325,000
>
> **Other (legal, property tax, and community obligations):** $3.3 million

Types of Financing: Equity investment and existing $5 million debt of land partners. Reinvesting sale proceeds until all debt is retired (approximately $800,000 remains). Current debt is about $1 million with $30 million in sales remaining (as of January 1997).

Lot prices: $220,000 to $475,000 for ocean view (1997 prices)

Total Costs: $14.1 million (as of October 1996)

Total Return on Investment: Net profits exceeding pro forma by approximately 90 percent. Net income, originally estimated at $12 million, is now estimated at $23 to $24 million (as of January 1997). Gross income is projected to be $44 million. ROI is expected to average between 30 and 35 percent. This is due to the reduced need for equity, based on infrastructure cost reduction from environmentally responsive measures.

Notable Green Development (GD) Features: Environmental preservation and restoration was a major focus in the design; 65 percent of land is held in a wildlife preserve. Vehicle-free island (except for golf carts) with pervious roads. Careful site planning and orientation. Natural ventilation and passive solar heating in homes. Healthy materials and indigenous vegetation. Water efficiency and water-quality strategies. Native seed harvesting project. Extensive environmental education programs, with a full-time ecologist and environmental educator, and promotion of local crafts to strengthen links with community. Architectural

Resource Board to monitor building designs. Forty hours of builder training is required.

Results: Energy- and environment-sensitive design requirements have led to a 50 to 80 percent savings in utility bills as compared with average. Wildlife has increased on the island. Land development and infrastructure costs reduced to 60 percent below the average. Workers are healthier, building with environmentally friendly materials, as are residents living in these homes. In 1995, the International Energy Agency Future Buildings Forum in Switzerland cited Dewees as an international model for how communities should be planned and developed. Keep America Beautiful honored Dewees with the 1995 First Place National Award for Environmental Excellence; this was the first time the organization had given an award to a private development. The development has received numerous other awards, and was the first development ever to be honored by the President's Council on Sustainable Development.

Project Name: Prairie Crossing

Location: Grayslake, Illinois

Owner: Prairie Holdings Corporation

Developer: Shaw Homes, Inc.

Contacts: Victoria Post-Ranney and Franklin A. Martin

Date Completed: Models opened February 1995. Fifty homes occupied and 30 more are being built (January 1997).

Project Size

    Site (gross land area): 667 acres

    Building (gross building area): 207 acres

Project Description: A new community of 317 single-family homes located on an old family farm in a Chicago suburb. Open space and 150 acres of farmland. Future plans for commercial (33 acres) and limited industrial (42 acres) adjacent to the development.

Hard Costs

    Site Acquisition Costs: $5.2 million

Types of Financing: Land acquisition financed by equity partnership comprised of the original owners, the Gaylord Donnelly family, and neighbors. Other costs financed by bank loan.

Cost of Each House: $194,000 to $409,000

Notable GD Features: Originally this site was slated to have 1,500 homes. The developer reduced density to 317 homes (20 percent of permitted density). Land planning types include large lot, cluster, and neotraditional neighborhoods. Restoration of several different native habitats and historic buildings on site; 150 acres of existing farmland to be kept in production. Site design involved planning the development around the existing hedgerows, wetlands, and terrain. Community-supported organic garden. Almost two-thirds of site retained as open space. Home features include high insulating values, low-VOC materials, energy-efficient appliances and lighting, built-in recycling bins. Trails for walkers, bikers, and horseback riders. One-half percent of each home sale goes to support the Liberty Prairie Foundation for environmental education and stewardship programs. Mass rail transit is adjacent to the site, providing service to downtown and the airport.

Results: Saved $1.4 million on infrastructure costs by using narrower streets ($4,400 per lot), and natural storm water drainage. Energy consumption for heating and cooling homes is reduced by 50 percent as compared with conventional new home construction in Chicago.

Project Name: Santa Lucia Community Preserve

Location: Monterey Peninsula, south of the Carmel Valley, California

Owner/Developer: Rancho San Carlos Partnership, Thomas Gray, general manager

Contacts: Jeffrey B. Froke, Michael Horst, and David Howerton

Date Completed: Project pending (See Chapter 7)

Project Size

> **Site (gross land area):** 20,000 acres

> **Building (gross building area):** 2,000 acres

Project Description: High-end residential real estate development with nature preserve; 300 homes to be built in ecologically defined clusters plus 50 units of employee housing.

Hard Costs

> **Site Acquisition Costs:** $70 million (1990)

> **Site Development Costs:** $100 million+ to date in planning and inventory (fall 1996)

Types of Financing: Financing/funding of preserve through a nonprofit conservation trust. Goal to raise $20+ million endowment with revenue-generating capacity. Creative feasibility helped secure original $80 million in equity. Japanese public institution invested $72 million, and the Rancho San Carlos Partnership invested the remaining amount.

Sale Price per Lot: $1 to $4 million (est.)

Average Lot Size: 2.5 acres

Notable GD Features: Preservation and restoration of 18,000 acres through the Santa Lucia Conservancy. Number of approved homes downsized from 11,000 to 300. Site sensitivity in placement of houses and roads, and in golf trail system. Renovation of an existing building to be used as a clubhouse and/or library. Extensive site analysis; developed a GIS system of 15,000 layers of information to guide design and long-term stewardship.

Results: Market research identified a market niche willing to pay a premium to live in an environmentally sensitive development in a legendary California landscape. Partnership between conservancy and developers will ensure financially sustainable preservation of land in perpetuity.

Project Name: Spring Island

Location: Barrier Island in Beaufort County, South Carolina

Owner/Developer: Spring Island Company

Contact: James Chaffin

Project Completion: 250 sites sold; 38 houses built and 46 in progress (February 1997)

Project Size

    Site (gross land area): 3,000-acre island

    Building (gross building area): 500 home sites

Project Description: Environmentally responsible development of 500 homes (1- to 10-acre lot size), par 72 golf course, 1,000-acre land preserve.

Hard Costs

    Site Acquisition Costs: $17 million

    Site Development Costs: $18 million

    Building Construction Costs: $12 million

Soft Costs

    Financing: $6.3 million

    Marketing/Leasing: $10 million

    Architectural and Other: $2 million

Types of Financing: $10 million in presales convinced NationsBank to lend $17 million in debt. $20 million in initial equity from joint venture Japanese investors, Nippon Landic. $13 million in infrastructure remained as of August 1996.

Total Costs: $90 million

Total Return on Investment: $40 million (10 years); approximately 23 percent after debt service

Notable GD Features: Downzoned from 5,500 homes to 500. Interdisciplinary team comprehensively addressed the needs of the site and the development impact on the ecosystem. Developed a land trust to manage and preserve 1,000 acres of the island. Land trust supported by a 1.5 percent fee on the initial sale of each lot and on each subsequent resale. Preservation of a historic ruin on the island. Architectural review board scrutinizes all aspects of home design and siting. Full time naturalist on staff. No hard-paved roads. Environmentally sensitive golf course design and maintenance.

Results: 1993 Conservation Award from the South Carolina Wildlife Federation, 1995 Award from South Carolina Department of Natural Resources, 1996 Award from Renew America, and numerous other awards. The golf course has earned certification by Audubon International.

Project Name: Village Homes

Location: Davis, California

Developer: Village Homes

Contacts: Michael and Judy Corbett

Date Completed: 1981

Project Size

　　Site (gross land area): 70 acres

　　Building (gross building area): 32 acres

Project Description: Planned community of single-family detached homes and apartments (240 units); 12 acres of greenbelts and open space; 12 acres of common agricultural land; 4,000 SF of commercial office space.

Hard Costs

　　Site Acquisition Costs: $434,000 (1975)

　　Site Development Costs: $2.3 million

Soft Costs

　　Marketing/Leasing: Marketed initially by word of mouth

　　Amenities: $313,107 for swimming pool, bike paths, landscaping

Initial Sale Price per Unit: $31,000 to $75,000

Types of Financing: Limited partnership for first 10 acres; infrastructure lender Sacramento Savings and Loan. Initial option on the land—$10,000; 13 investors raised $120,000; first bank loan $170,000 for first 10 acres (1973). Bought land in increments over a five-year period, developed in five phases.

Average Development Cost/SF: $38 (1980)

Total Return on Investment: Original investors made a profit of 30 percent per year.

Notable GD Features: Platted to ensure solar access. Active and passive solar home designs. Natural drainage systems based on Ian McHarg's model. Pedestrian-friendly design with bike paths and narrow streets. Edible landscaping and organic agriculture.

Results: Known as the "granddaddy" of green developments. In 1995 homes sold for $10 to $25/SF over standard homes in the area. Low turnover and faster sales. Very low crime rate. Lowered ambient air temperature by 15° by reducing paving. Surface drainage system saved $800 per lot, which was applied toward additional landscaping. By 1989, much of Village Home's residential food was produced in the neighborhood. Annual household bills range from one-half to one-third less than those of surrounding neighborhoods. Eighty percent of the residents participate in various activities promoted by the development. Average number of cars per household is reduced from that of surrounding Davis neighborhoods.

Hotel/Resort

Project Name: Boston Park Plaza

Location: Boston, Massachusetts

Owner: Boston Park Plaza/Saunders Hotel Group

Contacts: Tedd Saunders and Susan Silva

Date Completed: 1990

Project Size

    Building (gross building area): 75,000 SF

Project Description: Renovation of a 977-room hotel built in 1926.

Hard Costs

    Window Retrofit Costs: $1.2 million

Soft Costs

    Marketing/Leasing: $50,000 for advertising

Types of Financing: $4,000 in lighting rebates from local utilities.

Total Costs: $1.8 million

Total Return on Investment: 21.75 percent (1993)

Notable GD Features: Environmentally conscious operations. Initiated 125 hotelwide initiatives. Energy-efficient lighting. Water-efficient shower heads. Comprehensive recycling program. Installed 1,642 tighter, yet operable, thermopane windows. Upgraded insulation. Installed a $90,000 filtration system, allowing hotel to recycle two-thirds of its wash water and retain most of its heat.

Results: Green hotel image attracted about $2 million in new business and has achieved a higher occupancy rate (1994). Water consumption was reduced by 65 percent, saving $45,000 annually. Each retrofitted room saves $75 annually. Eliminated use of two million individual shampoo bottles per year by purchasing natural bulk amenities instead. Recycling has saved $67,901 (renovation—1994). $130,000 in energy savings (renovation—1994). Saves $51,500 each year in food/beverage eco-initiative. Received the President's Environment and Conservation Challenge Award. Hotel recently sold for $100 million and had a higher building valuation as a result of energy-efficient renovation.

Project Name: Inn of the Anasazi

Location: Santa Fe, New Mexico

Developer: Aspen Design Group/The Zimmer Group

Contacts: Robert Zimmer, Michael Fuller, and Jeff Mahan

Date Completed: 1991

Project Size

    Building (gross building area): 54,000 SF

Project Description: 59-room luxury resort hotel

Hard Costs

    Building Acquisition Costs: $1.5 million

Types of Financing: Bank of America construction loan. Refinanced permanent loan in late 1993 through ITT Real Estate Financial Services, Chicago. Only independent hotel in Santa Fe to get financing that year.

Building Construction Costs per Room: $198,000

Total Costs: $12 million

Total Return on Equity: 13 percent by 1994

Notable GD Features: Reused a building in downtown Santa Fe. Design reflects the diverse cultures of the region. Used locally sourced, nontoxic building materials. Daylighting throughout building. Extensive community connections and involvement. Green operations. Employees have paid time each week to work in the community. 70 percent of the food is sourced from organic farms. Kitchen wastes sent to the local pig farm and leftovers given to food shelters.

Results: Appraised at $14 million. Received an offer to buy the hotel at more than $14.5 million. Value increased by more than $2 million in less than three years. Has 83 percent average occupancy rate and 35 percent repeat traffic. Development team's attention to environmental and community issues has boosted the inn's and the restaurant's performance by 15 to 20 percent. Supports local organic land-grant Hispanic farmers. High employee retention and financial returns.

Project Name: Maho Bay

Location: Within the Virgin Islands National Park, St. John, U.S. Virgin Islands

Owner/Developer: Stanley Selengut

Contact: Stanley Selengut

Date Completed: 1992 (in 1974 took out a 31-year lease on land on St. John)

Project Size

> **Site (gross land area):** 14 acres

> **Building (gross building area):** 44,000 SF

Project Description: Eco-tourist resort of clustered tent-cabins (114 tent-cabins — 16'x16') located on an island where 75 percent of the land is National Park.

Hard Costs

> **Site Acquisition Costs:** $150,000 (1974)

> **Building Construction Costs:** $3,000 to $15,000 per unit

Soft Costs

> **Financing:** $250,000

> **Marketing/Leasing:** A lot of free press

Types of Financing: Owner financed

Average Development Cost/SF: $27.34

Total Costs: $3,000 to $15,000 per unit

Total Return on Investment: $15 to $20 million in assets over 20 years

Notable GD Features: Extremely site-sensitive placement of the tent-cabins and walkways. No roads were built, and construction materials were brought in by hand along walkways. Self-sufficient tent-cabins minimize impact of guests. All major trees were preserved. Low-flow or composting toilets. Water from the showers is collected and used to water the garden, and the compost is used for fertilizer. Focus on environmental education—island ecology, astronomy, and whale research.

Results: 7,000 guests per year. Very attractive returns in spite of no advertising. Very high occupancy rates have given developer net profits of 25 percent of his gross revenues. Developer surveys every guest, and respondents are very pleased with amenities. Developer has received 10,000 surveys back. Protecting environmental integrity of the island. Developer has gone on to create two other successful developments on St. John: Harmony and Estate Concordia.

Industrial

Project Name: The Body Shop Headquarters
Location: Wake Forest, North Carolina
Owner: The Body Shop
Contact: Gail A. Lindsey
Date Completed: 1993
Project Size
   Building (gross building area): 153,700 SF
Project Description: Warehouse and office building
Average Development Cost/SF: $21 for office/laboratories; $11 for warehouse
Total Costs: $2,107,457
Notable GD Features: Retrofitted existing building. Reuse and recycling of materials. Attention to low-toxic and low-embodied-energy material selection. Recycled materials. Daylighting strategies. Efficient HVAC and lighting systems. Operable windows. All existing vegetation preserved.
Results: Avoided tipping fees by reusing existing materials. Donated materials to Habitat for Humanity, for which the project received a tax credit. Increased natural light, beneficial to employees in office areas. Good indoor air quality. Periphery of existing vegetation helps in site cooling.

Project Name: Herman Miller SQA
Location: Zeeland, Michigan
Owner/Developer: Herman Miller

Contacts: Joe Azzarello, Keith Winn, and William McDonough

Date Completed: 1995

Project Size

    Building (gross building area): 290,000 SF

Project Description: Warehouse, manufacturing plant, and offices for 720 workers over three shifts

Types of Financing: Internal financing by corporation

Average Development Cost/SF: $48

Notable GD Features: Design team took a whole-systems approach. Site sensitivity in building placement. Maximized solar gain in orientation. Passive solar heating and natural ventilation. Building is entirely daylit. High-efficiency electric lights are controlled with electronic sensors. Adaptability—able to easily add on 100,000 SF addition. Good IAQ. Strove for zero off-gassing materials. Used natural drainage, native plantings, and constructed wetlands to break down pollutants. Designated recycling areas.

Results: Preliminary investigation revealed that on a square-foot basis, natural gas costs have decreased 7 percent, water and sewer costs have decreased 65 percent, and electric costs have decreased 18 percent in the new building versus costs incurred in the old building. In manufacturing operations 85 percent of waste is recycled. Striving to be a waste-free company. Employees are very satisfied with their new work environment. This facility is halfway through a three-year study conducted by Battelle Pacific Northwest Laboratory and funded by the DOE to determine the possible health and financial productivity improvements that can be realized using green development techniques.

Project Name: VeriFone Worldwide Distribution Center

Location: Costa Mesa, California

Owner: VeriFone Corporation

Contacts: Randolph Croxton, Kirsten Childs, and Bill Conley

Date Completed: 1993

Project Size

    Building (gross building area): 76,000 SF

Project Description: Offices and the worldwide distribution center

Hard Costs

    Site Development Costs: $480,000

Soft Costs

Financing: Internal

Types of Financing: $73,000 electrical rebate from Southern California Edison; $48,000 gas rebate from Southern California Gas.

Average Development Cost/SF: $39

Total Costs: $3.2 million ($1.2 M for HVAC)

Total Return on Investment: 7.5 year payback on energy-efficient technologies

Notable GD Features: Reuse of tilt-up concrete building in an industrial area. Design team took a whole-systems approach in decision making. Maximized utilization of daylighting strategies, energy-efficient lighting fixtures, high-performance glazing. Double-filtered air supply. Nontoxic and recycled building materials. Three times as many air exchanges as a typical office. Used 60 percent more insulation than used in a standard building. Selected office furniture that did not contain formaldehyde or outgassing chemicals, VOCs, or endangered species woods.

Results: 65 to 75 percent savings in energy; 59 percent lower energy use as compared with California Title 24 for new construction. Reduced utility costs from $1.54/SF (costs of a similar building) to $.43/SF. Building uses 50 percent of the energy required for the adjacent building. Good IAQ. Productivity increases: absenteeism dropped from 14.3 hours to 7.5 hours. Reusing an existing building saved about 880 metric tons of concrete.

Institutional

(Note: Dollar amounts in Canadian $.)

Project Name: C. K. Choi Building for the Institute of Asian Research

Location: The University of British Columbia, Vancouver, Canada

Owner/Developer: The University of British Columbia

Contacts: Freda Pagani and Eva Matsuzaki

Date Completed: 1996

Project Size

   Site (gross land area): 22,500 SF

   Building (gross building area): 30,000 SF

Project Description: Research offices with seminar spaces

Hard Costs

    Site Development Costs: $142,000

    Building Construction Costs: $4.8 million

Soft Costs

    Architectural and other: $1 million

Types of Financing: $4.5 million from Canadian and Asian donors and from the C. K. Choi family. B. C. Hydro PowerSmart Rebate of $42,000.

Average Development Cost/SF: $200

Total Costs: $5.9 million

Notable GD Features: Team-oriented, front-loaded design approach. Composting toilets and urinals. Subsurface, graywater recycling system to cleanse graywater and irrigate site. 50 percent of wood salvaged from demolition of campus building. Daylighting and stack ventilation. Recycled, reused, and sustainably derived materials. Adaptability in design scheme.

Results: Electrical savings of 191,603 kWh/yr, saving $15,000 per year. Water savings of 1,000 to 1,500 gallons/day. Healthful indoor environment. Attractive work environment.

(Note: Dollar amounts in Canadian $.)

Project Name: The University of Victoria Engineering Laboratory Wing

Location: The University of Victoria, Victoria, British Columbia, Canada

Owner/Developer: The University of Victoria

Contact: Terry Williams

Date Completed: 1996

Project Size

    Building (gross building area): 127,800 SF

Project Description: Four-story educational facility for electrical, computer, and mechanical engineering and computer science laboratories

Types of Financing: Funded by the Provincial Government of British Columbia, Canada. Received a $61,623 incentive from B. C. Hydro.

Average Development Cost/SF: $151

Total Costs: $19.3 million

Notable GD Features: Holistic approach to building design and an efficient building envelope. Eliminated perimeter heating and air-conditioning system. Heavy concrete structure for thermal capacity, light shelves, shading devices, and high-performance glazings. Structural, mechanical, and electrical systems designed to be as simple and effective as possible. Motion sensors, and sophisticated lighting and ventilation controls throughout the building.

Results: Saves 723,095 kWh/yr. Reduced operating costs by $36,150. Ninety percent reduction of light fixtures used 80 percent of the time (when it is light outdoors and people are working).

Project Name: San Francisco Main Library

Location: San Francisco, California

Owner: City of San Francisco, Public Library

Contact: Anthony Bernheim

Date Completed: 1996

Project Size

    Site (gross land area): 90,257 SF

    Building (gross building area): 381,000 SF

Project Description: Seven-story building located on an urban site in San Francisco Civic Center

Hard Costs

    Site Development Costs: $2.6 million

    Building Construction Costs: $97 million

Types of Financing: Municipal bond financing. Library Foundation of San Francisco was formed to raise money for non-bond-funded items.

Additional Costs for Building Commissioning: Unknown. Costs included in contractor's bid.

Total Costs: $142 million

Notable GD Features: Collaborative design with owner, architect, and consultants. Close attention to IAQ issues. Use of low-VOC building materials, including adhesives and paints. MSDS and emissions test data requested for some products. Commissioned building.

Results: Excellent IAQ and very happy librarians.

Project Name: The Way Station

Location: Frederick, Maryland

Owner: The Way Station

Contact: Greg Franta

Date Completed: February 1991

Project Size

    Building (gross building area): 30,000 SF

Project Description: Nonprofit mental health facility

Hard Costs

    Building Construction Costs: $3.3 million (1991)

Types of Financing: Corporate, governmental, and individual donors

Average Development Cost/SF: $111

Total Costs: $5.5 million

Additional Costs for Energy Efficiency: $170,000

Total Return on Investment: 22 percent, with a payback of 4.5 years

Notable GD Features: Whole-systems, front-loaded design. Careful attention to patients' needs in design. Innovative daylighting schemes. Heavy focus on energy and water efficiency. Nontoxic materials and products. Greenhouse provides a thermal mass for storing heat. High-efficiency lighting. Non-/low-toxic cleaning materials used in maintenance.

Results: Building does not seem institutional. Savings of $37,655 per year in energy costs as compared with base case. For lighting alone, the building uses 75 percent less energy than a conventional facility. The Way Station has put this savings to work in the local community by creating jobs.

Office/Commercial

Project Name: American Association for the Advancement of Science Building (AAAS)

Location: Washington, D.C.

Owner: American Association for the Advancement of Science

Contacts: George Wilson and Christina Bolinger

Date Completed: 1996

Project Size

    Site (gross land area): 22,110 SF

    Building (gross building area): 260,000 SF (includes parking garage)

Project Description: Twelve-floor office building. Three of the twelve floors will be leased to other nonprofit organizations. Two floors of meeting space and exhibit areas.

Hard Costs

Site Acquisition Costs: $16 million

Building Construction Costs: $26.5 million (includes tenant work on floors 3 through 5)

Soft Costs

Marketing/Leasing: $150,000

Architectural and Other: $1.5 million

Types of Financing: $52 million in District of Columbia industrial revenue bond sales (low-interest, tax-exempt bond sales).

Gross Development Cost/SF: $239

Total Costs: $62 million

Total Return on Investment: Estimated that municipal bond financing will save AAAS $40 million in interest over first 30 years of occupancy.

Notable GD Features: Integrated design approach. Daylighting and efficient lighting. Nonpolluting gas-fired absorption chillers and construction materials. Attention to IAQ through appropriate materials selection and good ventilation — 25 percent more outside air than conventional. Operable windows. Elimination of virtually all CFCs and HCFCs. Use of gas-fired absorption chillers. Flexibility built into the design. Energy and space savings through "intelligent elevator system." Close to mass transit hub.

Results: 50 percent energy cost savings above building code minimum. Reduced Btus/SF from 183,000 to 90,000 (as compared with conventional). 50 percent reduction in lighting energy to less than one watt/SF. 50 percent reduction in emissions. $150,000 to $200,000 in energy savings per year.

Project Name: Audubon House

Location: New York, New York

Owner: The Audubon Society

Contacts: Randolph Croxton, Kirsten Childs, and Jan Beyea

Date Completed: 1992

Project Size

Building (gross building area): 98,000 SF

Project Description: Renovation of 100-year-old Schermerhorn building for the National Audubon Society's office headquarters (five of the eight floors are occupied by Audubon; the rest are leased out).

Hard Costs

    Building Acquisition Costs: $10 million (1989)

    Building Renovation Costs: $14 million

Soft Costs: $2 million

Types of Financing: Industrial Development Revenue Bonds

Average Development Cost/SF: $122 (market rate $120 to $128/SF)

Total Costs: $24 million

Rebate: $72,000 from Con Edison for air-conditioning, $7,280 for high-efficiency motors, $30,895 for high-performance lighting

Total Return on Investment: Payback of five years on green features—reduced to a three-year payback because of utility involvement

Notable GD Features: Whole-systems, team-oriented, front-end planning and design. Attention to material selection and IAQ. $430,000 invested in energy-efficient and environmentally sensitive products. High level of fresh air ventilation —30 percent more outdoor air delivered to occupants. Decreased need for artificial lighting through exemplary daylighting strategies. Close to mass transit and other existing infrastructure. Attention to human factors in design. Internal recycling center. Least toxic maintenance procedures, as compared with conventional.

Results: Saved 27 percent over new construction costs by reusing an old building (a new building would have cost $33 million.) Saves $100,000/year in operating costs. Overall energy consumption cut by two-thirds. Cut electric lighting needs by 75 percent. Efficient lighting system reduced electricity bills by $60,000. Consumes 62 percent less energy than a standard building. 70 percent of office waste generated is sorted and reclaimed. Good IAQ.

(Note: Dollar amounts in Canadian $.)

Project Name: Crestwood Corporate Centre Building No. 8

Location: Richmond, British Columbia, Canada

Owner: Bentall Development Inc.

Contact: Bunting Coady Architects

Date Completed: 1996

Project Size

    Site (gross land area): 260,549 SF

    Building (gross building area): 84,000 SF

Project Description: Office building at the Bentall Crestwood Corporate Centre, a campus-style business park

Hard Costs

   Site Acquisition Costs: $1.5 million

   Site Development Costs: $7.1 million

Soft Costs

   Financing: $900,000

   Marketing/Leasing: $300,000

   Architectural and Other: $750,000

Incremental Costs: Hard costs: $272,727; Design: $74,606 (includes modeling); Envelope testing: $10,750; Monitoring: $46,392 + $100,000 over three years; Direct digital controls: $46,392.

Types of Financing: CANMET, Canada (under its C-2000 Program for Advanced Commercial Buildings) and B. C. Hydro (utility partner) provided $207,560 to cover extra design fees and capital costs associated with high-performance elements.

Average Development Cost/SF: $62

Total Costs: $5.2 million

Total Return on Investment: Simple payback based on energy savings only is 4.4 years and a net present value of $67,684. (This does not include environmental benefits, which were not valued in dollars.)

Notable GD Features: Innovative team approach integrating all disciplines through all stages of design. 50 percent more air exchanges for enhanced IAQ. Environmentally sensitive materials and technology choices. Attention to embodied energy. High-performance windows with good visible light transmittance. High insulation values. Energy-efficient lighting.

Results: High-performance commercial windows allowed nearly 60 percent of the building to be glazed and still achieve twice the energy performance of neighboring buildings. Whole-systems design process resulted in energy savings of 50 percent + over ASHRAE 90.1 standard.

Project Name: Southern California Gas Company's Energy Resource Center (ERC)

Location: Downey, California

Owner: Southern California Gas Company

Contact: Diane Morrison

Date Completed: 1995

Project Size

Site: 153,000 SF

Building (gross building area): 44,572 SF

Project Description: Reused a 1957 building to showcase the Gas Company's commitment to energy efficiency and environmental advancements.

Hard Costs

Site Development Costs: $452,757

Building Construction Costs: $6.7 million

Soft Costs

Construction Management Fee: $150,592

Types of Financing: 100 percent equity from Southern California Gas Company shareholders; $45,000 in rebates from the local electric utility for incorporating various energy-efficiency technologies.

Average Development Cost/SF: $153.61

Total Costs: $7.9 million

Notable GD Features: 80 percent of all construction materials and furnishings are recycled or products of recycled materials or renewable resources. Introduced the Interface "Evergreen Carpet Lease." Sensors optimize IAQ. Natural daylighting. Low-E windows. Drought-resistant plants for exterior landscaping.

Results: Saved $3.2 million over conventional construction by recycling the building. Exceeds California Title 24 by 45 percent. Engineers estimate the building will realize $21,000 to $30,000 savings in electricity annually.

Project Name: International Netherlands Group (ING) Bank, formerly the Nederlandsche Middenstandsbank (NMB)

Location: Southeast Amsterdam, the Netherlands

Owner: ING

Contact: Anton Alberts

Date Completed: 1987

Project Size

Site (gross land area): 467,742 SF

Building (gross building area): 538,000 SF

Project Description: Organic design for the bank's office headquarters.

Hard Costs

    Site Acquisition Costs: $4.9 million (1996)

    Site and Building Construction Costs: $49 million (1996)

Average Development Cost/SF: $100 (1996) ($200/SF with furniture, fixtures, and equipment, 1996)

Total Costs for Green Technologies: $865,200 (1996)

Total Costs: $53.8 million (1996)

Total Return on Investment: Three-month payback on investment in energy efficiency

Notable GD Features: Integrated design team process. Passive solar heating and ventilation. Cogeneration and waste heat capture. Daylit office space and interior cores. Water-efficient landscaping and rainwater cisterns. Flexible and adaptable design for changing uses. Site in proximity to a majority of employees' residences. Art integrated into the design.

Results: 92 percent reduction in primary energy as compared with conventional building of similar size. Productivity gains, absenteeism down by 15 percent. Bank's business has grown dramatically. Estimated energy savings of $2.9 million. Did not accurately estimate future needs of the people or plug loads (because of increase in computer use) and exceeded estimated energy use. Problem corrected following analysis.

Project Name: United Parcel Service Headquarters

Location: Atlanta, Georgia

Owner: United Parcel Service (UPS)

Contact: Gene Montezinos

Date Completed: 1994

Project Size

    Site (gross land area): 36 acres

    Building (gross building area): 623,000 SF (6-acre footprint)

Project Description: Office headquarters and corporate grounds for UPS

Average Development Cost/SF: $112

Landscape Preservation Cost: $2 million

Total Costs: $70 million

Notable GD Features: Team approach in the design of the building. Site-sensitive construction to minimize destruction of the wooded site. Strict protection of wetlands. Used solar design and shading features

Results: Paid a premium of 3 to 5 percent of the total building costs for site-sensitive construction, but did not have to landscape what was not destroyed, so saved money. Received the 1994 Global ReLeaf for New Communities Award for site sensitivity. Team approach resulted in a more cost-effective building.

Retail

Project Name: Real Goods Solar Living Center

Location: Hopland, California

Owner: Real Goods

Contacts: Jeff Oldham and Ecological Design Institute

Date Completed: Phase I — February 1996

Project Size

> **Site (gross land area):** 12 acres

> **Building (gross building area):** 5,000 SF showroom; 1,200 SF storage facility; planning a 1,000 SF visitor's center and classroom for 1997.

Project Description: Demonstration center and showroom for sustainable living

Hard Costs

> **Site Acquisition Costs:** $250,000

> **Site Development Costs:** $432,630 (Phase I)

> **Building Construction Costs:** $902,000

Soft Costs

> **Financing:** $1.2 million

> **Architectural and Other:** $110,000

Types of Financing: National Bank of the Redwoods construction loan; company assets for soft costs and site development

Average Development Cost/SF: $165 SF (for the 5,000 SF showroom)

Total Costs: $1.1 million

Notable GD Features: Reuse of a site that was a dump for California Department of Transportation. Comprehensive building and land design. Building is a learning tool that incorporates operable or exposed features. Green demonstration home, organic gardening, aquaculture ponds, sustainable landscaping, wetlands, and biological waste management. Used alternative building materials such as straw bales and sustainably harvested wood. Powered by grid-tied PVs and some wind power. Passive cooling and shading with trees and adjustable awnings. Daylighting models and wind tunnel testing used in design process. Not currently tied to mass transit but hope to link into the rail line. Have installed two electric vehicle charging stations to charge a total of four cars.

Results: Six hundred rice bales donated by California Rice Industries—multiple benefits of using an agricultural waste that would otherwise be burned off. PV panels donated by Siemens Solar. Visitors delighted with the interactive nature of the Center. Received $100,000 worth of free publicity due to the unique nature of the project.

Project Name: Tolman Creek Shopping Center

Location: Ashland, Oregon

Developer: Watson & Associates

Contacts: Dick Wanderscheid and John McLaughlin

Date Completed: 1991

Project Size

   Building (gross building area): 94,505 SF

Project Description: Four-building complex: grocery store (43,770 SF), drug store (35,000 SF), small business (12,000 SF and 8,000 SF)

Notable GD Features: Site sensitivity accommodated existing oak trees and a stream. Promotes bird habitat near stream. Used natural lighting strategies. Worked with the utility and the city of Ashland's Conservation Department for design assistance to achieve energy savings. Increased insulation, installed heat recovery system in refrigerator, and installed occupancy sensors. Recycling bins throughout plaza. Bicycle racks installed. Good pedestrian access on site to encourage walking between stores. Reduced number of parking spaces in lot.

Results: Energy performance is well beyond code (city of Ashland has a model energy code). Saves the grocery store $40,000 annually in energy costs. Increased HVAC efficiency and reduced lighting loads. Greater success and lower capital costs could have been achieved if energy measures had been discussed early in the design phase. Received Bonneville Power Authority's Energy Smart Award.

Mixed Use

Project Name: 2211 West Fourth Avenue

Location: Vancouver, British Columbia, Canada

Owner/Developer: Harold Kalke, Salt Lick Productions Ltd.

Contacts: Harold Kalke and Jean-Pierre Mahé

Date Completed: 1993

Project Size

    Site (gross land area): 55,000 SF

    Building (gross building area): 138,000 SF

Project Description: Four-story mixed-use project: 40,000 SF of retail, 29,000 SF office space, 69,000 SF of residential space

Hard Costs

    Site Acquisition Costs: $8.6 million

    Site Development Costs: $5.3 million

    Building Construction Costs: $15.4 million

Soft Costs

    Architectural and Other Consultants: $1.1 million

    Interest Fees, Utility Connections, Taxes: $2.2 million

    Tenant Improvements: $2 million

    Marketing/Leasing: Developer did own leasing—retail and commercial interests approached him.

Types of Financing: Owner equity: $10 million; bank construction loan: $19 million; long-term mortgage: $11 million

Sale Price per Apartment: $169,000 to $179,000

Average Development Cost/SF: Including land $212 (excluding land $150)

Total Costs: $29.3 million

Total Return on Investment: 12.3 percent for residual investment; long-term cash flow anticipated from office/retail components

Notable GD Features: Infill project maximizing the use of existing infrastructure. "Rainscreen" double exterior wall system and ground-source heat pump for heating and cooling. Natural or recycled materials. Thermostated gas fireplaces as primary heat source.

Results: Stores and offices pay higher rent because operating costs are lower as a result of a ground-source heat pump for heating and cooling. Design preserves the character of the Kitsilano neighborhood and helps to create community. Waiting list for both office and retail space. Project is widely recognized as highly successful from community, occupant, and owner perspectives.

Project Name: Civano

Location: Tucson, Arizona

Owner/Developer: Community of Civano LLC/Case Enterprises, Inc.

Contacts: City of Tucson—John Laswick; Case Enterprises—David Case, Kevin Kelly, Lisa Picard

Date Completed: In progress. Build-out anticipated by 2004.

Project Size

> **Site (gross land area):** 1,145 acres

> **Site (developable acres):** 916 acres

Project Description: A master-planned community developed in four neighborhoods, with a total of 2,600 units, 48 acres of commercial/retail, more than 200 acres of natural and enhanced open space, and a 65-acre environmental technology business park

Hard Costs

> **Site Acquisition Costs:** $2.7 million

> **Site Development Costs:** $22 million (excludes infrastructure costs financed by municipal bonds)

> **Building Construction Costs:** $400 million (est.)

Soft Costs

> **Financing:** $3 million for debt and equity

> **Marketing/Leasing:** $3 million

> **Architectural and Engineering:** $4 million

> **Sustainability Research:** $1 million

> **Legal/Taxes/Other:** $3 million

Types of Financing: Developer equity of $1 million for preacquisition, acquisition, and predevelopment costs. Other equity sources of $5 million for ongoing development costs. Conventional debt of $4 million for land acquisition and predevelopment. Municipal bond financing of up to $38 million by the city of Tucson for infrastructure. Grant of city funds for up to $3 million in off-site infrastructure improvements and construction of the primary boulevard. Additional city funds of up to $4 million derived from issuing general obligation bonds for the construction of the community center and park.

Total Return on Investment: 30 to 35 percent (est.)

Notable GD Features: The development concept focuses on a complete approach toward sustainability: economic, physical, social, and environmental. Project uses traditional neighborhood design principles and resource-efficient strategies to forward the sustainability concept. Land planning process applied from Ian McHarg's environmental overlay methodology as described in Design with Nature. The architectural and urban design of the project draws heavily from the local environment and attempts to use indigenous materials and building traditions. In fostering a balance of land uses, the project is expected to create more than 1,200 jobs on-site.

Results: A working public/private venture based on strong community support. More than $500,000 in annual savings from avoided infrastructure costs to the public. The city's $7 million investment will be repaid within eight years, and the city will receive an estimated annual increase in revenue of $1 million, net of operating expenses. Nearly 10 percent of the project's net profits will be placed in a trust to further sustainable research in Tucson and the region. Developing a green builder program for Civano similar to Austin's that will promote sustainable building techniques and educate builders, developers, residents, and the community.

Project Name: Denver Dry Goods Building

Location: Denver, Colorado

Owner/Developer: Affordable Housing Development Corporation

Contact: Jonathan F. P. Rose

Date Completed: 1994

Project Size

   Site (gross land area): 58,000 SF

   Building (gross building area): 350,000 SF

Project Description: Mixed use of retail, office, and affordable and market-rate housing in downtown Denver

Hard Costs

   Site/Building Acquisition Costs: $6.9 million

   Building Construction Costs: $18.5 million

Soft Costs

   Financing/Legal: $3.4 million

   Marketing/Leasing: $500,000. Leased all housing units within six months of opening; preleased all office and rental; $96,000 in saved interest as a result of free press.

   Architectural and Other: $860,000

Types of Financing: 23 different funding sources

Average Development Cost/SF $120.52

Total Costs: $30.1 million

Notable GD Features: Reuse of existing building, access to mass transit, energy- and water-efficient design. Project encouraged other developers to incorporate affordable housing into the downtown core.

Results: Savings of at least $75,000 per year on operating expenses, increasing the building's value by $750,000 when capitalized. Waiting list for apartment space.

Project Name: Hamilton

Location: Novato, California

Owner/Developer: U.S. Army, U.S. Navy, New Hamilton Partnership, managed by the Martin Group

Contact: Molly Gleason

Date Completed: Infrastructure construction completed fall 1996. Homes occupied by winter 1997.

Project Size

    Site (gross land area): 415 acres (Zone I)

Project Description: 950 homes, commercial, and retail. Mixed-use, mixed-income, intergenerational community; 250 acres of open space.

Notable GD Features: Cleaned up dump and disposal site, capped landfill—converted into community parklands. Cleaned up hazardous materials left on site after 60 years of contamination from aircraft maintenance and repairs. Conducted archaeological studies of the site. Renovated enlisted men's barracks to 80 senior housing units. Preserving historic 1930s structures, some of which are on the historical register. Providing affordable housing and encouraging an intergenerational mix of people. Protecting bats by supplying a secured bat roost.

Results: Brought the community together in a collaborative five-year process to help plan the project.

Project Name: Haymount

Location: Caroline County, Virginia

Owner/Developer: Haymount Limited Partnership/John A. Clark Development Company

Contact: John A. Clark

Projected Date of Completion: In progress. Broke ground spring of 1996. Expected build-out in 2005.

Project Size:

   Site (gross land area): 1,650 acres

Project Description: Compact development pattern of a mixed-use and mixed-income community with a projected population of 9,500. 4,000 residential units. 500,000 SF of office and light industrial space. 250,000 SF of retail. 50-acre college campus.

Hard Costs

   Site Acquisition Costs: $5 million

   Site Development Costs: $44 million (infrastructure, utilities, and proffers)

   Building Construction Costs: N/A. Most lots will be sold to builders.

Soft Costs: $62 million

   Marketing/Leasing: $14 million

Types of Financing: W.C. and A.N. Miller Company provided equity for site acquisition and predevelopment planning. The second round of financing will come from debt and/or equity from an institutional partner.

Total Costs to Date: $10 million for predevelopment activities (fall 1996)

Estimated Total Project Costs: $170 million

Projected Tax Revenues to County: $196 million

Total Potential Land Sales Profit: $288 million

Total Projected Revenues: $467 million after 22 years

Notable GD Features: Thorough project planning and site analysis. Almost 70 percent of the site will be preserved or reforested. Invited community involvement through numerous meetings. Plan elements include: connection to mass transit, pedestrian-oriented design, energy and materials codes, biological wastewater treatment system and biotechnical storm water management system. Promotion of environmental educational opportunities. Promotion of organic farming practices and a farmers market. Green builder program.

Results: Won a tough fight in rezoning of Caroline County's comprehensive plan to accommodate the Haymount project. Established a strict environmental precedent for other developers to follow in the county. Influenced State Department of Transportation's revision of road standards. Successfully obtained approvals on an alternative wastewater system and changed the storm water programs to biotechnical water management and storm water treatment.

Project Profile Contacts

Anton Alberts
Architectenbureau Alberts Nen Van Huut
Keizerscracht 169
1016 DP, Amsterdam
Netherlands
Phone: 31-20-622-0082
Fax: 31-20-624-0406

Joe Azzarello
Project Manager
Herman Miller
885 E. Main Avenue
Zeeland, MI 49464-0302
Phone: (616) 654-3907
Fax: (616) 654-5180

Anthony Bernheim
Architect and Project Manager
Simon Martin-Vegue Winkelstein Morris
501 Second Street, Ste. 701
San Francisco, CA 94107
Phone: (415) 546-0400
Fax: (415) 882-7098

Jan Beyea
National Audubon Society
700 Broadway
New York, NY 10003
Phone: (212) 979-3000

Christina Bolinger
Communications Manager
Pei Cobb Freed & Partners
600 Madison Avenue
New York, NY 10022
Phone: (212) 751-3122
Fax: (212) 872-5443

Bunting Coady Architects
171 Water Street, Suite 300

Vancouver, BC V6B 1A7
Canada
Phone: (604) 685-9913
Fax: (604) 685-0694

David Case, Kevin Kelly, Lisa Picard
Civano/Case Enterprises
6280 South Campbell Avenue
Tucson, AZ 85706
Phone: (520) 889-8888
Fax: (520) 889-6207

James Chaffin
Spring Island Company
P.O. Box 2419
Beaufort, SC 29901-2419
Phone: (803) 521-1807
Fax: (803) 521-1897

Kirsten Childs
Interior Designer
Croxton Collaborative, Architects, P.C.
475 5th Avenue
New York, NY 10017
Phone: (212) 683-1998
Fax: (212) 683-2799

John A. Clark
The John A. Clark Company
4910 Massachusetts Avenue
Washington, DC 20016
Phone: (202) 362-5088
Fax: (202) 362-5152

Bill Conley
Facilities Manager
VeriFone
3080 Airway Avenue
Costa Mesa, CA 92626
Phone: (714) 979-1870
Fax: (714) 434-2498

Michael and Judy Corbett
2417 Buckleberry Road
Davis, CA 95616
Phone: (916) 756-5941
Fax: (916) 448-8246

Randolph Croxton
Croxton Collaborative, Architects, P.C.
475 5th Avenue
New York, NY 10017
Phone: (212) 683-1998
Fax: (212) 683-2799

Ecological Design Institute
245 Gate 5 Road
Sausalito, CA 94965
Phone: (415) 332-5806
Fax: (415) 332-5808

Greg Franta
ENSAR Group
P.O. Box 267
Boulder, CO 80301
Phone: (303) 449-5226
Fax: (303) 449-5276

Jeffrey B. Froke
Environmental Director and President of
    the Santa Lucia Conservancy
Rancho San Carlos
P.O. Box 222707
Carmel, CA 93922
Phone: (408) 626-8200
Fax: (408) 626-8282

Michael Fuller
Conger Fuller Architects
720 E. Durant Street, Ste. E-8
Aspen, CO 81611
Phone: (970) 925-3021
Fax: (970) 925-3110

Molly Gleason
Hamilton, Director of Community
    Relations

Building 500, Hamilton Field
Novato, CA 94948
Phone: (415) 382-8696
Fax: (415) 884-0400

Michael Horst
InSpire Enterprises
177 Seadrift Road
P.O. Box 157
Stinson Beach, CA 94970
Phone: (415) 868-2580
Fax: (415) 868-2585

David Howerton
Robert Lamb Hart Planners &
    Architects
242 California Avenue
San Francisco, CA 94111
Phone: (415) 986-4260

Harold Kalke
Salt Lick Productions, Ltd.
2211 West 4th Avenue, Ste. 209
Vancouver, BC V6K-4F2
Canada
Phone: (604) 739-2500
Fax: (604) 739-2514

John L. Knott Jr., CEO
Managing Director
Island Preservation Partners
P.O. Box 361
Dewees Island, SC 29451-2662
Phone: (803) 886-8783
Fax: (803) 886-5836

John Laswick
Project Manager
City of Tucson
P.O. Box 27210
Tucson, AZ 85726-7210
Phone: (520) 791-4675
Fax: (520) 791-5413

Gail A. Lindsey
Environmental Consultant
Design Harmony
16 North Boylan Avenue
Raleigh, NC 27603
Phone: (919) 755-0300
Fax: (919) 755-0028

Jeff Mahan
Manager, Inn of the Anasazi
113 Washington Avenue
Santa Fe, NM 87501
Phone: (800) 688- 8100

Jean-Pierre Mahé
Hotson Bakker Architects
406-611 Alexander Street
Vancouver, BC V6A 1E1
Canada
Phone: (604) 255-1169
Fax: (604) 255-1790

Franklin A. Martin
Shaw Homes, Inc.
676 North St. Clair Street, Ste. 2200
Chicago, IL 60611
Phone: (312) 943-8800
Fax: (312) 943-8815

Eva Matsuzaki
Matsuzaki Wright Architects Inc.
2410-1177 W. Hastings Street
Vancouver, BC V6E 2K3
Canada
Phone: (604) 685-3117
Fax: (604) 685-3180

William A. McDonough
Project Architect
William McDonough + Partners
410 E. Water Street
Charlottesville, VA 22902

Phone: (804) 979-1111
Fax: (804) 979-1112

John McLaughlin
Director of Planning Department
City Hall
20 East Main Street
Ashland, OR 97520
Phone: (503) 488-5305

Gene Montezinos
Project Architect
Thompson, Ventulett, Stainback & Assoc.
2700 Promenade Two
1230 Peachtree Street, N.E.
Atlanta, GA 30309-3591
Phone: (404) 888-6600
Fax: (404) 888-6700

Diane Morrison
Manager, ERC
Energy Resource Center, ML ERC 1
9240 East Firestone Boulevard
Downey, CA 90241-5388
Phone: (310) 803-4700
Fax: (310) 803-7551

Jeff Oldham
Real Goods Trading Corporation
555 Leslie Street
Ukiah, CA 95482-3471
Phone: (707) 468-9292
Fax: (707) 468-0301

Freda Pagani
Campus Planning & Development
University of British Columbia
2210 West Mall
Vancouver, BC V6T 1Z4
Canada
Phone: (604) 822-8228
Fax: (604) 822-2843

Victoria Post-Ranney
Prairie Holdings Corporation
190 South LaSalle, Ste. 3604
Chicago, IL 60603
Phone: (847) 548-4062
Jonathan Rose
Affordable Housing Development
    Corporation
33 Katonah Avenue
Katonah, NY 10536
Phone: (914) 232-1396
Fax: (914) 232-1398

Tedd R. Saunders
Eco-Logical Solutions
6 St. James Avenue
Boston, MA 02116
Phone: (617) 426-2010
Fax: (617) 426-2060

Stanley Selengut
Maho Bay Camps, Inc.
17 East 73rd Street
New York, NY 10021
Phone: (212) 472-9453
Fax: (212) 392-9004

Susan Silva
Saunders Hotel Group
64 Arlington Street
Boston, MA 02116
Phone: (617) 457-2300
Fax: (617) 426-2060

Dick Wanderscheid
Manager of Conservation Department
City Hall

20 East Main Street
Ashland, OR 97520
Phone: (541) 488-5306
Fax: (541) 488-5311

Terry Williams
Project Architect
Wade Williams Young + Wright,
    Architects
914 Gordon Street
Victoria, BC V8W 1Z8
Canada
Phone: (604) 384-0504
Fax: (604) 380-6811

George Wilson
Project Manager
American Association for the
    Advancement of Science
1200 New York Avenue NW
Washington, DC 20005
Phone: (202) 326-6400

Keith Winn
Project Manager
Herman Miller
885 E. Main Avenue
Zeeland, MI 49464-0302
Phone: (616) 654-5180

Robert D. Zimmer
The Robert D. Zimmer Group
135 Grant Avenue
Santa Fe, NM 87501
Phone: (505) 986-8338
Fax: (505) 986-1678

Further Reading

Books

Climatic Building Design: Energy-Efficient Building Principles and Practices. Donald Watson and Kenneth Labs. Published by McGraw-Hill Book Company, 1983. Provides an introduction and reference guide to climatic design, the art and science of using the beneficial elements of nature to create environmentally sensitive buildings. Sections include a background in the scientific principles underlying climatic design, a designer's guide and catalog of the practices of climatic design and construction, and ways of analyzing local climatic data and applying strategies and principles for major United States locations.

Design with Nature. Ian L. McHarg. Published by John Wiley & Sons, 1992; reprint. Presents a thorough analysis of the relationship between the built environment and nature. This was one of the first books to bring forward planning concepts in environmental sensitivity.

Ecological Design. Sim Van der Ryn and Stuart Cowan. Published by Island Press, 1995. Discusses how the living world and humanity can be reunited by making ecology the basis for design. Ecological design, the marriage of nature and technology, can be applied at all levels of scale to create revolutionary forms of buildings, landscapes, cities, and technologies. Design principles are presented that can help build a more efficient, less toxic, more healthful, and more sustainable world.

The Energy Source Directory. Published by Iris Communications. Provides access to more than 500 products that help make homes energy efficient. Information about air barriers, heat recovery ventilators, sealants, heating and cooling equipment, solar water heaters, insulation materials, and so forth, is indexed by manufacturer, product name, and product category.

Environmental Design Charrette Workbook. Donald Watson. Published by the American Institute of Architects, 1996. Highlights intensive design workshops dealing with energy efficiency, building technology, environmental approaches to landscaping, waste prevention and resource reclamation, as well as planning and cultural issues. The workbook also contains guidelines for organizers and facilitators, a sample briefing booklet, and a discussion by expert practitioners on the art of community dialogue.

Environmental Resource Guide. The American Institute of Architects. Published by John Wiley & Sons, 1996. Provides a comprehensive guide to resources for environmental building and is updated three times a year. Project reports present case studies that incorporate environmental concepts and technologies. Material reports detail the environmental aspects and life cycles of building materials.

Green Architecture: Design for an Energy-Conscious Future. Brenda and Robert Vale. Published by Bulfinch Press, 1991. Provides an overview of resource-conscious building and an exploration of the relationship between the built environment and such critical problems as power supply, waste and recycling, food production, and transportation.

How Buildings Learn. Stewart Brand. Published by Viking Penguin, 1994. Discusses how buildings adapt over time. Photos of case studies are used throughout to show before/after states of buildings. Design principles are described for creating an adaptable/flexible building.

The Death and Life of Great American Cities. Jane Jacobs. Published by Random House, 1961. Offers valuable lessons not yet learned about building healthful, safe, and habitable cities.

The Next American Metropolis: Ecology, Community and the American Dream. Peter Calthorpe. Published by Princeton Academic Press, 1993. Places the "American dream" of a suburban home for the nuclear family in its historical and ecological context. It suggests mechanisms of transit-oriented development, including mixed-use, pedestrian-friendly pockets. Features case studies from across the United States.

A Pattern Language. Christopher Alexander, Sara Ishikawa, and Murry Silverstein. Published by Oxford University Press, 1977. Volume 2 of the Centre for Environmental Structure series. Illustrates a new architecture and planning theory that reflects the traditional ways in which people created their living environment. It explains the language of *The Timeless Way of Building* (Volume 1), discussing a range of subjects, from community to individual building elements.

A Primer on Sustainable Building. Dianna Lopez Barnett with William D. Browning. Published by Rocky Mountain Institute, 1995. Provides an overview for architects, builders, developers, students, and others interested in environmentally responsive home building and small commercial development. Topics include site and habitat restoration, transportation integration, food-producing landscapes, energy-efficient design, materials selection, indoor air quality, cost implications, and more.

Rural by Design. Randall Arendt with Elizabeth A. Brabee, Harry L. Dodson, Christine Reid, and Robert O. Yaro. Published by APA Planners Press, 1994. Advocates creative, practical land-use planning techniques to preserve open space and community character. Thirty-eight case studies are used to demonstrate how rural and suburban communities, among others, have preserved open space, established land trusts, and designed affordable housing appropriate for their size and character.

Sustainable Building Technical Manual. Cosponsored by Public Technology Incorporated, the U.S. Green Building Council, and the U.S. Department of Energy. Published by Public Technology, Inc., 1996. Addresses green building practice, covering predesign issues and site planning through operations and maintenance. Fifteen practitioners were asked to write sections of the book pertaining to their particular area of expertise. Checklists and a list of resources are also found in this helpful manual, which is available by calling PTI at (800) PTI-8976 or the U.S. Green Building Council at (415) 543-3001.

Sustainable Communities: A New Design Synthesis for Cities, Suburbs, and Towns. Sim Van der Ryn and Peter Calthorpe. Published by Sierra Club Books, 1986. Covers a range of issues dealing with sustainability for urban and suburban renovation through an in-depth look at several case studies, as well as essays focused on community sensitivity, transportation, and economics.

Visions for a New American Dream. Anton Nelessen. Published by APA Planners Press, 1994. Provides practical information to help planners and designers create small communities that combine the best design principles of the past with the technological advances of the present to combat suburban sprawl. Visual Preference Surveys™ and Hands On Model Workshops are thoroughly described.

Newsletters and Magazines

Environmental Building News. A monthly newsletter full of clear, concise information on environmental design and construction. West River Communications, Inc., RR 1 Box 161, Brattleboro, VT 05301; (802) 257-7300.

Indoor Air Bulletin. This monthly publication focuses on indoor air quality but considers all aspects of indoor environment important to occupant health, comfort, and productivity. Indoor Air Information Service, Inc., P.O. Box 8446, Santa Cruz, CA 95061-8446; (408) 426-6522.

Interior Concerns Newsletter. A bimonthly publication covering topics related to sustainable and healthful designing and building, geared to environmentally concerned design and build professionals. Environmental Resources, Inc., P.O. Box 2386, Mill Valley, CA 94942; (415) 389-8049.

New Urban News. This bimonthly newsletter provides current information on traditional neighborhood development and planning projects around the country. New Urban News, P.O. Box 157, Emmaus, PA 18049; (610) 965-4623.

On the Ground. A journal on community, design, and the environment, published quarterly. Issues cover topics such as housing, mixed uses, ecology, transportation, public space, and regional form. Thousand Words, a Publisher of Visual Information, P.O. Box 9034, Berkeley, CA 94709-0034; (510) 883-0433.

Solar Today. This bimonthly magazine covers innovative passive and active solar house designs, solar technologies, building performance, cost-effective designs, and case studies. American Solar Energy Society, 2400 Central Avenue, Suite G-1, Boulder, CO 80301; (303) 443-3130.

The Urban Ecologist. Published by Urban Ecology, an Oakland-based organization that focuses on sustainability and resource efficiency in urban areas. This quarterly newsletter is a compendium of actions undertaken by municipalities, institutions, and community groups, both nationally and worldwide. Urban Ecology, 405 14th Street, Suite 701, Oakland, CA 94612; (510) 251-6330.

Organizations, Resources, and Web Sites

Organizations

Alliance to Save Energy
1200 18th Street NW, Suite 900
Washington, DC 20036
(202) 857-0666
(202) 331-9588/fax

Provides materials on home energy rating systems, building codes, efficient new construction and design.

American Council for an Energy-
Efficient Economy (ACEEE)
1001 Connecticut Avenue NW, Suite 801
Washington, DC 20036
(202) 429-8873
(202) 429-2248/fax

Publishes books and papers on industrial, commercial, and residential energy efficiency.

American Institute of Architects
Committee on the Environment (AIA
COTE)
1735 New York Avenue NW
Washington, DC 20006
(202) 626-7300
(202) 626-7426/fax

Works to create sustainable buildings and communities by advancing, disseminating, and advocating environmental knowledge and values to the profession, the industry, and the public.

American Society of Heating,
Refrigerating, and Air-Conditioning
Engineers, Inc. (ASHRAE)
1791 Tullie Circle, NE
Atlanta, GA 30329-2305
(404) 636-8400
(404) 321-5478/fax

This not-for-profit organization provides research, standards writing, and continuing education. ASHRAE's sole objective is to advance the arts and sciences of heating, ventilation, air conditioning, and refrigeration for the public's benefit.

American Solar Energy Society, Inc.
(ASES)
2400 Central Avenue, Suite G-1
Boulder, CO 80301
(303) 443-3130
(303) 443-3212/fax

Disseminates and transfers research on practical uses of solar energy, wind power, and photovoltaics.

Building Environment and Thermal Envelope Council

National Institute of Building Sciences
1201 L Street NW, Suite 400
Washington, DC 20005
(202) 289-7800
(202) 289-1092/fax

Identifies and coordinates research and other programs on building envelope energy and the indoor environment.

Center of Excellence for Sustainable Development

U.S. Department of Energy
Office of Energy Efficiency and Renewable Energy
Denver Regional Support Office
1617 Cole Boulevard
Golden, CO 80401
(800) 357-7732
(303) 275-4826
(303) 275-4830/fax

Provides communities with world-class consultation in sustainable development, and helps them link to other public and private programs that can help them carry it out.

Center for Maximum Potential Building Systems, Inc.

8604 FM 969
Austin, TX 78724
(512) 928-4786
(512) 926-4418/fax

A nonprofit ecological planning and design firm that works with public entities, professional organizations, community groups, universities, and individuals in pursuit of sustainable development policies and practices for undertakings ranging from individual buildings to entire regions.

Center for Resourceful Building Technology (CRBT)

P.O. Box 100
Missoula, MT 59806
(406) 549-7678
(406) 549-4100/fax

Performs research and educates the public on a variety of issues related to housing and the environment, with particular emphasis on innovative building materials and technologies that place less stress on regional and global resources.

Energy Outreach Center (EOC)

Olympic Renewable Resources Association
512 East 4th Avenue
Olympia, WA 98501
(360) 943-4595
(360) 943-4977/fax

Provides information on efficient building design and construction, renewable energy, and transportation planning.

Environmental Protection Agency (EPA)

Public Information Center
401 M Street SW
Washington, DC 20460
(202) 260-2080
(202) 260-6257/fax

Provides an information service with referrals to various EPA hotlines and programs that address a range of subjects: radon, drinking water, indoor air quality, asbestos, hazardous materials, efficient commercial lighting, computers, and buildings (including the Energy Star Showcase Building Program).

Ernest Orlando Lawrence Berkeley National Laboratory
1 Cyclotron Road
Berkeley, CA 94720
(510) 486-5000

Provides information on building energy analysis, building science, modeling software, high-performance windows, lighting, and more.

Indoor Air Quality Information Clearinghouse
U.S. Environmental Protection Agency
P.O. Box 37133
Washington, DC 20013-7133
(800) 438-4318; (202) 484-1307
(202) 484-1510/fax

Provides information, referrals, publications, and data base searches on indoor air quality. Information includes pollutants and sources, health effects, control methods, commercial building operations and maintenance, standards and guidelines, federal and state legislation, and construction and maintenance of homes and buildings to minimize IAQ problems.

Local Government Commission (LGC)
1414 K Street, Suite 250
Sacramento, CA 95814
(916) 448-1198
(916) 448-8246/fax

Helps communities to be proactive in their land planning and encourages the adoption of programs and policies that lead to more livable land-use patterns. Center programs can help jurisdictions increase transportation alternatives, reduce infrastructure costs, create more affordable housing, improve air quality, preserve natural resources, and restore local economic and social vitality.

National Energy Information Center
U.S. Department of Energy
EI-30
1000 Independence Avenue SW
Washington, DC 20585
(202) 586-8800
(202) 586-0727/fax

Disseminates energy statistics to federal, state, and local agencies, the academic community, industrial and commercial organizations, and the public.

National Institute of Building Sciences
Building Environment and Thermal Envelope Council
1201 L Street NW, Suite 400
Washington, DC 20005
(202) 289-7800
(202) 289-1092/fax

Coordinates research and promotes publications relating to building, thermal energy performance, and new technologies and construction techniques.

National Renewable Energy Laboratory (NREL)
1617 Cole Boulevard
Golden, CO 80401
(303) 275-4099

A resource center that also maintains a library of technical and popular reports on residential, commercial, utility, industrial, and transportation uses of renewable energy.

Passive Solar Industries Council
1511 K Street NW, Suite 600
Washington, DC 20005
(202) 628-7400
(202) 393-5043/fax

Provides information on solar building design and retrofit issues, daylighting, insulation, and windows. It offers professional training, consumer education, and analysis tools nationwide, in addition to excellent publications, software, and videos on passive solar design.

Rocky Mountain Institute (RMI)
1739 Snowmass Creek Road
Snowmass, CO 81654-9199
(970) 927-3851
(970) 927-3420/fax

Conducts research and outreach programs and consulting to foster the efficient and sustainable use of resources. RMI has several areas of research: energy, water, transportation, green development, security, and economic renewal.

Southface Energy Institute
241 Pine Street
Atlanta, GA 30308
(404) 872-3549
(404) 872-5009/fax

Specializes in energy-efficient construction techniques for the southern climate. The institute offers a home-building school and energy audit and duct-sealing services.

Urban Agricultural Network
1711 Lamont Street NW
Washington, DC 20010-2601
(202) 483-8130
(202) 363-5824/fax

Promotes agricultural production in urban areas.

Urban Ecology, Inc. (UE)
405 14th Street, Suite 900
Oakland, CA 94612
(510) 251-6330
(510) 251-2117/fax

Works with communities to rebuild in balance with nature.

Urban Land Institute (ULI)
1025 Thomas Jefferson Street NW, Suite 500 West
Washington, DC 20007
(202) 624-7000
(202) 624-7140/fax

Urban Land Institute is the leading organization for developers in the United States. It produces a monthly magazine, *Urban Land*, which on occasion features case studies and articles on green development.

U.S. Department of Energy
Building Measurement and Verification Protocol
1000 Independence Avenue SW
Washington, DC 20585
(800) 363-3732

Promotes efficiency financing through a reliable means of measuring and ensuring savings from efficiency investments. Provides information on commissioning and recommissioning.

U.S. Green Building Council (USGBC)
90 New Montgomery Street, Suite 1001
San Francisco, CA 94105
(415) 543-3001
(415) 957-5890/fax

The USGBC is a nonprofit trade association whose primary purpose is to promote green building policies, programs, and technologies. Membership is offered to manufacturers, utilities, building owners, real estate advisors, scientific and technical organizations, and nonprofit trade associations that are supportive of green buildings.

World-Wide Web Sites

Note: While this is not an exhaustive list, many of these addresses are linked to other informative resource sites.

Center of Excellence for Sustainable Development — http://www.sustainable.doe.gov

Center for Renewable Energy and Sustainable Technology (Crest) /Sustainable Energy & Development Online (Solstice) — http://solstice.crest.org/

Ecology Web Enviro Links — http://www.pacific.net/~dglaser/ENVIR/LINKS/*links.html

Environmental Building News — http://www.ebuild.com/index.html

Environmental Organization Web Directory — http://www.webdirectory.com/

GreenClips Archives — http://solstice.crest.org/sustainable/greenclips/info.html

Indoor Air Quality Page — http://ttsw.com/AirJT.html

Iris Communications (Resources for Environmental Design Index) — http://www.oikos.com/redi/index.html

Rocky Mountain Institute — http://www.rmi.org.

Strategies and Checklists

Design Strategies to Make Density Livable*

Regional Scale

- Create a dense grid of public transit to provide residents a way to get around without cars.
- Plan for a hierarchy of parks, greenways, and bikeways throughout the urban region.
- Locate affordable housing throughout the region, requiring each city to build its fair share.
- Work to create a regional tax-sharing system that distributes funds fairly between jurisdictions and eliminates the fiscalization of land use.
- Plan for a sensible balance between jobs, shopping, and housing in each community.
- Concentrate development in existing urban areas by preventing sprawl beyond an urban growth boundary.

Neighborhood Scale

- Plan for a fine-grain mix of buildings to add character, interest, and diversity.
- Promote a mixture of land uses in the neighborhood to enhance walkability and community vitality.

*Source: Stephen Wheeler, *The Urban Ecologist*, vol. 1 (Oakland, Calif., 1996).

- Add bikeways, footpaths, and transit facilities to the design to encourage non-automobile travel.
- Locate parks, community gardens, and greenways within a five-minute walk of housing.
- Make streets livable by slowing traffic and adding trees, plants, lights, and signs.
- Restore natural landscape features such as streams, hilltops, shorelines, and tree groves as centerpieces of neighborhood identity.
- Promote diversity by including a variety of housing types, unit sizes, rents, and prices.
- Encourage individual small-scale development projects that add to neighborhood character.
- Work with existing residents and neighborhood groups to meet their needs and learn their perspectives.

Site Scale

- Pay as much attention to site design and landscaping as to the buildings themselves.
- Site new development near transit, stores, and services.
- Create a spectrum of outdoor spaces for the residents (private yards and balconies, semiprivate courtyards, sandboxes and gardens, public walkways and play areas).
- Reduce parking and put it below grade or in the back. For many housing types, one space per unit should be the maximum within an urban area. Cities can help by reducing parking requirements and making them more flexible. Some parking can be designed to serve as play space for children when not in use. New paving surfaces such as "grass-crete" or GrassPave™ can make parking less obvious.
- Make buildings relate to local streets and interior courtyards, thus improving safety by putting "eyes on the street." Provide porches, benches, and stoops on which residents can sit.
- Select building forms as well as landscape elements (trees and shrubs) to ensure adequate light to units and outdoor spaces, emphasizing sunny southern exposures.

- Integrate natural features such as streams, slopes, rock outcrops, and distinctive existing vegetation into the design.
- Respond to the scale and architectural character of adjacent structures.

Building Scale

- Provide high-quality detailing and design variation between buildings.
- Maximize natural light and southern exposure, for example, by using carefully placed windows and skylights to bring more light into interior rooms.
- Use roofs as open space, creating decks, pools, or gardens.
- Add porches, balconies, and decks to provide outdoor space to upper units.
- Provide a good public-private interface (sociable entranceways, front porches, no blank walls or monolithic building fronts facing the street).
- Ensure good soundproofing between units as well as between the building and outside (insulated walls and double-glazed windows help).
- Consider residents' needs and tastes when designing. Design in flexibility if possible.

Checklist for Environmentally Sustainable Design*

Design

- *Smaller is better.* Optimize use of interior space through careful design so that the overall building size—and resource use in constructing and operating it—are kept to a minimum.
- *Design an energy-efficient building.* Use high levels of insulation, high-performance windows, and tight construction. In southern climates, choose glazings with low solar heat gain.
- *Design buildings to use renewable energy.* Passive solar heating, daylighting, and natural cooling can be incorporated cost-effectively into most buildings. Also consider solar water heating and photovoltaics—or design buildings for future panel installation.
- *Optimize material use.* Minimize waste by designing for standard ceiling heights and building dimensions. Avoid waste from structural overdesign (use optimum-value engineering/advanced framing). Simplify building geometry.

*Source: Adapted from *Environmental Building News* 1, no. 2 (1992):8–9.

- *Design water-efficient, low-maintenance landscaping.* Conventional lawns have a high impact because of water use, pesticide use, and pollution generated by lawn mowers. Landscape with drought-resistant native plants and perennial ground covers.
- *Make it easy for occupants to recycle waste.* Make provisions for storage and processing of recyclables: recycling bins near the kitchen, undersink door-mounted compost receptacles, etc.
- *Look into the feasibility of using graywater.* Water from sinks, showers, and washing machines (graywater) can be recycled for irrigation in some areas. If current codes prevent graywater recycling, consider designing the plumbing for easy future adaptation.
- *Design for durability.* To spread the environmental impacts of building over as long a period as possible, the structure must be durable. Durable aesthetics ("timeless architecture") are also important.
- *Design for future reuse and adaptability.* Make the structure adaptable to other uses, and choose materials and components that can be reused or recycled.
- *Avoid potential health hazards: radon, mold, pesticides.* Follow recommended practices to minimize radon entry into the building and provide for future mitigation if necessary. Provide detailing that will avoid moisture problems, which could cause mold and mildew growth. Design insect-resistant detailing that will require minimal use of pesticides.

Siting and Land Use

- *Renovate older buildings.* Conscientious renovation of existing buildings is the most sustainable construction.
- *Create community.* Development patterns can either inhibit or contribute to the establishment of strong communities and neighborhoods. Creation of cohesive communities should be a high priority.
- *Encourage infill and mixed-use development.* Infill development that increases density is inherently better than building on undeveloped (greenfield) sites. Mixed-use development, in which residential and commercial uses are intermingled, can reduce automobile use and help to create healthy communities.
- *Minimize automobile dependence.* Locate buildings to provide access to public transportation, bicycle paths, and walking access to basic services.

Commuting can also be reduced by working at home — consider home office needs with layout and wiring.

- *Evaluate site resources.* Early in the siting process, carry out a careful site evaluation: solar access, soils, vegetation, important natural areas, etc.

- *Locate buildings to minimize environmental impact.* Cluster buildings or build attached units to preserve open space and wildlife habitats, avoid especially sensitive areas such as wetlands, and keep roads and service lines short. Leave the most pristine areas untouched, and look for areas that have been previously damaged to build on. Seek to restore damaged ecosystems.

- *Provide responsible on-site water management.* Design landscapes to absorb rainwater runoff (storm water) rather than having to carry it off-site in storm sewers. In arid areas, rooftop water catchment systems should be considered for collecting rainwater and using it for landscape irrigation.

- *Pay attention to solar orientation.* Reduce energy use by orienting buildings to make optimal use of passive solar heating, daylighting, and natural cooling.

- *Situate buildings to benefit from existing vegetation.* Trees on the east and west sides of a building can dramatically reduce cooling loads. Hedgerows and shrubbery can block cold winter winds or help to channel cool summer breezes into buildings.

Materials

- *Avoid ozone-depleting chemicals in mechanical equipment and insulation.* CFCs have been phased out, but their primary replacements — HCFCs — also damage the ozone layer and should be avoided where possible. Avoid foam insulation made with HCFCs. Reclaim CFCs when servicing or disposing of equipment (required by law).

- *Use durable products and materials.* Because manufacturing is very energy-intensive, a product that lasts longer or requires less maintenance usually saves energy. Durable products also contribute less to our solid waste problems.

- *Choose low-maintenance building materials.* Where possible, select building materials that will require little maintenance (painting, retreatment, waterproofing, etc.) or whose maintenance will have minimal environmental impact.

- *Choose building materials with low embodied energy.* Heavily processed or manufactured products and materials are usually more energy-intensive. As long as durability and performance will not be sacrificed, choose low-embodied-energy materials.

- *Buy locally produced building materials.* Transportation is costly in both energy use and pollution generation. Look for locally produced materials. Local hardwoods, for example, are preferable to tropical woods.

- *Use building products made from recycled materials.* Building products made from recycled materials reduce solid waste problems, cut energy consumption in manufacturing, and save on natural resource use. A few examples of materials with recycled content are cellulose insulation, Homosote®, Thermo-ply®, floor tile made from ground glass, and recycled plastic lumber.

- *Use salvaged building materials when possible.* Reduce landfill pressure and save natural resources by using salvaged materials: lumber, millwork, certain plumbing fixtures, and hardware, for example. Make sure these materials are safe (test for lead paint and asbestos), and do not sacrifice energy efficiency or water efficiency by reusing old windows or toilets.

- *Seek responsible wood supplies.* Use lumber from independently certified well-managed forests. Avoid lumber products produced from old-growth timber when acceptable alternatives exist. Engineered wood can be substituted for old-growth Douglas fir, for example. Do not buy tropical hardwoods unless the seller can document that the wood comes from well-managed forests.

- *Avoid materials that will offgas pollutants.* Solvent-based finishes, adhesives, carpeting, particleboard, and many other building products release formaldehyde and volatile organic compounds (VOCs) into the air. These chemicals can affect workers' and occupants' health, as well as contribute to smog and ground-level ozone pollution outside.

- *Minimize use of pressure-treated lumber.* Use detailing that will prevent soil contact and rot. Where possible, use alternatives such as recycled plastic lumber. Take measures to protect workers when cutting and handling pressure-treated wood. Scraps should never be incinerated.

- *Minimize packaging waste.* Avoid excessive packaging, such as plastic-wrapped plumbing fixtures or fasteners that are not available in bulk. Tell your supplier why you are avoiding overpackaged products. Keep in mind, however, that some products must be carefully packaged to prevent damage—and resulting waste.

Equipment

- *Install high-efficiency heating and cooling equipment.* Well-designed high-efficiency furnaces, boilers, and air conditioners (and distribution systems) not only save the building occupants money, but also produce less pollution during operation. Install equipment with minimal risk of combustion gas spillage, such as sealed-combustion appliances.
- *Install high-efficiency lights and appliances.* Fluorescent lighting has improved dramatically in recent years and is now suitable for homes. High-efficiency appliances offer both economic and environmental advantages over their conventional counterparts.
- *Install water-efficient equipment.* Water-conserving toilets, showerheads, and faucet aerators not only reduce water use, but also reduce demand on septic systems or sewage treatment plants. Reducing hot water use also saves energy.
- *Install mechanical ventilation equipment.* Mechanical ventilation is usually required to ensure safe, healthful indoor air. Heat recovery ventilators should be considered in cold climates because of energy savings, but simpler, less expensive exhaust-only ventilation systems are also adequate.

Job Site and Business

- *Protect trees and topsoil during site work:* Protect trees from damage during construction by fencing off the "drip line" around them and avoiding major changes to surface grade.
- *Avoid use of pesticides and other chemicals that may leach into the groundwater.* Look into less toxic termite treatments, and keep exposed frost walls free from obstructions to discourage insects. When backfilling a foundation or grading around a house, do not bury any construction debris.
- *Minimize job-site waste.* Centralize cutting operations to reduce waste and simplify sorting. Set up clearly marked bins for different types of usable waste (wood scraps for kindling, sawdust for compost, etc.). Find out where different materials can be taken for recycling, and educate your crew about recycling procedures. Donate salvaged materials to low-income housing projects, theater groups, etc.
- *Make your business operations more environmentally responsible.* Make your office as energy efficient as possible, purchase energy-efficient vehicles,

arrange carpools to job sites, and schedule site visits and errands to minimize unnecessary driving. In your office, purchase recycled office paper and supplies, recycle office paper, use coffee mugs instead of disposable cups. On the job, recycle beverage containers.

- *Make education a part of your daily practice.* Use the design and construction process to educate clients, employees, subcontractors, and the general public about the environmental impacts of buildings and how these impacts can be minimized.

Checklist for Protecting Trees and the Immediate Environment During Site Work*

1. Carefully survey building site prior to siting the building on it. Hire landscape architects, ecologists, and other specialists to inventory topography, vegetation, wetlands, and other natural features.

2. Determine placement of buildings, roadways, buried utility lines, sewer lines, and other infrastructure so as to impart minimal disturbance. In siting, consider orientation to take advantage of passive solar design, natural daylighting, and shading from trees so as to reduce energy consumption.

3. In selecting an excavation contractor, specify protection of trees, topsoil, and other natural features. Consider incentive or penalty clauses in contracts to encourage careful practices.

4. Remove trees and shrubs where buildings and roadways will be located. Depending on the specific site and excavating equipment used, trees within 15 or 20 feet of building excavations usually have to be removed, though in some situations trees as close as 5 feet can be kept. If certain trees or shrubs will have only marginal chance of survival, it may make sense to remove them, then replant the same species after site work is completed. In some cases, native plants from a building site can be salvaged and planted in other projects.

5. Erect clearly visible fencing around building areas, roadways, buried sewer lines, and leach fields and confine disturbance to this area only. Keep the fencing as close to the disturbance area as possible to avoid soil

---

Source: Adapted from *Environmental Building News* 1, no. 1 (1992).

compaction in the surrounding area. Do not permit construction vehicles to park, or building materials to be stored, outside this area. Alternately, areas to be protected can be fenced off.

6. In addition to erecting fences, flag important trees and lower branches that might be needlessly damaged when workers are dumping fill, excavating, or delivering construction materials.

7. Try to avoid having to raise or lower grade. When doing so cannot be avoided, valuable trees can often be saved by using walls to maintain the existing grade within the trees' "drip-line." With shallow ledge or heavy clay soils, the existing grade may have to be maintained farther out than the drip line.

8. Remove topsoil from the immediate area to be excavated. Store this topsoil where it will not damage other natural areas, then spread it over the site following construction. Chose the storage location to minimize soil compaction caused by excavation equipment. If the topsoil is to be stored for a long time before reusing, cover the pile or seed it with grass to prevent erosion.

9. On sloping sites, use terracing or retaining walls to maintain grades as close to the original as possible. Keeping existing trees on steep slopes is extremely important, as their roots help to stabilize soils and prevent erosion. When grading is necessary on steep slopes, protect soils with erosion-control plantings (ideally, native plants). "Hydraulic mulches" can be used to stabilize soils when seeding with turfgrass.

10. If the building site was created out of dense woodland, be particularly sensitive to stresses experienced by the remaining trees. Excessive sunlight exposure, dehydration, and loss of structural support are the most common problems. To reduce sun shock, thin deciduous trees during the winter months when they will be acclimated to higher levels of sunlight. Mulch and water trees during dry periods, and consult an arborist about the need for fertilizers or crown thinning.

11. If you plan to clear a large area but leave a few trees standing, consult an expert before felling trees. The biggest, tallest trees on a site might not be the best candidates for retaining. An arborist should be able to select trees most likely to survive the stresses of land clearing and the loss of nearby structural support. In deciding on which trees to remove, be sure to consider such issues as solar exposure.

12. Unless absolutely necessary, do not stump an area that will remain predominantly wooded. Pulling stumps with an excavator or backhoe will damage nearby trees and soil ecosystems.

13. Consider native groundcovers as an alternative to turfgrass. Along with the fertilizer, pesticide, and water requirements of turf, grass competes with trees for nutrients—grass roots often extend below the feeder roots of trees (which are quite close to the surface).

Checklist of Construction-Phase Activities

1. Is the project driver (developer, owner, or architect) clearly communicating the green development goals to key stakeholders, contractors, and consultants?

2. Are contractors being brought in as part of the green development team as early as possible to gain their valuable insights and perspectives?

3. Are detailed environmental guidelines and restrictions set up to inform contractors of the most environmentally sensitive and health-conscious ways to treat the site and to build?

4. Have specific contracts for subcontractors been drawn up and signed that outline responsibilities, liabilities, and potential rewards/penalties to ensure that the green agenda is coherently addressed?

5. Are effects on environment and community being considered in planning the staging of the construction process?

6. Are frequent construction meetings and inspections being planned to help answer questions and ensure quality of construction?

7. Are the green specifications that were written as part of building design being made known and followed in advertisements for bids, in prebid meetings, and in preconstruction meetings?

8. Are the most appropriate venders being located for the sourcing of low-toxic or nontoxic, sustainable, and local materials? Are the appropriate people being made aware of the longer lead times that may be required to obtain certain products?

9. Is there sufficient ventilation while the building is under construction? Are barriers installed (such as plastic sheeting) around the construction area to prevent dust and other airborne pollutants from migrating

outside the construction area? Is the construction sequenced so as to minimize contaminant sinks?

10. Are contractors being held financially responsible for all energy and water permits and consumption charges for the project?

11. Is a construction waste management plan being established to define procedures for material separation and handling, recycling, and hauling?

12. If the project is one of renovation, are existing materials being identified for reuse or salvage? Are the capabilities of the local recycling and salvage infrastructure being identified?

13. Is a commissioning agent being brought on board to carry out a commissioning plan and prescribe or carry out corrective measures? Are sufficient time and money being budgeted for commissioning to ensure optimal building performance?

14. Is the postconstruction cleanup crew being directed to use nontoxic cleaning products? Is the building's HVAC system or a separate ventilation system being operated to flush the building of harmful contaminants?

Bibliography

Note: Much of this book is based on an extensive amount of original research in the form of personal interviews, telephone interviews, questionnaires, and correspondence with the developers, architects, and other people mentioned throughout the various chapters.

Books

Aberley, Doug. *Futures by Design: The Practice of Ecological Planning.*Philadelphia: New Society Publishers, 1994.

Alexander, Christopher, Hajo Neis, Artemis Anninou, and Ingrid King. *A New Theory of Urban Design.* New York: Oxford University Press, 1987.

Alexander, Christopher. *A Timeless Way of Building.* New York: Oxford University Press, 1979.

Alexander, Christopher, Sara Ishikawa, and Murry Silverstein, with Max Jacobson, Ingrid Fiksdahl-King, and Shlomo Angel. *A Pattern Language: Towns, Buildings, Construction.* New York: Oxford University Press, 1977.

Arendt, Randall G. *Conservation Design for Subdivisions: A Practical Guide to Creating Open Space Networks.* Washington, D.C.: Island Press, 1996.

Arendt, Randall G., with Elizabeth A. Brabec, Harry L. Dodson, Christine Reid, and Robert O. Yaro. *Rural by Design.* Chicago: American Planning Association, 1994.

Audin, Lindsay, David Houghton, Michael Shepard, and Wendy Hawthorne. *Lighting Technology Atlas.* Boulder: E Source, Inc., 1994.

Barnett, Dianna Lopez, with William D. Browning. *A Primer on Sustainable Building.* Snowmass, Colo.: Rocky Mountain Institute, 1995.

Brand, Stewart. *How Buildings Learn.* New York: Viking Penguin, 1994.

Calthorpe, Peter. *The Next American Metropolis: Ecology, Community, and the American Dream*. New York: Princeton Architectural Press, 1993.

Calthorpe, Peter, and Sim Van der Ryn. *Sustainable Communities*. San Francisco: Sierra Club Books, 1986.

Center for Livable Communities. *Building Livable Communities: A Policy Maker's Guide to Infill Development*. Sacramento, Calif.: Local Government Commission, 1995.

———. *Participation Tools for Better Land-Use Planning*. Sacramento, Calif.: Local Government Commission, 1995.

Charter, Martin. *Greener Marketing: A Responsible Approach to Business*. Sheffield, England: Greenleaf, 1992.

Coates, Gary J. *Resettling America*. Andover, Mass.: Brick House Publishing, 1981.

Committee on Banking, Finance and Urban Affairs. *Regulatory Impediments to the Development and Placement of Affordable Housing*. Serial No. 101-153. Washington, D.C.: U.S. Government Printing Office, August 1990.

Committee on the Environment. *Designing Healthy Buildings: Indoor Air Quality*. Washington, D.C.: American Institute of Architects, 1992.

Corbett, Judy, and Steve Weissman. *Land Use Strategies for More Livable Spaces*. Sacramento, Calif.: Local Government Commission, 1992.

Corbett, Michael. *A Better Place to Live: New Designs for Tomorrow's Communities*. Emmaus, Pa.: Rodale Press, 1981.

Crosbie, Michael J., ed. *Green Architecture: A Guide to Sustainable Design*. Washington, D.C.: American Institute of Architects, 1994.

Demkin, Joseph A., ed. *Environmental Resource Guide*. New York: John Wiley & Sons, Inc., 1996 (updated three times a year).

Department of Public Works and Transportation, Environmental and Conservation Services Department. *City of Austin Sustainable Building Guidelines*. Austin, Texas, 1994.

———. *City of Austin Sustainable Building Sourcebook*. Austin, Texas, 1994.

Derman, Asher, ed. *Greening the Office: Issues of Waste and Indoor Air Quality*. New York: Green October, Inc., 1994.

Diamond, Henry L., and Patrick F. Noonan. *Land Use in America*. Washington, D.C.: Island Press, 1996.

Downs, Anthony. *New Visions for Metropolitan America*. Washington, D.C.: Brookings Institution, 1994.

Environmental Protection Agency, Office of Air and Radiation and the National Institute for Occupational Safety and Health. *Building Air Quality: A Guide for Building Owners and Facility Managers*. Washington, D.C.: EPA, 1991.

Ewing, Reid. *Best Development Practices*. Chicago: APA Planners Press, 1996.

———. *Developing Successful New Communities*. Washington, D.C.: Urban Land Institute, 1991.

Frank, James. *The Costs of Alternative Development Patterns: A Review of Literature*. Washington, D. C.: Urban Land Institute, 1989.

Girouard, Mark. *Cities and People*. New Haven: Yale University Press, 1985.

Hamel, Gary. *Competing for the Future*. Boston, Mass.: Harvard Business School Press, 1994.

Hanson, Chris. *The Cohousing Handbook: Building a Place for Community*. Vancouver: Hartley & Marks Publishers, 1996.

Hawken, Paul. *The Ecology of Commerce: A Declaration of Sustainability*. New York: Harper Business, 1993.

Hiss, Tony. *The Experience of Place*. New York: Vintage, 1990.

Jackson, John Brinckerhoff. *Discovering the Vernacular Landscape*. New Haven: Yale University Press, 1975.

Jacobs, Jane. *The Death and Life of Great American Cities*. New York: Random House, 1961.

Kasian, Kennedy Design Partnership. *Design Smart, Energy Efficient Architectural Design Strategies*. Burnaby, B.C.: BC Hydro Power Smart, 1995.

Katz, Peter. *The New Urbanism: Toward an Architecture of Community*. San Francisco: McGraw Hill, 1991.

Kunstler, James Howard. *The Geography of Nowhere: The Rise and Decline of America's Man-Made Landscape*. New York: Simon & Schuster, 1993.

Langdon, Phillip. *Better Place to Live: Reshaping the American Suburb*. Amherst, Mass.: University of Massachusetts, 1994.

Langdon, Phillip, with Robert G. Shibley and Polly Welch. *Urban Excellence*. New York: Van Nostrand Reinhold, 1990.

Leopold, Aldo. *A Sand County Almanac*. New York: Ballatine Books, 1966.

Loken, Steve, Rod Miner, and Tracy Mumma. *A Reference Guide to Resource Efficient Building Elements*. 4th ed. Missoula, Mont.: Center for Resourceful Building Technology, 1994.

Lyle, John Tillman. *Regenerative Design for Sustainable Development*. New York: John Wiley & Sons, 1994.

Mackenzie, Dorothy. *Design for the Environment*. New York: Rizzoli, 1991.

Mantell, Michael A., Stephen F. Harper, and Luther Propst. *Creating Successful Communities: A Guidebook to Growth Management Strategies*. Washington, D.C.: Island Press, 1990.

Marinelli, Janet, and Paul Bierman-Lytle. *Your Natural Home: The Complete Sourcebook and Design Manual for Creating a Healthy, Beautiful, and Environmentally Sensitive House*. Boston: Little, Brown and Company, 1995.

McCamant, Kathryn, and Charles Durrett. *CoHousing: A Contemporary Approach to Housing Ourselves.* 2d ed. Berkeley, Calif.: Ten Speed Press, 1994.

McDonough, William. *The Hannover Principles/Design for Sustainability.* New York: William McDonough Architects, 1992.

McHarg, Ian L. *A Quest for Life.* New York: John Wiley and Sons, 1996.

——— *Design with Nature.* New York: John Wiley & Sons, 1992.

McKenzie, Evan. *Privatopia: Homeowner Associations and the Rise of Residential Private Government.* New Haven: Yale University Press, 1994.

McKibben, Bill. *Hope, Human and Wild: True Stories of Living Lightly on the Earth.* New York: Little, Brown and Company, 1995.

McMahan, John. *Property Development.* 2d ed. San Francisco: McGraw-Hill Publishing Company, 1989.

Miles, Mike, Richard Haney Jr., and Gayle Berens. *Real Estate Development: Principles and Process.* 2d ed. Washington, D.C.: Urban Land Institute, 1996.

National Audubon Society and Croxton Collaborative, Architects. *Audubon House: Building the Environmentally Responsible, Energy Efficient Office.* New York: John Wiley & Sons, 1994.

National Science and Technology Council. *Bridge to a Sustainable Future: National Environmental Technology Strategy.* Washington, D.C.: White House, April 1995.

Nelessen, Anton C. *Visions for a New American Dream: Process, Principles, and an Ordinance to Plan and Design Small Communities.* Chicago: American Planning Association, 1994.

Norwood, Ken, and Kathleen Smith. *Rebuilding Community in America: Housing for Ecological Living, Personal Empowerment, and the New Extended Family.* Berkeley, Calif.: Shared Living Resource Center, 1995.

Pearson, David. *Earth to Spirit.* San Francisco: Chronicle Books, 1995.

———. *The Natural House Book.* New York: Simon & Schuster, 1989.

Public Technology, Inc. *The Sustainable Building Technical Manual: Green Building Design, Construction, and Operations.* Washington, D.C.: Public Technology, 1996.

Roelofs, Joan. *Greening Cities: Building Just and Sustainable Communities.* New York: The Bootstrap Press, 1996.

Romm, Joseph J. *Lean and Clean Management: How to Boost Profits and Productivity by Reducing Pollution.* New York: Kodansha International, 1994.

Roodman, David, and Nicholas Lenssen. *A Building Revolution.* Washington, D.C.: WorldWatch Institute, 1995.

Rousseau, David, W. J. Rea, and Jean Enwright. *Your Home, Your Health, and Well-Being.* Berkeley, Calif.: Ten Speed Press, 1988.

Saunders, Tedd, and Loretta McGovern. *The Bottom Line of Green Is Black: Strategies for*

Creating Profitable and Environmentally Sound Businesses. San Francisco: Harper San Francisco, 1993.

Scott Landis, ed. *Conservation by Design.* Easthampton, Mass.: Woodworkers Alliance for Rainforest Protection and Museum of Art, Rhode Island School of Design, 1993.

Schmidheiny, Stephan, and Federico Zorraquín, with the World Business Council for Sustainable Development. *Financing Change: The Financial Community, Eco-Efficiency, and Sustainable Development.* Cambridge: MIT Press, 1996.

Senge, Peter M. *Fifth Discipline: The Art and Practice of the Learning Organization.* New York: Doubleday/Currency, 1990.

Stein, C.S. *Toward New Towns for America.* Cambridge: MIT Press, 1989.

Sucher, David. *City Comforts.* Seattle: City Comforts Press, 1995.

Summerville, James, and Charles A. Howell III, eds. *Healthy Building for a Better Earth.* Nashville: Trust for the Future, May 1990.

Talbott, John L. *Simply Build Green: A Technical Guide to the Ecological Houses at the Findhorn Foundation.* Findhorn, Scotland: Findhorn Foundation Development Wing, 1993.

U.S. Department of the Interior, National Parks Service, Denver Service Center. *Guiding Principles of Sustainable Design.* Washington, D.C.: U.S. Department of the Interior, 1994.

Urban Land Institute. *Designing the Successful Downtown.* Washington, D.C.: Urban Land Institute, 1988.

Vale, Brenda, and Robert Vale. *Green Architecture: Design for an Energy-Conscious Future.* Boston: Bulfinch Press, 1991.

Van der Ryn, Sim, and Stuart Cowan. *Ecological Design.* Washington, D.C.: Island Press, 1995.

Walter, Bob, Lois Arkin, and Richard Crenshaw, eds. *Sustainable Cities: Concepts and Strategies for Eco-City Development.* Los Angeles: Eco-Home Media, 1992.

Wann, David. *Deep Design: Pathways to a Livable Future.* Washington, D.C.: Island Press, 1996.

———. *Biologic: Environmental Protection by Design.* Boulder: Johnson Books, 1990.

Watson, Donald. *Environmental Design Charrette Workbook.* Washington, D.C.: American Institute of Architects, 1996.

Watson, Donald, and Kenneth Labs. *Climactic Building Design: Energy-Efficient Building Principles and Practice.* San Francisco: McGraw-Hill Book Company, 1983.

Yost, Peter, and Eric Lund, National Association of Home Builders. *Residential Construction Waste Management: A Builder's Field Guide, How to Save Money and Landfill Space.* NAHB, Research Center, January 1997.

Articles, Journals, Magazines, and Papers

By Title

"Architecture in the Balance," *Architecture* 83, no. 6 (June 1993): 109–113.

"Back to the Hearth: Sustaining the Aging Industrial City," *Urban Ecologist* 2 (1995): 12–13.

Beyond Sprawl: New Patterns of Growth to Fit the New California, Bank of America Executive Summary (February 1995).

"CoHousing Is Sustainable," *Environmental Building News* 2, no. 1 (January/February 1993): 2–3.

"Commercial Building Energy Use on the Rise," *Environmental Building News* 3, no. 6 (November/December 1994): 3.

"Commissioning, Operation and Maintenance," *American Council for an Energy Efficient Economy Conference Proceedings,* Washington D.C., 1994.

"Dealing with Construction Waste: Innovative Solutions for a Tough Problem," *Environmental Building News* 1, no. 3 (November/December 1992): 1, 7–9.

"Demonstrations and Retrofits," *American Council for an Energy Efficient Economy Conference Proceedings,* Washington D.C., 1994.

"Designing Healthy Buildings: Indoor Air Quality," *American Institute of Architects, Committee on the Environment Conference Proceedings,* Washington, D.C., 1992.

"Designing the Successful Downtown," *Urban Ecologist* 2 (1995): 10.

"First Certified 'Sustainably Harvested' Plywood," *Environmental Building News* 1, no. 3 (November/December 1992): 2–3.

"From Waste to Resource," *Environmental Building News* 2, no. 3 (May/June 1993): 3.

"Green Builder Programs Proliferating," *Environmental Building News* 3, no. 1 (January/Febuary 1995): 6–7.

"Gunter Pauli Cleans Up," *Fast Company* 1, no. 1 (November 1993): 62–70.

"Heating with Wood Stoves," *Interior Concerns Newsletter* (September/October 1992): 6–8.

"Intelligent Design Skills Must Be Re-Taught," *Energy Matters* 1 (June 1994): 4–5.

"Leased Carpet—A Step to an Ecological Economy?" *Environmental Building News* 4, no. 3 (May/June 1995): 3.

"Light Shelves Increase Daylight Penetration" *Environmental Building News* 4, no. 3 (May/June 1995): 10.

"Lower Rates for Green Home Improvements," *Environmental Building News* 1, no. 3 (November/December 1992): 4.

"Mortgages Can Remove the Incentive for Sprawl," *Earthword* 4 (1993): 22.

"Neighborhoods Reborn," *Consumer Reports* (May 1996): 24–29.

"The New Green Gospel," *The GreenBusiness Letter* (May 1996).

"People Suing People for Eco-Neglect: An Interview with an Architect," *Interior Concerns Newsletter* (September/October 1991): 1–2.

"A Precedent-Setting Natural River Management Plan," *Urban Land* 54, no. 6 (June 1995): 62–63.

"Putting Our Communities Back on Their Feet: Towards Better Land-Use Planning," *Local Government Commission Conference Proceedings* (February 1994).

"Putting Our Communities Back on Their Feet: The Next Step," *Local Government Commission Conference Proceedings* (May 1995).

"Revitalizing Downtowns," *Urban Ecologist* 2 (1995): 1–4.

Redevelopment for Livable Communities. Washington State Energy Office, 1996.

Second International Green Building Conference and Exposition—1995. National Institute of Standards and Technology and the U.S. Green Building Council, August 1995.

"Solid Growth in Traditional Neighborhood Projects," *New Urban News* 1, no. 4 (November/December 1996).

Third International Green Building Conference and Exposition—1996. National Institute of Standards and Technology and the U.S. Green Building Council, November 1996.

Third National Conference on Building Commissioning. Milwaukee, Wis.: Portland Energy Conservation, Inc., 1995.

"Traditional Town, Traditional Buildings," *Progressive Architecture* (December 1993): 35–41.

"Understanding Formaldehyde," *Interior Concerns* (January/February 1993): 4.

By Author

Adair, Dorothy. "Jordan Commons: A Pilot Program for Sustainable Community-Building." *Solar Today* 9, no. 2 (March/April 1995): 21–23.

Addison, Doug. "Comfort Zones: Smart Designs Yield Homes That Work with Their Climate." *Weatherwise* (June/July 1994): 14–21.

Aitken, Donald, and Paul Neuffer. "Low-Cost, High-Value Passive Solar." *Solar Today* 9, no. 2 (March/April 1995): 30–32.

Alberts, Ton. "NMB Bank, Amsterdam." *Architect and Builder* (February 1991): 22–27.

Albrecht, Donald. "Urban Oasis: National Audubon Society." *Architecture* 83, no. 6 (June 1993): 62–69.

Albrecht, Virginia S. "The Wetlands Debate." *Urban Land* 51, no. 5 (May 1992): 20–23.

Allen, Greg. "A Sense of Belonging." *EcoDesign* (December 1994): 7–9.

Andersen, David. "Resort Development Goes Green: A Report from the First International Ecolodge Forum." *Interior Concerns Newsletter* (January/February 1995): 1–5.

Babbitt, Bruce. "Protect Our Landscape." *Architecture* 84, no. 7 (July 1995): 51–55.

Bacon, James A. "The Road to Haymount." *Virginia Business* (April 1991): 34–40.

Badger, Curtis J. "A Revolution in the Business of Conservation." *Urban Land* 54, no. 6 (June 1995): 40–45.

Bennet, Dick. "Graywater: An Option for Household Water Reuse." *Home Energy* 12, no. 4 (July/August 1995): 33–38.

Bledel, Irene. "The Market for Indoor Air Quality." *Urban Land* 54, no. 6 (June 1995): 36–39.

Bookout, Lloyd W. "The Future of Higher-Density Housing." *Urban Land* 51, no. 9 (September 1992): 14–18.

———. "Neotraditional Town Planning: Toward a Blending of Design Approaches." *Urban Land* 51, no. 8 (August 1992): 14–19.

———. "Neotraditional Town Planning: The Test of the Marketplace." *Urban Land* 51, no. 6 (June 1992): 12–17.

———. "Neotraditional Town Planning: Bucking Conventional Codes and Standards." *Urban Land* 51, no. 4 (April 1992): 18–25.

———. "Neotraditional Town Planning: Cars, Pedestrians, and Transit." *Urban Land* 51, no. 2 (February 1992): 10–15.

———. "Neotraditional Town Planning: A New Vision For the Suburbs." *Urban Land* 51, no. 1 (January 1992): 20–26.

Bourdier, Jean-Paul. "Dwelling with Spirit." *Progressive Architecture* (July 1994): 96–99.

Brewster, George Burton. "The Ecology of Development." *Urban Land* 55, no 6. (June 1996): 21–25.

———. "A Better Way to Build." *Urban Land* 54, no. 6 (June 1995): 30–35.

British Columbia Buildings Corporation. "A Case Study of Disposal Alternatives in the Demolition of a Public Institution." Vancouver, British Columbia, 1995.

Browning, William Dee. "Green Development: Determining the Cost of Environmentally Responsive Development." Master's thesis, Massachusetts Institute of Technology, 1991.

Burke, Michael J., and Barbara Eljenholm. " The Environmental Side of Military Base Reuse." *Urban Land* 55, no. 7 (July 1996): 63–66.

Campbell, Sheryl. "City Congregations Warm Their Toes." *Marketing Matters* (June 1995): 11–13.

Canty, Donald. "Earth Cycle." *Progressive Architecture* (June 1994): 84–91.

Carde, Margaret. "Flowforms." *Design Spirit* 2, no. 3 (fall 1993): 30–38.

Carnegie Mellon University, Center for Building Performance and Diagnostics. "The Intelligent Workplace Retrofit Initiative." 1994.

Carpenter, Erika. "The Recycled Lumber Option." *The Urban Ecologist* (winter 1992): 3.

Chen, Alan. "The Geographic Information Systems Laboratory." *Center for Building Science News* (spring 1995): 7.

Coe, Mike. "Smart Walls for Public Buildings." *NREL In Review* 16, no. 3 (fall 1994): 10–12.

Constantine, James. "Survey of Homebuyers Shows Interest in Traditional Neighborhood Development." *Land Development* 6, no. 3 (winter 1994): 5–7.

Corbett, Robert W. "Loops Along the Beltway: A New Geometry for the Urban Edge." *Urban Land* 54, no. 2 (February 1995): 23–27.

Cordaro, Mary. "Designing for Low Electromagnetic Radiation in the Home." *Interior Concerns Newsletter* (January/February 1995): 8–10.

Crosbie, Michael J. "A Maturing Green Architecture." *Progressive Architecture* (January 1995): 31–34.

Dauncey, Guy. "Germany Moves to an Eco-Economy." *EcoNews* (September 1996).

Dewees Island Chronicles. Newsletter. Island Preservation Partnership, Dewees Island, S.C. (monthly).

Dietsch, Deborah. "Green Culture." *Architecture* 84, no. 7 (July 1995): 15.

Dinsmore, Clement. "State Initiatives on Brownfields." *Urban Land* 55, no. 6 (June 1996): 37–42.

Dorris, Virginia Kent. "Land Stewardship." *Architecture* 83, no. 6 (June 1993): 99–105.

Dunphy, Robert. "New Developments in Light Rail." *Urban Land* 55, no. 7 (July 1996): 37–41, 87–88.

Early, David. "What Is Sustainable Design?" *The Urban Ecologist* (fall 1993): 1, 3.

Economics Research Associates. "Haymount Project Market Analysis." 1996.

Environmental Building News. Published Monthly. Brattleboro, Vt.

Epmeier, Jennifer. "Energy Saving Reflected in Retailing Retrofits." *Store Equipment and Design* 3, no. 5 (May/June 1994): 17–18.

Equitable Real Estate Investment Management, Inc. "Emerging Trends in Real Estate." 1996 (annual).

Fischer, Adelheid. "Coming Full Circle: The Restoration of the Urban Landscape." *Orion* 13, no. 4 (autumn 1994): 20–29.

Fisher, Thomas. "Escape from Style." *Progressive Architecture* (September 1994): 59–63, 100.

———. "Low Income Housing: Avoiding Our Past Failures." *Progressive Architecture* (May 1994): 49–55.

Foster, J. Dean. "Sustainable Development at Work in the Lowcountry." *Charleston Metro Commerce* (second quarter 1996): 22–33.

Franzen, Robin. "Oregon's Taking Tangle." *Planning* 60, no. 6 (June 1994): 13–15.

Fromm, Doris. "Cohousing: The First Five Years." *CoHousing* 9, no. 3 (fall 1996): 12–13, 30.

Gilman, Robert. "Restorative Design: An Interview with Bob Berkebile." *In Context* 35 (spring 1993): 9.

Green, Kay. "Adaptable Housing Makes Good Sense (and Dollars)." *Urban Land* 51, no. 4 (April 1992): 9.

Grupe, Greenlaw "Fritz," Jr. "Marketing the Dream." *Urban Land* 51, no. 4 (April 1992): 10–14.

Gunts, Edward. "Blueprint for a Green Future." *Architecture* 83, no. 6 (June 1993): 47–51.

Hare, Patrick H. "Accessory Units Can Provide Affordable Housing." *The Urban Ecologist* (winter 1993): 10.

Harriman, Marc S. "Indoor Ecology." *Architecture* 83, no. 6 (June 1993): 121–123.

Haymount Limited Partnership. "Haymount: a Traditional Town of the Rappahannock." July 1995.

Herman Miller, Inc. "Herman Miller and the Environment" (annual report). Zeeland, Michigan, 1996.

Hughs, Paul. "A Flexible Development Order for Cold Springs Villages." *Urban Land* 51, no. 9 (September 1992): 23–26.

Ivy, Robert A., Jr. "Against the Tide." *Architecture* 80, no. 5 (May 1991): 121–123.

Jantrania, Anish R. "Individual Home Wastewater Management Systems." *Land Development* 6, no. 3 (winter 1994): 22–26.

The John A. Clark Company. *Haymount, a Traditional Town on the Rappahannock* (quarterly newsletter). Washington, D.C.

Johnakin, Stephen G. "Declarations for Interconnected Mixed-Use Projects." *Urban Land* 50, no. 11 (November 1991): 16–21.

Kanavos, Peter J. Jr., "Avalon Park: Getting the Vision Approved." *Urban Land* (October 1994): 52–55.

Kaufman, Wallace. "Confessions of a Developer." *Orion Nature Quarterly* 8, no. 4 (autumn 1989): 8–15.

Kay, Jane Holtz. "The Greening of Architecture." *Architecture* 80, no. 5 (May 1991): 61–63.

Kennedy, Patrick. "An Infill Developer Versus the Forces of No." *Urban Ecologist* 2 (1995): 11.

Kingsbury, Jeff. "Sustainable Development at Prairie Crossing." *Urban Land* 54, no. 6 (June 1995): 72–73.

Kinsey, Ken, and Uri Avin. "GIS in Action." *Urban Land* 51, no. 3 (March 1992): 18–21.

Kinsley, Michael, and L. Hunter Lovins. "Paying for Growth, Prospering from Development." Rocky Mountain Institute, 1996.

Kjellman, Christie, Deborah Dodds, and Tudi Haasl. "A Building Commissioning Study in the Home Stretch." Third Annual Conference on Building Commissioning. 1995.

Knight, Nancy. "Creating a Green Zone for Vancouver." *The Urban Ecologist* (spring 1994): 7, 10.

Lacy, Jeff. "An Examination of Market Appreciation for Clustered Housing with Permanently Protected Open Space." Amherst, Mass.: Center for Rural Massachusetts, University of Massachusetts, 1990.

Langdon, Philip. "The Urbanist's Reward: Opportunities to Practice the New Urbanism Are Growing, But to Limit Sprawl, a Regionalist Approach Is Needed." *Progressive Architecture* (August 1995): 82–89.

———. "Learning from the Traditional City." *Progressive Architecture* (January 1995): 49–52.

———. "A Good Place to Live." *Atlantic* 261, no. 3 (March 1988): 39–60.

Latoff, Richard. "Monitoring Construction." *Urban Land* 51, no. 9 (September 1992): 36–37.

Lazarus, Chris. "LUTRAQ: Looking for a Smarter Way to Grow." *Earthword* 4 (1993): 23–27.

Levin, Ed. "Creating Healthy Houses." *Design Spirit* 2, no. 3 (fall 1990): 22–29.

Litvan, Laura M. "Going 'Green' in the `90s." *Nation's Business* (February 1995): 30–32.

Lockwood, Charles. "Suisun City, California: New Urbanism in the Real World." *Urban Land* 54, no. 5 (May 1995): 20–26.

Lovins, Amory. " Energy-Efficient Buildings: Institutional Barriers and Opportunities." E-Source: A Strategic Issues Paper, 1992.

———. "End-Use/Least-Cost Investment Strategies." Invited paper –2.3.1, 14th Congress of the World Energy Conference, Montreal, 1989.

Lovins, Amory, and William D. Browning. "Vaulting the Barriers to Green Architecture." *Architectural Record* (December 1992).

Lovins, Amory, and L. Hunter Lovins. "How Not to Parachute More Cats." Rocky Mountain Institute, 1996.

Lyman, Francesca. "Urban Ecology: The Eco-city Movement Offers a Greenprint for Downtown U.S.A." *E The Environmental Magazine* 2, no. 5 (September/October 1991): 33–35.

MacLeish, William. "Battle for the Countryside." *New England Monthly* (September 1990).

Major, Michael J. "A Comforting Future for Commercial Buildings." *Energy Focus* 4, no. 2 (March/April 1994): 12–16.

Malin, Nadav. "Performance-Based Compensation: Getting Paid for Good Design." *Environmental Building News* 4, no. 2 (March/April 1995): 1, 14–17.

———. "Carpeting, Indoor Air Quality, and the Environment." *Environmental Building News* 3, no. 6 (November/December 1994): 1, 13–18.

———. "Letting Floodplains Do Their Job." *Environmental Building News* 2, no. 5 (September/October 1993): 8–11.

———. "Recycled Plastic Lumber." *Environmental Building News* 2, no. 4 (July/August 1993): 1, 12–16.

————. "Embodied Energy: Just What Is It and Why Do We Care?" *Environmental Building News* 2, no. 3 (May/June 1993): 8–9.

Malloy, Susan. "EI [Environmental Illness] Political Action and Environmental Responsibility." *Interior Concerns Newsletter* (January/February 1993): 12–15.

Marsh, Lindell. "Habitat Conservation at Fieldstone/Carlsbad." *Urban Land* 54, no. 6 (June 1995): 52–56.

Mayer, Caroline E. "In Virginia, a Dream of Development." *Washington Post,* 22 June 1996, pp. E1, E6–E7.

Mays, Vernon. "Centre of the Earth: Boyne River Ecology Centre." *Architecture* 83, no. 6 (June 1993): 52–57.

McKee, Bradford. "Sustainable Cities: Can Architects Extend Ecological Design Beyond Buildings to the Urban Scale?" *Architecture* 84, no. 7 (July 1995): 61–65.

McNally, Marcia. "Sustainability Principles for the Bay Area." *Urban Ecologist* 4 (1996): 5–6.

McPherson, Gregory, and James R. Simpson. "Shade Trees as a Demand-Side Resource." *Home Energy* 12, no. 2 (March/April 1995): 11–17.

Meyers, Erik J. "Environmental Law: Back and Forth to the Future." *Urban Land* 54, no. 6 (June 1995): 25–29.

Middleton, D. Scott. "Where Is Resort Development Heading?" *Urban Land* 53, no. 8 (August 1994): 21–25, 78.

Miller, Naomi. "Seeing the Light." *Progressive Architecture* (December 1994): 82–85.

Molinaro, Joseph R. "Rethinking Residential Streets." *Earthword* 4 (1993): 18–19.

Mudge, Anne E. "Property Rights in the Courts." *Urban Land* 54, no. 5 (May 1995): 18–19.

Mumma, Tracy. "Reducing the Embodied Energy of Buildings." *Home Energy* 12, no. 1 (January/February 1995): 19–22.

National Association of Home Builders, Economics Department. "Builders Survey of Environmental Issues." Washington, D.C.: NAHB, November 1994.

Newman, Morris. "An Environmentally Correct Hotel for the Big Sur." *New York Times* 28 April 1991, p. 31.

Newman, Peter. "Restoring the Commons." *Earthword* 4 (1993): 4–5.

Novitski, B. J. "Energy Design Software." *Architecture* 83, no. 6 (June 1993): 125–127.

Okamoto, Ariel Rubissow, ed. "A Blueprint Action Agenda." *Urban Ecologist* 4 (1996): 7–8.

Okamoto, Paul. "Designing the Ecological Suburb?" *Earthword* 4 (1993): 20–22.

On the Ground: The Multimedia Journal on Community, Design, and Environment 1, no. 1 (fall 1994); 1, no. 2 (winter/spring 1995); 2, no. 1 (1996); 2, no. 3 (1997).

Patchett, James M., and Gerould S. Wilhelm. "Designing Sustainable Systems." Naperville, Ill.: Conservation Design Forum, 1995.

Payton, Neal, ed. *Proceedings of Nathan Cummings Roundtable,* AIA, 1992–1993.

Pease, Mike. "Sustainable Communities: What's Going on Here?" *Place* 9, no. 3 (winter 1995): 50–69.

Phelps, Priscilla. "Low Income Housing That Sustains Residents." *The Urban Ecologist* (winter 1993): 1, 3.

———. "Financing Low-Income Housing." *The Urban Ecologist* (winter 1993): 6.

Porter, Douglas R. "Multiparty Development and Conservation Agreements." *Urban Land* 51, no. 2 (February 1992): 21–25.

Romm, Joseph J., and William D. Browning. "Greening the Building and the Bottom Line: Increasing Productivity Through Energy-Efficient Design." Rocky Mountain Institute, 1994.

Romm, Joseph J., and Charles B. Curtis. "Mideast Oil Forever?" *Atlantic Monthly* (April 1996): 57–74.

Ruggiero, Steven. "Anatomy of a Sick Building." *Progressive Architecture* (August 1994): 82–86.

Salvesen, David. "Promoting Transit-Oriented Development." *Urban Land* 55, no. 7 (July 1996): 31–35, 87.

———. "Interest Growing in Green Homes." *Urban Land* 55, no. 6 (June 1996): 12–14.

Sarasohn, Dayle. "Environmental Illness: Madness, Myth or Malaise?" *Interior Concerns Newsletter* (January/February 1993): 9–10.

Sayer, Jim. "The Costs of Sprawl." *The Urban Ecologist* (spring 1994): 11.

Schomer, Victoria. "Carpet and the Eco-State of the Art." *Interior Concerns Newsletter* (May/June 1994): 1–7.

———. "San Francisco's Public Library and a Comprehensive Green Team." *Interior Concerns Newsletter* (May/June 1993): 1–2.

Schwolsky, Rick, Susan Bradford, and Linda Altman. "Building Green." *Builder* (February 1995): 136–144.

Selengut, Stanley. "Sustainable Development in Paradise." *Solar Today* 8, no. 5 (September/October 1994): 16–19.

Shields, Patsy. "Urban Gardens." *Land and People* 6, no. 2 (fall 1994): 9–13.

Sinclair, Robert. "Preserving Paradise." *Washingtonian* 31, no. 5 (February 1996).

Slack, Gordy. "Emerald Cities." *Land and People* (spring 1995): 17–22.

Smith, Larry. "Combining Ecology and Transportation." *Earthword* 4 (1993): 8–9.

Smith, Mark Rodman. "Ecologically Accountable Building." *Urban Land* 55, no. 6 (June 1996): 50–53, 65.

Sneider, Daniel. "Blue-Blood Development. Green Scam or Green Model?" *Christian Science Monitor,* 30 April 1996, pp. 1–2.

Snyder, Ryan. "Bicycles in Ecological Cities." *Earthword* 4: 6–7.

Solomon, Nancy B. "Green Software." *Architecture* 84, no. 7 (July 1995): 131–135.

Sullivan, Ann C. "Photovoltaics." *Architecture* 84, no. 7 (July 1995): 109–117.

Thayer, Burke Miller. *Buildings for a Sustainable America: Case Studies.* Solar Today, 1994.

Toevs, Stacy Witt. "Trends: Down to Earth." *Visual Merchandising and Store Design (VM&SD)* 125, no. 6 (June 1994): 42–48

Trewby, Mary. "Computer Model Simulates Building Energy Use." *Marketing Matters* (June 1995): 19.

Turner, Wood. "Creating the Blueprint." *Urban Ecologist* 4 (1996): 3.

ULI Wetlands Task Force. "Wetlands Permitting." *Urban Land* 51, no. 8 (August 1992): 37–38, 47.

Urban Land. Published monthly by the Urban Land Institute.

Vaughan, Nigel, and Phil Jones. "Making the Most of Passive Solar Design." *Building Services, The CIBSE Journal* 16, no. 11 (November 1994): 39–41.

Wagner, Michael. "Survival of the Forests." *Architecture* 83, no. 6 (June 1993): 117–119.

Walton, Dorothy. "The Challenges of Marketing Mixed-Use Properties." *Journal of Property Management* 56, no. 6 (November/December 1991): 30–34.

Warson, Albert. "Building Telecommunications." *Urban Land* 54, no. 5 (May 1995): 37–39.

———. "Born-Again Urbanism in Canada." *Progressive Architecture* (November 1994): 51–52.

Watkins Carter Hamilton Architects. "The Greening of MOBs [Medical Office Buildings]." *Interior Concerns Newsletter* (September/October 1993): 1–5.

Wheeler, Stephen. "Successful Downtown Projects." *Urban Ecologist* 2 (1995): 14.

Wilson, Alex. "How Green Is Your Building?" *Progressive Architecture* (April 1995): 86–91.

———. "Using Graywater for Landscape Irrigation." *Environmental Building News* 3, no. 2 (March/April 1995): 1, 10–14.

———. "Insulation Materials: Environmental Comparisons." *Environmental Building News* 4, no. 1 (January/February 1995): 1, 11–17.

———. "Stormwater Management: Environmentally Sound Approaches." *Environmental Building News* 3, no. 5 (September/October 1994): 1, 8–13.

———. "Keeping the Heat Out: Cooling Load Avoidance Strategies." *Environmental Building News* 3, no. 3 (May/June 1994): 1, 13–18.

——— "Perspective: Does It Cost More to Build Sustainably?" *Environmental Building News* 3, no. 3 (May/June 1994): 1.

———. "Building Design and EMF." *Environmental Building News* 3, no. 2 (March/April 1994): 8–11.

———. "On-site Wastewater Treatment: Alternatives Offer Better Groundwater Protection." *Environmental Building News* 3, no. 2 (March/April 1994): 1, 12–18.

———. "Heating Fuel Choices: Weighing the Alternatives." *Environmental Building News* 2, no. 6 (November/December 1993): 1, 13–17.

———. "Materials Alternatives." *Architecture* 80, no. 5 (May 1991): 113–118.

Wilson, Alex, and Dan MacArthur. "Protecting Trees and the Immediate Environment During Sitework." *Environmental Building News* 1, no. 1 (July/August 1992): 4–7.

Wilson, Alex, and Nadav Malin. "Ecological Wastewater Treatment." *Environmental Building News* 5, no. 4 (July/August 1996): 14–17.

Winburn, William A., IV. "The Development Realities of Traditional Town Design." *Urban Land* 51, no. 8 (August 1992): 20–21.

Woodhull, Joel. "Link Between Transit and Land Use: The Pedestrian." *Earthword* 4 (1993): 12–16.

Glossary

Absorption rate: The estimated rate at which properties for sale or lease can be marketed in a given locality.

Adaptable buildings: Buildings that can be easily remarketed, retrofitted, or reconfigured to better meet the changing needs of occupants, maintenance crews, and the larger community.

Amortization: A gradual paying off of a debt by periodic installments.

Appraisal value: An estimate of the value of property substantiated by various analyses. Used by developers in deciding whether to go forward with a project, to determine a reasonable sale price, or to allocate the purchase price to the land and improvements.

Biodiversity: The tendency in ecosystems, when undisturbed, to have a great variety of species forming a complex web of interactions. Human population pressure and resource consumption tend to reduce biodiversity to dangerously low levels; diverse communities are less subject to catastrophic disruption.

Biological wastewater management: Purifying wastewater in a natural or simulated wetland environment. Such systems are powered mainly by sunlight and achieve treatment through the combined action of living food chains, many of which are microscopic.

Bonding: A guarantee of completion or performance typically issued by an insurance company. For example, contractors are often bonded as assurance that they will complete the work specified.

Brownfields: Abandoned, idled, or underused industrial and commercial facilities where expansion or redevelopment is complicated by real or perceived environmental contamination.

Build to suit: Construction of land improvements and buildings to a tenant's or buyer's specifications.

Building codes: Municipal ordinances that regulate the construction and occupancy of buildings for health and safety reasons.

Building ecology: Physical environment and systems found inside a building. Key issues include air quality, acoustics, and electromagnetic fields.

Building envelope: Building elements (e.g., walls, roofs, floors, windows, etc.) that enclose conditioned spaces and through which energy may be transferred to and from the exterior.

Building valuation: The process of assessing the value or price of a building.

CFC: Chlorofluorocarbon. Used in refrigerants, foam insulation material, and many other consumer products. CFCs have been linked to the destruction of the ozone layer.

Capital: Money or property invested in an asset for the creation of wealth.

Capitalization rate (cap rate): The rate, expressed as a percentage, at which a future income flow is converted into a present value figure.

Change order: A form used by an architect or contractor to specify changes from the approved original plan.

Charrette: An intensive design process that involves the collaboration of all project stakeholders at the beginning of a project to develop a comprehensive plan or design. Although it may take place only over a few short days, it establishes groundwork for communication and a team-oriented approach to be carried throughout the building process.

Cistern: A tank to hold a supply of fresh water.

Codes, Covenants, and Restrictions (CC&Rs): A declaration filed by a developer to specify his or her intended restrictions on what one can or cannot build in his or her development.

Cohousing: Housing that combines the privacy of single-family dwelling units with extensive common facilities, such as kitchens, dining rooms, children's playrooms, and laundry facilities, thus enhancing a sense of community. Residents often come together to identify a site and raise predevelopment funds, making the development process much different from the usual development of communities.

Commissioning: The process of ensuring, verifying, and documenting that new equipment and systems are installed and able to operate according to the design intent.

Community: (Biological definition) An association of organisms of different species living together in a defined habitat with some degree of mutual interdependence.

Compact fluorescent lighting: A fluorescent bulb that is compacted to fit into an Edison light socket.

Comparable property (comp): Another property to which a subject property can be compared to reach an estimate of market value.

Composting: A waste management option involving the controlled biological decomposition of organic materials into a relatively stable humus-like product that can be handled, stored, and applied to the land without adversely affecting the environment.

Conservation: Efficiency of energy use, production, transmission, or distribution that yields a decrease in energy consumption while providing the same, or higher, levels of service.

Constructed wetland: Any of a variety of designed systems that are modeled after natural wetlands, use aquatic plants, and can be used to treat wastewater or runoff.

Construction loan: A loan usually made by a commercial bank to a builder for use in constructing improvements on real estate. It usually runs six months to two years.

Covenants: Promises written into deeds and other instruments agreeing to performance or nonperformance of certain acts, or requiring or preventing certain uses of a property.

Creative feasibility: Used during market research, this process involves using market indicators, such as the growing demand for green consumer products, and extrapolating these indicators to determine trends in demand in real estate markets. It can be used to identify markets for ecologically sensitive developments and convince financiers of their feasibility by combining primary market research, focus groups, and traditional supply (comparatives) and blending this information with analysis of the best practices used in a variety of environmentally responsible projects.

Culvert: A sewer or drain running under a road or embankment.

Daylighting: The use of controlled natural lighting methods indoors through skylights, windows, and reflected light.

Debt service: Periodic repayments of a loan, with a portion of the payment applied to interest and the rest applied to repayment (amortization) of principal.

Due diligence: During the assessment phase, investigation of all reasonable considerations and factors—financial, legal, environmental, and others—related to a project or property to prevent unpleasant future surprises.

Earth sheltering (also **earth berming**): Building below ground level. Soil temperature varies less than air temperature (deeper soil = more constant temperature); an earth-sheltered structure provides an interior climate that is generally closer to comfort level than a conventional interior space. Savings on heating and cooling bills are often in the range of 40 to 60 percent.

Ecology: In biology, it is the study of the relationship between living organisms and their environment. In sociology, it is the study of the relationship between the distribution of human groups with reference to material resources and the consequent social and cultural patterns.

Ecosystem: A complex set of natural, interconnected elements on which a habitat's survival depends directly or indirectly.

Eco-tourism: Partnerships between the tourism industry and conservation efforts to preserve natural and cultural resources in resort destinations.

Edible landscaping: Landscaping containing vegetation that is cultivated for its ability to provide items that can be eaten and digested by humans, for example, fruit trees and grape arbors.

Efficiency: The ratio of the amount of useful energy output to the energy input for a given device.

Embodied energy: The energy required to grow, harvest, extract, manufacture, refine, process, package, transport, install, and dispose of a particular product or building material.

End-use/least-cost: A decision-making tool that keeps a planning team focused on the end users' needs. It is a key component of green design and development because it identifies ways to achieve the *greatest* benefits at the *least* cost in financial, social, and environmental terms.

Energy: The capacity for doing work. Different types of energy may be transformed from one form to another. English units express energy in Btus or kilowatt-hours (kWh).

Energy or water efficiency: Using less energy or water to perform tasks. A device is energy efficient if it provides comparable or better quality of service while using less energy than a conventional technology. Building weatherization and high-efficiency shower heads are examples of efficiency technology.

Equity: That portion of an ownership interest in real property (or other securities) that is owned outright, rather than financed by debt.

Feasibility study: A combination of a market study and an economic analysis that provides an investor with knowledge of both the environment where a project exists and the expected returns on investment to be derived from it.

Floor area ratio (FAR): Typically used as a formula to regulate building volume. The ratio of floor area to land area, expressed as a percentage or decimal, that is determined by dividing the total floor area of the building by the area of the lot. A low maximum FAR of 0.3 results in a low-density building pattern.

Flow form features: Water features of a building that are not only viewed as artistic decorations, but also maintain a pleasant level of humidity and acoustics as part of the building ecology.

Focus group: Market analysis tool in which a moderator presents a set of carefully prepared questions to a group, usually eight to twelve people, in order to collect detailed and specific information on customer attitudes and preferences.

Fossil fuels: Fuels, such as oil, natural gas, and coal, formed from organic material deposited in the earth.

Geographical Information System (GIS): Detailed information on the soils, hydrology, land-use patterns, and plant and animal habitats of sites, plotted on maps or entered in data bases and employed to determine the appropriate location of buildings and infrastructure and to plan landscaping and other land-use considerations.

Glazing: Transparent or translucent coverings that allow light to enter rooms and solar collectors while providing weather protection. Window glass and clear plastic films are examples of glazing.

Global warming: A long-term gradual increase in the average temperature in climate systems throughout the world as a result of the greenhouse effect.

Graywater: Water that has been used for showering, clothes washing, and faucet uses. (Kitchen sink and toilet water is excluded.) This water can be reused in subsurface irrigation for yards in some states.

Green development: A development approach that goes beyond conventional development practice by integrating the following elements: environmental responsiveness—benefiting the surrounding environment; resource efficiency—using resources in the construction, development, and operations of buildings and/or communities in ways that are not wasteful; and sensitivity to existing culture and community—fostering community in design, construction, and operations. Bringing these elements together through the green development approach provides numerous environmental and economic benefits by capitalizing on the interconnections.

Greenfields: Undeveloped land.

Greenhouse gas: Any number of gases that trap heat in the atmosphere, including carbon dioxide, methane, and chlorofluorocarbons.

Green wash (also faux green): To falsely claim a product is environmentally sound.

Habitat: The environment in which an organism or biological population usually lives or grows.

Hard costs: In new construction, includes payments for land, labor, materials, improvements, and the contractor's fee.

Heat island effect: The rise in ambient temperature that occurs over large paved areas. Strategic placement of trees can reduce this effect and reduce energy consumption for cooling by 15 to 30 percent.

Heat recovery ventilator (or air-to-air heat exchangers): Exhaust fans that warm the incoming air with the heat from the outgoing air, recovering about 50 to 70 percent of the energy. In hot climates the function is reversed so that the cooler inside air passes by the incoming hot air and reduces its temperature.

Highest and best use: Conventionally defined as the property use that, at a given time, is deemed likely to produce the greatest net return in the foreseeable future, whether or not such use is the current use of the property. Green development defines highest and best use not just in terms of maximum return on investment, but also as the use that best reflects long-term social, cultural, and financial values held by a community.

HVAC: Heating, ventilation, and air-conditioning.

Indoor air quality (IAQ): The cleanliness or health effects of air in a building is affected by the amount of compounds released into the space by various materials, carbon dioxide levels, and microbial contaminants. IAQ is heavily influenced by both choice of building materials (and cleaning procedures) and ventilation rates.

Infill: Developing on empty lots of land within an urban area rather than on new undeveloped land outside the city. Infill development helps prevent urban sprawl and can aid in economic revitalization.

Infrastructure: Services and facilities provided by a municipality or privately provided, including roads, highways, water, sewage, emergency services, parks and recreation, and so on.

Insulation: Material having a relatively high resistance to heat flow and used primarily to retard the flow of heat.

Integrated design: A holistic process that considers the many disparate parts of a building project, and examines the interaction between design, construction, and operations, to optimize the energy and environmental performance of the project. The strength of this process is that all relevant issues are considered simultaneously in order to "solve for pattern" or to solve many problems with one solution. The goal of integrated design is developments that have the potential to heal damaged environments and become net producers of energy, healthful food, clean water and air, and healthy human and biological communities.

Internal rate of return (IRR): The true annual rate of earnings on an investment. Equates the value of cash returns with cash invested, taking compound interest factors into account.

Land stewardship: The act of managing the land and its resources in a sustainable or restorative manner.

Lease: A contract that gives a tenant the right of possession for a period of time in return for paying rent to a landlord.

Life cycle: The consecutive, interlinked stages of a product, beginning with raw materials acquisition and manufacture, continuing with its fabrication, manufacture, construction, and use, and concluding with a variety of recovery, recycling, or waste management options.

Life-cycle analysis: An objective assessment of the cost of a design feature that allows for production, sales, operation, maintenance, and demolition or recycling costs. The cost also encompasses all the environmental burdens of a product or process through its entire service life.

Light shelf: A daylighting strategy that allows natural light to bounce off a shelf located in a window and onto the ceiling to bring light deep into a space.

Locally sourced materials: Materials obtained from an area within a defined radius around a project site, helping to support the local economy and reducing transportation costs and energy.

Location-efficient mortgage (LEM): An innovative new type of mortgage designed to encourage and facilitate home ownership in transit-accessible inner-city and denser suburban neighborhoods. This model applies the money people save in transportation costs toward their mortgage payments in location-efficient areas, enabling them to buy a higher-priced "location-efficient" home than they could otherwise afford.

Louvers: A series of baffles used to shield a light source from view at certain angles, or to absorb unwanted light, or to allow selective ventilation.

Low-emissivity windows: Glazing that has special coatings to permit most of the sun's light radiation to enter the building, but prevents heat radiation from passing through.

Market niche: A particular subgroup within a market segment distinguishable from the rest of the segment by certain characteristics.

Mass transit: Conveyance of persons or goods from one place to another on a local public transportation system such as light rail, bus, or subway.

Miniperm loan: A short-term loan (usually five years) meant to be an interim loan between a construction loan and a permanent loan. It is usually securitized like any other loan.

Mixed-use: A development in one or several buildings that combines several revenue-producing uses that are integrated into a comprehensive plan, such as a project with elements of housing, retail, and office space.

Mortgage: A written contract that uses real estate as security for the payment of a specified debt.

Native vegetation: A plant whose presence and survival in a specific region is not due to human intervention or cultivation.

Neotraditional planning: Based on nineteenth-century American town prototypes, this type of planning minimizes automobile use and encourages a sense of community with a town center and open public areas.

Net operating income (NOI): Income from real estate property after operating expenses have been deducted, but before deducting income taxes and financing expenses (interest and principal payments). The formula is: NOI = gross income − operating expenses.

New Urbanism: A city planning movement that focuses on revitalizing the inner city and reforming the American suburb within an integrated regional structure. New Urbanists strive for a built environment that must be diverse in use and population, must be scaled for pedestrian use without entirely eliminating automobile access, and must have a well-defined public realm supported by vernacular architecture.

Nonrenewable resources: Natural resources that are consumed faster than can be produced. Thus, they are limited resources that could eventually be depleted.

Off-gas: The emission of chemical compounds from a newly painted, finished, carpeted, or furnished room into the air.

Operating costs: Costs directly related to the operation, maintenance, repair, and management of a property and the utilities that service it. These include insurance, property taxes, utilities, maintenance, and management expenses.

Orientation: The relation of a building and its associated fenestration and interior surfaces to compass direction and, therefore, to the location of the sun. It is usually given in terms of angular degrees away from south; that is, a wall facing due southeast has an orientation of 45 degrees east of south.

Passive solar: Systems that collect, move, and store heat using natural heat-transfer mechanisms such as conduction and air convection currents.

Payback period: The time estimated for a capital investment to pay for itself, calculated by relating the cost of the investment to the profit it will earn or savings it will incur.

Pedestrian pocket: A simple cluster of housing, retail space, and offices within a quarter-mile radius of a transit system. Smaller scale than new towns or Planned Unit Developments.

Pedestrian scale: An urban development pattern where walking is a safe, convenient, and interesting travel mode.

Permaculture: A unique approach to the practice of sustainable farming, ranching, gardening, and living, by designing constructed ecosystems that serve the needs of human populations without degrading the natural environment. Permaculture sites integrate plants, animals, landscapes, structures, and humans into symbiotic systems while requiring a minimum of materials, energy, and labor to maintain.

Permanent loan: A long-term loan on real estate from a financial institution. Subject to specific conditions, such as construction of improvements.

Photovoltaics (PVs): Solid-state cells (typically made from silicon) that directly convert sunlight into electricity.

Plenum: The surface between the ceiling of one floor and the surface of the floor above. HVAC ducts, variable air volume (VAV) boxes, pipes, lighting fixtures, and other building equipment are generally located in the plenum space.

Plug loads: Electrical loads created by the use of devices that are plugged into wall sockets. These include such items as computers, printers, photocopiers, refrigerators, water coolers, fans, microwave ovens, heaters, and other pieces of equipment.

Premium: The value of a mortgage or bond in excess of its face value. Buyers or renters sometimes pay a *premium* because the project has attributes for which they are willing to pay more than market rate.

Pro forma: A financial statement that projects gross income, operating expenses, and net operating income for a future period based on a set of specific assumptions.

Proffer: A developer's promises that are approved by the local municipalities and tied to the land in the zoning process. They include any financial commitments made by the developer to offset costs the county would otherwise have to pay.

Product differentiation: A function of advertising in which the aim is to convince the public that a particular brand of product is "different" from and "superior" to others.

R-value: A unit of thermal resistance used for comparing insulating values of different materials; the higher the R-value of a material, the greater its insulating properties.

Rainscreen: A method of constructing walls in which the cladding is separated from a membrane by an air space that allows pressure equalization to prevent rain from being forced in.

Rebate: A deduction from an amount charged or a return of portion of a price paid, as in a utility rebate awarded for an energy-efficient building.

Recycled material: Material that would otherwise be destined for disposal but is diverted or separated from the waste stream, reintroduced as material feed-stock, and processed into marketed end products.

Redevelopment: The redesign or rehabilitation of existing properties.

Renewable resources: Resources that are created or produced at least as fast as they are consumed, so that nothing is depleted. If properly managed, renewable energy resources (e.g., solar, hydro, wind power, biomass, and geothermal) should last as long as the sun shines, rivers flow, wind blows, and plants grow.

Renovation: The process of upgrading an existing building. Usually, there is an attempt to keep the same general appearance of the building with new materials or to return the building to its original appearance.

Restoration: The process of bringing back a structure or landscape to its original state.

Retrofit: The replacement, upgrade, or improvement of a piece of equipment or structure in an existing building or facility.

Return on investment (ROI): The annual return that can be expected on the equity funds invested.

Revitalize: To give new life or vigor to; for example, to *revitalize* inner-city neighborhoods.

Sealant: An adhesive agent used to close or secure something in order to prevent seepage of moisture or air.

Sick building syndrome (SBS): This sickness is characterized by the symptoms of an unhealthy building's occupants — dizziness, headaches, irritated eyes, nausea, throat irritation, and coughing. These reactions typically cease when the occupants leave the building.

Site assessment: The thorough environmental analysis conducted as a stage in planning to assess a variety of features, including soils, topography, hydrology, environmental amenities such as wetlands, wind direction, solar orientation, animal and plant habitat, connections to community, and so on. Geographical Information Systems can facilitate this task.

Site development costs: All costs needed to prepare the land for building construction, which may include the demolition of existing structures, site preparation, off-site improvements, and on-site improvements.

Soft costs: Expenditures associated with real estate development that are incorporated into construction costs. These include architect fees, legal

fees, marketing costs, interest, origination fees, appraisals, and other third-party charges.

Solar access: Access to the sun's rays by, for instance, restricting the location of shade trees or laying out the building so as to maximize the usefulness of solar energy.

Solar energy: Energy received from the sun in the form of electromagnetic radiation in the wavelength range from 0.3 to 2.7 microns. This includes all visible light as well as some ultraviolet and infrared radiation.

Spec house: A single-family dwelling constructed in anticipation of finding a buyer.

Specifications (specs): Detailed instructions provided in conjunction with plans and blueprints for construction. Specifications may stipulate the type of materials to be used, special construction techniques, dimensions, and colors.

Sprawl: An irregular spread of residential areas, shopping centers, and small industries beyond city boundaries.

Stakeholders: Those people who are or will be affected by a real estate development, financially and/or physically (i.e., occupants and users, investors and lenders, local community, local government, and other institutions).

Stretch ratio: In mortgage calculations, the percentage that lenders will "stretch" a mortgage (i.e., from 28 percent of the home buyer's salary to 30 percent) for homes that meet energy-efficiency ratings or other standards, realizing that other expenses such as operating or transportation costs will be lower.

Superwindows: Double- or triple-glazed window *sandwiches* that contain a center sheet of coated mylar "low-emissivity" film and are filled with argon or krypton gas. This construction and the coating on the film allow short-wave radiation (visible light) to pass through, but reflects long-wavelength radiation (infrared or heat) so heat cannot pass through. R-values of 4.5 or more are achieved.

Sustainability: Meeting the needs of the present without compromising the ability of future generations to meet their own needs, as defined by the Brundtland Commission, 1987.

Sustainably sourced materials: Materials that are acquired in an environmentally sound manner, emphasizing efficient and appropriate use of natural resources.

Swale: A hollow or depression on a wet, marshy ground through which water flows.

Thermal mass: Materials that have a high capacity for absorbing heat and change temperature slowly. These materials are used to absorb and retain solar energy during the daytime for release at night or during cloudy periods. These include water, rocks, masonry, and earth.

Tipping fees: Fees charged for dumping large quantities of trash into a landfill.

Topography: The physical features, including the configuration of the surface, of a place or region.

Traditional Neighborhood Development (TND): A basic unit of New Urbanism, which includes the following characteristics: a center that includes a public space and commercial enterprise; an identifiable edge, ideally a five-minute walk from the center; a mix of activities and variety of housing types; an interconnected network of streets and blocks, usually laid out in a modified grid pattern; high priority to public space, with prominently located civic buildings and open space that includes squares, plazas, and parks.

Transit-oriented development: A mixed-use community within an average 2,000-foot walking distance of a transit stop and core commercial area that mixes residential, retail, office, open space, and public uses in a way that makes it convenient for residents and employees to travel by transit, foot, bike, and so forth.

Triple-net lease: A lease in which the tenant pays all operating expenses of the property; the landlord receives a net rent.

Truth window (or wall): An exposed section of a wall or window that reveals the layered components within it.

Up-front planning: Comprehensive planning in advance of the development process.

Urban growth boundary: A boundary that identifies urban and urbanizable lands for a specified planning period, to be planned and serviced to support urban development densities, and which separates these lands from rural lands.

Variance: A special permission to vary a physical structure or use a property in a way normally prohibited by existing zoning.

Vernacular: In architecture, vernacular buildings are seen as the opposite of whatever is academic or high style; the traditional architecture of a region. Traditional architecture is often a result of response to the regional climate and land conditions.

Viewshed: Everything visible from a specific vantage point.

Visual Preference Surveys™: Photographic images of various planning and design elements, accompanied by questionnaires and other analysis techniques. First developed by Anton Nelessen.

Volatile organic compound (VOC): A class of chemical compounds that can cause nausea, tremors, headaches, and, some doctors believe, longer-lasting harm. VOCs can be emitted by oil-based paints, solvent-based finishes, and other products on/in construction materials.

Wetland: Land that is transitional between aquatic and terrestrial ecosystems and is covered with water for at least part of the year. These lands are important as buffer zones to help control flooding and also provide an ecosystem for a diverse number of species.

Whole-systems thinking: A process through which the interconnections of systems are actively considered, and solutions are sought that address multiple problems at the same time.

Xeriscaping: Creative landscaping design for conserving water that uses drought-resistant or drought-tolerant plants.

Zoning: A legal mechanism for local governments to prevent conflicting land use and promote orderly development by regulating the use of privately owned land through enforcement.

Case Studies Index

Note: This is an index of the main case studies featured throughout the chapters. Page numbers in italic refer to illustrations or captions.

General Index

Page numbers in italic refer to illustrations or captions.

503

Service(s):
of comfort, 408
municipal, 70
Sewage:
conventional treatment plant,
147, 149
effluent, 132
municipal treatment plant, 147
system, 51, 211
treatment plant, 147, 149
treatment system, 147
Sewer:
connection, 186
system, 211–212
Shading, 161
Shané, Roberto, Dr., 64
Shaw, Robert, 22
Shaw Construction Company, 302
Shaw Homes, Inc., 169–170, 240, 425
Shelburne, Ontario, 161
Shenoa Retreat and Learning
Center, *122*, 123, 374
Sheraton, 320
Shimuzu Corporation, 303
Shopping plaza, 222
Short, Ford, and Associates, 166
Shoulders, Mike, 288
Sick building syndrome (SBS), 16,
174, 295
Siemens Solar, 444
Sierra Club, 205
Silva, Susan, 429
Simon Martin-Vegue Winkelstein
Moris, 36
Sim van der Ryn and Associates, 57.
See also: Ecological Design
Associates, 443
Site:
analysis, 427
archaeological and historic, 152
assessment, 128–132
design to fit, 160
preservation, 291
sensitive construction, 293
sensitivity, 427, 444
Site protection, 291–293
during construction, 291
Skyscraper, 162
Slone, Dan, 199
Smith, Mark, 117
Snowmass, Colorado, 50
Social:
environment, 153
issues, 400

patterns, 9
values, 414
Socially responsible investment
funds, 263
Socioeconomic and demographic
profiles, 119
Sociographic and psychographic
research, 108
Soil erosion, 143
Solar:
electric power, 149. *See also* pho-
tovoltaics
exposure, 161
gain, 433
Solar access, 130, 429
ordinance, 220
Solar Aquatics systems, *148*, 149,
230, 404–405
Solar-powered pump, 374
Solar Today, 159, 364
Solomon, Dan, 78
Solution multiplier(s), 5, 37, 80,
147, 180
Sommer, Robert, 380
Sony Pictures Daycare Center, 214
South Carolina, 28, 127, 383
Lowcountry islands, 108
South Carolina Coastal
Conservation League, 211
South Carolina Department of
Natural Resources, 131
South Carolina Sea Grant Marine
Extension, 390
South Carolina Wildlife Federation,
131
Southern California Edison, 310
Southern California Gas Company,
112, 283, 287, 301, 342, 440
Energy Resource Center, 113, 283,
284, 287–288, 301, *341*,
342–343, 440–441
construction cost comparison
chart, *113*, *278*, 301
Southside Park, 389
Space:
efficiency, 44
efficient use of, 169–170
flexible, 54
open, 21, 86–90, 94, 111, 120,
205, 231, 246, 317, 377
quality of, 80–81
Specifications (specs), 215, 287,
288–290, 291, 299
Sprawl, 68–70, 78, 96, 194, 257

suburban, 92
Sprawling development, 400
Spring Island, 28–29, *29*, 107–109,
109, 123, 130–131, *131*, 135,
135, *151*, 152, 188–189, 209,
238–239, 242, 273–274, 357,
361, 381–384, *383*, 427–428
architectural review board, 428
Spring Island Company, 29, 427
Spring Island Handbook, 383
Spring Island Trust, 29, 238–239,
238, 273–274, 385, 428
Stack effect, 167
Staging area(s), 291, 292
Stakeholder(s), 197–201, 351
Standard Insurance Company, 234
Stanford Research Institute, 122
Stapleton Airport, 415
Stapleton Redevelopment, 415–416
Foundation, 415–416
Project, 415, *416*, *418*
Starwood Lodging Trust, 320
State Housing Authority, 233
Statistics, 105
Steelcase Corporation, 410
Steiner, Rudolph, 25
Stephen, Merry, 430
Stevenson, Berit, 161
Stewardship, 275, 427
Storm:
conventional sewers, 144, 146
sewer system, 12, 191
Stormwater, 134
infiltration systems, 141
roof-top, 144
runoff, 37, 97, 144
treatment, 449
Strategic analysis, 102
Straw-bale construction, 265, 290
Street(s):
narrower, 12, 37, 153, 246, 429
narrowing, 88
narrow tree-lined, 224
traffic-calming designs, 37
Strupp, Dean, 264
Stuart, Florida, 92, 317
Substitutions, 289
Summerfield, 317
Sunnyvale, California, 165
Suntempering, 56
Sun-tracking lighting system, 158
Superfund regulations, 85
Supermarket, 222
Supervision, 285–291